First-time Mum

First-time Mum

Surviving and enjoying your baby's first year

Hollie Smith

First-time Mum: surviving and enjoying your baby's first year

This first edition published in 2012 by Crimson Publishing Ltd, Westminster House, Kew Road, Richmond, Surrey TW9 2ND

© Hollie Smith 2012

The right of Hollie Smith to be identified as the author of this work has been asserted by her in accordance with the Copyright, Designs and Patents Act, 1988.

All rights reserved. No part of this publication may be reproduced, or transmitted in any form or by any means, stored in a retrieval system electronic and mechanical, photocopying, recording or otherwise without prior permission of Crimson Publishing Ltd.

British Library Cataloguing in Publication Data
A catalogue record for this book is available from the British Library

ISBN 978-1-90828-111-1

Typeset by IDSUK (DataConnection) Ltd
Printed and bound in the UK by Ashford Colour Press, Gosport, Hants

Contents

Note from the author

I owe a huge thank you to the members of my mums' panel, who once again have provided me with invaluable input by sharing their anecdotes, tips, and opinions. These are real women, with real babies, and real lives. Frankly, I doubt you'll get better advice anywhere, wherever you look.

Thanks also to Louise Cremonesini, Health Visitor, lecturer, wife, mum, and all-round superstar, for casting her expert eye over the book.

A brief note about gender: for convenience I've used 'he' for babies; 'she' for Health Visitors and midwives; and 'he' for doctors. Outrageously sexist. My apologies.

Where I've mentioned an organisation, charity, or source of further information, you'll find it listed in the Useful Contacts chapter at the back of the book.

If you'd like to read more from me, please drop in on my blog some time: www.holliesmith.co.uk/blog/

Introduction

Welcome to your first year of motherhood – possibly the most amazing and challenging 12 months of your life so far. After the drawn-out anticipation of pregnancy, your baby's here, and you're finally a mum. No doubt you're exhausted – and feeling a huge mix of emotions from joy to anxiety. Other mums will have told you how wonderful motherhood is: but also that it was harder than they anticipated. In truth, you can never really know how it feels until you're experiencing it. It's certainly challenging. But hopefully, with this book as your companion throughout the first year, you'll have the information you need to care for your baby, stay sane – and to actually enjoy it too!

I remember my first year of motherhood in vivid technicolour. I won't ever forget the smells, the sights, the sensations, and the emotions that made it such an incredible experience. I've got to be honest. A lot of it was hard-going: that stomach-churning feeling when you hit the sack, knowing you're going to be up in the cold, dark middle of the night three hours later, feeding the wee insomniac; the agony of hungry gums on raw nipples; the relentless, hours-on-end colicky crying; the poo that looks like korma sauce, in places you didn't think poo could reach. And while you're doing your utmost to fathom out the mysteries of baby care, you have to cope with your own emotional and physical changes: your body ravaged in all sorts of ways by birth; a catalogue of new emotions that's as likely to include anxiety and depression as it is joy and wonder; the demands of a third party and new roles on your relationship; and the inner turmoil involved in considering your return to work. And yet, it's a truly wonderful time, too.

The love and pride you and your baby's dad feel as you watch him evolve from a mewling infant to a lively one-year-old, and the sense of achievement in getting your first year of parenthood under your belts: well, there's nothing to beat it.

So, here's *First-time Mum*, a guide to the first year for modern mothers. I hope you'll find it's full of useful information and packed with reassurance. You'll notice I take a neutral stance on most things – modern mums have enough guilt and doubt to contend with, without being lectured by the very manual they're reading. You might also notice that my advice is rarely definitive or prescriptive. There's a good reason for that: all babies are different, and so are all mums. And if I've learned one thing as a writer, and as a mum myself, it's this: while there are very few absolute rights and wrongs in parenting, there *are* lots of maybes, sort-ofs, and perhapses. So what I'm offering here is a combination of basic facts, 'accepted wisdom', official guidelines, and, perhaps most importantly, word on the street. It's up to you to take it from there.

Part one

Starting out

1

What to buy for your baby

One of the first quandaries facing you as a new mum, no doubt, is what – amid the myriad products up for sale to new parents – do you need to buy for your baby; what can you get away with borrowing, and what should you probably just bypass altogether? Truth be told, there's very little that you *definitely* need at the outset, beyond a few absolute basics. Depending on what stage you're reading this, by now, you may have done a fair amount of acquiring already – and you may use this chapter as a checklist, or for some non-essential-but-nice ideas. Or you may be reading this in preparation, and can use these suggestions to save yourself a bad buy or two . . .

When it's your first baby, you might just want to make sure he has *absolutely* everything he could possibly need (even if you're not quite sure what his needs *are*, yet). And maybe you're enjoying the shopping opportunities so much it's hard to keep a lid on your purchasing. But still, it's a good idea to stick with what seems really essential to get you started. I've included a tick list of the absolute, initial essentials at the end of the chapter (pages 20–21) and go through the pros and cons of these, and everything else, just below. As time goes on, it should become clearer what you need and what you don't, and at that point you can order it: after all, eBay is but a mouse click away. You're bound to get at least some of what you need as presents, too (along with a fair few things you don't). Keep your receipts!

Whatever you've got on your acquisitions list, remember that almost all of it can be handed down, borrowed, or bought for a song second-hand via sources such as National Childbirth Trust (NCT) sales, local noticeboards, and online. There are two exceptions to this: car seats and cot mattresses, which safety experts recommend that you buy new. Think hard about anything you *do* fork out the full whack for, because it's easy to waste your money in this market. And bear in mind that, whatever the size of your home, it can seem very small once it's cluttered with baby equipment. Don't get more than you can actually house.

Ultimately, this is a subjective issue: one new mum's essential is another's total waste of money. In the end it's down to you what you decide you need for your baby. You'll almost certainly end up acquiring at least a couple of things you wish you hadn't – but hopefully, too, a good few that turn out to have been worth every penny.

Mums' panel round-up

Tips on buying for a baby

Don't buy anything new. Your baby will only spill/puke/poo on it anyway, or grow out of it in 30 seconds. eBay is your best friend. You can buy bundles of designer baby clothes for a quid, among other bargains – **Charlee C**

Let your baby try out expensive non-essentials like bouncers, slings, and Bumbos 'before' forking out for them. Some babies just don't want to be put in these things! – **Lucy R**

Freecycle, Gumtree, Netmums, and NCT sales are all brilliant places to find the essentials, cheap or even free – **Molly F**

I was the first of my friends to have a baby and I told everyone to get lots of muslins. Most of my friends have since said asked why. Turns out I just had a sicky baby! The moral of the story is every baby's different. Wait and see what yours needs – **Claire A**

Don't rip tags off clothes given as gifts. Shops are often really good about exchanging stuff that's the wrong size, or simply not to your taste – **Viv S**

Avoid the big baby shops. You'll walk round and see a zillion things you think you need, but actually don't. Research and buy online, instead – Lauren B

For dressing

You will definitely need . . .

- **Plenty of clothes.** Plain old **sleepsuits** are best at first, for day and night, because they're comfy, and – once you've mastered any poppers – easy to whip on and off quickly. Buy cheap, and have plenty, as you can get through several in a day at first when they tend to get frequently soiled. Some mums prefer to see their baby 'dressed' in the day, in which case **simple separates** in soft fabrics are the best alternative.
- **Some vests.** A thin extra layer is a good idea in cooler temperatures, and they can be worn on their own when it's hot, so these are useful all year round. Also very likely to get soiled, so have plenty.
- **Cardigan.** You'll need one of these for chillier days, and probably a spare as well. Traditional hand-knitted varieties are nice: don't buy if you've got an enthusiastic granny or friend who'd simply love to do the honours for you.
- **Jacket or coat.** For going outside on cold days.
- **Socks.** Good for keeping toes warm and a better bet than bootees as they're more likely to stay put, especially if you buy nice long ones. (And if not, you can always invest in a pair of 'Sock-ons', which claim to keep even the most slippery pair in place.)
- **Hat.** A warm one is necessary for going out in cold weather (do always take it off when you get back indoors so he doesn't overheat) and a sun hat is important when the sun's out, unless he's well covered by a pram hood, parasol, or carefully draped **muslin**.

> *"It's just not worth splashing out on fancy outfits of any description – you'll almost certainly get some as gifts, anyway, and if and when you do need to buy them yourself, it's easy to source good quality secondhand options, or seek out hand-me-downs."*
>
> *Lauren B*

You may or may not need . . .

- **Bootees and pram shoes.** Cute, but notoriously tricky to keep on. If you do have these, make sure they're made of soft, flexible fabric or leather as the cartilage in babies' feet is easily damaged.
- **Gloves.** Also difficult to keep on, although some brands claim to have staying power. Don't worry too much: cold hands probably won't bother your baby.
- **Pram suit/snow suit.** While a jacket or short coat is probably necessary for going out in cold weather, you may well find that a pram suit or snow suit – typically, a very warm but rather bulky all-in-one – isn't. They're a pain to put on and take off, and an extra blanket or two will do the job just as well when your baby's in the pram.

> *"Snow suits turned out to be a red herring. We thought we'd need one for our winter baby, but it just swamped him, and in fact layers of clothing and blankets work fine. (It did make for some funny photos, though.)"*
>
> *Clare F*

You really don't need . . .

- **Scratch mitts.** In theory, these little soft cotton gloves are supposed to prevent a baby from doing himself any damage with his own fingernails, but they always, always fall off. You're better off buying a pair of **baby nail scissors** or **clippers** (see below) and keeping his nails nice and short.

For changing

You will definitely need . . .

- **Nappies.** Your baby will get through lots and lots of these from the start, so you may want to consider buying in bulk. Disposables are the most popular option: get the best you can afford and make sure you've got the right size for your baby's weight to help avoid nappy rash (see page 156). If the environment and finances are a concern and you can face the laundry issues, look into cloth nappies: the initial outlay is more, but you'll save in the long run – and you can get good deals secondhand. You'll also need a bucket with a lid to store or soak the mucky ones in.
- **Cotton wool.** The nicest option for cleaning sensitive newborn bots, and also needed for topping and tailing and washing eyes (see page 60).
- **Wipes.** Significantly less bother than cotton wool for cleaning bums and definitely something you'll want to switch to eventually, anyway. Look for kinder brands that are alcohol and fragrance-free.
- **Nappy rash or barrier cream.** Sore bottoms are pretty common, so it's worth having this on stand-by from the start. Hints on preventing and treating nappy rash can be found on page 156.
- **At least one wipe-clean changing mat.** Get one for each floor of your house. You can put them on a table to change your baby (if you do, don't take your eyes off him for a second), or just use the floor. Neat, portable, fold-up versions are quite adequate, and these are often given away free with baby magazines or in other promotions. One to keep permanently folded up in your **changing bag** is also useful.
- **Big bag.** You'll certainly need a bag to put nappies (and a million and one other things) in when you're out and about: most mums find it's a good idea to keep one permanently packed and ready to go by the door. However, you *don't* have to fork out for a bag specifically designed for the purpose (which will usually have different compartments for nappies, bottles, and so on). A roomy rucksack or tote will suffice.

You may or may not need . . .

- **Nappy sacks.** Although not very environmentally friendly, nappy sacks are undeniably handy for sticking dirty nappies in if they're leaky, or you want to try and contain the smell a bit. You can of course just use supermarket carrier bags, instead.
- **Nappy disposal unit.** Some mums wouldn't be without theirs; others feel strongly they should be filed under 'useless'. Essentially, they simply mean fewer trips to the dustbin.

> *"Don't buy a nappy bin. No matter how well you clean them or how regularly you empty them, they give off the most repulsive and distinctive smell, which, in my opinion, is worse than the dirty nappies themselves."*
>
> *Jo W*

You really don't need . . .

- **Changing unit.** These tend to crop up most regularly in the list of 'most useless investment'. Assuming you keep it in the nursery, you'll have to trudge upstairs every time your baby does a poo, or one wee too many, downstairs.

> *"Can I reassure you that you do not need a nappy wipe dispenser? The wipes get jammed in the top, so they are useless."*
>
> *Rebecca F*

For sleeping

You will definitely need . . .

- **Cot.** Even if you don't put your baby in a cot at the outset because you prefer to put him in something cosier (see Moses baskets and cribs, below), you'll need one before too long.
  Cot beds are a good investment as they convert into something

he can sleep in for a good few years. (On the other hand, if you're planning to have another baby, who'll also need a cot, you might decide not to bother.) A **sidecar cot** may be a good compromise if you'd like to sleep with your baby but you're concerned about safety.

- **New mattress for any basket, crib or cot you've acquired secondhand.** The Foundation for the Study of Infant Deaths (FSID) recommends that, ideally, all new babies sleep on a brand new mattress. For safety reasons, mattresses need to be a very snug fit, so if you're buying one separately, make sure you get exactly the right size. See page 108 for more information on safe sleeping.
- **Some bedding.** You'll need a couple of **sheets** for whatever your baby's sleeping in – at least one spare is vital, as soiling is, you guessed it, pretty usual. Fitted sheets make life a little easier, but aren't essential. For warmth, one or two **blankets** will be needed on top, depending on the temperature: cellular blankets, which are loosely knit and therefore 'holey', are widely recommended because they allow air to circulate and are lightweight yet warm. At least one other blanket, perhaps the fleecy sort, is useful for trips out, or just for spreading on the floor for your baby to lie and play on.
- **Room thermometer.** Useful to help you work out whether your baby's room is a safe temperature (see page 109). Don't pay more than a few quid, if that, for a cardboard version. They're available cheaply from FSID and in fact they're often given away free with baby magazines, in promotion packs, or by big stores.

> *"You don't need special sheets. Babies lying on their backs don't care what their bedding looks like. A pillowcase fits a Moses basket mattress, and a single sheet cut or folded in half fits a cot. And those silly lacy frilly things that go over the side are fiddly and unnecessary."*
>
> *Abi M*

You may or may not need . . .

- **Moses basket.** Some parents wouldn't be without a Moses basket; some reckon they're unnecessary. They're said to provide a cosier, more comforting sleeping environment for newborns, but their main advantage is that, being small and portable, you can position them right by your bedside, and also move them from room to room – which is a help in the early months when your baby's kipping a lot in the daytime. However, they're only useful while your baby fits in it (three to four months tops – with some big babies outgrowing them within a month or two) so they're definitely not worth buying new. Make sure you also get a **stand**, to keep your baby away from drafts, and so you can easily pick him up.

- **Crib.** A sturdier but less portable precursor to a full-sized cot, these give more service than a Moses basket as they're usually good for up to six months. They often come with a rocking or gliding facility (as do some Moses baskets) and although some parents find that handy, others may well warn you about the perils of setting up a 'sleep association' (see page 119) that you wish you hadn't!
- **Sleeping bag.** Classed by many parents as an essential, a baby sleeping bag can be a real aid to sleep, as they keep a baby warm all night. They're suitable from birth but it's important, for safety reasons, to get the right size, as well as the right tog rating for the time of year – so you may well need to buy several as your baby grows, or the seasons change, and you may also want to have a spare in case of accidents.
- **Swaddle blanket.** Some say these make for a good night's sleep – others say there's no point forking out when an ordinary baby blanket, snugly wrapped, will do. For more on swaddling, including some important health and safety advice, see page 110.
- **Baby monitor.** There's a vast choice of these electronic systems, which allow you to listen to (or even watch) your baby while he's sleeping in a different room. Latest models include high-tech digital or video versions, and they come with all sorts of added features such as room thermometers, night lights, and 'talk-back' facilities. Some even play lullabies. Many first-time parents find the peace of mind these offer make them worth the money, others reckon they're pointless – after all, if you're following safe sleep guidelines you'll have your baby near your own bedside for the first six months and the rest of the time (unless you live in a very big house) you're going to hear him when he cries anyway. You

can also buy **movement monitors**, which sound an alarm if a baby stops breathing for a pre-set time (usually 15 to 20 seconds), and some first-timers say these are hugely reassuring. However, experts tend to urge caution as there's no evidence they definitely prevent cot death – and because they can spark stressful false alarms.

- **Travel cot.** By no means a necessity, but a portable travel cot that collapses into a neat cuboid that fits easily in a boot is a boon for holidays or nights away. They also serve as a playpen a bit later on when your baby's mobile and you need somewhere to stick him for short bursts when you're not in the room.
- **Black-out blinds.** Two opposing schools of thought on these: a) they are an undoubted aid to sleep that some parents swear by; and b) they set up a certain condition that your baby will always need to drop off. You decide!
- **Cot mobile/musical toy.** May well offer distraction for your baby and could even become a reliable sleep association (see page 119). However, they can also end up filed under 'rod for own back' if you need to get up in the night to wind it up again – although, these days you can actually get ones with remote controls, so at least you won't have to get out of bed to restart it.

“A really good buy for your baby is a disco ball. Seriously, they love watching the swirl of lights on the ceiling – gets them to sleep in no time!”

Abi M

You really don't need . . .

- **Cot divider.** Marketed as an aid to keeping your baby in the feet-to-foot position, but really not necessary if you always tuck him up at the bottom of his cot – or use a baby sleeping bag. (Some parents of twins reckon they're handy for putting both babies down in the same cot.)
- **Frilly skirts, 'bumpers', and canopies for your cot, crib, or Moses basket.** Unless you really like the look of them, of course.

For feeding

You will definitely need . . .

- **Bottles and teats.** Essential, that is, if you're formula feeding, or if you're breastfeeding and plan to offer expressed milk. Some breastfeeding mums reckon it's worth having them on standby, anyway – as well as a steriliser – just in case of problems or a change of heart. (Others reckon that's a bad idea, in case it influences your resolve to keep feeding yourself.) There's a bewildering array of bottle types and teats out there, so ask your mum-friends for recommendations and be prepared to try out more than one. The most important thing is making sure they fit in the steriliser you choose. For more on formula feeding, see pages 34 and 87.
- **Bottle/teat brush.** Really important for getting these items very clean, which you should, as milk can so easily harbour germs and babies are so vulnerable to tummy infections.
- **Steriliser.** Vital if you're going to be giving your baby a bottle at any point in the first year, when his immune system is still developing, and also useful for keeping the worst of the germs off dummies and teething toys. Most popular are electric steam or microwave models. (If storage space is an issue in your kitchen, go for the latter as you can keep it tucked away in there when not in use.) There's also the more traditional method of dunking items in cold water and sterilising solution. For this you can buy a **sterilising unit** – essentially a lidded bucket – or you can just use any large, clean container with a lid. (For more on sterilising, see page 88.)
- **Bibs or muslins.** Handy, even in the pre-weaning months. Milk feeds in the early days, particularly with bottles, can involve a lot of leaking, spillage and regurgitation, and a small plastic-backed bib will absorb the worst and save you having to change him completely after a messy meal. The muslin, tucked into the neck of his sleepsuit, gives even better coverage – and they're also good for general mopping purposes, covering up when breastfeeding, and as a potential comforter (see page 120) for your baby.

> *“Go straight for full-sized bottles and don’t waste your money on those ‘mini’ ones for newborns. Why? They’ll be drinking 8oz before you know it.”*
>
> *Celine G*

You may or may not need . . .

- **Breast pump.** A worthwhile acquisition if you’re keen to keep giving your baby breastmilk, but you need, for some reason, to give it to him in a bottle. Expressing can be done by hand, but with a pump it’s easier to decant it straight into a bottle or storage pouch. The two main sorts are manual and electric. The latter are pricey, and can also be hired via the NCT or other private companies. There’s more on expressing on page 81.

You definitely don’t need . . .

- **Bottle warmer.** Truly unnecessary. A jug of boiling water will do the job as well, and most parents are happy to take their chances with a quick blast in the microwave and a jolly good shake (although official advice is not to, in case it causes hot spots – see page 91).

For travelling

You will definitely need . . .

- **Car seat.** You won’t be allowed to leave the maternity unit without your baby in one of these (and in some hospitals, that’s policy *even* if you’re planning to walk home). Always buy your car seat new, unless you’re acquiring it via a very good friend, as a damaged seat could compromise your baby’s safety. And make sure you’ve got the right sort and the right size for your baby: you need a rear-facing infant carrier for a newborn, although you can also buy models that will later convert to face forward and are suitable for older babies and toddlers. Your best bet is to go to a reputable purveyor of car seats like Halfords or Mothercare, where they'll give you free advice and fit the seat for you, too. Remember not to put your baby's seat on the front seat of your car if you have air bags fitted.

- **Pram or buggy.** A pram or pushchair of some description is undoubtedly an essential and may be in use for several years to come. Some parents feel a high-end, heavy-duty 'travel system' is an investment worth making – and actually good value in the end, because there's usually a car seat thrown in, and maybe a carry cot, foot muff, changing bag, and/or rain cover too. Plus, of course, you should get further use out of it if you go on to have more babies. Others reckon a good quality but basic, lightweight, collapsible 'stroller' is a far better bet: as you can buy models that recline and are suitable from birth (or just use a sling for the early months); in theory you could get one that will see you through the pre-school years, too. Whatever you plump for in terms of a pram or buggy, do consider practicalities like how light and sturdy it is, how well it 'handles', how easily it can be collapsed and put up, how much shopping you can fit into it, and whether you've got enough room to store it in your boot, and at home.

> *“Don't spend hundreds on a big travel system: four months down the line you'll abandon it in favour of a lightweight stroller, never to be used again.”*
>
> *Emily D*

You may or may not need . . .

- **Sling/carrier.** Useful to have for days when you could do without the hassle of a pram – or you just want to keep your baby close to you. Walking a baby in a sling or carrier can be a good way to soothe him when he's suffering from colic (see page 143), and useful if you need to get stuff done, but he's demanding your attention. There are various designs, but shop carefully, as it's important to get one with good head support. The main drawback is that carrying your baby in one for too long can give you backache – and it's tricky getting him in and out without a second pair of hands.

> *“Get a good sling. They’re a lifesaver when you need to pop out quickly, or indeed to do anything with a baby that won’t be put down!”*
>
> *Rebecca F*

For washing and grooming

You may or may not need . . .

- **Baby bath.** Considered by many to be a waste of money. Newborns can simply be topped and tailed, or washed in the sink (taking care to avoid the taps, obviously), and when a bit bigger, put in the big bath, either with a grown up in there too to hold him, or with the aid of some kind of bath support (see below). One positive thing to be said about a baby bath is that, if you get one with a stand, it’s good if you have a bad back. (On the other hand, you’ll still need to empty it which, if you have a bad back, you’ll need to ask someone else to do for you.) **Bucket-style baby baths** are available, and some parents say these are good.
- **Baby bath support.** Handy if you want to put your baby in a full-size bath but you’re worried about him staying put, or need both hands to wash him. For newborns, these are typically foam wedges, and for older babies who are sitting up well, there are plastic seat-style versions.
- **Bath thermometer.** Some argue these are the only way to really safely test the temperature of your baby’s bath. Others are confident that common sense and a dunk with an elbow should ensure you get it right.
- **Nail scissors or clippers.** Handy, as babies will often scratch themselves with their own nails – and contrary to popular advice, it’s not really a good idea to bite them off. For more on this, see page 65.
- **Baby toiletries.** Warm water alone will usually get a baby clean enough, but still, these do make your baby smell divine. Look carefully at the labels to make sure they’re clinically tested, and

suitable for infant skin. Bear in mind too that you only use them in tiny quantities, and most products are suitable for washing both skin and hair – so a single bottle will no doubt see you good for quite a while. For more about bathing your baby, see page 61.
- **Baby sponge and baby towel.** Not remotely essential, but it's nice to have these as they're especially soft. Lots of mums recommend the towels with little hoods, which provide extra warmth and cosiness after bath time.
- **Baby hairbrush and/or comb.** Not essential, unless you've got a real mop-top on your hands – and even then, you could probably use a normal comb or a hairbrush with very soft bristles. A narrow-toothed comb of some sort can be handy for tackling cradle cap (see page 62).

"We were given a brilliant contraption: a plastic bath support that can be used for newborns up, which means you can easily wash them in a normal bath."

Molly F

You really don't need . . .

- **Top-and-tail bowl.** Really no need to bother, as two clean plastic bowls will suffice (for more on top and tailing, see page 60).

"We had something called a baby toiletries box, and never used it. It has proved handy for keeping my sewing kit in though."

Sarah C

For everything else

You will definitely need . . .

- **A bottle of fever-reducing medicine such as Calpol or Nurofen for Babies.** To keep in the medicine cabinet for times of teething, immunisations, and fever. There's more on baby health on page 147.

You may or may not need . . .

- **Soft floor blanket or mat.** Handy to pop your baby on for changing or play – and for protecting your carpet during 'nappy-free time' (see page 157)!
- **Bouncy chair.** Generally considered to be very useful acquisition indeed, a bouncy chair – also known as a **cradle chair** – gives you somewhere to safely leave your baby while you get on with something. The gentle movement is soothing and the upright view of the world reassuring. Many have some kind of activity bar for added interest.
- **Vibrating rocker chairs** or **swing seat.** Sometimes described by parents of colicky babies (see page 143) as a godsend. The potential drawback is that, for a while at least, it might become the only thing your baby will *ever* settle to sleep in. It's recommended you never leave your baby unattended in a rocker or bouncy chair on a high surface, as the movements can nudge them forward. Experts also warn against leaving a baby in them for too long, to help avoid flat-head syndrome (see page 158).
- **Baby gym.** These bright arches with dangling toys can keep a baby amused for a while – however, they're not much cop once they're rolling, unless very carefully monitored, as they could easily roll out from under it, and into trouble. Rather space-consuming – although the fabric, fold-up variety can at least be easily stored away.
- **Comforter.** Some people still think they're the devil's work, but lots of parents find that **dummies** are a helpful aid to soothing a baby – and they're really not harmful if used responsibly. Little **comfort blankets** can also become very popular with some babies – you could buy or ask for one of the commercial versions, or you could just give your baby a little square of cellular blanket or a piece of muslin, and that will offer the same service, for nothing. (There's more on dummies and other comfort objects on page 65.)

- **Baby thermometer.** Well worth having for peace of mind, so you can easily assess your baby's temperature when he has a fever (see page 150) – in fact, many parents would consider them an essential. There are several varieties available and prices vary quite a bit, but the safest, most accurate, and easiest to use is probably a digital thermometer that can be popped under your baby's armpit. There's also a variety that can be put in your baby's ear.

> *"I'd highly recommend a bouncy chair. Mine allowed me to wash up or have a shower while my little boy was happily strapped in, but could still see me and hear me talking. It doesn't need to be flashy, as long as it offers a different view of the world."*
>
> *Lara S*

And not for now, but for later

You will definitely need . . .

- **Highchair.** You'll need one once your baby starts on solid food, and is strong enough to support himself comfortably while sitting up. Best to look for something neat that will fit in your dining room, both aesthetically and physically, and that will pull right up to the table, so your baby can join you for meals. A **portable highchair** that folds up and can be fixed either to a table or a chair can be handy when you're out visiting. (There's more on weaning and weaning equipment on page 94.) Some mums reckon a **'Bumbo' chair** is useful during weaning but this moulded foam seat, suitable from four months, seems to be loved by some babies and hated by others, so is definitely a 'try-before-you-buy' product.
- **Plastic weaning equipment.** Advisable, because it's always possible your baby will knock his plate or bowl to the floor and, where spoons are concerned, they're more comfortable in the mouth than metal.

- **Plenty of good-sized bibs.** Find ones that cover as much clothing as possible, as you won't believe how much mess your baby gets in while getting to grips with proper food (or just stick with those handy old **muslins**, as an alternative).

> *"I ended up regretting the pricey plastic highchair we bought for our first baby, because it turned out to be a huge, ugly, eyesore that tripped me up every time I walked past it. I wish instead we'd gone for the same neat little real beech, Scandinavian design that our friends had, and which – usefully – converted into something a toddler could also use. You live and learn."*
>
> *Lauren B*

You may or may not need . . .

- **Playpen.** Useful once your baby's on the move, and you need somewhere to put him for short bursts when you can't be in the room (and would rather not lug him around with you), but only if you've got the space. A collapsible **travel cot** (see above) doubles up effectively as one.
- **Baby walker.** Essentially a seat and tray in a wheeled frame, which allows a baby to trundle around under his own steam. Suitable from four to six months, or once your baby's got a strong back, and good head control. Safety campaigners warn against them because they can cause accidents if they tip, or allow a baby to grab at potentially dangerous objects. Over-use also could also hinder development – he's better off having the freedom to practise rolling, crawling and cruising. However, lots of parents – and babies – think they're great. If you do have one, check it complies with current safety standards as these all have an anti-tipping mechanism. Always supervise your baby when using one, keep stints in it limited to 15 minutes at a time, and get shot of it once he's showing signs of walking. (You can also get **static activity stations**, an alternative that's probably less fun, but undoubtedly safer.)
- **Door bouncer.** Like baby walkers, these can keep a baby independently entertained for a while once he's got good head control, but they also come with developmental and safety

disclaimers: they need to be very firmly fixed to a very solid doorframe, and it's best to limit use to short (and supervised) bursts. You can also get bouncers that have their own frame and sit on the floor, such as the 'Jumperoo'. They cost a lot of money, though, and not all babies enjoy being in them.

- **Back carrier.** Generally only suitable for babies from six months who have good head control. They're hard work on your back and, as your baby's likely to be pretty hefty by then, probably only good for your other half to take charge of.
- **Non-slip baby bath mat.** Once your baby's old enough to sit up and splash around in the bath, it's a good idea to pop him on one of these to stop him slipping. Some are heat sensitive and change colour if the bath water's too hot, which is handy.
- **Toys.** Something you may not need to bother buying for your baby at all, as you're very likely to come by them as gifts and hand-me-downs. You certainly don't need to get them new, as they're so readily available at NCT and boot sales, and on eBay. Smaller toys can be dunked in sterilising solution and larger ones wiped down with some antibacterial cleaner, if you're worried about hygiene.
- **'Baby-proofing' aids.** There's a vast range of these, including **window and cupboard locks, stair-gates,** and **socket covers,** and if you bought it all, you could end up spending a fortune. You'll have to decide for yourself what you want to invest in – but you probably don't have to worry about most of these things until your baby's determinedly moving around, because that's when the (potential) trouble starts! There's more about home safety on page 162.

> *"Baby toys are the biggest rip-off ever. My son's favourite toy was a wooden spoon with a knotted ribbon on it. And if you gave him a few pots and pans, and a plastic tub of rice, he'd be happy for ages!"*
>
> *Kathryn E*

Absolute essentials: what you need to start

- A cot and/or a Moses basket, or crib (with new mattresses if acquired secondhand)
- A sheet and two blankets, or a sleeping bag

- Eight to 12 sleepsuits; or sets of comfy, simple separates
- Eight to 12 vests
- One or two soft cardigans
- Several pairs of socks
- Coat, hat and gloves
- A car seat
- A pram and/or a sling
- Nappies, wipes, and nappy rash cream
- Cotton wool
- Changing mat
- Bottles, teats, bottle brush, and steriliser, if you plan to bottle feed
- Some bibs or muslins
- Room thermometer

2

The early weeks

So you've had your baby. Congratulations! Now you've got the exciting but extraordinary early weeks of motherhood ahead of you. Your best bet for this period is to take one day at a time – maybe even one moment at a time.

However the birth panned out, it's going to take a while to recover from it, and to get your head round your new status: mum. As for that small human you've incubated for so long: you may have wonderful feelings, mixed feelings, or no feelings at all about him, that's totally normal. Then, of course, there are the physical consequences of birth to deal with, which for many women is akin to recovering from a car crash. It's a lot to get to grips with all at once. But don't worry. You will.

> *"The first few weeks are etched in my memory forever. I was hit with a rush of love more powerful than I had ever felt, but I was terrified of her. Scared to go from hospital and having to cope at home. Scared of being alone with her. Scared I was doing everything wrong."*
>
> *Verity N*

When can we go home?

Unless you're among the tiny proportion of first-time mums who deliver at home, you and your partner will begin life as parents in hospital, or at a birth centre, which means you've got the advantage of having professionals on hand to help you make sense of those early hours. These days, if your delivery was normal and you and your baby are both doing OK, you should be discharged pretty swiftly, usually within 12 to 24 hours. Depending on when you gave birth, this may entail an overnight stay, and if so, you'll have to kiss your birth partner goodbye for a while and face a night alone, exhausted (and quite possibly sleepless, since post-natal wards and new babies are notoriously noisy), and no doubt awe-struck – a little freaked out, even – by the presence of your recently dispatched offspring in his clear plastic cot beside you.

> *"My god, I didn't get a wink of sleep that night, in spite of the fact I was knackered. My baby cried all night, it seemed to me, and I didn't have a clue how to stop it. I was so glad when morning came and her dad walked back into the ward."*
>
> ***Jess T***

Before you're discharged, a doctor or midwife will examine your baby for any obvious problems with his eyes, heart, lungs, spine, hips, mouth, and genitals. Now's the time to pipe up if you have any concerns. They'll probably ask if he's had a poo, to make sure his bottom is in working order. (Don't panic, by the way, if your baby's first few waste deposits look more like black treacle than poo: this is meconium, and it's the perfectly normal gunk that's built up in his intestines while in the womb.)

You may also be asked by medical staff if they can give your baby an injection of vitamin K. That's because babies are born with low levels of the stuff, making them vulnerable to a very rare, but serious, condition called vitamin K deficiency bleeding, or VKBD. However, if you have a particularly speedy discharge from hospital, the vitamin K injection, and the examination, too, can be carried out once you've got home by a visiting midwife or GP.

There'll be a few routine medical checks for you as well before you can leave. Your midwife will want to know that you've had a wee, that your blood pressure, pulse, and temperature are OK, and that you're fairly steady on your feet. She'll also feel your tummy, to make sure your uterus has begun the process of contracting back to its normal size.

You may have one foot out of the door as soon as you're allowed, but if you'd rather stick around at hospital for a while instead of going home, try not to feel panicky. You'll have one or more community midwives looking out for you – it's usual for one to call the very next day, and then again on several occasions afterwards (see page 43) – and in the meantime, you can always get her on the phone (make sure you've got a telephone number for the community midwives' office before leaving hospital), or even contact the maternity ward if it's out of hours and you need some fast advice.

A longer stay than you'd like

If there were complications during the birth, and either you, your baby, or both of you need extra care, or just a little further monitoring, you'll have to hang around in hospital a while longer – or be transferred there, if you had a home or birth centre delivery. You may also be asked to stay awhile if you're trying to breastfeed but it's just not taking off for some reason (see page 26).

After a C-section, you'll typically need a three- to four-day stay in the post-natal ward, although if you really want to leave before then and you seem to be recovering well, you may get the nod to leave after 24 hours.

> *"I lost a lot of blood and so spent six days in hospital after my C-section. But I was happy to be there as I had help when I needed it – particularly when I passed out. They wanted to monitor my son, too, as he was small and had low blood sugar levels, so I felt we were in safe hands. Mind you, it was good to get home."*
>
> *Amanda G*

Try to look on the bright side if you do need to stay in hospital for longer than you'd like. You may well long to be at home, where the food's edible, and the floors don't squeak. But on the other hand, you've got medical help to hand and you don't have to do anything else but lie there and take things easy while your body recovers from the shock a bit.

> *“I had to stay in hospital for a few days, and it was awful. I got no sleep due to other babies screaming, staff walking in and out constantly, and lights left on. I was so glad to be home, although I remember thinking, 'OMG, there are no staff to help, I can barely walk, and I have twins to care for!' The first thing I did was to take a photo of them and post it on Facebook with the caption: 'What do we do now?!'”*
>
> ***Dani B***

If he was born too early, or is unwell, your baby may be admitted to the nearest available neonatal care ward. It's sure to be distressing to see your new baby looking vulnerable and tiny in an incubator, or relying on special equipment to help him breathe or feed, and miserable to be spending any of your post-natal days in a the clinical surroundings of a hospital ward. An excellent source of support at times like this is Bliss, the special-care baby charity. Details (along with all the other sources of further information and help that are mentioned throughout) are in the back of the book.

> *“My son was taken to the special-care baby unit because he'd contracted an infection during the birth, so the first few days he was in the care of the neonatal nurses, rather than mine. It was desperately upsetting, knowing my baby was in there, and that I couldn't do what other new mums were doing for theirs.”*
>
> ***Marianne O***

First feeds

Feeding your baby is one of the first things you'll have to do for him, and arguably the most important. He needs food to grow, thrive, and survive, which is why feeding can be such an emotive issue for new mums – and one that can cause unnecessary stress and worry.

All your baby needs for the first six months or so is milk – either direct from you or made up from infant formula – and once you've got feeding sussed (whichever method you choose), you'll find it comes easily. Until then, it's a matter of following this particular learning curve as best you can.

There's lots more detail about feeding in Chapter 3, but here's what you need to know to get you started . . .

Getting going with breastfeeding

If, as the majority of new mums do, you've decided to have a bash at breastfeeding, you'll no doubt be encouraged to offer up your boobs at the earliest opportunity. You almost certainly know already about the benefits of breastfeeding so I won't bang on about them here, but suffice to say that breastmilk is good stuff, because it's rich in antibodies which can help keep bugs at bay; it's always the right composition and temperature; and it's thought it can help protect against the onset of allergies, which is why breastfeeding is particularly recommended for babies with a mum or dad who suffers from an allergy or atopic condition such as eczema.

It's really important to understand that, at this stage, your milk is not the full-flowing, mature stuff, which 'comes in' a few days after birth (see page 29), but the much less abundant, high-protein, antibody-rich, creamy early milk, known as colostrum. It may seem that your baby is only taking tiny amounts of this 'gold-top' but that's fine, as it's so highly concentrated. It's not unusual at first for brand new babies to be disinterested when presented with a nipple, or just too sleepy to feed. All you can do if that's the case is to keep on offering.

TIP If you're worried about milk flow, it's worth trying with your kit off: this is known as skin-to-skin contact, and it's believed to aid bonding as well as boost your flow. However, please don't fret if you can't feel maternal love flowing through you right now. For a lot of mums, this doesn't come until later.

> *"On the second night home, I rang the labour ward in tears and told them that I didn't have enough milk. I thought it must be because I had the world's smallest boobs. They told me I had plenty, it just hadn't come in yet. So I persevered, and on day five, my milk came in. It was brilliant!"*
>
> **Charlee C**

You may find there's pressure from staff to get your breastfeeding technique sussed before you've even left hospital. In fact, they'll usually want to know you and your baby are at least on the right track before discharging you. 'I remember sitting in hospital with a midwife yanking my boob trying to "encourage" my son to feed, thinking to myself that it wasn't quite the picture of motherhood I'd had in mind,' remembers Caroline S. 'Luckily, though, he quickly got the hang of it.'

Unfortunately, this pressure can lead to much despair when it just doesn't seem to be taking off for some reason. And the sad reality is, difficulties in getting breastfeeding established can persist after you've got home from hospital, anyway – or, you can make a good start, only to falter a little further in. I don't mean to be negative about breastfeeding when I say that. I think it's a great way for a mum to feed her baby: free, ready-to-serve, immunity-boosting, and always a good excuse for a prolonged sit-down. And I know from personal experience that early difficulties can often be overcome – twice, I gritted my teeth through the pain of cracked nipples and went on to breastfeed for four months (at which point, admittedly, my commitment foundered – but that's another story). What I want to make clear is that, while some women sail through the start of breastfeeding, for many, it's no picnic. And it's better to go into it with realistic expectations and then find it's easier or more enjoyable than you thought, than imagine it will be some kind of rose-tinted rush, only to experience the absolute opposite.

> *"Establishing breastfeeding was a nightmare. My daughter didn't latch on properly and my nipples were shredded. I swear a whole chunk just fell off at one point. It took a lot of perseverance and manhandling by assorted healthcare workers and I was disappointed: it wasn't the warm, fuzzy experience I'd expected."*
>
> ***Jo W***

Getting the latch right

You'll no doubt hear much about getting the 'correct latch' when trying to get to grips with breastfeeding, and it has to be said, the correct latch is pretty darn important because without it, your baby will be sucking the bejesus out of your nipple without getting what he needs out of it – and that's going to be an unhappy situation for you both. Here are some tips on how to do it.

- Get your positioning right. Make sure your baby can easily get a good mouthful. Some kind of support to help you bear his weight and raise him to the right level is vital: try sitting in a chair with arms, or use one of those v-shaped breastfeeding pillows, or just a simple stack of cushions.
- Make sure that you're as comfortable as possible, too. A pillow behind your back and a footstool are useful aids.
- Hold your baby close to your body with his head and body in a straight line, facing you, with his nose in line with your nipple.
- If you've got very big boobs, are sore from a C-section, suffering from a bad back or piles, or are just plain knackered, you might find it easier to try while lying on your side. Put your head on a pillow and your shoulder flat on the bed, your body curled round your baby, and support him so he's lying on his side, too, facing you.
- Alternatively, try the 'rugby ball' hold, which means tucking your baby's body under your arm. Some mums, in fact, say this position is far more comfortable anyway. You'll probably need to use a (very steady) pile of cushions to lay him on so that he's the right height to comfortably quaff.
- Wait until your baby's mouth is really wide open so you can get as much boob into it as possible. Aim to get all of the areola (the darker skin round your nipple) in, if you can.

- Guide your boob in with your hand (or, of course, allow your midwife to shovel it in on your behalf) and, if necessary, wobble your nipple right under his nose. Babies have a rooting reflex which means it's instinctive for them to make a beeline for a boob, but you sometimes need to give them a head start.
- Once he's on, his bottom lip should be visibly curled out and his cheeks rounded. If he's feeding well his sucking will be rhythmic, and his ears will wobble.
- Check out your nipple when he's finished, too: if it's misshapen and squashed-looking, that's an indication the latch isn't right.
- Avoid pulling your nipple clear from your baby's mouth if you don't think the latch is right and you want to try again: that way, severe pain lies. Break the suction with your finger first.

Is it supposed to be this painful . . .?

Accepted wisdom is that breastfeeding only hurts if you've got the latch wrong, but actually it can hurt like hell anyway when you're getting started. The moments after those determined gums clamp down, and the 'let-down' (the reflex action, stimulated by hormones, that kicks off milk flow) gathers powerfully behind the areola are often to be heard described as 'excruciating' by new mums. You may also experience some fairly intense cramping, or 'after pains' (see page 170) in your uterus while breastfeeding at first, because it triggers a release of the same hormones that help the womb contract back to normal size.

Most women also report a fair bit of discomfort, too, when their body begins to produce actual breastmilk (as opposed to colostrum). This process, kicked into action by the hormone prolactin, typically between three and five days after birth, is generally known as your milk 'coming in'. It's common for it to happen overnight, which means you could wake up one morning with a whole new pair of boobs attached to your chest. 'I'm well-endowed anyway, and when my milk came in my breasts felt like boulders – hard, hot and swollen,' recalls Jo W. 'My daughter found it very hard to latch on: she tried in vain to get to grips with these huge objects that were twice the size of her head!'

When your boobs are swollen, tender, and full to bursting like this, it's known as engorgement. It's a problem that can be eased simply by feeding your baby (and avoided in the future by always feeding him for as long and as often as he seems to want, or expressing if necessary – see page 81). Some also say that a cold compress applied after feeds can bring relief and, yes, they do say that cooled cabbage leaves slipped into the bra can help, although needless to say there's no scientific evidence for this. If it's really bad, you could try popping a couple of paracetamol or ibuprofen. Babies will often struggle to get their mouths round a boob that's full to bursting and slippery with leaking milk, and you may have to help yours out by gently using your hands to squeeze a little excess into the sink. This overflow shouldn't last long, as the supply and demand system settles into a pattern.

TIP You may find you're soaking your way through an awful lot of breast pads right now. Do get the best-quality, most absorbent brand you can afford, and change them really regularly, as soggy nipples are very likely to become sore nipples.

Unless there's a specific problem, though, the pain will be temporary. Honest. Accounts vary, but it should ease after a couple of weeks, and eventually it will cease altogether – thanks no doubt to a combination of tougher nipples, improved technique, and an increasingly positive mindset on your part. However, if things become worse rather than better, you may well be looking at an issue such as cracked nipples, blocked ducts or infection. There's more about all of those things on page 77.

> *“My milk came in on day three. I was talking to a visiting friend, who didn't like to point out that my t-shirt was being rapidly saturated! I was shocked by how sore they were – and how big. I truly believe that if breastfeeding campaigners explained that it does hurt at first, but should get better, then more people would stick with it.”*
>
> *Claire A*

. . . and are they supposed to feed this much?

New mums are generally advised to 'demand feed' at first, which means offering up your breast (or a bottle – see below) whenever your baby seems hungry. Breastfeeding runs on a supply-and-demand system, which means you have to keep on emptying your breasts very regularly if you want your milk to keep on coming.

How do you know when he's hungry? Well, you don't always, at first. But in these early weeks and months, it may be more often than you'd bargained for because new babies have tiny tummies and can't fill themselves up very effectively. So they'll typically feed little, but often – perhaps every hour, or even more often than that, at first. Within a few months or more, they invariably settle into a more widely spaced pattern of feeding, so you can start *expecting* them to be hungry at certain times and typically, this will be every three to four hours. In the meantime, you'll just have to watch out for his 'hunger cues' – if he's opening his mouth, smacking his lips, gnawing on his fist, rooting around near your boob, or generally fussing, they're all good signs. Crying will often indicate hunger – but of course there are other potential reasons for it including tiredness, thirst, a dirty nappy, illness, or colic (see 143), so you may have to address those things one by one if the offer of a feed doesn't cheer him up.

TIP It's generally agreed that you can't overfeed a breastfed baby, however often they seem to want to munch. This is probably because they're in control of how much they take in. Sucking on a boob's quite hard work, so they're not inclined to take more than they definitely need. If you're worried about your baby not getting enough, see page 70 in Chapter 3.

Making sure each breast is completely drained as often as possible is also important, so always let your baby drink long and hard from one breast before swapping to the other. It means he can fill up on the fat-rich 'hind' milk, which only comes down after the less filling 'fore' milk. Doing this is often cited as a way to avoid colic (see page 143), and will also help to avoid problems such as blocked ducts and mastitis (see page 79). If he makes a start on the second breast, too, but doesn't empty it, then offer it first at the next feed – you should be able to feel the difference as it will be fuller, but if not, the well-worn trick of attaching a little ribbon on a safety pin to the relevant side works well.

Feeds can take forever at first, as babies usually take a while to hone their technique, and also because they often enjoy chomping on a boob for the comfort factor, long after they've actually taken their fill. That combined with the frequency of early feeds means that initially, breastfeeding mums can find themselves amazed (and often, very fed up) by the sheer proportion of their life spent releasing their breasts from their bra. Like the pain, the sense that you are in fact little more than a human milking machine should decrease over the first few months, as your baby's tummy grows and his technique improves, allowing him to take larger amounts, less often. Meanwhile, a good maternity bra with quick-release front opening, is handy, along with a wardrobe full of loose tops that you can either just lift up, or can easily open down the front. (Hint: buttons are a nuisance. I recall asking my mum to sew zips in the front of a whole load of jersey tops, which she duly – and very kindly – did.)

> *“I just couldn't believe how much she fed at first. It felt like I had my boob in her mouth for at least half the day. In between, thankfully, she slept a lot, giving me a chance to lie there with my naked boobs in the air, caked in Kamillosan, trying to let them recover a bit in time for the next feed.”*
>
> ***Lauren B***

What about what Gina says?

Of course, not everyone agrees that baby-led demand feeding is the only way forward with a newborn. Proponents of strict routines would no doubt say that it's daft to spend more time than necessary letting your baby nibble at will on your boobs, or a bottle for that matter – and equally, that it's silly to let him snooze through when he ought to be awake and feeding.

These schedule-based strategies tend to get frowned upon by health professionals, who feel they may stop mums responding to a baby's natural 'cues'. And for many of us, the sheer efficiency required make them seem like more work than they're worth. However, there's no doubt that Gina Ford has a great many fans among mums who swear she really did help them to have a 'contented baby', so if you think it could be the way forward for you, pick up a copy of her book, or check out her website, and give it a go.

Otherwise, though, rest assured that some sort of structure to your baby's feeding and sleeping schedule is almost certain to develop in a fairly natural way eventually – usually once the dust has settled on the first few months – making for a more settled and predictable life.

> *"I found the Gina Ford routines to be a real lifesaver. I also found they were wonderfully compatible with breastfeeding – they allowed me to go on with it when I might have given up, because he was feeding so much, it was depressing. I know these routines get a lot of stick, mostly from people who haven't read the books, so I decided early on that I wouldn't give a toss what anyone thought."*
>
> ***Lucy J***

Getting help

Sadly, the often difficult nature of getting breastfeeding established can really mar the early days for some new mums. One thing you'll need in spades is support and practical help from your partner, or other reliable loved ones. You need someone to bring you food, drink, and anything else you need while you're permanently pinned to the sofa with your breasts out, for starters. And if for some reason you're struggling to get started, you'll need plenty of sympathetic, non-judgemental practical guidance, either from the health professionals at hand, or a source of specific help such as an NCT (National Childbirth Trust) breastfeeding counsellor, or breastfeeding clinic. There's more about this on page 80.

Don't overlook the help that's available online, however, if you'd rather work out how to breastfeed for yourself. 'YouTube is a brilliant repository of video instruction on the subject which is great if you don't fancy being manhandled by a scary midwife-type at a workshop,' recommends Charlee C. 'Watching online tutorials during the mammoth feeding sessions in the first few nights after the birth has the added bonus of giving you something to concentrate on when you feel you might just fall asleep halfway through.'

> *"Get help if you're struggling to get breastfeeding established. Demand it! And yes, it really is a good idea to lie in bed naked with your baby while trying. You can't possibly work it out while desperately trying to stuff an engorged boob into a screaming baby's mouth while your brother-in-law tries to maintain eye contact with you. And feeding needs to be pretty constant in those early days so you need loads of time, space and privacy."*
>
> *Rebecca F*

Formula feeding

Feeding your baby formula from a bottle also has its benefits. Chief among them is that you will always be able to ask your partner (or anyone else, for that matter), to take over. For most modern mums, that's a big plus.

> *"I planned to breastfeed, but the agony of latching on, the misery of cracked nipples, an unhappy baby, and hopeless midwives made me lose my incentive, and I gave up pretty quickly. I'm no martyr. I found the switch difficult, though. Not one midwife would advise me on what to do. So I just went by the instructions on the tub, tried a variety of different bottles and types of formula, and we muddled through."*
>
> *Jessica P*

Please don't feel guilty about it if you've decided to formula feed your baby, or if you end up formula feeding because breastfeeding didn't work out for you. Sadly, it's a common reaction. But formula is a perfectly good alternative to breastmilk, as long as you always get the maths right and you've got the hygiene issues sussed. Both are crucial for your baby's good health, so you do need to make sure you're familiar with the instructions on the tin, and that you know all the rules about sterilising and making up bottles (see page 88).

TIP Statistics show formula feeding is a popular choice. While the Department of Health recommends that mums breastfeed exclusively for six months and up to 81% of UK mums make a start with breastfeeding, the most recently available official figures – from the 2005 Infant Feeding Survey – show that only 21% are still breastfeeding exclusively at six weeks. So the vast majority of mums have offered formula by then.

Setting up for formula feeding

Before you get started with formula feeding, you'll need the right equipment: at least four bottles and teats (but, realistically, several more besides in the early days, when feeding is on demand and often frequent, and you're too tired to keep up with more than one daily cycle of washing and sterilising); a bottle cleaning brush; and some form of steriliser. And you'll need formula, obviously, although it may not be clear exactly which sort to go for, as the number of brands and types on offer is bewildering and other mums will no doubt offer up many different recommendations.

Cost may also be a significant factor for you, as it's surprisingly expensive stuff. You may even come to discover that your baby himself has preferences, or just 'gets on' with one better than another, in which case you can only really use a process of trial and error. Pick one arbitrarily for now and see how you go. But do make sure you've got the first-stage stuff – steer well clear of second-stage, 'follow-on' or 'hungrier baby' varieties, as they're not suitable for newborns.

Ready-made formula in cartons is a convenient option, since you just pour it straight into a sterilised bottle and it's good to go, which means you can't get the proportions wrong and, as it can be stored (when unopened) at room temperature, you probably won't even need to warm it (helpful, if you've got a very hungry, very cross baby in your arms). Naturally it's more expensive than the powdered stuff: you may not be able to afford to use it all the time but it's still great for days out, or occasions when you just can't be bothered with making bottles in the usual, more long-winded way.

> *"My son was constantly sick so we kept changing formula brands, to try and resolve the issue. I found information on the different brands hard to come by as the Health Visitor didn't want to be seen to recommend one over another. As it turned out, the problem was caused by a hernia."*
>
> *Clare A*

Even if you're not breastfeeding, your breasts will still produce milk at first. It will subside and dry up, but there's likely to be a painful few days for you in the meantime: a hot flannel, snug bra, and a painkiller or two, if necessary, should see you through. Beyond that, the only major problems you're likely to have in getting formula feeding up and running is the whiff of disapproval from certain other people. Try to ignore that kind of attitude if it rears its head. He's your baby. How you feed him is your business.

> *"I struggled to feed my twins myself, there just didn't seem to be any milk in there for them. It was inferred by my charming feeding nurse that it was probably due to me not feeling emotionally connected to them. Eventually I offered them both a bottle, instead. Formula rocks."*
>
> *Natasha H*

How to bottle feed

Make sure you and your baby are both comfortable for bottle feeds. He'll need good head support, and to be able to swallow and breathe freely. Hold the bottle upright, so the teat is always full and the bottle neck always covered with milk – otherwise, he may take in air and that could make him windy. Allow him to take bottle feeds at his own pace, with pauses throughout if he seems to want them.

Winding your baby

Whether breast or bottle fed, a gentle rub on the back after a feed is a good way to bring up any extra wind. You can sit them up or pop them over your shoulder – but put a muslin over it first! You may get a lovely big burp for your troubles. Better out, than in, as they say.

How much formula?

As a formula-feeding mum, you're no more likely to know when and how often to feed your newborn than a breastfeeding mum, and you too will probably have to be led by your baby and offer a bottle whenever he seems hungry. (You'll get just the same sort of cues as you would from a breastfed baby – see above.) Little and often is normal at first – typically, you'll find he only drinks a few ounces at a time, but wants to feed fairly regularly, but as time goes on a pattern will emerge, and he'll drink larger quantities, with longer and more regular intervals in between. Chuck anything he hasn't drunk, rather than trying to save it for later, because bacteria can quickly develop. You may have to accept some wastage for a while. There's more advice on formula feeding in Chapter 3.

Reality bites

Don't be surprised if, having strapped your new baby lovingly into his car seat, driven him home at seven miles an hour, and placed him gently down on the sitting room carpet, it all feels a bit anti-climactic. 'We got back after a five-day stay in hospital and to be honest, it was rather weird and a bit horrid as we didn't know what to do, either with him or ourselves. We just sat down in silence, staring numbly at him in his car seat,' recalls Sarah R.

For some mums, the full force of maternal love hits home from the start. 'I spent the first few days in (happy) tears, just looking at him and crying because I was so proud that I'd made something so perfect,' says Jemma P. 'I didn't want to put him down, or even hand him over to visitors for a cuddle'. Alex G felt similarly gobsmacked after the birth of her daughter: 'I held her and was just in complete awe of what I had just done, and also of this little creature that I was holding. That first day home was amazing. I went to bed when she did, in a Moses basket next to me, and I held her hand all night. It was daunting, confusing, and wonderful all at once. I spent the first few weeks just staring at her, feeling overwhelming love.'

All of which is wonderful. But it's quite possible you won't feel the same way. If you're looking down at your new-born baby and feel absolutely nothing, rest assured that it's *not* abnormal. Bonding's a funny old business, but one thing's certain: it's by no means automatic. Lots of mums say it was days, weeks, or even months down the line before they felt like they really loved their baby. My own memories are a tad blurred, but I do recall that for me, motherly love only kicked in a little way down the line – and in a gradual way, rather than in one big rush.

> *"I felt like death, to be honest. The birth had been long and traumatic. I was numb, utterly exhausted, in pain. I cried loads. I had no feelings for my son at all, no rush of motherly love. I just wanted it to go away. We had to go back into hospital because he had jaundice, and that was hellish. Back home, I felt like I'd made the worst mistake of my life. Grim, I know. It did get better!"*
>
> ***Lucy J***

The baby blues

Most new mums experience the 'baby blues' to some degree in the first few days and weeks. Sometimes the urge to burst into tears hits all of a sudden a week or so in. It's hardly surprising, really: shock and exhaustion hit home, your hormones are all over the shop, your body aches, and you're probably wondering if you can actually pull this whole motherhood thing off. If you're also preoccupied by a difficult delivery, a poorly baby, breastfeeding worries, or any sort of external stress, that's just going to make it worse. So, ricocheting between elation and despair is in fact really quite normal right now. 'I was an emotional wreck for the first few weeks,' reveals Lara S, 'although most of the time it was just happy tears, or tears of pure exhaustion.'

Please don't be alarmed if this emotional barrage occurs. It's very normal, and it doesn't mean you have post-natal depression (see page 202).

These ups and downs should lift within the first few weeks and in the meantime, you'll just have to ride them out as best you can. Get as much rest and sleep as you can, eat well and make sure you're getting all the sympathy and practical support you can from your nearest and dearest. If you're not, seek support from the friendliest health professional you know.

You may be feeling very anxious a lot of the time, and it's hardly surprising when you consider the weight of the responsibility the stork has just delivered, and the distinct possibility that you have no clue whatsoever how to actually care for this tiny thing. As Molly F recounts, 'I felt a strange mixture of calm and content, punctuated by extreme nerves. The house was quiet as she slept so much, which made me feel as if I was living in a cosy bubble. But then I'd get these panics about breastfeeding, and the huge responsibility of keeping a little person alive.'

Do, please, keep on top of difficult feelings post-birth. Talk them through with your partner, or a good friend. For some women, these relatively minor 'baby blues' or feelings of anxiety can give way to actual post-natal depression (PND) or post-natal anxiety (PNA), and those things require help, so talk to your midwife, Health Visitor (HV) or GP if you're showing the signs. Be aware too of birth trauma, which can strike after a difficult delivery and cause serious emotional problems. There's more about all these issues in Chapter 6.

> *“I felt numb and indifferent in those early days, and I even felt angry, at times. I felt happy only fleetingly, but in a completely overwhelming way. Please don't worry if you feel the same. It will get better. It just will. Not quickly, but gradually, and most definitely. Hold that thought in your mind.”*
>
> *Rebecca F*

Taking it easy

Outside looking after yourself and your baby, it's a good idea to do as little as you can get away with in the early weeks. Let your other half take charge of domestic chores, and if your mum insists on helping out while she's visiting, make the most of it. That way, you can concentrate on resting and recovering. 'You and your baby have some steep learning to do in those early days. Go with the flow and don't even try to run to schedule,' is Nicola L's advice.

Don't bother with cooking, either. If your partner's a bit of a Jamie Oliver and happy to spend his paternity leave rustling up sustenance, that's well and good, but otherwise, rely on ready meals and easy snacks as much as possible. Whatever you do, don't skimp on eating, though, and try to make sure you're getting a reasonably healthy balance of foods. You need fuel to keep you going – particularly if you're breastfeeding – and to boost your physical recovery.

> *“Having a baby is the biggest shock ever to your body, your life, everything. Of course, everyone says sleep when the baby sleeps! Yeah, right: no matter how knackered you are, chances are that when your baby sleeps, you'll be wide awake! But if that's the case, at least try to rest: make a cuppa, put the telly on, and put your feet up.”*
>
> ***Emily D***

Don't be afraid to stay in your PJs, or simply to stay in bed altogether, if it suits you. It will make it easier to grab some shut-eye when your baby does, or at the very least to catch up on rest, reading, or a spot of social networking. If wallowing around in bed seems rather an indulgence, remember this: you probably won't get a chance to do so with your next baby, because you'll be too busy running around after your (now-mobile) first born. Try to get up and about at least a couple of times a day though, as moving around can help get your blood moving, boost your recovery – and make you feel a bit more human.

> *“Like many women I made life hard for myself in the early days, worrying about the house being tidy for the Health Visitor, and the sleepsuits being perfectly folded. I wish I'd chilled out a bit. Try to channel your inner Earth mother, even just for a few days: stay in your pyjamas, let loved ones pamper you, and keep the rest of the world out for a while. Enjoy being in the cocoon. It's a special time.”*
>
> ***Jo W***

Safe sleep: a warning

Wonderful as it is to be snuggled up in bed with your baby, do please be wary of falling asleep when he's next to you – and that particularly goes for dropping off on the sofa or armchair, all too easy as it is when you're knackered. It's a controversial subject, and the truth is that lots of parents *do* sleep with their baby, either by design or by default, but official advice is not to, for safety reasons. Most experts are pretty firm in their convictions that the best place to put your newborn down for sleep is in a Moses basket, cot, or crib, positioned close to your own bedside. If you are certain you *do* want to sleep with your baby, there are guidelines that can minimise the risks. They're included, along with other safe sleep advice, in Chapter 5.

Up and about

Of course, staying in your PJs or lolling in bed is not an idea that appeals to all new mums, as Heidi S can vouch. 'Oh God, the thought of getting into bed with my baby and staying there for days horrifies me,' she says. 'I would have gone stir crazy.' So by all means, if it makes you feel better, then take a shower and get dressed at your first opportunity (albeit, no doubt, rather later in the day than you're used to).

Some fresh air can also be a tonic, and there's no reason why you can't take a brand new baby out and about, if you've got the energy. As Clare F recalls: 'One thing that really helped me was to shower and freshen up every day with clean clothes and a bit of make-up. Sounds easy but it can be a major achievement early on. After about a week I also started going out for a walk every day, just for ten minutes. It did us both the world of good.' Don't go mad, though. Now's not really the time for shopping trips or long journeys. A pootle down the road with the buggy or sling is probably a good aim to begin with.

> *"You should do what you feel like doing, not what you're supposed to do. If you want to slob around all day, do it, but if you're the sort of person who needs to be up and dressed and nice and clean, then make the effort if it'll*

make you feel better. Everyone copes with the early days differently. Though I've yet to find anyone who thinks going to the London Aquarium with a two-week-old is a good idea, which is what I did for some reason.”

Lucy J

Dealing with visitors

Friends and relatives will want to share in your happiness – it's only natural. And many of them will want to do this in person, mainly so they can get their mitts on your new arrival. For some new parents, the right visitor, at the right time, doing the right things, will prove a downright boon. 'My sister came to stay for a week after the birth, and having her there was invaluable,' Molly F recalls. 'She cooked all the meals, kept the house clean, and stayed on top of the mountains of washing, which meant I could focus totally on my new baby.' Unfortunately, not all visitors are such a delight. 'I remember sitting there, as my baby slept in a Moses basket, watching two friends slowly get pissed while toasting her birth,' says Rebecca F. 'All I could think about was how I could have been asleep for those three hours.'

“Don't hesitate to ask someone else to take over and hold your baby while you grab a break – even the monster-in-law! You might be a bit reluctant to let go at first, but trust me, the novelty of holding your newborn will soon wear off.”

Natasha H

You may have to adopt a fairly forceful policy on visitors if you're finding it all a bit much. If you personally can't bear to turn people away, then ask your other half or someone else with a thicker skin than yours to do it for you. A little white lie, such as 'they're both sleeping' can go a long way in these circumstances. Putting a note on the door to that effect means you can ward off the cold-callers at least.

“Be assertive. If someone says you should be taking the baby out to meet the family and you don't feel up to it, tell them so. If they come to see the baby then sit on their arse

holding your precious bundle and expecting you to make tea, plonk yourself down and ask them to put the kettle on. If they outstay their welcome, don't just hint, tell them. You're allowed to be rude. Blame it on the hormones."

Abi M

Paying for help

If you don't have much in the way of reliable (or desirable) extra help, and you can afford it, consider buying some in. An independent maternity nurse will charge, on average, £10 to £15 an hour (although you may also have to add agency fees and expenses on to that) and will usually be happy to take on long shifts, living in if necessary. As well as helping with feeding, changing, and generally caring for your baby, they're usually happy to wash bottles, take on a baby's laundry, and do some light housework too, all of which will allow you to sleep, rest and recover.

Alternatively, and perhaps a little more cheaply, you could consider hiring the services of a post-natal 'doula'. Doulas aren't usually qualified or medically trained but generally have kids themselves and can offer practical and emotional support to new mums.

"*We had an independent midwife helping out, both pre- and post-birth. She visited us daily for the first month, as I had no family around and we were clueless. It was fantastic having someone with a logical, experienced head on her shoulders to make sure our baby was fed, watered, and the right temperature. I'd thoroughly recommend forking out for professional help.*"

Celine G

Your post-natal care

According to guidelines from the National Institute for Clinical Excellence (NICE), you and your baby should receive post-natal care courtesy of the NHS for six to eight weeks after the birth. That means, in theory, a number of home visits from members of the healthcare team looking out for you and most likely a series of appointments at, or an open invitation to attend, your local baby clinic. Precisely what you can expect and when can't be generalised: it can vary wildly according to where you live, and any individual needs you may have. A community midwife will usually call the day after you get home from the hospital or birth centre (or the day after birth, if you had your baby at home), and she, or a colleague, will generally call again at least a couple of times during the next ten days or so. She'll want to make sure your recovery is going OK, that your baby is feeding well, and that you're coping in general.

Responsibility for you and you baby will then be passed to one or more HVs, who'll make the first of a series of home visits and provide you with a red book in which important health and development notes will be made over the next year and beyond. HVs will also want to keep on top of feeding issues, and make sure your baby is gaining a healthy amount of weight – she'll bring scales to do this, or direct you to the nearest clinic. (Bear in mind that new babies usually lose some weight at first and, typically, are expected to regain it within the first fortnight.) She should also be able to advise you on your baby's general care, health, and development – or refer you elsewhere, if not. And she should be asking after your emotional well-being, too, and offering help if she suspects yours is under par.

> *“I felt completely at sea, especially as I found breastfeeding difficult and didn't know who to turn to. The midwife was vague about visits – she didn't turn up at all for her second appointment so I ended up going to a weekend drop-in centre instead, and I had to chase for the next – she'd obviously forgotten. I would have loved a daily visit in that first week or so. I didn't have a clue.”*
>
> ***Alex G***

Most HVs are efficient, well-informed, sympathetic, and a huge help when you're floundering in the early weeks. However, some can be a bit 'old school', lack empathy, or come across as judgemental – no doubt heightened if you feel over-sensitive or defensive about things. 'I was really happy with my Health Visitor and felt her advice was very useful most of the time,' recalls Molly F. 'But I do think that their approach to advice can sometimes be a bit one-sided and 'by-the-book', with not much appreciation that all babies are different.'

There's not a lot you can do about it if you're lumbered with a HV who's more hindrance than help: you don't need to see her beyond the routine visits and appointments, and if you really need to talk to someone, you can always request another member of the team. Don't take it lying down either if you don't seem to be getting the checks you're due – after all, just because something is laid out in NICE guidelines, that doesn't mean it will always happen in reality and the sad truth is that a lot of community care teams are understaffed and overworked. Be proactive: get on the telephone and make any necessary appointments yourself. And if you need advice in between visits, don't hesitate to call and ask for it, or to arrange for someone to come and see you if necessary.

Newborn tests

Your midwife will want to carry out a minor medical procedure on your baby, known variably as the 'heelprick', 'bloodspot', or 'Guthrie' test. This speedy bit of screening is usually carried out a week or so after birth, and is used to detect a number of rare but serious conditions that are far better off picked up early, including congenital hypothyroidism, cystic fibrosis, and sickle cell disorders. It involves a little blood being taken via a small pronged device, from his heel – he'll probably cry horribly, and you might too, but it's over quickly. A swift follow-up cuddle or feed should see him right soon enough.

At some point within the first few weeks, your baby will also get to have his hearing tested. This quick, painless automated process may be carried out at home or in a clinic (or sometimes even before you're discharged from hospital). Don't fret if it turns out your baby is required to have a second test: it's fairly common, as there are a variety of reasons why the first lot of results aren't reliable, and won't necessarily indicate a hearing problem.

Sleep in the early days

Brand new babies will often spend a large proportion of their day asleep. Some new parents find it hard to believe quite how much – and then find themselves constantly checking their baby's breathing, just in case they aren't asleep, but unconscious. But they really can and do sleep for long stretches at first. For a little while, it may seem as though your baby only wakes for a feed, a burp, a poo, and a change, before falling straight asleep again.

Unfortunately, since a newborn's body clock (or circadian rhythm, to give it the correct term) has not yet settled into anything resembling a normal pattern, and because their tummies are tiny, and need fairly frequent filling, this cycle of waking, feeding, and sleeping will usually just carry right on through the night. So, from the start, you will come to experience one of the very worst bits about having a new baby: the hell of interrupted sleep. As Laura K puts it, 'Baby-induced sleep deprivation is very much like jet lag: and I don't mean the sort where you've got a holiday to look forward to the other end'! There's more about sleep in Chapter 5.

> *“If you find yourself up at all hours in the night, try not to stress about your lack of sleep. Sky-plus some of your favourite programmes, take your baby downstairs, and chill. The calmer you both are, the quicker you'll go back to sleep.”*
>
> *Emily D*

It may help to try and find a positive spin in those dark night time moments when you're breastfeeding, or taking your turn with the bottle. 'I found the interrupted sleep with my first baby sort of weirdly magical,' recalls Heidi S. 'I used to get up and make a cup of tea and a cosy nest on the sofa for the long night feed, and loved the sense that we were the only ones awake in the world.' Meanwhile, try to make the most of any long slots of daytime peace you get in these early weeks by grabbing a kip yourself – or at the very least, resting the bits of your body that hurt the most.

On the other hand, you may find as Jenny C did that your new arrival is bright-eyed and bushy tailed from the start. 'She didn't sleep, at all – or at least, not in her Moses basket, or her cot, or her car seat unless the car was moving,' Jenny recalls. 'She cried every time we tried to put her down. So we didn't. We had to hold her in four-hour shifts, and I breastfed on demand – which seemed to be every half an hour. We took it in turns to get sleep whenever we could!'

> *"My daughter slept loads for the first few days. I remember thinking she must be the most beautiful, angelic, perfectly behaved newborn in the world. After a few days, though, she woke up properly and reality kicked in! She was still beautiful, but she made her presence felt, and my little bubble burst somewhat."*
>
> *Jo W*

Can I do anything to make him sleep better?

What with their wonky body clocks, tiny tummies, and frequent need for physical reassurance, there's probably no point in trying too hard to influence when or how your baby sleeps in these early weeks. Unless you're determinedly following a Gina-style routine that involves structuring his sleep/wake times right from the start, your best bet is to let your baby lead the way, allowing him to nap whenever he wants during the day, and getting up to give him whatever he needs in the way of food or comfort when he wakes at night.

Well-meaning onlookers may warn you against setting up 'bad habits' like rocking or feeding your baby to sleep, and it's true that you can end up indulging some tendencies that, a bit later on, may require a little work to undo. But my advice is not to worry about that right now. If you have no choice but to rock, cuddle, or feed your newborn to sleep because it's the only thing that will reliably send him off to the land of nod, then you pretty much have to go with that, really. There are, however, some 'good' sleep habits you can aim to get set up, even from the start, if you want to: they're outlined on page 119.

Why is he crying?

Good question. Babies cry a lot. It's their way of communicating their feelings and needs to you in the absence of any talking skills. Some say that babies have different types of cries, which a tuned-in mum can learn to identify and pinpoint – and maybe you too will develop this skill in time and with a bit of experience under your belt. But generally, when it comes to working out why your baby's crying, all you can really do is use a process of elimination to work out what he's in a tizz about, and what you need to offer to soothe him. If he's not hungry, perhaps his nappy needs changing? Maybe he's simply tired, and needs to be put down in his cot or taken for a walk or drive so that he can drop off. If wind's bothering him, a good rub on the back may solve the problem. Or it could be he's just bored or fed up, in which case you may find a cuddle helps. Do seek medical help if your baby's crying is accompanied by any worrying symptoms (see pages 150–151). But bear in mind that if it's excessive and inconsolable and there doesn't seem to be any clear reason for it then it's very likely to be colic. There's more about that on page 143.

Newborn characteristics

While your new baby is no doubt beautiful to you, he may also boast one or more weird newborn characteristics and you may need reassurance that these are OK. If you're in any doubt at all about anything, don't hesitate to ask your midwife or HV: she won't laugh at you, however neurotic you may fear you're being.

Odd heads. The outward journey through the birth canal and vagina is a bit of a squeeze, and the plates that form the skull still soft, so don't be surprised if your baby has an elongated or otherwise strangely shaped head, especially if a ventouse or forceps were involved in his birth. The soft spot at the top (the fontanelle) will gradually close up over the course of his first year as the skull bones fuse: meanwhile, it's covered by a pretty tough layer of membrane, so it's only in your nightmares that anyone would really be able to push a finger through it.

> *"He was stuck for a while during the latter stages of labour; as a result, he was born with a bruised and cone-shaped head. His dad recently said something about him being an ugly newborn, but I didn't see it that way! I still think he was gorgeous. I suppose I was wearing hormone-tinted spectacles!"*
>
> *Clare F*

Dreadful skin. If your newborn seems spottier than the average adolescent, fear not. Baby skin is often sensitive and may well be blotchy, pimply, or very dry. Little white 'milk spots' (milia), are particularly common around the nose and cheeks. Check with your HV if you're worried, but on the whole, spots and pimples will usually clear up on their own and in the meantime, are best left alone. If his skin seems rather greasy, it will just be remnants of vernix, a creamy white coating that develops in the womb and acts as a kind of moisturiser. Yellow-ish skin could indicate jaundice, a common sign of an immature liver: your midwife should be well on top of this, as severe cases may require treatment, but if you're worried, make a call and ask if someone can take a look.

An excess of hair. Don't worry, you haven't given birth to a primate. This hairy covering is just lanugo, which helped to protect him in the womb. It will drop off eventually, but may hang around for a little while longer. Hair on the head is very variable: some babies have little or none, others a luxuriant mop. Whatever he does have will probably fall out in the coming months and grow back, and quite possibly in a completely different colour or texture.

> *"My daughter was so hairy! Even the back of her ears were covered in fur. She still is, eleven months later. We call her Monkey Child."*
>
> *Charlee C*

Swollen nipples and genitals. Although slightly freaky, this very normal occurrence is down to hormones, passed on by you during pregnancy and birth. For the same reason, baby girls sometimes have a little blood in the nappy – her very first period, if you like.

Squinty eyes. When a newborn appears squinty, it's usually because the muscles are underdeveloped, although sometimes it's a pure optical illusion, caused because the bridge of the nose is so flat. Either way, it won't last long. (You should, however, get medical advice if a squint persists.)

> *"His eyes went in different directions, which really worried me! But the Health Visitor explained that babies are born without the ability to control their eyes at the same time, and that by six weeks, it would be fine which, almost to the day, it was."*
>
> ***Lara S***

Birthmarks. These coloured patches on the skin come in many different forms, from pale pink 'stork bites' to dark red, raised 'strawberry marks', and are extremely common. Some birthmarks fade and disappear with time, some don't. And sometimes they can be problematic, for medical or cosmetic reasons. Your GP should be able to advise you.

Cord stump. This black, shrivelled thing is what remains of the umbilical cord and will hang down from your baby's navel for up to a fortnight. It may look red and sore which is usually normal, however, infection can develop so keep it clean with plain water, and turn down the top of his nappy to avoid rubbing. Get some advice if it starts to look very sore or weepy, and/or smells really bad.

> *"I'd gone through childbirth, with all its blood and gore, but what really horrified me was the cord stump. It is truly a gross thing. The day it dropped off, we breathed a sigh of relief."*
>
> ***Nicola L***

Making the most of it

So, all in all, those first few weeks are a pretty amazing time. With hindsight, you'll probably look back and remember it as both awful and awesome in equal measures. The thing to remember is that these weeks are just one very small part of you and your baby's lives together. Take each day as it comes, and meanwhile, make sure you and your other half wallow in whatever time you have to spend with the newest member of your family. You won't believe how quickly he's about to grow up.

Part two

Your baby

3

Basic babycare

So, you need to know how to care for this tiny and totally dependent new member of your family. And yes, it's true – as that amusing observation goes – they don't come with instructions. If you've never really spent time with a new baby before, there's no reason why you should know how it's done, which is where the advice of a good babycare manual such as this one, a decent health professional, or a trusted loved one who's been there and done it (and whose advice is offered only when solicited), will come in handy. And failing that, of course, there's an abundance of instructional videos on everything from changing a nappy to getting your baby dressed on YouTube.

Meanwhile, try to relax when it comes to caring for your baby. Sure, it's not always obvious what you need to do and how, but instinct will get you a surprisingly long way. Confidence and know-how will come with time. Until then, take comfort in the fact that you're extremely unlikely to cause him any lasting harm with your incompetence.

> *“There were so many things I could not make head or tail of! I was completely baffled by how best to dress him, and also how to keep him the right temperature. A lot of stuff you just have to learn by trial and error, but they're pretty resilient. He's survived!”*
>
> *Clare F*

Mums' panel round-up

What did you find trickiest at first?

Getting her dressed. I gave up trying to get her coat on properly for the way home from hospital. I couldn't bend her little arms far enough back to do it – **Jane H**

Trying to keep her the right temperature. It was October, and I had no idea how many layers to dress her in. She seemed either to be bright blue or bright purple, never a sort of normal skin colour – **Charlee C**

I was nervous of taking care of her umbilical cord properly, and unsure about her swollen genitalia, and the changes in her poo – **Alex G**

Bathing. My daughter screamed throughout. In the end I gave her jug-showers, or had her in my bath with me – **Abi M**

Changing a nappy was terrifying – and trying to dress or change this fragile baby. I couldn't even entertain leaving the house. The thought terrified me – **Emily D**

Not knowing why my boys were crying. I soon found out that it was all down to guess work – **Dani B**

How to handle him

It's very normal to feel nervous about picking up, holding and handling your fragile new offspring. Perhaps you're convinced you'll squash him or drop him, or hurt his neck, as you cack-handedly attempt to administer cuddles, or simply move him from A to B. As with so much else, it's really just a question of building up a bit of confidence, but in the meantime, remember to: a) hold him nice and close to you, and fairly firmly, so that he feels secure; and b) always support his head, since he won't have the strength to do so himself at first, and it will wobble and loll most uncomfortably if you don't. (However, don't panic if this does happen occasionally, as it's unlikely to cause injury.) If you can't get on with the traditional 'cradle' hold, try holding him upright against your chest, supporting his bottom with one hand and his head with the other. Lots of babies seem to prefer this outlook on life.

Dressing is a skill that can take a bit of practice. The key aim here is to put the garment on your baby, rather than your baby into the garment. So, rather than bending his arm into the armholes, scrunch up the fabric of the sleeves before pulling them down over his arms, and widen necks with your outstretched fingers before bringing them swiftly over his head. It's also a good idea to go for the simplest combos, as Sharon F wisely recommends. 'Resist the fancy outfits you've been given by family and friends,' she says. 'Just keep them in sleepsuits – it's so much easier.' I myself clearly recall dressing my new daughter one morning in an extremely cute and clearly expensive two-piece, since the kind friends who'd gifted it to her were coming round that afternoon. Naturally, she'd brought up a feed on it long by mid-morning, and was back in an Asda all-in-one when they arrived.

> *“Oh, those sodding sleepsuit poppers. Remember to pop from the bottom up, people, that's my advice.”*
>
> *Rebecca F*

Nappies

What's in a nappy

If he's producing plenty of wet and dirty nappies, it's a sign your baby's healthy and feeding well, so try to look on the bright side when changing time comes round. And please don't be surprised if you find yourself wondering if your baby's poo is quite normal. It can come out in all sorts of surprising colours and textures at first.

Breastfed baby poo is typically a bright, mustardy colour, often with a seedy texture, and extremely soft – indeed, it can be alarmingly runny, copious, and, at times, quite explosive, although on the plus side it doesn't usually smell too bad. Regularity can be pretty erratic too: breastfed babies will usually produce several nappyfuls a day, but they sometimes go for several days or more without doing a poo at all, without it causing a problem. Formula-fed babies usually do poos that are a pale yellow or beige colour, firm in texture, and pretty whiffy – and they will generally need to get one out every day, if they're to avoid constipation.

TIP Don't worry too much if the colour and texture of your baby's poo seems to vary quite a bit, it's normal. However, it's a good eye idea to be alert to any major changes in his waste-dispensing habits, as it could be a signal that something's up. There's more about poo problems in Chapter 7.

Changing time

It's important to keep on top of very wet or dirty bottoms, to avoid soreness or nappy rash developing (see page 156): so aim to change your baby as soon as possible after he's pooed (trust me, you *will* know when this is – giveaway signs include the look of intense concentration on his face while in the act, and the unmistakable smell) and whenever the nappy seems rather soggy. Modern disposables are very absorbent, so you may have to rely on how heavy it seems to be to work out whether it needs changing or not.

> *"I really didn't like newborn nappies, and neither did my husband. We had a turn system and tried to persuade anyone else we could to change him in between."*
> *Claire A*

A bum job: tips for nappy change time

- Have everything you need within reach before attempting to change a nappy: it's a job that requires two hands. Make sure you've worked out which way round it needs to go beforehand, too.
- Wipe off the worst of the mess with the old nappy (and do then put it in a safe place, and not somewhere you might kneel on – or where your baby might put his hand in it), tackling the rest with cotton wool and warm water, which is what's usually

recommended for sensitive newborn bottoms. If you go for wipes straight away, stick with unfragranced brands.

- When cleaning little girls, wipe from the front to the back, rather than the other way round, to avoid spreading germs. And with little boys, don't try to pull the foreskin back – it's still attached at this stage.
- A little petroleum jelly can help prevent nappy rash (see page 156), but more important is letting the skin dry completely and, if you've time, exposing it to the air for a while, before putting on a new nappy – babies often enjoy the chance for a little semi-naked kickaround, too.
- Watch out for surprise wees at this point, particularly if your baby has a penis.
- Don't forget to wash your hands before and after nappy changes, for obvious reasons of hygiene.
- Bung the nappy in a scented nappy bag to help keep the smell contained and put it in your dustbin at the earliest opportunity.
- Whichever type of nappy you go for, get the best quality you can afford (the more you pay, the more absorbent it's likely to be), and make sure the fit's good: too loose and you'll get leakage, too snug and it could cause chafing. Hold on to any money-off or free sample vouchers that come your way, to make nicer nappies a more affordable option. Look out for supermarket deals too, and buy in bulk where you can.

“I really wasn't expecting such an impressive trajectory when he weed for the first time during a nappy change. A good trick is to lie a muslin across his bits to soak up the worst – or just stem the flow with the nappy you were about to put on.”

Alison M

TIP Do your homework if you're considering reusable or 'real' nappies and weigh up the pros and cons before making the investment. Fans of reusables argue that they're cheaper in the long run, greener, and kinder to babies, being chemical-free. On the flipside, they're undoubtedly more hassle – and some argue that the extra energy required to wash them means they're not as environmentally friendly as all that. A compromise may be to opt for one of the more eco-friendly brands, which tend to contain more natural materials and are usually at least partially biodegradable (but don't seem to feel quite as soft).

Keeping him clean

You may be surprised at how much cleaning up your newborn requires. It's normal for babies to bring up some of their last feed (there's more on 'posseting' on page 92), and this regurgitated milk can gather in places you might not even realise need checking: in and behind his ears, and under his chin and armpits, for instance. I remember being horrified to discover that dribbled milk had made a home under my first-born's chin and – since it had clearly been there a couple of days – had more or less formed cheese. Poo can also find its way into all sorts of places you'd rather it didn't, and may linger even if you've shown due care during nappy changes (tip: don't attempt to change a dirty nappy in the dark at night). It's also important to keep the area round the umbilical cord stump clean to avoid the risk of infection.

So, all in all, a daily clean-up is a good idea. However, some newborns are a little freaked out by baths (see page 61) so if this particular task seems too daunting during the early days, just 'top and tail' him instead.

Wash and go: how to top and tail your baby

- Get everything you need ready and to hand: cotton wool, a soft towel, a clean nappy and clothing, and a clean bowl full of warm water, as well as a separate container of water that you've boiled and cooled, for his eyes.
- Undress him and put him securely on a changing mat (drape a towel or muslin over it first to take the chill off) or your lap. Cover him with a towel to keep him warm. Make sure the room is a nice toasty temperature, too.
- Wash his eyes first: use a clean bit of dampened cotton wool – discarding and changing it for each eye – and wipe once, from the inside corner of the eye outwards.

- Using a fresh piece of cotton wool for each 'bit', gently wipe the face, neck, hands, bottom, and genitals, in that order. Don't forget to wipe away any milk that's ended up behind the ears and under the armpits.
- Gently pat him dry.

All about baths

Don't worry if you feel a bit wobbly when it comes to bathing your baby. Most new parents lack confidence when it comes to this particular challenge – not helped by the fact that some babies are initially distinctly unimpressed by the prospect of a dunk. It's a skill you'll pick up as you go along, and with experience under your belt, you'll very soon be doing it like a pro. You might even find it becomes a routine bit of babycare you both love.

Getting a grip

Whether you decide to do it in a baby bath, in the sink, or just an ordinary tub with the aid of a support or accompanied by another adult, your main aim is to make sure he's securely held so he feels comfortable and confident, and there's no risk of his head dropping under the water – admittedly easier said than done, as a wet baby can be as slippery as a fish and you need to keep one hand free to wash him. Unsurprisingly, lots of parents find a bath support comes in very handy here – although the drawback is there's less freedom for him to splash around.

> *"I always found bath times a bit tricky. Our baby loved the water from the word go but dealing with a slippery little wriggly baby could prove quite tricky – especially when she couldn't even hold her head. I was terrified she'd slip out of my grasp and I'd lose her in the bubbles!"*
>
> ***Molly F***

Good, clean fun: all you need to know about bathing your baby

- You don't have to bath your baby every day. Two to three times a week is sufficient – although you should probably 'top and tail' (see page 60) all the really dirty bits daily. On the other hand, a daily bath often becomes an established part of a bedtime routine so if you find it fits well in yours, carry on.
- Make sure the water temperature is right. It should be 'comfortably warm', and if you're not confident about guessing that, use a thermometer. Around 37°C is what you're aiming for. Always make up the bath and test the temperature before dunking your baby in it to avoid scalding. Tradition has it you use your elbow or wrist to do this, because they're more sensitive to heat than your hand. Choose a good time for bathing. He won't enjoy it much if he's hungry or very tired.
- Spend a few minutes gathering everything you need and have it close to hand so you never have to take your hands off your baby (it goes without saying that for safety reasons you should always stay right beside him while he's in the bath).
- Before putting him in the bath, wrap him in a towel and wash his eyes, ears, face and neck with water and cotton wool (turn back to page 60 to be reminded how). If you're washing his hair, keep him wrapped up and hold him firmly in one arm, so that his head's over the bath. Use your other hand to rub a little baby shampoo in, and rinse carefully with handfuls of the bath water.
- Use baby bath products sparingly, and stick with those specially formulated for infant skin. If what you're using dries or irritates your baby's skin, stop, and stick with plain water instead.
- For even more clean, slippery fun, simply step in to the big bath with your baby. Don't forget to adjust your usual temperature to suit – and get a second party involved to hand you your baby and take him out again, rather than trying to clamber in and out with him in your arms. It could be disastrous if you slip.
- Have a warm, soft towel ready to wrap your baby up in after his bath. Cuddle dry. And don't forget the creases!

Cradle cap

If your baby develops a covering of greasy, flaky scales on his head, don't panic: it's almost certainly 'cradle cap', a harmless and extremely common skin condition. Doctors seem a bit confused about what causes it, but it's widely assumed to be due to overactive sebaceous (oil-producing) glands – a lingering consequence of a mum's pregnancy hormones – which cause old skin cells to stick to the scalp rather than fall off as they normally would. It's definitely nothing to do with poor hygiene habits or anything else you could possibly control, so please don't worry if it's something that affects your baby. It won't cause him any pain or discomfort, either. It just looks a little gross.

What can I do about it?

There are no definitive cures for cradle cap – but plenty of things you might like to attempt, on a trial and error basis, halting immediately if it seems to cause a problem. Some mums say certain remedies don't work; others that they caused irritation. You'll find dozens of different recommendations if you check out the online parenting forums on this one – and there are some ideas listed below.

> *"My son had horrible cradle cap. We found the most effective thing to be apricot oil, made by an online company called Burt's Bees. The downside is that it left oily stains in his Moses basket, but the upside was that it kept his head nicely moisturised and helped get rid of the cradle cap quickly. It also smelt lovely."*
>
> ***Ruth D***

Cradle cap can hang around for a quite a few months (and sometimes a couple of years), building up to a pretty thick crust over time, and occasionally spreading down to the eyebrows. If you do manage to get rid of one lot, it may come back. But, although it isn't pretty, it will eventually go on its own (and will also be less noticeable as your baby's hair grows), so you can choose not to bother with treatments at all and just dress him in a cute hat whenever you leave the house.

Do keep an eye on it in the meantime though because if it becomes inflamed or sore, or really seems to be bothering your baby, it could be that an infection has developed, or it may be that a more serious skin condition such as eczema is at play – in which case you should ask your GP to take a look.

> *"My son's cradle cap was horrendous. It covered his whole head and he even had it in his eyebrows. I'd been recommended everything from olive oil to Vaseline but after reading other people's experiences online, I wasn't so sure. My HV prescribed an emollient cream called Epiderm which was fantastic. I rubbed it in and combed it through before his bath, then washed it off, and combed his damp hair with a gentle zig-zag motion which lifted the scales off. After two or three treatments, it was gone."*
>
> Marianne O

Scaling back: tips for tackling cradle cap

- Slather on a suitable emollient (moisturising) cream. Ask your pharmacist to recommend one, or your GP to prescribe one. Some say good old Vaseline works a treat (although it can be a pig to get out afterwards).
- Try one of the medicated shampoos that are marketed specifically to tackle cradle cap; for instance, the one made by Dentinox.
- Rub in a little olive oil and leave overnight (be prepared for your baby to smell a bit like a chip pan) before washing off any residue with the aid of a little baby shampoo. You could also try rapeseed, coconut, or plain old baby oil. Official advice is to avoid nut-based oils, in case of the risk of allergy.
- For an old wives' approach, try applying a paste of water and bicarbonate of soda, leaving it on for ten minutes, then washing off.
- Use a soft brush or fine-toothed comb to carefully lift loose flakes away, once you've softened up and loosened them with any of the above treatments.

TIP Most of the solutions listed above will need to be done more than once before the problem clears. Don't pick at the scales unless they're already nice and loose – however tempting – because it could cause soreness, and may even lead to infection.

Cutting your baby's nails

Another small task that can become disproportionately terrifying, cutting your baby's nails is something you'll probably have to do to avoid him scratching his face – or exposed bits of whoever's cuddling or feeding him, for that matter – when he's too little to know better.

Get yourself the right tool for the job: a pair of baby nail scissors or baby nail clippers (preferences vary), and pick your moment. Most parents say it's best to wait until he's feeding, or better still, deeply asleep. Don't cut the nail to close to the skin. And steer clear of the age-old recommendation to bite or chew nails off yourself – it's too easy to rip off more than you intend to.

> *"I remember trying to cut her nails for the first time. I nicked one tiny finger and it bled, and I was distraught. My mother arrived to find me sobbing over her hands and berating myself for being the worst mother ever. I've never nicked one since though."*
>
> *Jo W*

Dummies, and other comfort habits

If your baby isn't easily settled, or if he likes to comfort suck and you'd prefer he used something other than a piece of you to do so, you may find that offering him a dummy (also known as a comforter or pacifier) provides a helpful solution.

Dummies get a bad press. Lots of mums feel they're to be avoided at all costs, or feel guilty about introducing one – even if it *does* make life a little easier. And it's true that there are certain potential drawbacks – speech and language therapists aren't keen, for instance, and argue that a baby who's too busy sucking on a dummy won't have enough chance to move his mouth around and practise speech sounds, which is important for speech and language development, and some dentists warn that too much sucking, for too long, could eventually cause misalignment of the teeth.

However, in both cases, we're talking about *truly* excessive dummy-sucking habits. *Sensible* dummy use – as outlined below – won't cause any problems (other than sniffy looks from snobby mums – and the potential for being woken at night by a baby who can't find his comforter and needs you to do so for him). So, if you want to give your baby a dummy, do. The only other main drawback is that at some point, you'll have to take it away. But you can always cross that bridge when you get to it.

> *"I couldn't have survived early infanthood without dummies. No mother plans to use them and we all like to think our babies will be too brilliant to need anything so 'chavvy', but some babies are very sucky which means it's either a dummy, or a baby hanging off your boob 24/7, and I know which option I prefer."*
>
> ***Heidi S***

Comforting stuff: tips for sensible dummy use

- Try to avoid offering a dummy to your baby if you're still trying to get breastfeeding established. He may need a month or more without distraction to get his boob-sucking techniques sussed, and a dummy might put him off.
- Restrict use from the start. Offer it only when your baby needs comforting, or settling to sleep, and put it away the rest of the time. Don't pop it in for no good reason.
- Aim to wean your baby off his before his first birthday – the earlier you try taking it away, the easier it's likely to be. Most parents find a 'cold turkey' approach at this stage is the best bet: whistle it away, offering cuddles and distractions for a while instead. Chances are it'll be a less painful process than you feared. (Alternatively, you could just let him keep it until he's old enough and rational enough to understand why it's time to take it away – or he simply chooses to drop it himself. It won't cause harm in the meantime if you continue to restrict its use sensibly.)

- Be sure to sterilise your baby's dummies daily, store them in sterilised pots, and always have several spare in case one falls to the floor, as dummy use can increase the risk of ear and tummy infections. (NB, putting your baby's dummy in your *own* mouth will actually make it *dirtier*.) Throw away any cracked or damaged dummies, because they're more likely to harbour bacteria.
- Choose an orthodontic dummy if it makes you feel better – however if you're already being sensible about restricting use, your baby shouldn't be affected by dental problems in the future. Never dip his dummy in anything sweet, though. He could end up with tooth decay.
- If you're keen to give your baby a dummy at night in line with recommendations from the Foundation for the Study of Infant Deaths (see pages 110–111), remember that you need to consistently give it *every* night. If you can't or don't want to give your baby a dummy in spite of these guidelines, but you're following all the other safe sleep advice, there's probably no need to worry.
- Bear in mind that some babies simply don't take to dummies, however hard their parents try to interest them in one. Hey, that's life. At least you won't ever have to go 'cold turkey'!

“I have friends who were so against dummies it was unreal. Both of mine were soothed by their dummies, mainly just at night time, and I couldn't understand what all the fuss was about. I took my daughter's away at six months, and she transferred her affection to a soft toy which she then chewed to death. But I didn't try taking my son's away until he was 18 months old, mostly because I was a walking zombie then and would do anything for an easy life.”

Alex G

Thumbs, fingers, and blankets

If your baby takes to sucking his own thumb or fingers or develops a close attachment to a manky old bit of blanket or a particular soft toy, don't worry: it's completely normal. In fact, it may even be an advantage, because it takes the pressure off you to help him settle. However, some mums become quite worried that these sorts of 'comfort habits' might be problematic in the long term, perhaps picturing a childhood blighted by buck teeth, or a permanent obsession with a transitional object (so called by psychologists, because he's transferred part of his dependence for comfort from you to it) that will lead to teasing in the playground.

At this stage, there's really no need to worry about any comfort habits your baby has developed, so let him suck away on his thumb when he wants to, and give him his blankie, snuggly, muzzy, Taggie, Cuski, or whatever it may be, whenever he really seems to need it – and as with dummies, avoid when he doesn't. Your only real worry is replacing it when it (inevitably) gets lost – and trying to get the smelly article in the washing machine once in a while. (If he's got a strong attachment to it by the time you apply for an infant school place, then maybe you'll want to apply some gentle discouragement tactics – but the truth is, he'll probably stop on his own accord as long as you *don't* try to make him.)

> *“We gave our daughter a little square of cellular blanket which she'd put over her face at night, without fail, before sighing contentedly and dropping off. Now she's older and it's all frayed around the edges, she likes to tickle herself to sleep with it.”*
>
> **Lauren B**

4

Feeding

It's likely to be your number one priority: making sure your baby is well fuelled. It may also be one of your greatest challenges, through the early weeks into the first months. If you're breastfeeding, getting it established is only the start, as worries about milk flow and specific problems such as mastitis can then strike. And formula feeding – although technically easier to get up and running – is by no means an obvious science, either. Then, just as you've got milk feeds sussed, you need to start thinking about weaning – and with it, a whole new batch of issues, and a bank of muddled advice. One thing is sure: any difficulties you encounter are likely to be resolved with a little time and experience. You'll be feeding like a pro – and so will your baby – before you know it. I know it's easy for me to say, but in the future, you'll look back to this anxiety-ridden time and realise you probably didn't need to worry so much after all.

TIP We discuss starting to breastfeed or formula feed and the immediate challenges you might face in Chapter 2, page 26. Turn back if you're just starting out.

“I remember feeling so desperate to get the feeding right. But with hindsight, I can see that I didn't have to put myself under such enormous pressure. Now that my 'babies' are a bit older, it all seems entertainingly irrelevant.

And, by the way, the trickiest of them is the one who had the most breastmilk!"

Rebecca F

Is he getting enough milk from me?

You might be worrying about providing enough milk for your baby if you're breastfeeding. The frequency and the often long duration of early feeds (anything up to 45 minutes is cited as normal, some mums find they can be longer still) may well cause you to question your supplies – after all, if he's getting what he needs, how come he seems to constantly want more?

If you're fretting, you're not alone. It's common for breastfeeding mums to become convinced they're starving their baby because, unlike formula, breastmilk can't be measured and it's impossible to know how much is actually going in. Added to which, breastfed babies naturally tend to have a slower weight gain, and be – on average – a bit lighter than their formula-fed counterparts, anyway. And if your baby seems to be making slow progress on his centile chart, those public weigh-in sessions down at the baby clinic will no doubt worsen any anxiety you're feeling.

Accepted wisdom has it that almost all mums should be able to make enough to meet their babies' needs (although, anecdotally speaking, there's no doubt that many are quite certain their milk supplies are insufficient). The key – it's said – is offering up your boobs whenever, and for however long, your baby seems to need them, in the first couple of months, at least. It's tedious and tiring having to be so committed when the supply-and-demand system is being cranked up, but if you're worried about milk production, you're advised to keep on trying to feed your baby at every opportunity – and perhaps express whenever you have a chance as well (see page 81). This may mean waking him for a munch sometimes, if he's sleeping for stretches of longer than three or four hours – in spite of what they say about not waking a sleeping baby. Getting naked and getting into bed together, preferably for a whole day or two, can provide a good opportunity to get the milk flowing. And you might find help in the form of fenugreek tablets, which are available from health food shops and are said to help boost milk production (although by all accounts, it's pungent stuff and can produce the distinct odour of curry in your wee and sweat). Please do also bear in mind that if, like me, you are not well-endowed in the chest department, it definitely won't have any bearing on the extent of your milk flow. Breasts of any size and shape will usually be up to the job!

Offering formula feeds instead of, or as a supplement to, breastmilk feeds will have the knock-on effect of decreasing your own supplies, so it's something to avoid if you're keen to keep on exclusively breastfeeding, unless a health professional has serious concerns about your baby's health and urges you to. Don't despair, though, if you have to offer formula as a supplement, but didn't really want to. You may still be able to boost your supply a little later by feeding or expressing whenever possible, and getting lots of skin-to-skin contact. There's also the much overlooked option of mixed feeding (see page 86), which means you can do a bit of both.

I know it's easier said than done, but please try not to worry too much about whether you're feeding your baby enough. *Most* mums who fret about supply are actually doing fine. Ask for help and get your baby weighed if you're truly anxious about his growth, and do go with whatever the health professionals advise if there really is a shortfall in milk flow, but meanwhile, try not to dwell on every single fluid ounce of milk he's taking in and every little bit of weight lost or gained. If he's feeding regularly, putting on weight gradually, and keeping you busy with lots of nappy changes (you're looking for an average of six wet nappies per 24 hours, and as a general rule, a poo at least every other day – there's more on poo on page 154), then you haven't got anything to worry about.

> *“Sam always fed very quickly once we got breastfeeding established. He'd be done within ten minutes, whereas some books said he should be at it for 40 minutes or more. It made me worry he wasn't taking enough. I now know that as long as they put on weight, everything is OK.*

Breastfeeding mums need to liberate themselves from all that 'how many fluid ounces has he taken?' fretting. ❞
Emma H

Looking after yourself while breastfeeding

If you're confused about what you should – or shouldn't – be eating, drinking, or otherwise consuming while breastfeeding, here are the basic guidelines.

Eating well

There's debate about this: some experts stress you don't *have* to eat healthily while breastfeeding, and that your body will produce milk regardless. Others reckon that eating well is important to maintain a good-quality supply. 'An extra 400 calories a day' is often cited as a necessity for breastfeeding mums – truth is, most find they're absolutely ravenous and are automatically filling up on as much as their body needs, anyway (and then some). Still, it stands to reason that if you eat well and get a good balance of foods inside you, it will help give you the strength and energy you need to breastfeed.

Beating thirst

You may find you feel very thirsty while breastfeeding, because water from your body is being co-opted to make milk, so drink whatever you need to quench your thirst. Water, milk and juice are the healthiest options.

Fish

You're advised to limit oily fish such as salmon, trout, and fresh tuna to a couple of portions a week, because of potential pollutants. Shark, marlin, or swordfish (should you have a passion for these) are best avoided, as they contain high levels of mercury.

Colic-causers

Some foods are said to be likely causes for colicky symptoms – strongly flavoured vegetables like cabbage and cauliflower, onions, caffeine, wheat, citrus fruits, dairy products, and anything very spicy are the usual suspects – so if your baby's suffering you might want to try avoiding each of these in turn, to see if it helps. Don't cut out any major food groups without checking with your GP first. (There's more on colic on page 143.)

Peanuts

It used to be thought wise to avoid peanuts or peanut products when breastfeeding just in case it triggered an allergy to them in your baby – and particularly so for mums from high-risk families. New evidence has changed doctors' thinking, though, and these days the official line is that breastfeeding mums – irrespective of a family history of allergies – should feel free to indulge in all things nutty.

Caffeine

There's no evidence that too much caffeine will definitely cause a problem for your baby if you're breastfeeding. However, some mums do notice a link between caffeine and colicky symptoms or restlessness, and others swear their baby sleeps better when they steer clear of the tea, coffee and cola.

Alcohol

Dreary, but true: it's best to stick to limited amounts of booze when breastfeeding, as alcohol does pass through into your milk – and although the tempting possibility that this might actually improve your baby's sleep, the fact is it's more likely to have the opposite effect and make him unsettled. It may also inhibit your 'let-down' and make your milk taste funny. Of course, you can still enjoy the odd drink – and in fact, there's a strong argument in favour of that because it aids relaxation, and that can boost milk production – particularly if you aim to get the timing right by squeezing your tipple in after a feed. This should give you a couple of hours until the next, by which time the alcohol will have passed out of your system entirely (it takes an hour for your body to process one unit of alcohol: once you're clear of it, your milk is too). If you can master the art of expressing (see page 81) – and assuming of course there's another responsible adult around who'll look after your baby for you while you're gone – you can still have a big night out when you want one: you may have to plan ahead and freeze several sessions-worth in advance, and perhaps 'pump and dump' if you need to. On the plus side, you'll find it easier to cope with a baby with a clear head – and once you do stop breastfeeding, you'll be a cheap date for a while.

> *"I enjoyed drinking moderately. A glass of red in front of the telly of an evening was the only way to cope with a baby stuck to my bosoms. I never got properly drunk – mainly because I wasn't getting enough sleep to entertain a hangover. Once I knew they wouldn't wake up at night, my usual drinking habits were resumed!"*
>
> ***Rebecca F***

Keep taking the tablets: are vitamins really vital?

What's the current advice?

The Department of Health says that if you're a breastfeeding mum, you should take an extra 10 mcg of vitamin D daily, to help boost your baby's early stores as it's vital for the development of strong bones and teeth. Guidelines also state that breastfed babies over six months should be getting extra vitamin D (as well as extra vitamin A, and C) in the form of drops, or from one month, 'if a mum's vitamin status during pregnancy was considered low'. Formula-fed babies, meanwhile, will be fine as these vitamins are added to formula, but only for as long as they're getting at least 500ml (16 fl oz) a day – after that, they too should take a supplement of these vitamins. And all children should, in theory, continue taking these until the age of five.

Why do they say this?

Experts are increasingly worried that many children (and adults) are just not getting enough of the important vitamins they need and in particular, vitamin D, which we get a small amount of through food sources like oily fish, fortified cereals and margarine, and eggs, but mainly from exposure to summer sunlight. Some areas of the country have even seen a re-emergence of rickets, a grim disease caused by vitamin D deficiency which, at worst, can lead to a painful softening of the bones. Of course, not all mums and babies will be lacking vitamin D, and some – those with dark skin and those who are always covered up, perhaps for cultural reasons – are particularly vulnerable. It may also be that some people living in the north of the country simply don't get enough sun in the winter months to see them through the year. So this 'blanket' health recommendation is really just to make sure *everyone's* OK.

What should I do?

Continue taking an ante-natal supplement, if you took one in pregnancy, or buy one specifically for breastfeeding mums, and ask your pharmacist about suitable daily multivitamin drops for your baby. Sticking with own-label brands can help keep the cost down. The NHS offers free Healthy Start vitamin supplements for low-income breastfeeding mums and for their babies and children, usually distributed via clinics or GP surgeries, and in some areas, these may be available cheaply to non-eligible mums, so it's worth asking your HV for more information.

Does it really matter if we don't bother?

If you're confident that you and your baby get enough sun when it's out to see you through the months when it isn't, and that you (and your baby, once weaned) get a good range of foods, then you may both be OK to go without supplements.

But isn't the sun dangerous?

Cancer specialists warn that it's still important to keep your baby protected from direct exposure to the sun. There's more detailed advice at the website of Cancer Research UK's SunSmart campaign.

Feeding in public

One drawback of breastfeeding is that you'll almost certainly have to get your whammers out in front of people you wouldn't normally: your father-in-law, for instance, and random members of the public. While many mums are happy to do so with pride, others feel embarrassed, or simply afraid that someone will complain about it. If you're shy, don't be ashamed to take off into another room to feed your baby, or seek out a quiet corner when you're out and about. Covering up with a muslin or pashmina may boost your confidence (and you can even buy shawl-like garments specifically for the purpose, such as the 'Hooter Hider'). However, going to pains to be discreet can actually make you more obvious, and with a bit of practice, a baggy top, and a front opening, or easily shifted bra, most mums find they can feed their baby in public without anyone even realising. 'I was pretty concerned about the whole feeding in public thing but in the end it was no problem,' reveals Caroline S. 'You're so concerned with feeding your baby you really don't care.'

TIP Keep in mind that you cannot legally be stopped from breastfeeding in a public place. If you are, you're well within your rights to kick up a stink about it with the management.

> *"Breastfeeding when out and about is scary at first. It feels like everyone is staring. You hear so many stories of women being asked to leave places or being told to use the toilets. Thankfully, I never came across any of that. I used a blanket to cover us. She'd fall asleep, I'd put everything away, then I pull the blanket down to reveal my sleeping baby. Anyone watching would assume I'd covered her to soothe her to sleep."*
>
> ***Rachel G***

When breastfeeding hurts

It's normal for breastfeeding to be painful or at least uncomfortable at first, while you seek to get your latch right, and your nipples man up to the task of being sucked long and often by your hungry baby. But if you're suffering from breastfeeding pain that just won't go away, or rears its head a bit later, having got it sussed, then there's probably a specific cause at play. The main ones are outlined below.

> *"I got dry, cracked, very sore nipples. I was given two tips which worked like a dream. 1) Never put away a wet nipple (cue lots of wandering around the house post-feed topless!); and 2) Squeeze out a drop or two of milk once baby is finished and smear it over your nipple. No idea why, but the combination works better than any fancy cream you can buy."*
>
> *Clare F*

As a rule (torturous though it sounds), you're advised to carry on feeding as best you can through all these problems. It won't harm your baby to drink from an infected or bleeding breast (although it may affect the taste a little and be off-putting for him), and in the case of a blocked duct or mastitis, keeping your boob well drained will aid recovery. Of course, if you stop or slow down, it's likely to affect your flow as well. Expressing for a while (see page 81), instead, is usually a less painful option. A comfortable, well-fitting bra that's snug but not too tight, can also ease discomfort.

It may also be a good idea to try and limit any pure comfort sucking your baby is doing – if he's drained a whole boob or more, that's a good sign he's had his fill, and you'll know he's just munching for the heck of it because his suck won't be as furious. If he's a 'sucky' baby who seems disgruntled at having this particular service withdrawn, you could always offer a clean finger, or dummy (see page 65) instead – although they say it's best not to offer a dummy until breastfeeding is well established.

Please don't feel bad about it (or let anyone else make you feel bad) if a breastfeeding problem turns out to be insurmountable and you end up reaching for the formula instead. It's a brave woman who battles through potentially toe-curling issues like mastitis or thrush. And if you're really struggling, remind yourself that what's 'best' for your baby, may not be the best thing for you. What your baby needs most of all is a happy, pain-free, and non-stressed out mum.

Sore, cracked or bleeding nipples

These are usually said to be a sign that the latch isn't right – although many mums suspect deep down that might not be entirely true. 'I just don't believe that you only get sore nipples if you're doing it wrong. I think if you have a baby feeding more or less constantly then it's bound to happen anyway,' admits Rebecca F. I'm with her on that. I was so sure I'd got it right – but ended up nevertheless with a very livid red weal across each of my nipples, making gritted teeth a necessity at each feed for a time. Still, it's certainly a good idea to check your positioning, or ask a health professional or breastfeeding counsellor to check it for you if you're not sure. Swapping to a 'rugby ball' (see page 28) hold if you've been using the more conventional nursing hold might help. Meanwhile, you could try generously applying nipple cream to any sore bits. The one most widely recommended by the experts is Lansinoh, which is organic, so you don't have to wipe it off before you feed your baby. Some mums also swear by the antiseptic properties of a little breastmilk itself, rubbed in gently. Keeping your boobs as dry as possible will help with both cure and prevention, so buy really absorbent breast pads and change them very regularly. Giving them a little 'air time' can also be beneficial. (Just remember to cover up again before opening the door to the milkman.) Some mums find nipple shields can really save the day – others that their baby was distinctly unimpressed by them.

> *“I ended up with cracked, bleeding nipples, and needed a lot of help from the midwives and the Health Visitor. I invested in a pump and some bottles and expressed for a day or two, which let me heal. I also found that lying down*

to feed helped him latch on without causing me pain, so we went with that until he was a little bigger. But I went on to breastfeed him for nine months, in the end.”

Nicola L

Blocked milk ducts

Caused by a build-up of milk, blocked ducts can cause a painful lump in the breast, and sometimes a red, inflamed patch of skin above it. The problem should go on its own after a few days, and gently massaging the affected breast, either during feeds or during a hot bath or shower, can help solve the problem. Do keep a close eye on an infected duct and get medical advice if you're worried, as the problem can develop into mastitis.

Mastitis

A painful inflammation of the breast, mastitis can either be caused by an infection, when bacteria enter the breast tissue, or by a simple build-up of milk. It can also cause a fever and other flu-like symptoms such as chills or aches. Sometimes it will go on its own, sometimes it will need antibiotics to clear it up, so always consult a health professional if you're suffering and meanwhile, ibuprofen will ease pain and reduce inflammation. Occasionally, a breast abscess can develop as a result of repeated or untreated bouts of mastitis, so it's important to keep on top of it.

“I got mastitis. My breast was painful and red, and I was sweating and shivering. I managed to keep on feeding through the pain. Once I'd worked out what it was, I took myself straight to the GP for antibiotics – none of your messing around with cabbage leaves – and that sorted it very quickly.”

Rebecca F

Thrush

A fungal infection, thrush can develop in a baby's mouth and then affect a mum's breast. If you've been taking antibiotics for some reason, or if your breasts are sore and cracked anyway, it can make you more vulnerable. It can cause extremely sore, sensitive, itchy nipples, and sometimes shooting pains deep in the breast itself and, in a baby, white or curd-like sore patches in the mouth which may make feeding painful for him. However, it can also be symptomless so it's tricky sometimes to diagnose. Antifungal cream or tablets will be needed to clear it up, along with an oral gel for your baby. You'll probably both need treating at the same time, to make sure it doesn't come back to haunt you.

Tongue-tie

It's worth getting your midwife or GP to check out this possibility if you're experiencing serious pain and your baby's really struggling to latch on. Known medically as ankyloglossia, this condition means babies have an abnormally short frenulum (the little bit of skin that joins the tongue to the floor of the mouth) and it can cause real problems in breastfeeding. Some health professionals prefer to take a 'wait-and-see' approach as long as your baby's gaining weight OK; however, a simple surgical procedure is available which can solve the problem immediately.

Getting help with problems

Don't suffer in silence – look for help if you're struggling. Mums who overcome breastfeeding problems often say it was thanks to extra support they received from the right person. It may be your HV, but they are busy people, and there are numerous other sources of help out there. National telephone support lines include those run by the NCT, the La Leche League, the Association of Breastfeeding Mothers and the Department of Health, and you can also get information from them online. For hands-on guidance, seek out a local breastfeeding counsellor (all three of the charities mentioned above offer this service) or see if there's a breastfeeding clinic or cafe running in your area.

Bear in mind, though, that not all sources of breastfeeding help are that helpful, as Lucy J found. 'The breastfeeding support group I went to was rubbish. It consisted of 15 weeping women sitting on hard, armless chairs, shoving breasts into screeching babies' mouths,' she recalls. 'I have massive tits so I needed a chair with arms. And they wouldn't let my husband in, the poor sod had to go and sit in the car.' If you find, like Lucy, that one option fails you, seek out another and give that a go, instead.

> *“Breastfeeding is really, really hard. Probably the hardest thing I ever did in my life up to that point. And I don't think we get the support right in this country. There's way too much emphasis on this whole 'breast is best' thing and not nearly enough practical, useful, unbiased advice.”*
>
> *Charlee C*

All about expressing

You may want to give your baby breastmilk in a bottle sometimes: to give your boobs a rest, perhaps; because you need to go somewhere or do something without your baby; or simply because your other half would like to play a part in feeding, too. And actually, it's a really, really good idea – even if you're exclusively breastfeeding and very happy with that arrangement – to offer your baby a bottle at quite an early stage if you know you'll need him to take one in the future, perhaps when you return to work, or maybe when you've had enough of breastfeeding and decide to offer formula instead. And this is where expressing comes in.

> *“I'd really recommend expressing and doing the odd bottle feed once feeding is established enough. I didn't bother because there didn't seem much point and it seemed like a lot of bother when it was easier to feed him direct. But because I didn't persevere with a bottle then, he*

now flatly refuses breastmilk from anything but the source, which means I've had to put him to bed every night for nine months and I would really like an evening out. I wish I'd tried when he was younger."

Lucy R

Won't it cause 'nipple confusion'?

If you're exclusively breastfeeding and hoping to continue to for a while, you might be worried about offering your baby a bottle of expressed milk (or formula sometimes, for that matter, if you want to: see mixed feeding, below) for fear it will interfere with breastfeeding. It's true that some babies seem to suffer from 'nipple confusion' – in other words, deciding they prefer the comparatively easy flow of the teat, and refusing the boob as a result. But many are more flexible than given credit for and will happily switch between one and the other. 'We decided to get our breastfed baby used to a bottle for occasional expressed feeds,' reveals Clare F. 'It took perseverance and determination to get it to work and about two weeks of very difficult evenings, but once it happened we didn't look back. It never caused any problems with "nipple confusion" either. He was more than happy to latch back on to me given the chance.'

If you're going to offer a bottle instead of a boob, bear in mind the standard warning that it's best to wait for four to six weeks, or until breastfeeding is 'well established' before trying. Equally, though, you probably shouldn't put it off much beyond that, because it's generally reckoned that the window in which you'll get a result is a small one – there's no hard evidence for it, but some say you should really do it before six to eight weeks is up, if you don't want your baby to be so boob-loyal he simply won't countenance a feed from any other source. And while this won't matter if you're happy to keep breastfeeding for as long as *he's* happy to (or perhaps, later on, you can get him to accept milk in a beaker or cup – see page 104), it could prove to be a matter for regret if – some months down the line – you find you would *kill* for the chance to bugger off for a while, knowing someone else can take over feeding duties while you're gone. There are tips for introducing a bottle on page 85.

> *“I always planned for my daughter to take a bottle, so that I could return to work without worrying, and have the odd night out with my husband. I was so worried about nipple confusion, I waited for six weeks, as advised, and she flatly refused to take one. Although I enjoyed breastfeeding, I did find it exhausting. I could never be away from her for more than an hour or so, and I admit I felt a bit suffocated. With hindsight, I wish I'd tried to introduce a bottle a bit earlier. Being the only one to do all the night feeds does have its drawbacks!”*
>
> *Molly F*

What you need to express

Mums in the know say that if you're serious about expressing, you should go straight for an electric model instead of faffing around with a manual. They're pricier, but if you look around you should be able to source a second-hand bargain, and you can always hire if you don't want to buy: details for the NCT breast pump hire line are in the back of the book. It's also possible to express by hand, using a massaging technique, and although this may sound like hard work, it's often said to be the most effective method of all.

> *“Try hand expressing, straight into a wide-necked bottle – it's far more efficient and feels far more natural. I hold the bottle with my nipple pointed into it, and use my fingers to push downwards, from the top of the milk ducts. When the milk slows, I move my fingers round a bit, and push there. Think hard about your baby, or look at a picture of him, to encourage your flow.”*
>
> *Abi M*

How much should I be getting out?

Don't be surprised if you don't seem to produce much when you express. You may need to pump over several sessions to get a whole feed's worth, at first. But mums who did express with success say that persistence pays off: if you pump regularly at points when you've got milk to spare, you should see a gradual increase in supply as a result. Early in the morning is said to be the most fruitful time.

Breastmilk can be stored in sterilised bottles in the fridge for between three and eight days (it depends on how cold your fridge is), or put in pre-sterilised bags and frozen, then defrosted, either gradually in the fridge or under running water if you're in a hurry. For more information on this issue, check out the comprehensive guide to expressing and storing breastmilk that's available for download on the website of the Breastfeeding Network.

> *"Expressing: I loved it! I know not everyone finds it easy, and it does take practice. You need to stick with it for a good few days before your supply starts to go up. I soon realised that the more I expressed, the more milk I made. Eventually I was putting a bottle in the fridge every day, for my husband to do the final feed. And soon I had so much stored in the freezer I could go out for an evening."*
>
> **Lucy J**

Mums' panel round-up

Did you manage to express with success?

I never got the hang of expressing. No matter what I tried, I could never let down without my baby there. I could only ever express from one boob while she drank from the other, which was tricky, annoying and somewhat pointless – **Charlee C**

I had a massive oversupply, and any time I needed to, I could produce a couple of bottles. Positive thinking and bloody-mindedness helped: she was premature and I was determined to express for her – **Abi M**

I tried, but only ever ended up with teaspoon-sized amounts after expressing for up to half an hour. Bah! – **Celine G**

I found expressing stressful. Couldn't do it, hated trying. I always felt like a cow on a machine – **Amanda G**

You need perseverance: at first I got hardly anything but as time went on, I could express at least 9 fl oz every time. My advice (and pardon the pun) is to go with the flow – **Dani B**

I had a nightmare with expressing. I kept at it for three weeks, but never expressed more than 3 fl oz a time – **Lara S**

When to stop breastfeeding

Your baby will need either breastmilk or formula until he is one. Many breastfeeding mums choose to make the switch to formula quite a while before their baby's first birthday, for lots of different reasons: getting dad involved in feeding, perhaps, an easier return to work, or just a need for more than a single glass of wine sometimes! Some mums are happy to carry on breastfeeding for as long as their babies want to, beyond a year or more. There's no reason not to if you enjoy it. After all, you hear of mums still breastfeeding five-year-olds!

Going from boob to bottle

If you're breastfeeding but want to offer expressed milk or water from a bottle, switch to formula, or attempt mixed feeding (see below), you'll need to get your baby sucking from a teat – and this can be easier said than done if he's grown a little set in his ways. You might find he takes to it with gusto, and little encouragement, but more than likely, you'll need to try one or more of the tricks below. (And *keep* on trying!)

Suck it and see: tips for introducing a teat

- Experiment with different sorts of teat – there's lots on the market. Latex varieties are softer and more nipple-like than silicone, while some offer a faster flow than others. Don't go mad, though. You could end up spending a fortune.

- Get the timing right. Try when your baby's fairly hungry – but not so hungry he'll be upset and unreceptive.
- Check the temperature of what you're offering. If your baby's used to breastmilk and you want him to take formula, he may prefer it slightly warmed (see page 91).
- Ask someone else to offer the bottle. If your baby can smell your breastmilk, it's likely to be a distraction. Leave the house, if you can't cope with the upset it's causing.
- Try offering the bottle in the dark, or in a different location if you always tend to feed him in the same place.
- Don't force it, or get upset if your baby isn't playing ball. Give up and try again in another few days.
- Some babies who are accustomed to a boob just won't ever accept a bottle. You may find you have to be philosophical about that – or try interesting him in milk from a beaker instead (see page 104).

Mixed feeding

You may find a happy compromise in mixed feeding, with some breast and some formula if your baby's happy to switch from boob to bottle and back again. That way, you can still pass on the benefits of your own milk, but get a break sometimes. In particular, it suits some working mums to leave a bottle behind for the day, while continuing to offer the boob morning and night. Be aware that once you swap a regular breastfeed with a bottle of formula, it won't take long for your body's supply and demand system to adapt accordingly. After a while, there'll be no going back.

> *“We mix fed, from about four weeks in. It totally saved my bacon when I was exhausted. A lot of my breastfeeding friends were warned off bottles, and it really made things difficult for them.”*
>
> *Charlee C*

More on formula feeding

If you're formula feeding, prepare to be flummoxed by the many and varied guidelines on bottle preparation. Check out the internet forums, and you'll see parents have many different ideas out there about how it's done – and needless to say, some of those views are at odds with the official advice. As the risks involved are all about your baby's health, you may as a first-time mum decide to play by the rulebook, just to be sure.

Making up feeds

These days, formula-feeding parents are advised to make up feeds as and when they're needed rather than making up several in advance and storing them in the fridge for up to 24 hours (as was the usual practice only a few short years ago). That's because of new fears that tins of formula may contain rare bacteria, which could cause serious problems. You can kill any harmful bugs by always adding water of at least 70°C to formula (so, once you've boiled it, don't allow it to cool down in the kettle or bottle for any longer than half an hour before making up the feed), but if you then let the feed hang around for any length of time – even in the fridge – there's a risk that bacteria will develop and multiply.

> *“I looked at the guidelines about making up each bottle at the time, applied a little of my own scientific knowledge and instinct, and um, ignored them.”*
>
> *Rebecca F*

This advice has been perplexing new parents since it was issued because it's rather complex and pretty inconvenient if you need to get a bottle quickly down a hungry baby, or if you're out and about (in which case, you are now advised to take a flask of freshly boiled water, a pre-sterilised lidded bottle, and a sterilised container of formula with you, and make up your bottle when needed, but only while the water's still hot, in other words, within about four hours or so).

Department of Health guidelines do concede that it's OK to make feeds in advance when 'not practical' to make them up when required – and this includes times when you need a child-minder or nursery worker to give your baby a bottle. If you do this, though, they advise that you still aim to store formula feeds in the fridge for as short a time as possible, making them in the morning, rather than the night before, for example. Your fridge temperature should be below 5°C, and bottles stored at the back, where it's coldest. If you need to give a feed on the go, make sure it's been cooled in the back of the fridge for at least an hour first, transport it in a cool bag with an ice brick, and use within four hours.

> *"We spent a fortune on ready-made milk in cartons, as the advice for making up bottles was so bonkers, and I was too shattered to follow it! Other times, I would boil the water, put it in sterilised bottles, add the powder later and microwave it. I've also been known to nuke a bottle before going out, then keeping it hot for half hour or so in a thermal bag. Probably all wrong!"*
>
> ***Marie L***

Sterilising and hygiene

It's important to pay careful attention to hygiene, as your baby's immunity has yet to develop and bacteria can easily find their way into his system, making him vulnerable to all sorts of bugs and illnesses. Official advice is that, for the duration of your baby's first year, all bottles and teats need to be thoroughly cleaned (using a bottle cleaning brush to make sure you've removed any milk lurking in the nooks and crannies), rinsed, and then sterilised before you feed your baby from them. It's generally reckoned that after six months, it's fine to sterilise bottles and teats in a dishwasher, as long as you run it on its hottest cycle. It does however tend to ruin and stain teats, somewhat – and it's still a good idea to hand wash first with a bottle cleaner and very hot soapy water.

You'll need either a microwave or steam steriliser, or a cold water unit. It's also worth knowing that you can sterilise bottles and teats by boiling them in a saucepan of water for ten minutes: probably not very practical on a permanent basis, but handy if you're stuck somewhere without the proper equipment for some reason.

Technically, you should probably sterilise each time you make a bottle, too – but this would be impractical and, frankly, a waste of electricity, and most parents probably aim to get away with one cycle of sterilising a day. If you're using sterilising fluid and a sterilising unit you can keep your bottles and teats bobbing away in there until you need them (you don't have to rinse equipment that's been in sterilising fluid, but if you do, you're advised to use water that's been boiled), and leaving them where they are in a microwave or steam steriliser once the cycle's over will keep them sterile for a certain period (it varies, you'll need to check the instructions). Failing that, if you remove them all and assemble them then put the lids on, you should be able to confidently make a feed in them at any point the same day. Don't forget to wash your hands really well, and to make sure the surface you're using is really clean, too before preparing bottles.

It's easy to get in a bit of a pickle over sterilising rules and regulations, and of course, no-one wants a baby with a poorly tummy. If you're worried that you're not being scrupulous enough, you may be reassured to hear that some parents don't sterilise at all, considering a wash in very hot soapy water or a run through the dishwasher to be sufficient. And interestingly, it's standard procedure to take that approach in the United States.

> *“It's a nightmare how many opinions there are on the 'right' way to sterilise and make up formula feeds. We used bottles that self-sterilised in the microwave, boiled the water, filled the bottles, put the lids on, and left them until needed. Then we just added the powder when a feed was required. I never bothered warming them, just offered it at room temperature. When he was screaming at night, there was no way I was waiting for a bottle to warm up!”*
>
> *Clare A*

By the book: more official guidelines on bottle-making

- Carefully read and digest the manufacturer's instructions before using your steriliser.
- Always clean and disinfect the surface before preparing bottles, and wash your hands thoroughly. (But try not to let the teat or bottle cap touch the surface, anyway.)
- Only use fresh tap water, recently boiled, and use within 30 minutes of it boiling. Steer clear of bottled water, as it will often contain too much salt, or sulphate. If you do use it, perhaps when abroad, it will still need boiling.
- Make sure you always get the quantities right, by carefully following the instructions on the tin. Too much powder and your baby could end up constipated or dehydrated; too little and he could be going hungry.
- Shake the bottle well to make sure the contents are well mixed.
- Give your baby the bottle as soon as possible once it's made. You can cool it speedily by holding the bottom half of the bottle under cold running water.
- Throw away any milk left over after your baby's finished. Don't offer a feed again, beyond an hour (some say two) after you made it.

How much formula should he be drinking?

There are no hard and fast rules on how much formula you should offer and when – all babies are different. If he's typical, yours will take six or more feeds of around 3 fl oz (90ml) per 24 hours at the start, progressing to an average six feeds of up to 7 fl oz (210ml) by the time he's four months; and four feeds of 8 fl oz (240ml) by six months – at which point it's time to get weaning underway, and after that he'll gradually start to drink less (see page 105). But it's ever so variable, and of course, different babies have different needs.

All you can do is follow the suggestions on the tin, and be guided by your baby. If there's always a little bit of milk left in the bottle when he's finished, you'll know he's had his fill, and if he's draining it completely (and looking round expectantly for a second course), you should try offering a bit more the next time. Look out for growth spurts: if he seems extra hungry for a day or two, you may just have to offer whatever extra will satisfy him.

As with breastfed babies, the overall picture will help you see if your formula-fed baby's doing OK: a steady curve on his growth centile chart, and plenty of wet and dirty nappies. He should be making around six soggy per 24 hours, while his poos will typically (but not necessarily) be produced less frequently than in a breastfed baby, on average once a day, or every other day. There's more about poo on page 154.

TIP It **is** possible to overfeed a baby on formula. Make sure you stick with the appropriate stage, and make up very carefully according to the instructions. Look out for those hunger cues (see page 31) before offering a feed, let him drink from the bottle at his own pace, and allow him to take in only as much as he seems to want, never more.

What sort of temperature?

Assuming you're making a feed up from freshly boiled water, as advised, you'll need to cool it down before offering. Squirt a little on your wrist, to make sure it's not too hot. The general assumption is that babies prefer their feed to be slightly warm – breastmilk is, after all – but truth is, they may well be fine with milk that's room temperature or even chilled, if you get them used to it.

If you do need to warm up a bottle, most guidelines urge you to do so by letting it sit in a jug of hot water, and to avoid the microwave for fear of creating 'hot spots' that will burn your baby's mouth. In reality, many parents do warm bottles in the microwave without causing their baby any lasting harm. Anywhere between ten seconds and a minute may be required, but it will depend on how cold your milk is to start with, how much is in the bottle, and how powerful the microwave, so do always proceed with caution, shake the contents like mad, and test before offering.

Extra drinks of water

If your baby's formula fed, you may need to offer him extra drinks of water sometimes – either in a bottle or, when he's ready, in a beaker (see page 104). Don't let him drink too much, though, as you don't want it to affect his appetite for milk feeds: a few fluid ounces a time is plenty. Some extra water is a particularly good idea if the weather's hot, if he's constipated (see pages 154–156) or when he's poorly and has a fever, is off his milk, or if he's suffered vomiting or diarrhoea, all of which can leave him dehydrated. Make it with plain tap water – best boiled and cooled before six months – and avoid bottled water which can have various additives, including sodium, which aren't good for him.

Bringing it back up again

Whether bottle or breastfed, it's normal for a baby to chuck up some of his feed – making those several dozen muslins you bought a worthwhile investment. You may hear this referred to variably as posseting, spitting up, regurgitation, or reflux (also known sometimes more fully as acid reflux, or gastro-oesophageal reflux), and it happens because a baby's digestive system is immature, and because his tummy is of limited size, making him unable to cope with large quantities of milk.

There's not a lot you can do to avoid all this vomiting – although, if you're bottle feeding, changing to a teat with smaller holes can stop your baby gulping it down too fast. If he's bringing up an awful lot, you may find he's hungry again sooner than he would have been, and that you have to offer another feed a little later.

Mostly, reflux is harmless, and babies simply grow out of it as their tummy capacity expands. Things often improve, too, when they're on solid food, and spending more of their life upright. For some, however, it can be painful and problematic, causing serious feeding difficulties and misery all round. Chat to your GP if you're concerned that your baby is affected by problem reflux, as medication and specialised formula is available that may help. There are also various measures you can try yourself which are said to ease the problem, for example, holding your baby upright during and after feeds. Be warned, though: some health professionals can be a bit dismissive about this issue, stressing that it's normal, and will pass with time. There's more information on the website Living With Reflux.

> *"Gracie fed every two hours for the first three months, then promptly refluxed the lot. We found it helped to hold her upright, in a baby sling, for half an hour after each feed. She detested lying flat in her Moses basket, maybe because it was so uncomfortable for her, and insisted on sleeping on our chests."*
>
> *Celine G*

You might also wonder if lots of vomiting could indicate a cows' milk allergy, thought to affect up to 7% of babies. It's pretty unlikely if it's the only symptom, but definitely worth getting checked out if there are one or more other issues at play, such as dodgy poo (see page 154), weight loss, or eczema. Don't be tempted to try and diagnose or treat an allergy on your own, though: it's really important to get medical advice on this one.

Double helpings: feeding twins

- It's quite possible to breastfeed twins as, in theory, those clever old breasts will make enough to nourish two (or more) babies if you always offer them whenever they seem needed. 'It took a lot of determination, practice, and support to achieve,' says Amanda G, who breastfed her twins for an impressive nine months.
- Most breastfeeding mums of multiples feed their babies separately at first while getting the hang of it, before moving on to a tandem technique. 'I found the "rugby ball" hold worked for me, with a baby under each arm, aided by a v-shaped back support pillow,' reveals Dani B.
- If you've got multiples, you'll more than likely find you have to experiment with a variety of approaches – and a bit of both breast and bottle is an option that works for many. 'I went through many different scenarios: feeding both on the breast, one on the bottle propped up with pillows while the other was

on the breast, both in car seats with bottles,' recounts Nadine M. There's more on mixed feeling on p86.

- Many mums with multiples decide that 100% formula feeding is the only way forward, for the sake of their sanity. 'I gave breastfeeding a go but it just didn't take off for me, and with hindsight it was a relief,' admits Natasha H. 'At least with bottles you can ask someone else to help. The thought of either feeding separately or sitting there topless to tandem feed just wore me out.'

When to wean

At some point, you'll need to start the gradual process of introducing solid food to your baby, known as weaning. He'll reach a point where breast or formula milk alone does not provide enough calories and nutrients to ensure he grows and develops well – although he'll continue to need regular feeds of one or the other, in addition to solids, until he's one. (And he will still need a couple of daily milk drinks for a while after that because of his calcium needs, but you can then switch to regular, full-fat cow's milk, or offer the equivalent in calcium-rich foods such as cheese or yoghurt. Of course, you can also carry on breastfeeding if you're still doing that and enjoying it, for as long as you like.)

Unfortunately (but probably of no surprise), confusion and controversy surrounds the issue of when to start offering solids. Department of Health guidance, issued in 2003 and based on recommendations from the World Health Organisation, is that you should wait until your baby is 26 weeks old (or, about six months) to wean, because at that point he'll be physically ready to sit up, chew and swallow, his digestive system will be mature enough to cope, and there'll be a lower risk of him developing allergies or infections. Breastmilk or formula feeds alone should provide enough for his energy and nutritional needs in the meantime.

The reality is that as many as half of mums start sooner than that, choosing to stick with earlier advice that anything between four and six months is an acceptable window. And in fact, the most recent research available suggests that weaning from four months is no more likely to be harmful than if you wait until six months. One 2011 study even flagged up the possibility that some exclusively breastfed babies really do need to get cracking on iron-rich solids a bit before six months, if they're not to be at risk of problems like iron-deficiency anaemia. (This is unlikely to be an issue for babies who are on formula, as it has more iron in it.) There's also an as-yet unproven theory that early weaning may protect against, rather than cause, food allergies.

Scientists are still beavering away as I write, trying to establish the truth of the matter, and until they know for sure, the official guidelines will remain. Meanwhile, some recently published advice from the British Dietetic Association's Paediatric Group, based on a review of 'the best available evidence', aims to offer guidance to parents who are bewildered about weaning. I've summarised and simplified its main points in the box below, but I'd recommend you Google and download the full statement and give it a read if you're worried. I'd also urge you not to tie yourselves in knots about this issue. It's supposed to be an enjoyable step forward! And if nothing else, remember the following crucial points.

- Don't start weaning before your baby is 17 weeks (four months) old. His gut needs at least that long to become ready for solid food. If you suspect he's hungry for more before then, offer extra milk feeds instead.
- All babies are different: use your instincts and look for signs that yours is ready and able to wean, rather than at the calendar – and ignore pressure from well-meaning onlookers. If you've offered extra milk feeds but he's draining every drop and still looking for more, and if he's trying to 'eat' anything he can get in his mouth, maybe he really is hungry. He needs to be developmentally ready, too: in other words, sitting up well, and with good head control so he's able to swallow and chew his food. Waking more at night isn't necessarily a sign of hunger – although anecdotally speaking, some mums do suspect that solid food and sleeping through are linked.
- Don't delay the start of weaning much beyond six months. Your baby starts to need extra iron and other nutrients by then, and he's

most likely to be receptive to the concept of new tastes and textures at this point.

- Breast or formula feeds should continue until he's one, as they remain the main source of nourishment for your baby during weaning and beyond.

Expert opinion: what the BDA says about weaning

Breastfeeding offers the healthiest start in life for babies, and breastmilk alone can provide complete nutrition for the first six months for some babies – although it may not be enough for others.

Full-term infants should begin weaning by six months, but not before 4 months (17 weeks).

All infants should be considered individually when considering when to wean. Developmental signs of readiness and 'parental opinions' are factors that matter.

New evidence suggests there may not be any benefit in waiting until six months or beyond before introducing potentially allergenic foods – even to babies from high-risk families.

If you wait until six months to wean, you should move on fairly swiftly to the second stage of weaning, which includes lumpy textures, soft finger foods, and iron-rich meals.

Babies who were born pre-term need special consideration and specific medical advice when it comes to weaning, as anything from five to eight months after their birth date is likely to be a good time to start.

More research is required to clarify these issues!

Mums' panel round-up

Did you wait to wean?

No. They'd just changed the rules from four months to six months, which was confusing. He was feeding a lot, at night too, and I was exhausted. So I started weaning at four months. He was so much happier once I started – **Claire A**

Yes. In spite of a lot of pressure from 'helpful' grandparents who said it would help with sleeping – **Rebecca F**

My son was so hungry, I started at five months. I knew that as long as he was breastfed, something a bit more substantial as well would not do him any harm. I don't take official guidelines as gospel. Every baby is different – **Nicola L**

No, I weaned at around four and a half months. He'd started waking in the night again, and it seemed madness to regress to night feeds. He was also showing all the signs of being ready. My HV didn't approve but I could see I had a hungry baby – **Heidi S**

I waited until six months to wean, mainly because he was so obviously flourishing on milk alone: great weight gain, very content, sleeping well, and no particular interest in food – **Lucy R**

We started with a few tasters of things at about four and a half months. Even before that, though, I let her feel and smell stuff that I was eating, to try and give a sense of sharing and enjoying food. She's a fussy eater now, though, so my best intentions didn't really make any difference – **Charlee C**

Getting going with weaning

Ok, so you're sure your baby's ready to wean. What next? There are two main ways to wean these days: the traditional route, offering smooth, runny purees on a spoon and gradually progressing to lumpier textures and finger foods, and the more modern approach of 'baby-led weaning', which means giving them ordinary foods from the start and allowing them to feed themselves with it. Of course, if you're not sure which way to go about weaning, it's worth remembering that many parents find a compromise, with a bit of both theories served up to their baby once he's ready, works well.

If you decide to wean the traditional way, you'll find it's easy enough to make first purees from scratch: cook fruit or veg until tender if necessary (offerings like banana, avocado or peach are soft enough to be mushed up as they are), then blitz with a handheld blender, mouli, baby food mill, or by pushing through a sieve. (Bear in mind that babies often have a natural inclination for sweet tastes – so it's important to offer both.) Good first purees include those made from:

- sweet potato
- carrot
- parsnip
- squash
- apple or pear
- banana
- avocado
- peach.

Take things gradually at first, especially if you're weaning sooner than six months. It's a brand new experience for your baby, and it may take him a while to get his head round the whole idea. If he's not interested, ditch it for a day or two, and try again a little later. He'll probably only take in tiny quantities at first, but once he's got to grips with that, you can gradually move through the first phase of weaning, working up to one whole solid feed a day (an early lunchtime, in between naps and milk feeds, may be your best bet so that he's alert, and nice and hungry), and from there gradually introducing breakfast, and then finally tea.

Once he's got simple fruit and vegetables purees under his belt, you can start mixing flavours together, then adding protein or iron-rich ingredients, like meat, fish, and pulses.

TIP See *Weaning Made Easy* by nutritionist Rana Conway (White Ladder 2011) for more on the different methods of weaning, and how to decide which one is right for you. It's also got some excellent recipe ideas, and example meal plans.

If you think it all sounds rather labour-intensive, well, yes it is. Cooking large quantities of puree in one go and freezing the rest in ice cube trays for future use is one obvious way forward. Alternatively, you can of course select from a huge range of pre-packaged options: some people are sniffy about commercial baby foods, but there are lots of high-quality, fresh and frozen brands available that promise all-natural ingredients. (And ready-to-eat jars or pots are undoubtedly convenient for when you're out and about – if pricey.)

> *“I made purées and quite enjoyed it. At least when it's homemade you know exactly what's in it. But I do also think there's absolutely nothing wrong with the bought stuff. I sometimes got those fresh sachets which always tasted really good, although they are expensive. A bit of both is fine.”*
>
> *Lara S*

Moving on

If you're taking a pureed approach to weaning, you'll need to move on to what's known as stage two after a little while, offering your baby food that's coarsely mashed and lumpy, rather than blitzed to smooth, and 'finger foods', too. Timing wise, your aim is to have introduced and got your baby well used to these things before he's eight or nine months old – leave it any later, and you might find he rejects them altogether. If you haven't already, you should look to expand your baby's diet so that it includes a good balance of tastes and textures from across the food groups. Offering a healthy second course such as stewed fruit, rice pudding or a yogurt after his main meals can provide valuable extra nutrients.

If you went by the book and waited six months to wean, aim to crack on to stage two as swiftly as possible. Fortunately your baby should have all the necessary skills needed to negotiate lumps, chunks and finger foods by now so a speedy move forward should be entirely possible. And of course, if you're taking the BLW route, you'll be making a start from this stage anyway. Read on to find out more.

Weaning the baby-led way

If you prefer, you can bypass the blender altogether, and go for baby-led weaning (BLW), instead. It's a school of thought that's increasingly popular with parents and it certainly seems like a good idea to me – if for no other reason than it's a lot less bother. I've tried to sum up the main points about BLW in the box below.

> *"BLW was a real success for us. It meant we got to share meals together as a family, including my daughter in the whole experience. It also meant I got to eat my food while it was still hot and didn't have to muck around pureeing her meals. The only downside was the mess (although it did give us a few brilliant photo opportunities). Now, as a toddler, she's great eater and I'm sure that's because she trusts the food put in front of her – and because mealtimes have always been enjoyable."*
>
> *Molly F*

Well fed: the basic facts about BLW

- Baby-led weaning is all about letting your baby move onto solid foods at his own pace. There's no spoon-feeding, and no need for purees: you put pieces of suitable, normal foods in front of him, and let him use his fingers and hands to feed himself. He can then take as much or as little as he fancies.
- For successful BLW, it's especially important that your baby is physically ready to wean – in other words, sitting up well, with good head control, and able to reach out and hold food, and to chew and swallow it well. For most babies this won't be until they're around, or at least pretty close to, the six-month point.
- With BLW, you can offer your baby almost anything to eat, if he's ready and willing: chunks of raw or cooked fruit and

vegetables; pieces of meat or boneless fish, or veggie alternatives like tofu; cubes of cheese, slices of egg, cooked pasta, fingers of bread or toast, for example. As with weaning the traditional way, there are a few foods you should avoid (see below), and it's sensible to introduce potential allergens (see page 102) one at a time.

- Advocates of BLW stress that it's no more likely to make a baby choke on his food, as long as he's ready. Gagging can occur – it's a natural safety mechanism that allows babies to bring up what they can't get down – which can sometimes be a little frightening, but if you give your baby a moment or two, he'll be OK.
- Because BLW is all about ordinary food, you don't have to go to the trouble of cooking and preparing meals especially for your baby. Central to the concept is the notion that your baby joins you at the table and you share the same meal whenever possible, as a family. In theory, this should foster a good attitude towards mealtimes and, they say, means you're less likely to end up with a fussy eater. Obviously you need to be eating a suitable, fairly healthy diet yourselves: some say it's a great way to change your own eating habits for the better.
- You may find BLW a rather messy business (and also, unfortunately, rather wasteful). Cover the floor with a plastic sheet and your baby with a large bib, and take a deep breath.

What not to offer

Whichever way you wean, there are a few foods you should avoid or limit for your baby.

- **Salt.** Not good for tiny kidneys, and also causes dehydration. As it's already in many everyday foods that your baby will be eating like bread, cheese and cereals, it definitely shouldn't be added to anything you cook for him. In particular, avoid very salty pre-packed items, such as stock cubes. Pre-packaged baby foods are fine, though: the law states that manufacturers must leave salt out of these altogether.
- **Sugar.** Better not to encourage a sweet tooth, really: let's face it, sugar is a slippery slope. Nutritious milk or fruit-based puddings

that contain sugar are fine, but you'd be wise to steer clear of the choccy buttons for as long as you can.

- **Honey.** Don't let your baby have honey at all as it may contain bacteria which is linked to a rare but potentially serious infection called infant botulism (as well as being a form of sugar).
- **Whole nuts.** Best avoided altogether (now, and for the first five years) because they're a choking risk. (For more on nut products and allergies, see below.)
- **Shark, swordfish and marlin.** These types of fish contain mercury which isn't a healthy ingredient as it could affect growing nervous systems.
- **Raw shellfish and raw or undercooked eggs.** Simply because of the increased risk of food poisoning.
- **Low-fat products.** Babies need plenty of high-fat foods for their energy needs, so make sure yours gets the full-fat option every time.

What about allergens?

Official advice is that potential allergens such as eggs, cows' milk, wheat, soy, sesame seeds, nuts, citrus fruits, strawberries and tomatoes shouldn't be introduced to a baby's diet until after six months. Unofficially, the jury's still out on this issue. Research is ongoing and the latest thinking is that it may not make any difference whether you introduce these foods at four to six months or delay until six months, or beyond.

If your baby is 'high risk' because you or your other half are affected by allergy or an atopic condition like eczema, or because your baby himself has already shown signs of one of these problems, you may well feel anxious about introducing risky foods – but confused because the available advice is muddled and ever-changing. At the moment, what does seem clear is that you should do the following.

- Chat to a health professional before you start weaning.
- Introduce new foods gradually one at a time.

- Ideally breastfeed, and keep breastfeeding while weaning, as it may have a protective effect against the development of some allergies.

TIP Family history or not, you should get immediate medical advice if your baby does appear to react badly to something he's eaten. An itchy rash, sneezes, red eyes, wheezing, diarrhoea and/or vomiting and swellings round the mouth are all typical signs. Rarely, allergic reactions can cause breathing difficulties and be life threatening, with peanuts the most likely trigger, and in this instance you should dial 999. After any reaction, you should get a referral to an allergy specialist to get the specific help you need.

What if he doesn't like solid food?

Some babies take to weaning like ducks to water, some just aren't that keen. Seek advice from your HV or GP if it gets to a point where you're worrying, but meanwhile, don't panic. As long as he's still getting regular milk feeds, he'll survive well enough. Try something different, keep offering, and take a break for a day or two before giving it another go.

> *"We started offering solids at six months, but she just wasn't interested. Every few days, we'd try again. Finally at ten months she started eating finger foods – and she hasn't stopped eating since. I wasn't overly worried about the delay, because she was still drinking plenty of formula and still gaining weight. They'll eat in their own time."*
>
> *Rachel G*

Hygiene and safety

Bear in mind that babies are vulnerable to bacteria that can cause food poisoning. There are lots of guidelines, but the main ones are as follows.

- Keep surfaces, chopping boards and your hands really clean when preparing food for your baby.
- Wash weaning spoons and bowls well in very hot soapy water, and dry them with kitchen paper rather than a tea towel. (There's no need to sterilise weaning spoons and bowls – on the basis that food won't be sterile anyway, and because at this stage your baby is undoubtedly shovelling a fair few germs in every time he puts something in his mouth, anyway.)
- Make sure any food you're reheating is piping hot all the way through before offering it to your baby. But don't be tempted to reheat more than once – throw it away if it's uneaten. Be sure it's completely cooled before offering it.

Introducing a beaker

It's a good idea to start offering your baby drinks of water in a beaker with meals when you begin the weaning process. Water's good for him, for one thing. But getting him used to a cup early on is also a wise move because ideally, you want him to be off the bottle by the age of one or soon afterwards (experts advise this, for dental and developmental reasons). And if you're breastfeeding, it could prove useful if you've never been able to interest your baby in taking milk from a bottle, and the time's come for you to stop or reduce breastfeeds: it may be that you can persuade him to take his milk from a beaker instead. Don't put any other sort of drink in his cup, though, except perhaps very well diluted fresh fruit juice (about one part juice to ten parts water is what's recommended), and only ever give that at mealtimes, for the sake of his teeth.

It might take your baby a while to get to grips with drinking from a cup, but he's sure to get there with practice. There are loads of different sorts on the market, but as a rule your best bet is to go for a simple lidded design with a couple of holes in the spout. You might be tempted by one of the many 'non-spill' designs available, but these can be harder work as they require sucking rather than sipping (and that's the skill you want your baby to learn here).

Don't be dismayed if you can't interest your baby in milk from a cup: it's a common story – naturally there'll be a big comfort factor for him in having his milk feeds the way he always has. Keep persevering – he might change his mind. But if nothing's doing, don't fret. Once he's past one, he can get always his recommended daily three-quarters of a pint of milk through food sources like cheese and yogurt, as well as on his cereals and in puds and sauces (and at that age, it's OK to swap to ordinary full-fat cow's milk). And if he really loves a bedtime bottle past one – as so many babies do – rest assured that it's hardly likely to cause harm. It's only pretty serious bottle habits that lead to problems.

TIP Your baby will probably start to refuse one or more of his daily milk feeds once he's well established on solids. It's important that – for the whole of his first year – he still gets two or more breastfeeds, or 500–600ml (16–21 fl oz) of formula, daily. But if he's drinking much more than that, and you suspect it could be spoiling his appetite for solids, try cutting back.

5

Sleep

If there's one thing you're likely to be as a new parent, it's tired. *Very* tired. One of the less wonderful things about babies is that they will insist on waking in the night – and then demand that *you* provide them the means to drift back off again. And while some babies are considerate enough to start sleeping 'all the way through' within a matter of months, most will continue to wake at night – at least once, but very often more – for a long time to come. It's exhausting, no question. But I can reassure you that: a) the day will come, eventually, when you sleep well at night again; b) there are steps meanwhile that you can take to improve the situation, if you want to; and c) over time, you'll adapt to, and cope with, whatever disruptions the nights have in store for you. Honest!

> *“You do adjust really quickly to the lack of sleep. And quality of sleep becomes more important than the amount you're getting. Four hours' solid sleep feels so much better than eight interrupted hours.”*
>
> *Lara S*

Why babies sleep a lot . . .

We all need sleep to function. During sleep, physical growth and brain development happens – so babies need more of it than everyone else. Typically, they require:

- 16–20 hours' sleep per 24 hours as a newborn
- 15 hours' sleep per 24 hours at three months
- 14 hours' sleep per 24 hours at one year.

But of course, all babies are different. So it's best not to take 'average' charts like this too seriously, and better to look for general indications that your baby's getting enough sleep. If he's alert and fairly happy in his waking hours, then he's probably doing fine. Although it might all seem a bit mysterious at first, you'll very soon get to know the signs that your baby is in need of sleep or not. And most babies are pretty good at taking the overall amount of sleep they need – although it's true that some need a little nudging in the right direction, sometimes.

. . . and why they wake a lot

While they do a lot of sleeping, babies also tend to do a lot of waking. Initially it's because their circadian rhythms – in other words, their internal body clocks – are underdeveloped, and can be all over the shop in the first three months of life: hence there may not be much difference between his day and night time patterns of sleep at first. Babies also spend more time in rapid eye movement (REM) sleep (also known as dream sleep), from which it's easier to be roused, than older children and adults. And of course, they also wake frequently because they have small tummies that need regular top-ups of milk – so for a while, it's absolutely normal for them to be up and looking for the boob or a bottle several times a night. Once his internal clock has settled, and his tummy has grown, your baby will start waking less frequently.

And when he's past six months, you can safely assume that if he's still waking you up at night, it's from habit rather than hunger, and do something about it, if you wish.

Sleeping safely

You'll soon discover there are lots of 'safe sleep' guidelines. They exist because, every year, around 300 babies die for no clear reason while sleeping – it's known as Sudden Infant Death Syndrome, or, more commonly, cot death. Doctors don't really know for sure why these rare tragedies occur, but there are various theories and a number of likely risk factors – hence the long list of recommendations for parents, aimed at reducing the danger to an absolute minimum. (And since these guidelines were introduced, the number of cot deaths that occur has fallen dramatically – so it's definitely not empty advice.) Here's a summary of what the Foundation for the Study of Infant Deaths (FSID) and the Department of Health say on the subject.

Always put your baby to sleep in his own cot – and keep it in your room

Experts are convinced it's the safest combination of sleeping arrangements: putting your baby in his own cot (or crib or Moses basket) and keeping that cot in your own bedroom for the first six months of your baby's life. Past six months, the risk of cot death becomes very small (90% of cot deaths have occurred by this age), so you should be fine to move him into his own room after that.

Kit him out correctly

Make sure your baby's mattress is clean and dry (it's advised you always buy one new), that it's firm and that it snugly fits the cot or crib. Don't give him a pillow or a duvet.

Make your home a smoke-free zone

Exposure to smoke is thought to be a high risk factor for cot death (as is smoking in pregnancy), so don't let anyone light up near your baby, or in your home.

Get the position right

Put your baby to sleep on his back and in the 'feet-to-foot' position: in other words, make up his bed at the very bottom of his cot, so that there's no risk of him wriggling under his covers. Putting him in a baby sleeping bag cuts out this possibility altogether. If he flips over onto his tummy of his own accord, while under six months, you can gently try to roll him over – but don't fret too much about this or feel you have to get up in the night to do so.

> *“I paid heed to all the positioning advice, but both my babies soon started wriggling over to sleep on their tummies, and I wasn't going to go wrestling them back the other way.”*
>
> ***Heidi S***

Steer well clear of the sofa

Aim never to fall asleep with your baby on a sofa or armchair. It's easily done if you're tired – and ironically, lots of parents do this while feeding at night because they believe it's safer than doing so in bed – but it's proven to be a particularly risky factor. If you do feed or cuddle your baby this way, stay well awake.

Keep an eye on the temperature

Overheating is thought to be a definite risk factor for cot death, so make sure your baby never gets too hot. Bear in mind the following.

- His room should be about 16–20°C: if in doubt, use a room thermometer.
- There are no absolute guidelines on how much bedding or nightwear he needs, and when, so you'll have to use your nous. One to two cellular blankets should usually be enough even in chillier temperatures and when it's warm, he may be fine with nothing more than a vest and sheet. If in doubt, lay a hand on his bare tummy, and if it's very hot or sweaty, remove a layer or two.
- Sleeping bags are great, but if you use one, make sure you've the appropriate tog rating for the time of year, and that it's the right size for your baby's age. Some mums swear by 'swaddling' a baby to create a warm, secure sleeping environment: if you try it, use a lightweight or purpose-made blanket, and leave his arms free so there's no risk of him overheating. It's also crucial to leave him plenty of room to move his legs around: too tight and it could cause hip problems.
- Don't put your baby to sleep near a radiator or heater, or in direct sunshine.
- If you've been outside in the cold, remove outer layers of clothing once you're indoors again.

> *"Getting the temperature right was impossible! Has he got the right amount of bedding? Long-sleeve or short-sleeve vest? And does he need a cardigan? One night his hands were like blocks of ice; another he was sweating under his blankets."*
>
> *Clare F*

Give him a dummy at night

This fairly recent guideline is a tad controversial, as experts have traditionally warned against setting up long-term pacifier habits. It's based on a number of studies that found babies who were always given a dummy at night were at reduced risk of cot death (and although it's unclear exactly why, it may be because they keep the mouth, and therefore the airways, open).

If you do give your baby a dummy, aim to: a) wait a month or so if you're breastfeeding, so it doesn't interfere with that; and b) remember to make sure he has it every night, since consistency in this seems to be key. (Although the FSID guidelines stress that you don't have to worry about getting up to replace a dummy in the night.)

If your baby isn't interested in taking a dummy, or if you prefer not to offer one – perhaps because it's a habit you'd rather not have the hassle of breaking later down the line, or maybe because you'd rather avoid getting up in the night to find it every time your baby wakes and wants it – you probably don't need to fret about this particular piece of advice, as long as you're doing everything else right. (For more on dummies, see page 65.)

Breastfeed

Research suggests that babies who have been 'at least partly breastfed' are less likely to be victims of cot death, perhaps because it increases resistance to infection.

Seek help if he's poorly

Get medical attention if you're in any way worried about your baby's health. (There's more about coping when your baby's ill on page 148.)

TIP There's no doubt it's safer for babies to be put on their backs to sleep: since this advice was routinely given to new parents, thankfully, cot death figures have plummeted. One minor drawback, though – coupled with the amount of time spent in car seats and baby bouncers these days – is that a lot of modern babies develop plagiocephaly, or 'flat-head' syndrome. It's largely an aesthetic issue, but in severe cases, it can really bother parents. There's more information about it on page 158.

Sleeping with your baby

It's one of the golden rules of safe sleep: don't have your baby in bed with you. But as with so many 'rules', plenty of parents do it, anyway. Some don't plan to; it just works out that way. Others choose to quite consciously, having carefully weighed up the issues involved. As Heidi S recalls: 'Bed-sharing sometimes happened for us, by accident rather than design. When you're really knackered and do night feeds without even really waking it's all too easy to fall asleep with your baby still in the bed.'

I'm not going to tell you that you're crazy to bed-share with your baby if it's something you're set on doing – or if it's just something that happens sometimes, when it seems like the only way you can get some more shut-eye. I ended up with one or other of my babies under the duvet beside me on occasion, and I can see that it's easily done. It's also true to say that not all experts are opposed to bed-sharing: some think it's a good way to promote bonding and encourage breastfeeding, and point out that in many other cultures, it's a happy norm. And they stress that it's probably not bed-sharing in itself that's dangerous, rather, sleeping with a baby while one or more other risk factors are also at play, in particular, a mum and/or dad who's been smoking, drinking or taking drugs.

Bottom line, though, is that the FSID is pretty emphatic in its warnings on this, echoed by official advice from the Department of Health and the NHS. So do please consider it very carefully if bed-sharing is something you want to try. In particular, remember it's definitely to be avoided if:

- you (or your partner, or both of you) have been drinking, smoking, or taking drugs or medication that could make you drowsy
- you are 'unusually tired'
- your baby was premature, or a low birth weight
- your baby is poorly or has a fever.

And if you *do* have your baby in bed with you, do always take care to:

- sleep on your side, with your body curled around your baby in a protective 'c-shaped position'
- make sure – as with all the usual safe sleep rules – he is never too hot, or in any danger of being covered with a duvet or pillow. Don't overdress him, and check your room's the right temperature
- only sleep in a bed that's big enough – if the three of you can't fit, then maybe one of the adult occupants needs to take to the spare room
- check there's no way he could roll out or that there are no cracks between the wall and bed he could fall into
- avoid putting him to sleep in your bed alone, as even very small babies can wriggle their way into danger.

And if you still want to bed-share . . .

Bear in mind one other really good reason not to invite your baby into your bed: you won't easily get him out again. Some bed-sharing mums (and dads: though often, not so much) are happy to carry on indefinitely – even once their 'baby' is a strapping toddler. But most reach a point in the future when they'd like their bed to be an adult-only zone again. So if you do set up a heavy bed-sharing habit, be prepared to initiate a concerted turfing-out campaign, perhaps with the aid of a sleep-training technique (see page 127), a bit later down the line. And do also make sure, if you're keen on bed-sharing, that your partner is too. For the sake of your relationship, it needs to be something everyone agrees on.

> *"I never let any of my babies sleep in our bed. Partly because of the safety issues, but mainly because I didn't want to end up with children who would only ever go to sleep in mummy and daddy's bed. It's my pit, not theirs!"*
>
> *Amanda G*

Napping needs

Unlike the rest of us, babies can't squeeze in all the sleep they need at night time, so they have to take some of it in the day, too. Hence, you'll find that naps are an essential daily feature of your baby's first year, and probably beyond: he simply won't be able to get through the day without one or more bouts of extra kip. In fact, most parents find that 'sleep breeds sleep' – in other words, a baby who naps well is likely to be more easily settled in the evening, because if he's 'overtired' he may put up a fight come bedtime.

To be honest, naps – how often, when, where, and for how long – are something you're likely to find your baby controls, rather than you. Most babies will naturally take whatever sleep they need to refresh themselves in the day, whenever they decide they need it, particularly in the early months when their body clocks haven't got an established rhythm, and when they will often drop off regularly and randomly anyway, triggered perhaps by the soothing ritual of a feed or the comforting motion of a spin in the buggy, sling, or car seat.

As with feeding, a pattern will usually start to emerge and most mums find that by three to six months, they can rely on their baby becoming ready for a nap at similar times each day, and that usually makes life a lot easier to plan. Until then your best bet – unless you're committed to a structured, Gina-style routine – is simply to be guided by your baby and let him nap whenever he seems to want to. You'll soon start to know when he's ready for one, because the signs of a tired baby are fairly obvious: crying, grizzling, ear-rubbing, yawning, and general crabbiness are all common.

> *“It's a real fight sometimes, but I try to ensure he gets at least one big nap, or two small ones otherwise he's overtired, and the evening routine becomes really tricky. Equally though, if his afternoon nap is too late, then it's hard to settle him to bed. We've found that a car or buggy ride won't necessarily do the trick, as he's always far too interested in his surroundings. But a firm cuddle very often works.”*
>
> ***Clare F***

Not all babies nap with ease. Some will only drop off if you rock them in your arms, take them out in the buggy or sling, or drive them around town for at least half an hour. You may find you just have to do whatever it takes to get your baby to nap at first. But with time and a bit of persistence, 'bad nappers' will usually improve. As Charlee C recalls, 'She was a great sleeper at night, but a crap napper for the first six or seven months. She'd kip for 20 minutes here and there, with no discernible routine. Suddenly, though, at about seven months, she got the hang of it.'

> *"Naps were a struggle at first. I Googled 'baby sleep patterns' constantly, trying to work out how to get her to sleep at reliable times every day. All the different advice was confusing, and I kept changing my mind about how to deal with it. One day I'd leave her to cry for a bit, the next I'd give up and rock her to sleep. In the end, she worked it out for herself, and settled into a pretty good daily routine without help."*
>
> *Molly F*

How much should he nap?

It's impossible for me to say how much nap time your baby should have, since babies have such different needs and different habits. His napping patterns are bound to naturally change several times over during the first year, but even on a daily basis they can differ – not least because they may have to fit round whatever *you've* got planned for the day. What I can confidently tell you is that a *typical* baby is likely to:

- nap frequently, for long stretches, but without much pattern, in the early weeks
- adopt a more settled rhythm to his napping, perhaps three times a day, by three months
- be in the habit of napping twice daily, by six months
- consolidate his daytime sleeps into a single, longish burst, usually in the middle of the day, at the age of one, or more.

When it comes to how long his naps should be, again, it's usually best left down to him. Some babies will only grab brief snatches of kip here and there – and there probably won't be much you can do to make them sleep for longer. Others slumber soundly for several hours at a time – which is always handy when you need to get things done – and should generally be allowed to do just that. The exception is if late or long afternoon naps are preventing him from being nicely tired at bedtime, in which case you might want to try cutting them short, or avoiding them altogether after about 4p.m.

Where should he nap?

Getting your baby used to going down for naps in his cot and developing a regular time schedule for them is likely to encourage 'good' napping, it's true. On the other hand, many mums don't want to be tied down at home for nap times and would prefer their baby to be happy napping in a buggy or car seat so that visits, car journeys or shopping trips can be slotted in around them. You'll have to decide for yourself how you want to play this one. (It may be that getting your baby used to it both ways will make him flexible on the matter.)

> *"I put him in the cot for naps from the start. In the early days this meant a lot of jiggling and singing, before gingerly slipping him into his cot – only to have him wake the second his head touched the pillow. But I persevered and eventually he took to it like a charm and I could just plonk him down in his cot and leave him there, he'd chat happily to himself and eventually doze off. I like to think that's because those cot naps when he was tiny paved the way."*
>
> ***Heidi S***

Sleeping through

It's the million-dollar question for new parents. But I can't tell you when your baby will sleep through the night, I'm afraid. Babies are hugely variable in this and yours will do it when he pleases – or when and if you score success with a firm action plan like controlled crying (see page 130). And even when he does tick off this particular milestone, there's still every possibility that something like hunger, teething, a holiday or illness will start waking him up again in the future.

It's a fact that 'sleeping through' has different meanings for different people: while most parents think of it as an uninterrupted night from early evening through to a reasonable hour of the morning, some health professionals define it as nothing more than an (infinitely achievable) six-hour stretch. And it's also notable that 'sleeping through' is a bit of misnomer anyway, since everyone – babies and adults alike – wakes during the night while moving in and out of different sleep cycles. The difference is that, as adults, we tend to grunt, turn over, and nod off again, while babies, once roused, will usually come to, decide they need food or attention before going back to sleep, and then loudly demand it from you. This is where the significance of self-settling comes in (see pages 120–121).

> *"At ten months, he regularly sleeps from 8p.m. to 7a.m., which is a blessing. However, when he's poorly, teething, or just not in the mood, it all goes up the spout and I can end up getting up to him twice or more in the night."*
>
> Clare F

Unfortunately, a full night's sleep tends to become something of a holy grail on the mums' circuit, so you can pretty much guarantee that some other baby will get there well before yours does – and that you're going to hear about it when they do. Try to take any boasting from well-rested parents with a pinch of salt. And no, it is not OK to punch them.

Mums' panel round-up

When did your baby sleep through?

She was nine months old. I thought it would never happen. When other mums boasted that theirs had slept through at three months, I felt like strangling them – Nicola L

Ours woke more, not less, as time went on, presumably because of hunger, then teething, too. We had regular bouts of broken nights for 18 months. You get used to it – and learn to lean on coffee! – Heidi S

On the night we brought her home from hospital, she slept from 11p.m. until 5a.m. – and that was the worst it ever got. She went completely through, with a dream feed at about 10p.m., from about six weeks and by three months was sleeping from 6.30p.m. to 7a.m. – **Rebecca F**

From three weeks, he only woke once a night. But he wasn't showing signs of stopping that, so at six months we used the controlled crying method, and he was sleeping through within a week – **Rachel G**

She slept through at 11 weeks and I thought, yay, we've cracked it! But it was a one-off. She didn't do it again until she was over a year old – **Jane H**

My daughter didn't reliably sleep through the night for eight months. I was constantly hearing stories of all these other babies who slept through much earlier but I wish I hadn't got myself into such a state because she was fine eventually – **Molly F**

How to get more sleep

There *are* things you can do to get your baby sleeping more and waking less: some of which you can start putting into practice right from the start. Yes, it's true. But let me first tell you that you don't *have* to take these measures if you don't want to. Plenty of parents accept that having a baby = getting less sleep than they used to, and are happy to wait for their baby to settle into good sleep habits of their own in their own time. If, however, the bags under your eyes are getting bigger than the ones you put your shopping in, or you would simply like to boost your chances of improving your baby's sleeping habits as best you can, then maybe you would prefer to look at the various ways you can do so.

“Sleep, what's that?! Our daughter was a terrible sleeper. She would sleep fine in our arms but if we put her down she'd wake up. For the first six months she would sleep on my husband's chest in the evening while I went to bed, then he would go to bed at about midnight and I would spend

the rest of the night cuddling her and trying to put her in her cot so I could get some more sleep."

Jenny C

Setting up 'good' sleep habits

Most experts advocate a baby-led, 'go-with-the-flow' approach to sleep in the first few months. Let's face it, most of us are too dazed to attempt anything more structured, so it's got to be good advice. And this early on, it's only fair to offer him whatever he genuinely needs in the way of food or comfort when he wakes in the night. However, if you're canny, you can set up some good sleep habits from the start, which will help your baby to settle and sleep well and, eventually, get through the night without waking you.

- Teach him the difference between night and day. Newborns don't know the difference until their body clocks adjust to a more normal rhythm, but in the meantime it will help if you make night feeds quiet, swift, and business-like, and keep the lights low. And in the daytime, pull back the curtains, get him dressed, and take him downstairs for lots of active play and conversation.
- Get him used to being put down in his cot or basket right from the start. You'd be hard pushed to completely avoid him falling asleep in your arms in the early days, when they tend to drop off readily and frequently, and often after being lulled by a feed or a rock. And some babies really object to being put down, which is understandable, really, as there are few places more enjoyable to be than in a parent's arms. But do be resilient in your efforts to get him used to his own bed. Persistence should pay off.
- Try to put him down while he's awake. If you do this, it will help him learn the magical art of self-settling, which is absolutely key to everyone getting a good night's sleep a little later on. There's more about it below.
- Don't tiptoe round him. Get him used to dropping off with some noise and disruption in the background. If he always needs complete silence to drop off and stay asleep, you might find it a hard condition to maintain.
- Take him outside for regular walks. Fresh air helps boost production of melatonin, the sleep hormone.

- Set up a bedtime routine. You may want to let the dust settle for several weeks after birth before trying this, but if you can get one of these in place as early as feasible, it could just be the best sleep habit you ever started. There's advice on how on page 122.

Self-settling: the key to good sleep

Why is it important?

If your baby can go into his cot awake, and drop off on his own accord, unprompted by a feed, or a cuddle from you, it honestly will make your life so much easier. Come bedtime, you can plop him in his cot, kiss him goodnight, and walk away in good time for *Eastenders*. Better still, when he wakes up in the middle of the night (beyond the point when he's still waking from hunger, that is), he won't need to call on your attentions to get himself back to sleep if he's able to do so quite well enough without you. So, self-settling is a skill I can strongly recommend you help your baby acquire as soon as you can.

How is it done?

Essentially, you need to get your baby into the habit of being put down for sleep, or for naps, while nice and tired, but still awake. Admittedly, this can be easier said than done with a newborn, who may flatly refuse to go to sleep without some sort of comfort from you, or is very likely to just drop off mid-feed or -cuddle, before you have the chance to put him down awake. That's fine – newborns should generally be indulged. But do keep on trying. One way round the problem if it's a final feed that always makes him drop off, is to offer it a little earlier instead. The other is to gently rouse him before putting him down (which sounds a bit bonkers, admittedly, but if he's tired he'll soon drop off again). Give him time to practise self-settling, too: don't jump up immediately if he wakes and then whines or snuffles for a while, give him a bit of time to see if he can get himself back off again. You may find yourself pleasantly surprised when he does.

Will a comforter help him self-settle?

It might do. Babies can often be persuaded to transfer their need for you to settle them, to a comfort object like a little blanket, or by sucking on a dummy, or one of their own fingers or thumbs. It can certainly be a relief if your baby becomes content to rely on a smelly old bit of muslin (stick it down your bra for a while first, to boost its appeal), or just a good old suck on his own fingers, to get himself to sleep. However, you can't force a comforter on a baby: he'll either cosy up to one or he won't (and even if you help him 'find his thumb' by gently guiding it into his mouth, you can't ensure he keeps it there). There are potential pay-offs, though: a comforter can be a mixed blessing if it turns out you have to get up to offer it in the middle of the night because your baby can't locate it. And there could be hassle in store later if you want him to give it up, and he doesn't. (For more on dummies and other comfort habits, see page 65.)

What if he won't self-settle?

If your baby simply refuses to drop off without you around to help him, you may just have to accept that for a while and keep on doing whatever he needs you to do to settle him. If you want to, when he's reached six months, you can use a sleep-training technique (see page 127) to teach self-settling. In other words, he won't have much choice.

“At night I used soft LED plug-ins so it was just light enough to get about. I found sleeping bags were brilliant as they kept him warm, and tried not to disturb him too much getting him out of sheets. I wouldn't change nappies religiously, only if really necessary. Then after a feed, wind, and cuddle I would always put back down when he was still awake, so he'd become used to dropping off without any help.”

Kathryn E

Midnight feast: is a 'dream feed' a good idea?

Lots of mums swear that 'dream feeding' is a good way to get your baby sleeping for longer at night. The theory – generally attributed to babycare guru Tracy Hogg, aka, the 'Baby Whisperer' – is that you gently pick your sleeping baby up just before you turn in yourself at around 10 or 11p.m., and offer him a quick refuel with either bottle or breast. Ideally you do this without rousing him at all, or at least only partially, and since even a sleeping, or half-asleep, baby will instinctively root and suckle, this should be quite possible. Clearly, it's a good idea to keep all the lights low and everything very quiet. With his tummy full and his body clock 're-set', you tip him gently back into his cot (there's no need for winding as the relaxed nature of the feed means he won't have gulped in any excess air), and hope he'll then slumber on through to a reasonable hour of the morning, skipping that pesky 2 or 3a.m. waking, and giving his parents a decent chunk of sleep in the process. According to the theory, a little way down the line – typically at some point after six months, once he's on solids – you simply drop the dream feed and he sleeps right through. Result.

Some experts are a bit sceptical about dream feeding, arguing that it could upset the body's natural rhythms – and frankly that it just seems a little crazy to disturb a sleeping baby. And not all parents find it works: some who try dream feeding say their baby just wouldn't go for it, or that he did, but woke up again as usual anyway, a couple of hours later. (It's worth noting that you may have to keep at it for a week or so before it makes any difference.) But dream feeding certainly has plenty of advocates. Give it a go if you want.

The all-important bedtime routine

Sleep experts bang on incessantly about how useful it is to set up a good bedtime routine and, by God, they're right. It's the next best thing you can do – after helping your baby learn to self-settle – to ensure he goes down without a fight in the evening. It's also the best way forward if you and your other half would prefer a baby-free evening. (And – believe me – even if this isn't something you're bothered about right now, you probably will be later.)

> *“A bedtime routine is the one thing I really believe in. You're doing your baby a massive favour by getting this right, because they so badly need their sleep – and later too, as kids. Even if you put them to bed at seven, with the whole bath, book, cuddle, feed malarkey and it doesn't*

work at first, I think you have to keep trying, for the sake of your sanity. Eventually, it falls into place.”

Rebecca F

Nighty-night: all about bedtimes

- Set up a consistent bedtime routine and you'll be setting up series of 'positive cues' for sleep. Your baby will soon start to understand that bath, nosh, and PJs mean the end of the day is nigh.
- You can start a bedtime routine whenever you feel ready to. The earlier the better – although you may find it's not worth trying in the first month or two, when your baby's habits are still erratic, and you're still at the 'simply-coping' stage.
- Do it every night, and always at the same time. And try to stick with it as best you can even if you're staying with friends or on holiday. It's tedious at times, but the pay-off is worth it. There should be scope to be a bit flexible occasionally, once it's well established.
- Make bedtime whenever your baby seems to be ready for it – somewhere between 6p.m. and 8p.m. is typical – and aim to get the right window of tiredness. There's no point trying to put him down if he's not tired, but if he's overtired, he may not settle well. Your starting bedtime doesn't have to be set in stone, though, because you can budge it forward or backwards a bit later on, if you want.
- Design your own bedtime routine. Bath, pyjamas, bottle or boob, song or story and lights-out is fairly typical (although some mums find the bath isn't very calming, or just not particularly necessary every night). Aim to put him down while very tired, but relaxed – and still awake.
- Make bedtime happy, calm and cuddly. Keep the lights dim, and the room warm. If you make his bedtime cues positive ones, they're likely to remain so for years to come.

“I'm absolutely militant about our bedtime routine, which I started when the twins were three months. At 6.30p.m. I get them both into clean nappies and PJs, and we feed them in a dimly lit room. Then they're winded, and put in their sleeping bags, then in the cot, either awake or

sleepy. Rarely do I have to go back in. We've been lucky with sleeping. A lot came naturally. But the bedtime routine definitely helped."

Dani B

The three-month corner

Three months is often a bit of a turning point. By then, daytime patterns of sleep and feeding are usually more settled, and your baby's body clock should have got the difference between day and night sussed. His tummy will have grown too, so the nights of *very* frequent waking should soon be consigned to a thing of the past if they're not already. And if colic or excessive crying (see page 143) has been a problem that's brought chaos to your evenings or night, you should find that it starts to ease now – or will do very soon.

All that said, some babies carry on steadfastly waking up every couple of hours at this point – and if yours is one of them, you undoubtedly feel pretty wretched about it. The truth is that, once past three months, a baby who's feeding well in the day should be physically capable of getting from early evening to a reasonable time of the morning on a maximum of one or two (at a pinch, three) night feeds. So if you find you're bobbing back and forth between his cot and your bed more often than that, it's quite reasonable to look at ways of doing so less, and the best option at this stage is a very gradual process of 'spacing out' feeds. Here's how to do it.

- Don't jump to attend your baby straight away when he wakes. Buy yourself some extra minutes by waiting a while as he snuffles and whinges.
- Once you're up, don't immediately offer a feed. Give him a cuddle or stroke for a while, sing to him for a bit, or offer him a suck on your finger or a dummy instead. Sometimes a bottle of water will appease for a while.
- Keep up the delaying tactics, aiming to extend the gaps in between feeds by up to 15 minutes at a time. Once he's accustomed to not

getting a feed at the normal time, his waking schedule should adjust accordingly. Then you can look to widen the gap by a further 15 minutes, and then a further 15 minutes. And so on . . .

- Once your baby does completely drop a feed at night, don't go back: if he starts waking again where once he slept through, offer comfort, but not a feed. (If you're worried that it's a growth spurt making him hungry offer more milk in the daytime instead.)
- If all that seems like a lot of bother, you can take a cold turkey approach, in conjunction with a sleep-training technique. But it's only fair to wait until your baby is six months old before doing so, when you can be sure he's not waking through hunger. There's more advice in the section on sleep training below.

Can I fill him up?

An obvious option – if it's hunger that's waking your baby at night and you wish it weren't – is to look for ways of filling him up a bit more. So you might consider – if you've been breastfeeding until now – giving formula as his last feed, instead, or maybe if he's past the four-month point you'll be tempted to whip up some baby rice and offer that at teatime in the hope of tanking him up.

Formula is more filling than breastmilk, it's true, and some mums are certain their babies sleep better on it. Try it by all means if you want, but don't assume it will definitely help: there's no real evidence in its favour. The same goes for solid food: weaning your baby *might* buy you more sleep, but it might not (and by the same token, there's no certainty that a baby who begins waking having once slept through, is definitely doing so from hunger).

TIP However knackered you are, it's definitely not a good idea to introduce solids before four months (see page 94). Don't be tempted to add cereal to formula or make up feeds with extra powder, either. You could end up with an overweight, dehydrated, or constipated baby if you do.

Withdrawing night time services

So. You have a healthy baby of six months or more who's eating solids, and still taking several milk feeds a day, but routinely continues to wake once or more at night time. Most experts will tell you that, at this stage, continued waking is almost certainly down to habit: whether it's a feed, or just your attention that he demands every time to get back to the land of Nod, he doesn't actually *need* it. And if you want to, you can teach him as much, by ceasing to offer what he's looking for until he gets to the point where he realises he might just as well roll over and go back to sleep again instead.

If you're lucky, you might get away with simply withdrawing your night time services, with a minimum of grumbling as a result – as did Jane H when she decided the time had come to stop offering her daughter a customary night time breastfeed. 'My other half went through to her when she woke for milk, and cuddled her instead,' she recalls. 'He had to do it for two nights before she realised that milk would no longer be forthcoming at night, and she slept through after that.'

> *"She went through without that much effort on our part in the end. One night I was feeling too poorly to jump up and go into her when she woke, so I just left it for a while, and when I went in five minutes later, she was sound asleep. Giving her the chance to get used to getting herself back to sleep instead of me feeding, or daddy patting her, was the turning point."*
>
> *Nicola L*

On the other hand, you may find your baby kicks up a right old stink when you refuse to offer him the feed he's used to, or pick him up and cuddle him back to sleep – in which case, you may need a steely approach and a more sustained campaign: in other words, 'sleep training'. (You can also use sleep training techniques at bedtime if your baby still hasn't got to grips with settling on his own at the start of the night.)

I'll stress again here that if the idea of withdrawing your services, or 'training' your baby to settle himself doesn't sit well with you, and you're happy to keep on meeting his demands for as long as he makes them – or maybe just until he's old enough to be reasoned with – that's absolutely your choice. Please don't allow anyone to make you feel like you are some kind of mad tree-hugging type because you're determined to be baby-led on this matter. And your baby *will* get to a point where he doesn't wake you at night, in his own sweet time (although you may have to accept that time may be a long way away!)

> *"My son became dependent on the boob to drop off, leading to inevitable night wakings. We couldn't face sleep training, so I gave him what he wanted. The most stressful thing was the feeling that I'd failed – and every time I met someone with a baby younger than mine who claimed they'd slept through, I felt worse. Then one day I had a revelation. It was the sense of failure that was getting me down, not briefly being woken in the night. And my baby was blooming. I felt loads better!"*
>
> *Emma H*

Equally though, if you've got to the point where disturbed nights or evenings are just not doable anymore, because the knock-on effects of sleep deprivation mean you can't function properly in the day, you're snapping at your partner, or you've gone back to work and you can't do your job effectively, then you should seriously consider taking firm action.

All about sleep training

There are a number of different sleep-training techniques, but mostly they're variations on two basic themes:

- 'gentle' or 'no-cry' gradual withdrawal, in which you don't give in to your baby's night time demands to be fed or picked up, but do keep a presence nearby to avoid him getting too upset

- the more hardcore 'controlled crying', in which you leave the room altogether for periods of time.

Gradual methods are more time-consuming, tedious, and will usually take longer to achieve results – perhaps several weeks or more – but you may feel that's a pay-off worth making if you can't handle the alternative. Controlled crying, which will usually work within a week or two, and sometimes just a couple of nights, can be tough going, and is not for the faint-hearted. Some experts aren't keen on it, either, as there's a theory that the release of stress hormones could cause emotional damage in a baby who's left to cry for too long. However, if you do decide to take this approach, rest assured that it's still endorsed by many sleep gurus and health professionals. There's guidance on both methods below.

> *"I have a friend who did controlled crying with her son at six months and he never woke them in the night again! But even so, I just couldn't bring myself to do it."*
>
> *Alex G*

Whatever route you take, you need to be comfortable it's an option that you, your other half, and your baby can handle – so do your research carefully, ask around, and talk to each other about it. As Molly F wisely puts it, 'the thing to remember is that all babies are different, as are all parents. If you try and follow a technique that isn't in line with your own way of doing things, then it won't work. End of.'

TIP If you've got the cash, consider bringing the professionals in. The services of a sleep clinic or specialist may set you back a few bob, but they won't mess around, and they'll almost certainly get the situation sorted for you. It may also be worth asking your HV if there's an NHS-run sleep clinic in your area.

By and large, most parents who do make a success of sleep training tend to say it was 'the best thing they ever did' or that they 'never looked back' and their baby has been a 'brilliant sleeper ever since'. I can personally vouch for it, as we sleep trained both our babies (with controlled crying – although there were fewer concerns about it back then, and perhaps I would have gone for a gentler approach if I'd done it more recently). And it really did work – they have slept well to this day. On the other hand, some parents do end up admitting defeat when their efforts to sleep train founder: although whether they failed because they didn't do everything right or because they just didn't try for long enough, I couldn't say.

Before you embark on sleep training, make sure all the conditions are right first.

- Your baby should be six months old and have made a good start on solids, and still be getting regular milk feeds in the day. That way, you know for sure he's not likely to be crying from hunger.
- Choose a good time. Make sure he's well and healthy – and not suffering from teething, a cold, nappy rash, or anything that could legitimately be making him wakeful and cranky. Avoid periods where there's something going on in his life that might unsettle him – you going back to work, for instance, or a bout of separation anxiety (see page 141). It will help if you're in a good place, too – you might need to be mentally strong to see you through. (On the other hand, if lack of sleep is contributing to emotional difficulties for you, perhaps you shouldn't wait.) If one or both of you can take time off work for the duration, so much the better.
- Be prepared. Do your research, so you know exactly what your chosen technique involves and how you're going to put it in to practice.
- Sleep training's easier done as a team, so make sure your partner is completely on board. (If you're a lone mum, take whichever option that you think you can cope with by yourself – or co-opt a good friend to help out.) If you're trying to give up night time breastfeeds simultaneously, it's definitely a good idea to have an accomplice: one whiff of your leaky boobs and your baby is unlikely to play ball.
- Warn your neighbours if the walls are thin.
- Get other good sleep habits – as outlined above – in place first, if you haven't already: a comforting, early bedtime routine; whatever he seems to require in the way of daytime napping (bearing in mind that for some babies, sleeping too long or too late in the day can stop them from being tired enough to settle at bedtime); and, aiming to always put him down while awake, to encourage self-settling.
- Steel yourself. Be determined. Sleep training only works when you're truly committed to it and are prepared to see it through to a successful conclusion.

How it's done: controlled crying

- When your baby's grizzling or whining turns to crying, ignore it.
- Leave him to cry for three to five minutes, then go to his cot to check he's alright. Speak briefly and reassuringly to let him know you're there but don't hang around for more than a minute or two. In some variations of this technique, it's OK to put a comforting hand on him but generally you're advised not to make physical contact.
- Leave him again, slightly increasing the length of time you stay away, before coming back to briefly check him again. If you can't bear the sound of him crying, go to another room and do something else, or put your head under the pillow.
- Lengthen the amount of time between checks, but don't leave him for more than ten to 15 minutes at a time.
- Keep going. He'll drop off eventually. Repeat the following night and until he realises there's no point in crying anymore, because you definitely aren't giving in.
- If he becomes too distressed for you to bear it, give up and vow to start again the next night, or simply to reconsider your options altogether.

How it's done: gradual withdrawal

- When your baby wakes and cries for you, go to him and sit on a chair by the side of his cot, offering verbal reassurance that you're there.
- If he continues to cry or grumble, keep up the soothing words. In some variations of this technique, you can opt to offer him a kiss, a stroke, or even a very brief cuddle. But mainly you're advised not to touch him or even make eye contact: in other words, you're there, but you're unavailable.
- Keep going until he drops off. After a couple of nights, move the chair a little way away from the cot.
- Carry on moving the chair a little further away from the cot as the nights progress. Eventually, you can sit right by the door, and then just outside it. By then, in theory, your baby will have worked out that he's no choice but to settle himself!

Early to rise

So your baby wakes you at 5.30a.m. every morning? I'm afraid that's pretty normal. Babies may need plenty of sleep, but there are limits to their requirements, and if he's going to bed at 7p.m. and napping in the day, it's hardly surprising if he wakes at an ungodly hour. You might be able to buy yourself a bit more sleep by considering very early rising to be night waking and responding to it as such (and whether that's by feeding, cuddling, popping him into your bed, ignoring him, or responding with a sleep-training technique, will depend on how old he is – and your parenting style). And there are one or two other things you might like to try – outlined below. But more than likely, the fact of the matter is that your baby has had his full quota of sleep and is ready to start his day.

> *"My son woke up ridiculously early for a while, but doesn't anymore. I'm pretty sure it's because we didn't put up with it! We just kept putting him back, and never gave in at 5a.m. or whatever ungodly hour it was."*
>
> *Rebecca F*

Up with the lark: tips for coping with an early riser

- Black-out blinds. Some parents swear by them as a way to keep the early morning light from pouring in and buying an extra hour or two to lie in. Others say it's better to get him used to sleeping well in any conditions.
- Make him wait. Don't rush in. Many babies are content to amuse themselves in their cot for a little while after waking – you may get a few minutes more shut-eye if you use these delaying tactics, and you might also be able to increase the number of minutes you leave him each day until you've worked up to something significant.
- Get good nappies. A soggy bum is a common cause for needing attention in the morning. Fork out for the most absorbent kind you can and it might help.
- Put him to bed later. If you're happy to swap adult-only evenings for later morning wakings, this might work –

particularly if you take a gradual, long-term approach to any change in schedule. (It might not, though: some babies wake up early, however late they're put to bed.)

- The same goes for trying to reduce the amount of daytime sleep he's getting by cutting short your baby's naptime: it won't *necessarily* make him sleep longer at night, but it might be worth a try.
- Take turns with your other half to do the 'early shift'. Give your baby some toys or – if he's old enough – prop him up in front of the telly, and loll on the sofa with a large mug of tea. (Some energetic mums claim it's also a good time to actually get things done!)
- Remind yourself it's temporary. He'll gradually take to waking at a more human hour as he takes less sleep in the day (by which time you may be being woken up by your next baby, of course: but that's another story) and – as the cliché goes – one day you'll be shaking him awake in the morning to get him to school on time. (On the other hand, some babies steadfastly remain early risers into childhood – at which point, they can at least be relied upon to amuse themselves until you see fit to get up yourself!)

6

Development

No doubt you'll be keen to tick off your baby's various developmental 'milestones' when he reaches them. It's reassuring to know he's doing all the things he's expected to do at certain points in his first year (and beyond). I've outlined in very broad terms the main first-year milestones, and when you can expect your baby to achieve them, just below. But please don't allow the matter to cause you unnecessary angst. Having spoken to many mums about their baby's development, I've come to realise that the scope of what's normal in real life is not always made clear in some of those milestones charts. And even if your baby is 'behind' other babies you know, it's in no way an indication of what he'll achieve later – and no reflection of your parenting skills, either. The truth is that the vast majority of babies do everything they're supposed to at some point – and it doesn't really matter when. (And with the benefit of hindsight, I can tell you that what seems so important now in terms of first smiles, words and steps, will eventually become a distant – though fond – memory.)

> *“Whenever you go to mums and tots groups, this seems to be the first thing that comes up! My son was absolutely average: he sat up at six months, and crawled at eight months, but I then got very anxious about walking – even though when he eventually walked he was still well within the expected timescale for 'normal'. I realise now they cannot learn everything in one go, and we have to stop putting so much pressure on them (and ourselves) to achieve everything quickly.”*
>
> *Lara S*

Boosting your baby's development

In case you're really keen, I've also included tips for boosting your baby's development. Truth is, though, if you're already spending time talking, cuddling, playing and generally having fun with him (and I'm sure you are), you'll be helping him without even trying. There's no particular need to fork out on special toys or daft DVDs in a bid to hasten his development either. Nothing's better for him than a bit of knockabout time with you, and play sessions with your pots and pans or a scrunched-up magazine are just as likely to enhance his skills as that all-singing, all-dancing activity station. As for classes like baby gym and music and movement sessions, they're most definitely optional. If you don't fancy them or can't afford them, don't feel you must go. (Although the fact remains, they can be great for getting you out of the house and meeting people.)

Who's a clever boy: things to bear in mind when development-boosting

- Don't *overstimulate* your baby. He needs plenty of time just to relax, too – stop with the 'sit-ups' if he seems tired or ratty.
- Let him lead the way. Don't try anything outlined below until you can see for sure that your baby's strong enough and ready (and as it's bound to be very variable, you'll have to assess when this is for yourself).
- Think of it as playing with your baby, rather than 'boosting his development'. It should be enjoyable for you both so include lots of smiles, chat and singing while you're at it and always stop if he doesn't seem to be finding it that much fun.
- Always supervise closely, particularly when your baby's propped up with cushions, or on his tummy.

TIP If your baby was born pre-term, don't forget to adjust your expectations accordingly. As a general rule you need to measure his development against his adjusted age (when he should have been born) as opposed to his actual age.

Smiling

Typically begins: somewhere between four weeks and three months, although some parents are convinced they get a grin even earlier still – it's hard to know for sure as 'wind' can often cause a reflex action that for all the world looks like smiling!

Help him get there by:

- Smiling at *him*, as much as possible. Simple as that.

Head control

Typically begins: somewhere between a month and three months for those first few wobbly moments of independence, and generally mastered – so that he's strong enough to sit up – with a bit of support, somewhere between four months and eight months.

Help him get there by:

- Sitting him upright on your lap, holding him firmly and allowing him to lean on you for as long as he needs the support.
- Popping him on the floor, or on your own chest, for 'tummy time' as soon as he's up for it – usually from a month onwards. Once he's gained enough strength in his neck, he'll start to pull his head up slightly so he can take a look around. And later still, he'll probably use his arms to push himself up even further: a sort of 'mini press-up'.
- Pulling him gently up by his hands from a lying position to a sitting position, and back again. You can try this from three months onwards, once he's gained some strength in his neck muscles.

Rolling over

Typically begins: somewhere between three months and nine months. He'll probably flip from front to back first as this is a little easier. Once he does get to grips with it, he'll be chuffed, as it can actually get him places. (Some babies don't bother with rolling over at all, though.)

Help him get there by:

- Letting him lie on the floor with lots of space either side so he can practise.
- Putting something interesting a little way away from him, so that he has to roll in order to reach it.

TIP As soon as he starts rolling over, your baby's on the move – so be on your guard, and make sure any risks are out of his way. It's best never to leave a baby of any age alone on a high surface, but it's definitely not a good idea once he's a few months old as 'rolling over' is a skill that can take you both by surprise.

Sitting up without support

Typically begins: somewhere between four months and ten months. Once mastered, it's an interesting step forward, because it means your baby can sit in a high chair.

Help him get there by:

- Sitting him on your lap, pulling him up from a lying position, and giving him lots of tummy time – as outlined above.
- Propping him (very carefully) up into a sitting position using cushions, or in a baby nest, or inflatable 'doughnut' (which will usually need cushions wedged in it too, for firm support).

Crawling

Typically begins: between six months and a year, with crawling backwards often coming before crawling forwards. Some babies don't crawl at all though, favouring another method of propelling themselves forwards: for example, 'bottom shuffling', commando-style wriggling on the tummy, or bear-walking, on hands and feet. A few just skip the stage altogether and move straight from sitting to pulling up, standing and cruising.

Help him get there by:

- Giving him lots of tummy time, to help strengthen the muscles he needs.
- Placing an interesting object just out of his reach so he's motivated to move forward for it.

Grasping

Typically begins: from four months on, progressing so that he'll usually be able to grasp an object in two hands by nine or ten months. 'Pincer grip' movements – using his finger and thumb to pick up very small objects – will usually be under his belt before he's one.

Help him get there by:

- Making sure he's got lots of safe appropriate bits and bobs to practise grabbing. Early on, a mobile, baby gym, or any sort of dangly toys that can be attached to something just above him to allow him to bat at and swipe, will give him a head start.
- Playing games that involve picking things up, putting things in containers, etc.
- When he's ready, giving him appropriate finger foods (see page 99) for meals and snacks.

Standing, cruising, and walking

Typically begins: from five or six months, with lots of support from you (early standing skills and strong leg muscles are usually honed by bearing his own weight and 'bouncing' up and down while a grown-up holds on tight). Standing with support will usually come somewhere between eight months and a year, followed by 'cruising' – moving round while grabbing onto furniture, or the nearest pair of adult knees, for support – and then standing alone. Some babies begin walking before their first birthday, but the majority master it somewhere between 13 and 18 months.

Help him get there by:

- Allowing him loads of freedom to explore in a clear, safe area at home. Let him go barefoot as it's better for grip and balance, and give him free rein (watched carefully, of course) if he wants to climb stairs or 'cruise' the room.
- Getting him a sturdy push-along toy, like a cart on wheels.
- Holding his hands firmly while he practises his steps.
- Standing just ahead of him with your arms out and smiling encouragement.
- Chucking out his baby walker or door bouncer if he has one – or at least, being sure to keep stints in it to a minimum. Experts suspect they may interfere with walking skills.

Talking

Typically begins: at two or three months, in the form of cooing, gurgling and giggling, and progressing, at any point between three months and a year, to 'babbling' – in other words, joining together consonant and vowel sounds repetitively. (Mama and dada are among the easiest babble sounds, hence many parents believe their babies have mastered their names somewhat before they truly have!) A few babies come out with their first few recognisable words (or attempts at words) before their first birthday, but for most it will happen at some point during the following year, typically before they're 18 months old.

Help him get there by:

- Talking to him, whenever you get the chance – but shut up sometimes, so he can 'talk' to you. And this goes right from the very start: join in with any cooing and babbling he's coming out with, listen to what he's 'saying', and make sure you respond.

- Avoiding baby language. Keep it simple, by all means, but use the real word, not a made-up one.
- Using body language in the form of actions and gestures alongside words – it will help him get to grips with meanings. Some mums swear by signing as a means of communicating with their baby, and say it boosts talking skills, later on as well: you could look into classes if you're interested.
- Singing, reading to him, and reciting nursery rhymes. All these things will help him learn about language.

What should I do if I'm worried?

If you're worried, there's a very good chance you don't need to be. Your baby may just be taking his time about hitting his milestones. Equally, you shouldn't feel ashamed to ask if something's really bothering you – maybe a call to your HV or an appointment with your GP is all you need to set your mind at rest. And yes, just occasionally, a developmental delay could mean a significant problem's afoot. So it's a good idea to contact your HV or GP for a chat if your baby hits his first birthday and still isn't:

- sitting up on his own
- moving across the room in some way, shape or form
- grasping large objects with his hand, and smaller objects between thumb and finger
- babbling.

Meanwhile, try not to compare your baby with other babies. Talk to other mums and check out what they're saying on the forums by all means, if it helps prove what a huge variation in normal there is when it comes to baby development. But steer clear of those excessively proud types and their over-achieving babies. Who needs it?

“I got sucked into worrying about my daughter’s development. Other mums were so keen to boast about their babies’ achievements, I ended up trying to ‘keep up’ with them, surreptitiously propping up my non-sitting daughter, and lying about how great she was at crawling and rolling. In truth, she didn’t even sit unaided properly until she was around eight months, and didn’t crawl until she was one. At 18 months, she’s still not walking, but I’m more laid back now. I know she’ll get there eventually.”

Molly F

Mums’ panel round-up

Did you worry about developmental milestones?

I tried hard not to get caught up in the competitiveness of it all. It’s probably not until you have a second baby that you realise they do things when they’re good and ready – and they’re all different – Rebecca F

I’m taking it all in my stride and letting my twins do what they want when they are ready. At six months, one will stand with a bit of help, and the other just bends his legs like a frog when you support him – Dani B

He was three or four months behind average, probably because he was ill and spent so much time in hospital. So yes, it was a worry. It’s right to be relaxed, but don’t be complacent. Instinct is precious so if you have concerns, don’t be afraid to raise them – Clare F

We’ve been pretty laid back. She’s lazy about movement so she crawled fairly late, at ten months, but I try not to compare because they’re all so different – Charlee C

My son was a bit later than average – he sat up at seven months, stood at ten months, and crawled at eleven-and-a-half months. At first I couldn’t help worrying that he was behind, but eventually I realised you have to trust your instincts on this. Rip up the guidelines and relax! – Ruth D

My first baby was late with all the milestones. I wasn’t worried. I was late with mine, and my mum was late with hers. None of us have any problems walking or talking now – Abi M

Separation anxiety

Don't be dismayed if, at some point from six months onwards, your baby takes to bursting into tears when you leave him – even if it's only to exit the sitting room to make a cup of tea. This is an issue called separation anxiety and it's very common. There's a slightly complicated psychological explanation for why it occurs: it happens when a baby reaches a developmental stage in which he's getting to grip with the concept of 'object permanence'. In other words, he comes to understand that a person or thing continues to exist, even after it's disappeared from his view. But with that notion, comes the possibility that they may not return – and hence he can get pretty upset about it.

> *"She got her first bout of separation anxiety at nine months, and I could NOT put her down. My husband says it lasted about three weeks, but it felt like at least six to me. If I went to the loo, she screamed. If I went to the kitchen, she screamed. If I gave her to my husband to hold, she screamed. If I gave her to anyone else, she kicked and screamed. I ended up wearing her in a sling pretty much constantly, as it was the only way to get anything done. At her age and size, it was back-breaking."*
>
> *Charlee C*

Separation anxiety is – you guessed it – just a temporary phase which shouldn't last more than a couple of months at most. You may just have to get used to your baby being a more or less permanent appendage during this period, and a certain amount of sobbing when you have no other choice but to peel him off you for a while. Meanwhile, you can help him understand that 'object permanence' isn't necessarily a bad thing, with a simple trick that comes recommended by Jane H. 'We played a lot of peek-a-boo when my daughter developed separation anxiety at ten months,' she recalls. 'I'd hide for a moment or two then reappear, so she learned that, even though I might be leaving the room, I would return.'

Of course, if your baby's got used to you being the main person in his life, and he cries when you walk away after leaving him with a sitter, a daycare provider, or even his dad, there may be a less complex explanation: he loves you like crazy, and he just doesn't want you to go.

Either way, it's a tough one – and something that can make a return to work painful for many mums. Rest assured that your baby will get used to you walking away and, after a while, it will cease to upset him. In fact, most childminders and nursery workers say that babies usually stop crying very soon after their mum has left them. Your best bet is to keep your own chin up (let's face it, if you cry, he's bound to), and walk away without looking back. He'll be fine without you, eventually. (Even if a little part of you doesn't really want him to be.)

> *"Separation anxiety comes and goes. I think you've got to just go with it when it pops up. There's not much you can do about it, apart from being with them when they want you. And if you can't be there, then keeping your goodbyes swift, straightforward and the same each time helps, I think."*
>
> ***Rebecca F***

7

Health and safety

Making sure your baby stays safe and well is bound to be at the top of your to-do list. Common conditions like colic and constipation may well blight your baby's life (and yours) for a little while, and it makes sense to be prepared for the host of minor illnesses which they're pretty vulnerable to at this age. It's also worth knowing – God forbid – what to do if things take a serious turn. And of course, at some point this year you'll need to check out your home and make a few tweaks so it's a safer place for him to explore. So here's what you need to know about your baby's health and safety.

Coping with colic

Colic isn't a medical condition, as such. It's a term that doctors use to describe a common pattern of excessive, inconsolable crying by an otherwise healthy baby, for no clear reason. Of course, all babies cry a lot, anyway – it's how they communicate their needs – but colic tends to be relentless, persisting for several hours at a time on a regular basis for a while, in spite of all your efforts to soothe him. Both my babies had colic for what seemed like forever (although looking back, it was probably only a matter of weeks) so it's a problem I can empathise with entirely.

As a rule, colic can kick in a few weeks after birth and affects babies only in the first three to four months of life (six at the maximum), before the phase comes to an end. It can strike at any time, but typically it's at its worse in the late afternoon or evening. And it seems to affect both breastfed and formula-fed babies alike.

> *“The worst thing was the crying in the evening. She was like clockwork, screaming from around 5p.m. to around 9p.m. I thought it would go on forever, although it must have only been for a few weeks.”*
>
> *Jo W*

Is he in pain?

Often it can seem that pain or discomfort is the root cause of the crying – you may notice your baby pulling his legs up or his face reddening, as he cries. But sometimes, there just doesn't seem to be a particular cause at all, and even the experts admit that they're a bit baffled. So there's no real explanation, just a handful of theories. The main one is that colic is indeed the result of pain or discomfort, due to an immature digestive system and a short-term intolerance to his milk, or more simply to trapped wind (which would explain the red faces and drawn-up legs – and why a huge fart may bring relief). But there are other schools of thought too. Some say it's a sign that a new baby is struggling to cope with the shock or overstimulation of life outside the womb (which might help explain why it occurs at the end of a long day, when it all gets a bit much for him); others that it's down to a big, bad, headache, caused by structural pressure on the brain during birth. One argument goes that it's more psychological than anything – a baby 'picking up' tension vibes from his main carer. (And yes, you're spot on: in my case *that* certainly seems a possibility.)

> *“My son had terrible colic and I'm quite sure that it's an excess wind issue. He clearly had trouble bringing it up, and screamed a lot. I used to lay him on my lap, grab his feet together with one hand and push them as far towards his bottom as I could. With the other hand, I massaged his belly – which was always hard with air – until he brought up some of the wind. Infacol drops before every feed helped, too.”*
>
> *Rachel G*

Colic and sleep

You may well find that, for a while, colic makes it impossible to set up any good sleep habits you'd like to, with little hope of settling your baby quickly back down when he wakes, or of establishing an early, regular bedtime. And you may find too that you need to do whatever you can to settle him, which means setting up some frankly undesirable sleep associations: desperate parents have been known to drive into the next county, or to spend hours at a time rocking, jiggling, or vibrating a colicky baby to sleep. It may not be ideal, but if it's your only option, your best bet is just to do if for as long as you need to. You can always tackle any bad habits later down the line when he's more settled (see Chapter 5).

The cure for colic

Trick heading, I'm afraid. There is no cure – it's really just a question of trying out different methods of soothing him, and getting through the phase as best you can. I've outlined some things to try below.

TIP It's worth consulting your GP before assuming that your baby's problem is colic. He may want to rule out a number of medical possibilities such as reflux or an allergy (see page 92). Be alert if your baby's crying inconsolably in a pitch you've never heard before – particularly if there are other worrying symptoms going on (see page 151). If in any doubt, get a speedy appointment with your doctor.

Hush little baby: things you can try to ease colic

- Gently massage his tummy in a clockwise direction, or push his knees up to his chest and move his legs round in a circular motion.
- Rock or jiggle him in your arms, or hold him in your arms while walking up and down the stairs.
- Take him out in the pram or sling, or for a drive in the car.

- Invest in a vibrating chair or swing seat. Some parents swear by them – although a potential disadvantage is that he may refuse to settle without one.
- Play him some soothing music or let him listen to the washing machine or vacuum cleaner. Some colicky babies apparently respond well to rhythmic or 'white' noise.
- Offer him something to suck on – a boob if you're breastfeeding and not averse to providing a comfort chew, or a dummy if not.
- Make sure he's well winded after feeds.
- If feeding with a bottle, hold it well up so the neck is always covered in milk, which will help him avoid gulping in air, or try one of the many 'anti-colic' brands of bottle or teat on the market, which usually work by controlling and slowing the flow. If you're breastfeeding, check he's getting as much of the hind milk as possible rather than filling up on fore milk (see page 31).
- Watch your diet, if breastfeeding. Some foods are said to cause problems for sensitive babies: you could try cutting out the main culprits (see page 73) to see if it helps. If you're formula feeding, it may help if you change to an 'easy-digest' brand.
- Try a herbal remedy. Camomile, fennel, and peppermint teas are said to ease colic: offer in a teaspoon to your baby, or diluted in a bottle of water, or, if you're breastfeeding, drink a cup yourself. Gripe water, available from chemists, also contains fennel – there's no evidence it works, but plenty of parents say it helps.
- Check out the over-the-counter preparations available that claim to help. These include Infacol and Dentinox, which contain an ingredient called simeticone, and work to reduce trapped wind; and Colief, which aids digestion.
- Look into cranial osteopathy or craniosacral therapy. As these are 'alternative' treatments, they're not available on the NHS and you'll have to go private if you want to try one of them. Anecdotal reports are often positive.

“We took our son to see a craniosacral therapist for his colic. We were lucky that the person we saw offers a free first session for babies, so you can make a decision about whether it's for you or not without having to spend a fortune. I can't explain how it works, but we saw a noticeable improvement immediately.”

Ruth D

Getting help for yourself

It can be nightmarish trying to cope with colic as a first-time mum. When the crying doesn't let up, and nothing you can do for him seems to help, you might reasonably assume something's terribly wrong. I remember vividly how difficult it was to cope with. But first-time round it was particularly tough because I didn't really know what it was, why it was happening, and when it would end. To be frank, I would often end up crying, too.

If colic, or indeed any excessive crying, is driving you round the bend, look for whatever help and support you need to get through the problem yourself. Please bear in mind that you are no way to blame for the situation and you do not have to feel guilty about it. Make sure your partner understands what the issue is all about (shove this book under his nose if he doesn't seem clear), and beg for help from anyone else willing to give it, if you need to.

If you're really stuck, or you're on your own, pick up the phone and call a helpline like Cry-sis or Family Lives. And don't feel ashamed if you feel like chucking your baby out the window sometimes. When it gets too much, put him down somewhere very safe – in his cot, perhaps – and leave the room for a few minutes. He'll be fine without you for a while. Above all, keep telling yourself that colic is a temporary phase. I appreciate this is easier said than done when you're in the midst of it, but it will pass. Honestly. It will.

Your baby's health

No doubt you'll find yourself fretting about your baby's state of health more than once in his first year. They're vulnerable to problems like coughs, colds and tummy bugs while their immature immune systems are still being built up, and because they're so small, potential complications can also be significant: feeding problems because of a blocked nose, for instance, dehydration caused by vomiting and diarrhoea, or difficulty breathing as a consequence of a viral infection.

If in doubt, get it checked out

It's horrible when your baby's unwell. And it's often hard to know what to do about it. Are you being neurotic in taking him to the doctors – or just sensibly trying to rule out anything serious? The bottom line is that you should never be afraid to seek help if your baby's poorly – and to be assertive about it, if necessary. As a new mum, you can't possibly expect to know whether something needs checking out or not, so it's better to be safe than sorry.

If it's non-urgent, but you need advice all the same, keep in mind all your options. Make sure you've written or printed out telephone numbers, addresses and opening hours for any likely sources of help and stick them somewhere prominent for easy reference – preferably well before you actually need them. They might include the following.

- **Your GP surgery.** Don't forget to register your baby with your GP, at your earliest opportunity. Most family doctors will give priority to young babies, so you should be able to get yours seen the same day if you feel you need to. At the very least you should be able to get a telephone consultation. Your surgery's nurse practitioner may also be able to help, so it's worth asking if you can speak to or see her if a doctor isn't available. All surgeries operate some kind of out-of-hours service, so you should always be able to contact someone, regardless of the time of day.
- **Walk-in centre.** These will often be open seven days a week, 365 days a year, and outside normal GP surgery hours. Find out where your nearest is (and whether it offers treatment to babies, as some don't), in case you can't get to see your own GP but would like to get your baby seen by a doctor sharpish.
- **Your Health Visitor.** She's qualified to help with a whole range of health issues, so it may be worth contacting her by telephone to ask her opinion before attempting to get a doctor's appointment.
- **NHS Direct (or NHS Direct Wales, or NHS 24 in Scotland).** This telephone service can be accessed any time of day or night and whoever picks up the phone will advise you on your baby's symptoms, and whether or not you need additional help. If you've got time to go online, you can also use the NHS Direct symptom checker.

- **Your pharmacist.** Often overlooked, he'll have knowledge of many minor ailments, and can advise you on any over-the-counter treatments that could help.

Coughs and colds

Sometimes, your baby will be poorly and all you can really do is give him a little special attention at home. In the case of colds, offer plenty of fluid, either in the form of extra breastfeeds, or bottles of water, to help keep him hydrated (if he's on solids, but doesn't seem keen while ill, it won't harm him to go without as long as he's drinking). You may be able to offer a little relief from a blocked nose – particularly if it's making feeding difficult for him – with the help of saline drops, which are available from chemists, or by sitting with him in a steamy bathroom for a while. If he's also got a high temperature, and is over three months, you can offer the appropriate dose of anti-pyretic medicine (see below). But steer clear of any other kind of cold or cough medication as they're not suitable for babies.

Ear infections

Bear in mind that colds often lead to ear infections in babies. You probably won't know for sure if your baby's suffering from one of these, but if he's miserable and touching or rubbing his ear, it's likely. See your doctor if this is the case, as antibiotics may be required.

Tummy bugs

Bugs which cause diarrhoea, vomiting, or both are also common in the first year. If your baby comes down with one, it's important to keep a close eye on him as they can lead to dehydration which could be dangerous: as a general rule, you should take your baby to see the GP if he suffers more than six bouts of diarrhoea, or is sick three times or more, in 24 hours. Get attention, too, if there are other symptoms at play too, for instance fever or listlessness; if vomiting is projectile, bloody, or bile-like (in other words, green); or if diarrhoea is bloody.

Treating fever

As a general rule, your baby has a fever if he has a high temperature that's reached 37.5°C or more. A fever is actually a good thing: it's the body's way of battling infection, by stimulating the immune system. But it's important to keep a close eye on a baby with a fever because they can cause febrile convulsions (fits) – and because they can sometimes be a sign of serious illness. Offer drinks of water or extra breastfeeds to keep him cool and well hydrated, take off some layers of clothing if need be and keep the room at a comfortable temperature, opening a window if necessary.

If your baby is more than three months old and has a high temperature, you can bring it down by offering a dose of an infant anti-pyretic (fever-reducing) medicine, better known under brand names such as Calpol (which contains paracetamol) and Nurofen for Children (which contains ibuprofen). Both also work as analgesics: in other words, they give pain relief too.

TIP Do check the labels carefully or ask your pharmacist before offering your baby any kind of medicine to make sure you've got the right stuff for the right age group, and that you're always offering the right dose.

A fever in itself may not be a cause for major concern, but a fever that's accompanied by any other types of symptoms, such as drowsiness, a rash, or vomiting, is something to take seriously and get checked out at the first opportunity. In a baby under three months, you should in any case seek medical advice in the event of a temperature beyond 38°C – and likewise when a temperature reaches 39°C or more in a baby over three months and under six months, or 40–41°C in a baby over six months. Some kind of thermometer (see page 18) is a useful thing to have in your medical cabinet.

When you need help, quickly

It's hard to give definitive guidelines on when you should seek medical help for your baby. Your instincts as a parent will usually be the best yardstick. But here's what NHS Direct advises are the symptoms that should be regarded as 'serious' and checked out, pronto.

- A high-pitched, weak or continuous cry.
- A lack of responsiveness, reduction in activity or increased floppiness.
- A bulging fontanelle (the soft spot on the head).
- Refusal to drink anything for more than eight hours.
- A temperature of more than 38°C for a baby less than three months old, or over 39°C in a baby over three months and under six months. In particular, seek help in the case of a high temperature coupled with other symptoms, for example, cold hands and feet, or listlessness.
- Any sort of fit, convulsion or seizure.
- Turning blue, very pale, mottled or ashen.
- Difficulty breathing, very fast breathing, or grunting while breathing.
- Being unusually drowsy, hard to wake up or stay awake or doesn't seem to know you.
- A spotty, purple-red rash anywhere on the body (a potential sign of meningitis – see page 153).
- Repeated vomiting or bile-stained (green) vomiting.

It goes without saying that if you're really frightened about your baby's health and can't get to see a doctor immediately, or if he's been harmed in an accident, you should get him to the nearest accident and emergency unit immediately, or dial 999 and ask for an ambulance. In particular, the NHS advises urgent action if your baby:

- stops breathing
- is struggling for breath
- is unconscious or seems unaware of what's going on
- won't wake up
- has a fit for the first time, even if he seems to recover
- has a fever and is persistently lethargic despite taking paracetamol or ibuprofen.

TIP The medical advice offered in this chapter is far from comprehensive. For a good overview of infant health issues, buy a good family health guide, or look at the advice offered on the NHS Choices website. And don't forget: if in doubt, get it checked out.

Vaccinations

Your HV or someone from your GP surgery will let you know when the first lot of your baby's routine vaccinations are due. This series of injections is not compulsory, of course, but as they will immunise your baby – and help to protect the wider community – against a long list of very nasty illnesses, you'd be well advised to take up the invitation. Bear in mind that you won't necessarily get an invitation back to the surgery or clinic for subsequent jabs in the schedule, so it's a good idea to know what's due and when, so that you can call for an appointment if you don't hear anything.

Just a small prick: injections offered in the UK vaccination schedule

- At two months, your baby's due his first shot of the 'five-in-one' DTaP/IPV/Hib vaccine, which protects against diphtheria, whooping cough (pertussis), polio, tetanus, and Hib, a dangerous bacterial infection. He'll also be given his first shot of pneumococcal conjugate vaccine (PCV), which protects against pneumococcal disease, a major cause of a range of life-threatening conditions that include strains of pneumonia, septicaemia, and meningitis, as well as less serious but common illnesses such as ear infections and bronchitis.
- At three months, your baby's due a second jab of DTaP/IPV/Hib, and his first of the MenC vaccine, which protects against meningitis and septicaemia caused by meningococcal group C bacteria.
- At four months, your baby's due his third jab of the DTaP/IPV/Hib vaccine, a second shot of MenC, and a second shot of PCV vaccine.

- Within a month of his first birthday, your baby is due a single shot 'booster' of a combined Hib and MenC vaccine; a third dose of PCV; and the first of two MMR jabs, which protect against measles, mumps and rubella.

TIP It's important to remember that although the vaccinations mentioned here offer some protection against meningitis – a potentially deadly inflammation of the lining around the brain and spinal cord and septicaemia (the blood poisoning form of this disease) there are many forms, and vaccination does not guard against all of them. So it's well worth knowing the signs and symptoms of this potentially deadly condition: check out the website of the Meningitis Trust for more information.

Getting his jabs

Your baby may or may not be bothered when you take him in for his jabs, which your GP, or a practice nurse, will deliver swiftly into his thigh. Any pain is fleeting and, if he's upset by it, you should be able to easily soothe him with a feed or a cuddle. You'll then be asked to hang around in the surgery or clinic for a short time, as a precaution against the – very rare – possibility of a serious allergic reaction, or a febrile convulsion (fit). Your baby may develop a high temperature and be a bit poorly for a while after vaccination, in which case you'll no doubt be advised to offer him a dose of anti-pyretic medicine (see page 150) – but do check with the health professional involved first, before assuming it's OK to do so.

Are vaccinations safe?

Ask any doctor, and they won't hesitate to recommend you get your baby along to the clinic for all his vaccinations as soon as they are due, and to assure you that all the vaccines are safe and effective. No-one can promise you that they are *totally* risk-free (and it's true that there are small pockets of worried parents out there who feel sure that jabs could be more dangerous than the diseases they protect against), but the fact is that cases of badly adverse, proven consequences of immunisation are extremely rare indeed, while no-one is any doubt about the dangers of the diseases they protect against, which can cause brain damage, disability, and deadly infection.

Poo problems

It's a good idea to keep an eye on your baby's poo, and seek medical advice if anything about it seems very unusual.

Diarrhoea

Runny poo isn't abnormal, especially in a breastfed baby, but it could be diarrhoea if it just keeps coming, if it's watery, particularly explosive, very smelly, or streaked with mucus; or if there are other symptoms going on, such as vomiting or a high temperature (see above).

Usually, diarrhoea will be caused by some kind of bug such as gastroenteritis, but it can also be a symptom of a food allergy or intolerance. Bear in mind, too, that diarrhoea (and/or vomiting) can cause dehydration which can quickly become quite dangerous in small babies: your GP may want to prescribe an oral rehydration solution to replace lost fluid. Do also seek immediate help if you notice red, black, or bloody bits in your baby's poo, or if it seems extremely pale or whitish in colour.

Constipation

Lots of babies suffer from constipation, although it's generally said to be a rarity in exclusively breastfed babies, because breastmilk is so easily digested and because it produces such soft poo. In fact, it's not abnormal sometimes for a perfectly healthy breastfed baby to go for several days or more without passing a motion. It won't necessarily mean they're constipated, although you might reasonably assume that they were – as Molly F recalls. 'My daughter once didn't fill her nappy for more than a week,' she says. 'In a panic I rang NHS Direct and the HV, only to be told not to worry if she wasn't in pain as it can be perfectly normal for breastfed babies not to go for a while sometimes. It all came out in the end.'

It is, however, more common in bottle-fed babies – sometimes it can be the consequence of poorly made-up formula, or of offering 'hungry' or 'stage two' brands before a baby's ready for them: two good reasons to take care when making up bottles and selecting the right stuff. And it's also common for it to occur during weaning, as your baby's digestive system adjusts to the shift to solid food.

Constipation can occasionally be a symptom of a specific medical problem (including – very rarely – a handful of congenital conditions). But usually, it's what doctors call 'idiopathic', which means there's no particular cause; it's just 'one of those things'.

> *“We used baby rice when weaning our son at five months, but it made him constipated. We found that adding a little prune juice helped – and then once he was six months we started offering a multigrain porridge for babies. There were no further problems.”*
>
> *Ruth D*

You'll know when your baby's constipated, as it will be pretty clear from the look on his face when he's straining to pass anything – and because anything he does produce will be hard, and perhaps pellet-like. His tummy may feel solid, too. All that pushing can naturally cause a very sore bottom – and sometimes even small fissures (tears), with the unfortunate result that a baby may hold a poo in, causing it to harden, which of course just makes everything worse. And then you've got a vicious circle on your hands.

> *“My daughter started suffering from constipation at around six months. It was so upsetting to watch her, rolling around on the floor screaming in pain because she couldn't poop. It took a while before our doctor took it seriously but eventually she was prescribed a laxative solution. She continued to suffer, though, so they switched her to a powder medication and referred us to a specialist.”*
>
> *Rachel G*

Feeling the strain: how to cope when your baby's constipated

- Try to help things move along your baby's system by gently massaging his stomach in a clockwise direction or pushing his legs round in a circular motion (as with colic, p143).
- Offer extra drinks of water in between feeds, in a bottle or sip cup – or on a spoon, if he's breastfed and not interested in drinking from either of those. Some suggest adding sugar to water, but as it may encourage a sweet tooth, it's probably better avoided.
- Check you're making your formula up right, and that you've got the right 'stage'. It may also be worth switching to a different brand to see if it helps.
- Once weaned and eating solids, try offering your constipated baby more fruit, veg, and high-fibre cereals, or drinks of very well diluted fruit juice. Prune juice, in particular, can be pretty effective.
- See the doctor if your baby's constipation goes on for more than a day or two, to save the problem worsening and becoming really painful for him. Treatment in the form of a laxative solution may help, and stronger medication is available for more severe cases. If the problem persists, you should ask to be referred to a specialist.

Nappy rash

Sore bots due to nappy rash are very common, affecting around a third of babies. It's usually due to prolonged contact with the ammonia that's produced by wee and poo, causing a baby's delicate skin to become irritated, and can result in bright red, painful looking blotches or spots. Nappy rash will often crop up during or after a bout of diarrhoea, and – although there's no proven medical link – lots of mums are convinced there is a connection to teething (see page 159).

Usually you can clear up nappy rash yourself, with aid from one of the many over-the-counter nappy rash ointments available: recommendations vary, so it's probably a case of experimenting to find out which one works best for your baby. Don't forget to avoid wipes while he's recovering, as they can be pretty unforgiving on sore skin – stick with cotton wool and warm water for a while. Of course, there'll be less pain all round if you can manage to avoid nappy rash occurring in the first place. There are some tips that may help below.

A more serious cause

Keep in mind that, sometimes, nappy rash can be caused – or worsened – by either a fungal or a bacterial infection. This may not be obviously different from ordinary nappy rash, but if it's pretty bad, or refusing to clear up, do get your doctor to have a look, as he'll be able to prescribe treatment if it is infected. He may also want to rule out the possibility that an underlying skin condition is at play, such as eczema, or allergic dermatitis (in other words, a reaction to a particular substance).

Getting to the bottom of it: tips for preventing nappy rash

- Change his nappy really regularly. Don't let it get very soggy, and whip it off as soon as possible after he's done a poo. Splash out on the most absorbent nappies you can afford.
- Give him 'nappy-free' time whenever you can: let him kick, roll, or crawl around with his bot exposed to the air – naturally, a large, waterproof floor covering of some kind will be helpful.
- Make sure he's 100% dry whenever you put a new nappy on. Some say a quick blast with a hairdryer, on a low setting, works a treat.
- Regularly apply a little barrier cream, like petroleum jelly, or zinc and castor oil ointment, to his cheeks. (And I don't mean the ones on his face.)

Mums' panel round-up
How did you deal with (or avoid) nappy rash?

An ointment called Metanium always seemed to solve the problem. Although be warned, it's bright yellow and does stain clothing if you're not careful – Lauren B

I swapped to an organic nappy brand when my daughter had persistent nappy rash. I don't know if it was significant or not, but it cleared up and she didn't get it again – **Jess T**

We used real nappies and discovered that putting silk liners in them cured nappy rash, after Googling nappy rash + miracle cure! – **Eleanor H**

Tui bee balm by a company called Songbird Naturals is magic. I use it myself, too, as a moisturiser – **Kate R**

Always, always make sure the bum's dry every time, that's my tip. Even if it's just a bit damp from the wipe residue. Pat it dry first – **Rebecca D**

Bepanthen cream. It works a treat – **Mel D**

Positional plagiocephaly or 'flat head' syndrome

Increasingly these days, parents are noticing that the back or side of their baby's head begins to flatten at some point in the first year. It's a problem known as positional plagiocephaly, or 'flat-head syndrome', and it happens because the separate plates of the skull don't become fused for a year or two after birth, making them vulnerable to pressure.

The problem is pretty widespread now, no doubt because babies are automatically put down to sleep on their backs, on firm mattresses, in line with safe sleep guidance, and perhaps because they spend lots of time in car seats and bouncy seats as well. It can also be the upshot of a condition called torticollis, which is a tightening of the muscles on one side of the neck, caused by the way a baby's positioned in the womb, or during a difficult labour, which can make the head to tilt to one side. (And you should certainly see your doctor if you suspect this is a problem, as referral to a physiotherapist may be required.)

Flat-head syndrome doesn't cause any pain and is essentially a cosmetic problem. If you ask your GP about it, he'll probably tell you the misalignment will naturally correct itself over time, or at least become so well camouflaged by hair, it doesn't matter anyway. There are 're-positioning' techniques which can improve matters – as well as serving as a preventative measure. (They're outlined below.)

Correctional treatment is available, which involves wearing a helmet or band, more or less permanently, for at least a couple of months, but as the general feeling among doctors is that this causes unnecessary discomfort, it's not widely available on the NHS. However, there's no doubt that some babies are pretty seriously affected, and can end up with an extremely wonky head, which might bother you as his mum.

On me 'ead, son: tips for tackling and preventing plagiocephaly

- Keep periods of time your baby spends in his car seat or bouncy chair to a minimum whenever possible.
- Put him down on his front for 'tummy time' as much as you can while he's awake, to take the pressure off his head. Always stay to supervise, though.
- Watch to see if your baby tends to rest his head to one side when lying or sitting. If so, fix an interesting toy or picture to the opposite side to encourage him to look the other way sometimes, too. In his cot, you can influence the way he rests his head by placing a rolled up towel *under* the mattress, on one side or another. Never put anything above the mattress for safety reasons.
- Don't, whatever you do, stop putting your baby to sleep on his back. It's one of the most important measures in preventing cot death.

Teething

It's hard to say what you can definitely expect from teething: it's an experience that seems very variable. Six months is average for the first of a baby's teeth (also known as 'milk teeth' or 'the deciduous indentation') to appear, but for some it's earlier than that and for others, it can be a whole year or more. In any case, genetic factors are usually at play, so it's not something you can control, or indeed something that matters. Typically, the two middle teeth at the bottom (correctly known as the lower central incisors) come through first, followed by the two at the top (the upper central incisors), and an average baby may have around eight teeth altogether by the time he's one (with the full set of 20 in place by the time he's three).

Will it be horrible?

It might be. The phrase 'cutting teeth' is a bit of misnomer because what actually happens is the gums separate to allow a new tooth to come through; however they can certainly become tender and inflamed in the process. Reports from the frontline reveal that some babies have a miserable time of teething, while other, luckier babies, aren't too bothered. Along with the tenderness and discomfort, you might find that teething makes your baby irritable, and that his sleeping or feeding is affected. He may also have a red rash or inflamed patch on his cheek, and take to dribbling like a loon.

> *"She got all her teeth early, with the first coming through at three-and-a-half months. Sometimes when teething she gets bad tempered, and chews her own hands to bits. At night, she'll toss and turn a bit and might occasionally need a dose of ol' faithful – Calpol – but mostly it doesn't affect her sleep too badly."*
>
> *Charlee C*

Other symptoms

Many parents (and I include myself here) feel sure it's no coincidence that further symptoms such as fever, colds, diarrhoea, and nappy rash seem to crop up at exactly the same time a tooth comes through. However, according to the experts, there's no proven medical link to these things (although it's agreed that teething may lead to a 'slightly' raised temperature – and there is a theory that all that excess saliva can make stools looser and more acidic, which could explain the sore bums and runny poo).

TIP Health professionals urge against making assumptions here: according to research carried out in one hospital, a significant number of babies were admitted with a medical problem their parents had initially passed off as connected to teething. If in doubt, get it checked out.

> *"Teething came as a shock. He got his first tooth at six months and pretty rapidly gained a further seven. We use teething gel occasionally, but frankly, haven't messed about much before reaching for the Calpol, especially at night. I don't see the point in letting him suffer. We know the signs now: he gets a much thicker, more persistent dribble, is grumbly, and goes off his food. Sometimes he gets a red rash on the corresponding cheek and diarrhoea."*
>
> *Clare F*

Biting at mealtimes

For breastfeeding mums, teething can bring a rather painful new dimension to the activity. If you're vigilant, you might be able to pre-empt a bite by breaking the latch with your finger whenever you sense he's about to go in for the kill. You may also be able to 'teach' your baby – however young – that biting's not on, by issuing a loud 'no' and stopping the feed for a while, as Abi M did. 'It was a problem,' she admits, 'but I solved it simply by breaking the latch if I got bitten, then putting baby down for a minute or so with no attention.'

Tooth-fully speaking: how to ease teething pains

- Offer him a teether toy. Pop it in the fridge to cool first if you like (but never the freezer, as that could actually cause damage to the gums). If your baby's weaned and enjoying finger foods, a nice piece of chilled cucumber will have a similar effect.
- Gently massage his gums with a very clean finger.
- Give him Ashton and Parsons homeopathic powders. This may sound a bit cranky, but mums recommend them time and again. Reportedly, they're not always easy to source these days,

so you may have to shop around. (And be warned: according to Abi M, these little wraps of white powder could bring you under suspicion during handbag searches in nightclubs.)

- Dose him up with Calpol. A spoonful is guaranteed to ease pain, which could be a particular blessing in the middle of the night when sore gums are stopping him from sleeping.
- Rub in a little teething gel. These work by numbing the area, if only for a short while. Can also be cooled for extra relief in the fridge. Some mums say that smearing a little on a dummy is a good way of administering it. They're only suitable for babies over four months old.
- Apply a little barrier cream or emollient if dribble is causing facial soreness.
- Cuddle him. It might help take his mind off the misery.

Caring for your baby's teeth

It's a good idea to get into a regular habit of cleaning your baby's teeth right from the start to help protect against tooth decay. Even though it's his first set, to be replaced a few years down the line with a more permanent mouthful, they're still really important – if he loses any, it will make chewing his food tricky and could affect the alignment of his adult teeth. So, aim to brush twice a day, either with a tiny, soft baby toothbrush or a little piece of soft fabric wrapped round your finger. Using a small smear of infant-friendly toothpaste that contains 1000ppm (parts per million) of fluoride is a good idea, as it helps prevent decay, but steer clear of normal, adult brands as these tend to contain more fluoride than is good for them (as well as being rather strong, taste-wise). Ask your dentist for advice if you're not sure.

Making your home safe

Before you know it, your baby will be rolling around on his own steam, exploring the corners of your house he didn't know existed, and making a grab for items you'd rather he didn't. It's time then to have a think about his safety at home, and what you can do to ensure it – because trust me, once your baby begins to mobilise, he will be on a mission: a mission to explore his environment, to put his exciting new skills into place, and yes, to cause chaos.

You could, of course, keep your baby safe from harm by holding him permanently on your hip, or locking him up in a playpen 24 hours a day. But if you want him to develop in a healthy way, you have to allow him to run riot a bit. Hence, you need to be wary of what the main risks are, or could be, and you should (probably) put a few measures in place to prevent them. And because you can't ever hope to make your home a completely safe place for your baby (the difficult truth is, he's bound to have an accident or two somewhere along the line), you also need to do your best to teach him about potential dangers and how to avoid them, whenever, and as soon as, you possibly can.

> *“The only baby-proofing equipment we used were stair gates. For the rest, there was gaffer tape: you can put it on table corners to make them less sharp, and across kitchen cupboards and drawers to keep them closed. To be honest, I don't think there are many gadgets out there that compensate for teaching your child not to do or touch things they shouldn't.”*
>
> ***Natasha H***

How can I 'baby-proof' our home?

First off, I just want to say that you almost certainly couldn't 'baby-proof' your home comprehensively – you're bound to miss something out you hadn't thought about. And some say you'd be foolish to try. After all, if you thought your home was totally safe, you might be tempted to leave your baby to it, when really – unless he's very well secured in one very safe place – he ought always to have someone in the room with him.

"We put stair gates at the top and bottom of our stairs, locks on the cupboards containing risky products, put all valuables up high, and installed a foam guard round the edge of our fireplace. There'll always be stuff you can't prepare for, though. Once, when my daughter was in the bathroom, strapped into her bouncy chair as I showered, she reached out and started eating a leaf from my peace lily plant. I got out, moved her away, and looked it up in my baby book, only to read that peace lilies were poisonous. Cue a call to NHS Direct. So we moved house plants, too."

Jane H

That said, it's hard work hovering permanently over your baby. So it's a good idea to have a careful think about all the possibilities for danger or disaster, and make any adjustments you can that will give you peace of mind while allowing him a little freedom.

Think carefully about what you'd really like to invest in before you rush out to stock up on gates, locks, guards, covers, and any of the other myriad devices available on the market. Most safety measures are more about being aware and making small adjustments, than fitting pricey pieces of equipment. And lots of mums look back with hindsight and realise they got a bit ripped off by the retailers in their anxiety. Some even argue that you're better off *not* removing risks (or drawing a baby's attention to danger spots by fitting a piece of equipment over it) but rather, aiming to teach him what they are and how to avoid them – on the basis that life's a risky business anyway and you're better off learning that sooner rather than later. I've included a long list of baby-proofing measures below which should give you some pointers – but these are all just suggestions. In each case, you may alternatively choose to go down the vigilance/education route instead, keeping your beady eye on him at all times, while teaching him to negotiate danger areas with the help of gestures and body language. Simple words such as 'no' and 'hot' – and their meanings – can come to be understood by even young babies.(And one good reason for taking this line is that, while you can do a lot to make your own home safe, there's nowt you can do about the risks in other people's.) Some sort of balance between the two schools of thought is probably a wise aim.

Whatever you do to improve safety in your home, don't forget to keep reassessing the situation regularly. The risks are likely to increase as your baby gets older, develops new skills and becomes increasingly curious.

TIP The information here should provide you with a starting point. For further information, see the websites of the Royal Society for the Prevention of Accidents (RoSPA), and the Child Accident Prevention Trust (CAPT). There's also lots of advice about safety and other sorts of equipment at the website of Which?

"I'm not convinced you need to do anything other than the blindingly obvious (i.e., don't let your baby near hot stoves or hot drinks, and keep sharp knives out of reach). Kids learn fast and cotton wool kids will only get hurt when they visit a household without little kids and without safety measures."

Abi M

Safety first: measures you may want to take to reduce risks at home

- **Make your stairs safe.** Stair gates are among a small handful of safety items considered essential by the Child Accident Prevention Trust – and you need one at the bottom, as well as at the top. Talking of stairs: keep them clear of clutter. And check your banisters are sturdy, too.
- **Avoid trapped fingers.** It's a common injury in babies. Door jammers are an inexpensive way of doing this – or you could just use heavy door stops.
- **Watch out for choking risks.** Keep floors and surfaces clear of small items he could put in his mouth and make finger foods appropriate.
- **Assess your furniture.** Cover sharp corners that are at his head level. Make sure wardrobes, shelving units, large televisions, and lamps or large ornaments are firmly fixed in place and can't be pulled over. DVDs and other expensive entertainment centres are best kept out of reach (for their sake as much as his).

- **See to anything that dangles.** Cables, wires, tablecloths, blind cords, anything with a string or a ribbon attached: make sure anything that your baby could pull at or get around his neck is carefully tucked out of reach.
- **Make sure upper-storey windows are secure.** Locks or restricters are also one of the items recommended by CAPT. It's a long way down – and even if your baby isn't yet capable of climbing up to a window and opening it, he will be at some point.
- **Prevent burns.** Get a fire guard – or be extra vigilant when your fire is on; keep your baby away from radiators that get very hot; never put cups of tea or coffee within his grasp; always put the cold water in first when running a bath; take care with still-hot appliances like hair straighteners or kettles. And make sure your baby stays well away from the cooker – in particular, keep pans with the handles turned backwards.
- **Fit locks on cupboards and drawers.** At least, on those that contain anything dangerous. Sharp knives and utensils, breakable items, plastic bags, and medicines, alcohol and cleaning products are the obvious ones. Otherwise, simply move dodgy contents out of reach.
- **Consider your garden, too.** Ponds are a major hazard and if you've got one you should cover it – or be extremely vigilant at all times – and likewise, paddling pools need very careful supervision. Look for holes in the fence. And pull up poisonous plants.
- **Shop wisely.** Be sure that everything you buy for your baby is safe – if in doubt, look for British Standard or other safety marks on products and in the case of second-hand stuff, be absolutely certain it's in good nick. Be scrupulous in following any installation instructions, too.
- **Have a 'safe place'.** Set up a playpen, travel cot, or well secured room corner so you've always got somewhere you can put your baby for a few minutes if you need to leave the room (and let's face it, it's tiresome having to always take him to the toilet with you).

Part three

Being mum

8

Your body after birth

Bits of you are going to hurt after having your baby. It's inevitable: giving birth was a big, big deal for your body, whatever the nature of your labour and delivery. It's impossible to say how long you personally will take to physically recover, because experiences differ wildly. Some women are pleasantly surprised by how speedy the process can be; others are miserable to discover it's a long haul. However you feel, and for however long, aim to take things as easy as possible while you get back to normal. Seek advice from your midwife or GP about anything that's worrying you or causing you grief. And do try to take life at the slowest pace possible until you're back on form.

> *"You get lots of info on pregnancy, birth and what to do with your new baby, but no warning of how painful it can be afterwards. I had a second degree tear and stitches, and I swear that was worse than the birth itself. I felt like a bowling ball was about to fall out of me. I kept asking if it was normal. Apparently, it is."*
>
> *Emily D*

Mums' panel round-up
How long did it take to recover from birth?

I'd had a water birth and I'm sure it was one of the reasons I was feeling OK within days – **Maggie H**

It was a few months before I felt normal again, although I'm not sure how much of that was due to the section, and how much to new-baby shock – **Jane H**

I think I'd made a full recovery by six weeks. It took that long to stop bleeding, and to heal down below – **Kathryn E**

Four weeks until I could move around comfortably, six months until I could stand for long periods without feeling certain bits might fall out, and ten months before I felt completely normal again – **Charlee C**

Even after the worst of the pain had subsided after my C-section, I felt a dull ache for a further three months, and the occasional twinge for up to a year – **Julia W**

About six weeks, in spite of my HV's rather gloomy prediction that it would take nine months to recover from my Caesarean – **Caroline S**

After pains

Not everyone does, but you may find you suffer from 'after pains', which can occur as the womb contracts back to its usual size in the weeks following birth. They're usually only intense for up to a week, and can feel particularly strong while breastfeeding due to a release of oxytocin – the same hormone that triggers contractions (it's nature's way of helping to speed up the whole process, which is known as involution). Some new mums don't feel them at all (and they're said to feel more obvious with subsequent births) but for some, like Heidi S, they can come as a shock. 'The after pains were astonishing, and no-one had warned me about them. Somehow, labour I could handle because it was "productive" pain but these were just agonising,' she recalls.

If after pains are bothering you, try wallowing in a warm bath, cuddling a hot water bottle or heat pack, or popping a couple of painkillers. Let your midwife or GP know if the pains persist beyond much more than a week, or if they stop, only to begin again a little later, as it could be a sign that an infection's developed.

Post-natal bleeding

Properly known as lochia, your post-natal bleeding is likely to last for up to six weeks. The blood will be heavy and bright red to start with, decreasing and changing colour to pinkish-brown and eventually becoming white or colourless. Don't be too alarmed if there are clots in it, as some clotting is normal. 'I was horrified,' admits Dani B. 'I can only describe it as looking like bits of my liver were falling out of my vagina.' Do mention it to your midwife or HV, though, if the clots are numerous, or if they seem very large, as that can sometimes be an indicator of infection. Grim as it sounds, it's a good idea to keep one on a pad or in the toilet to show her, if you're concerned.

Major blood loss – what's known as a secondary postpartum haemorrhage – can occasionally occur. You'll know about it if you're unlucky enough to experience it, because you'll be soaking pads within minutes – seek medical attention, urgently, if this is the case. An unpleasant smell is also something to watch out for, as it's a potential sign that an infection has developed. And sometimes, an increase in lochia flow after it's begun to slow down is a sign that you're overdoing it, or of an infection developing.

> *"A friend had warned me about the bleeding, but I was still shocked. My first shower looked like a cross between Psycho and a vampire movie."*
>
> *Clare F*

Low iron levels in your blood (anaemia) can occur – particularly in women who suffered from it during pregnancy or who lost a lot of blood during the birth – and this can cause exhaustion and other symptoms such as breathlessness, headaches, and feeling faint. It can also affect the quality of breastmilk. If it's a problem for you, try to eat lots of iron-rich foods like red meats, fish, eggs, pulses, dried fruits and green veg, wholemeal bread, dark chocolate and fortified cereals, and aim to get plenty of vitamin C down you at the same time, as it boosts iron absorption (drinking a glass of orange juice alongside an iron-rich meal is ideal). Your doctor can also prescribe iron tablets if he thinks you need them.

You'll need a good supply of maternity pads to see you through the bleeding. Ordinary pads just won't cut it, and it's important to keep them changed regularly to prevent infection (for the same reason, tampons definitely aren't a good idea), being sure to wash your hands before and after every change. Big, loose, cotton-gusseted, dark-coloured pants are pretty much essential: get yourself a job lot from somewhere cheap, as you'll no doubt want to throw them away once they've had their use. You can buy disposable paper maternity pants, too: although word on the street is that these can be rather scratchy.

> *“I was surprised at how long I bled for, a good three or four weeks. I remember the midwife at ante-natal classes advising us to invest in some incontinence pads and thought then it was a bit far-fetched. I was glad I did though, because I'd have been lost without them – they're enormous, and very absorbent!”*
>
> *Molly F*

Vagina and perineum

For many women who have a vaginal birth, a torn perineum (the area between the vagina and bottom which inevitably gets stretched during delivery) is par for the course. While small tears can heal naturally, some will require stitches, as will an episiotomy (a cut made purposefully by a midwife or doctor to aid a baby's exit). Stitches will take several weeks to heal and should eventually dissolve of their own accord, but meanwhile can be sore and/or itchy. Your midwife will want to check them several times during home visits, to make sure they're still in place, that they're healing OK, and that there's no sign of infection. (Keep an eye out yourself for any oozing or weeping, throbbing pain, or nasty smells or discharge and flag it up to a health professional as soon as you get the chance.)

Meanwhile, aim to keep the area clean by washing it regularly in plain warm water – you'll probably find you want to dive into a bath or shower a couple of times a day, anyway, just to feel fresh. Stick with plain water, as soap or gel could be irritating, and use tissue to gently pat yourself dry, rather than a towel – or better still, expose the area to the air for a while and allow it to dry naturally. (You may want to make sure you're the only person in the room at the time!) There are some more tips on dealing with post-natal pain in the box below.

> *"My stitches became very painful and I just assumed it was normal. But it turned out they had burst and got infected (or possibly the other way round) so I needed a really strong course of antibiotics. Once the infection cleared I had a look in the mirror, and could see random bits of stitching sticking out, which I ended up simply picking out myself. Not pretty."*
>
> *Marianne O*

If you were unlucky enough to suffer a more serious third- or fourth-degree tear – which affects the anus, too – the healing process will probably last for months, rather than weeks. Hopefully, you'll get all the follow-up care you need, but don't suffer in silence if any pain or discomfort persists, if you experience any bowel problems, or if it just doesn't look or feel right down there. Talk to your midwife, GP, or consultant about it and insist on being referred to a specialist if necessary.

A sore subject: some tips for tackling pain down below

- Sit in a bath of plain, warm water. Some say a little salt added can aid healing, others swear by a drop or two of lavender or tea tree oil (and there's no harm to be had in trying either). Soap, shower gel or bubble bath are best avoided as they'll cause irritation.
- Pop an over-the-counter painkiller such as paracetamol or ibuprofen. Both are fine to take while breastfeeding.
- Try a little 'cold therapy'. You can buy gel-packs specifically for the purpose from Boots or Mothercare, chill them in the fridge, and pop them in your pants. A chilled maternity pad will also

offer cooling comfort, as will a bag of ice or frozen peas – but don't let anything that's come out of the freezer make direct contact with your skin as it could cause ice burn: wrap it in a clean towel first.

- Apply a local anaesthetic spray or cream. These are available over the counter, so ask your pharmacist.
- Take Arnica tablets. This homeopathic remedy, available from chemists and health food shops, is said to reduce bruising or swelling and stimulate tissue repair. There's no medical evidence that it really works – but many new mums are convinced it does.
- Sprinkle when you tinkle. Urine passing over your sore bits can really sting, so wait until you're in the bath to wee, or have a sports bottle full of water on hand near the loo, to squirt over your bits while in mid-flow. Drinking lots of fluid will reduce the concentration of your urine and make it less likely to sting (some say barley water is particularly effective).
- Sit comfortably. Look into hiring an inflatable 'valley cushion' if it hurts to sit down. The National Childbirth Trust (NCT) runs a specific phone line for this. Two rolled up towels – one under each buttock – offer a makeshift (and free) alternative.
- Get going on your pelvic floor exercises. They'll help stir up blood flow in the area and promote healing – among other important things. (Keep reading to find out what they are!)

“I had a nasty tear and stitches which left me in a lot of pain for several days. I had to sit on a rubber ring and take lots of salt baths. Arnica seemed to make a big difference, too. As if dealing with Jordan boobs and a new human wasn't enough!”

Heidi S

How you feel about sex

If the state of your nether regions leaves you feeling like sex is a very distant prospect, don't worry, you're far from alone. You might also find yourself fretting about some very normal changes to the way your lady bits look and feel – reduced elasticity, or raised scar tissue, for instance, are commonplace. These changes don't mean you need surgery for a 'designer vagina'. They simply mean you've had a baby, and it's made you look and feel a little different now. Meanwhile, doing your pelvic floor exercises can help tighten things up down there and – when you do get your mojo back – can enhance your sex life, too. There's more on sex lives after birth in Chapter 10.

> *"I was strict about doing my pelvic floors! Having had an episiotomy, I wanted to do my best to feel 'normal' down there."*
>
> *Kathryn E*

Recovery after a C-section

While some women sail through C-section recovery, others find it hard going. As a general rule, getting back to anything resembling normal will take up to six weeks – it's major abdominal surgery, after all – but some women say that twinges of pain continue for many months beyond that. Recovery from an emergency C-section is likely to take longer than if you had an elective op.

> *"I can't really remember there being that much pain after my C-section. I healed very quickly, probably due to high doses of Arnica. Not being able to drive for weeks afterwards was probably the worst thing about it."*
>
> *Alexis B*

Most C-section veterans report that the pain is pretty severe initially, and many that they're shocked by how debilitating it can be. 'My belly felt like I'd gone ten rounds with Mike Tyson. Once the epidural had worn off I didn't realise how painful it was to even attempt to get out of bed, let alone walk,' admits Dani B. 'I found it difficult just to put one foot in front of the other, so I mastered what I referred to as the bent-over shuffle!'

You'll be offered painkilling medication while in hospital, and should also be given a supply to see you through for as long as necessary once home. A physiotherapist will show you some simple exercises, and urge you to walk around at least a little bit every day, to keep circulation going and prevent the formation of a blood clot. You'll probably be shown how to support your wound with your hands or a pillow, which will come in handy if you need to cough or laugh. Painful trapped wind is a common consequence, as the digestive system can be affected by the surgery – peppermint tea is reckoned to be the best cure.

Basic stuff like sitting up and walking can be a struggle for a little while post-Caesarean, and even giving your baby a cuddle or feeding him may be a challenge, so you'll need lots of help in the early days (if you're a lone mum without a partner, you may need to find a willing volunteer who'll move in for a while). As for your wound, you should get plenty of advice from your midwife on how to care for it and prevent infection. You'll need loose, comfortable clothing for a while (and big pants, naturally), and you'll need to lay off any lifting or other unnecessary activities that could be a strain – strenuous household chores, for starters and – yes – all but the gentlest of sex sessions. Driving's usually out for up to six weeks, because you need to be in full control of your car – and often because your insurance company will insist on it.

> *“I thought I recovered well from my emergency C-section. I was out of bed by day two but, to be honest, it took a few weeks before I was back to 'normal'. I couldn't walk that well for about three weeks – after half an hour on my feet, I would feel sore and tired. And I couldn't do the housework or drive for six weeks.”*
>
> ***Sarah T***

Your scar's likely to look very red for a while, but in most cases it will shrink and fade to a fine, pale line over time, usually under the bikini line, anyway. 'I was surprised at how small and neat my scar is,' reports Dani B, reassuringly. 'In all honesty you would not know that I'd had a Caesarean.' It's normal to experience itching and also very usual for the area to feel numb. Do seek advice if it becomes red, very sore, or inflamed, in case it's caused by an infection developing.

> *“The worst bit post-Caesarean was struggling to hold her, and trying to feed her at night. When my husband was*

asleep (as he always was!), I couldn't even get out of bed to pick her up. It was very painful for a while, and I had to hold my tummy with my hand to support the muscles that had been cut."

Jane H

For some women, having to undergo unplanned surgery they weren't prepared for can bring with it psychological trauma that just adds to the physical challenges. 'I think recovery is to do with how much control you need over your life,' says Pippa B. 'Someone I knew had an emergency C-section and it took her five months to get over it – she said she couldn't cope with it not going to plan, whereas, thankfully, I naturally roll with the blows. So, after a horrendous labour and an emergency C-section, my recovery was better than expected. It took me three days to sit up, a week to stand up and shuffle, two weeks to walk and from then on there was no stopping me.'

"*I do remember going for a reasonable walk during week two, and thinking I'd managed pretty well, only to do the same walk a month later in half the time! People say you're too busy thinking about your baby to notice the pain, and I found that true. I think it helped that I felt fairly positive: I didn't 'mind' that I'd had to have a section. And taking my baby for a walk in the fresh air every day helped, too.*"

Caroline S

Call the midwife: serious post-birth symptoms

Occasionally, medical complications can arise after birth and more occasionally still, they can be dangerous, so it's a good idea to get immediate advice from a midwife or GP if you're experiencing one or more of the following symptoms.

- Prolonged or sudden very severe bleeding (it's excessive if you're soaking more than one pad an hour); especially large or numerous clots; bleeding that begins again after stopping or slowing down; or bleeding with an unpleasant smell.
- Feeling faint, dizzy, or feverish.

- Swelling or pain in the legs.
- A severe, persistent headache – particularly if you're also vomiting and/or suffering blurred vision.
- Persistent, severe abdominal or perineal pain.
- Chest pains or shortness of breath.
- Severe pain when weeing.
- Swelling, redness or oozing round a C-section incision.

Bladders and bowels

Weak and leaky bladders are pretty normal right now. It's not really surprising when you consider how hard your pelvic floor – the layer of muscle and ligaments that form a supportive 'hammock' for your bowel, bladder and uterus – had to work during birth (as well as during pregnancy itself, and labour, which is why women who've had C-sections may not escape, either). In most cases, this situation will gradually resolve itself within a few months, but please don't just assume it will and hope for the best: for quite a few women, the problem of bladder control can persist or can return to haunt you after subsequent births, or just a bit later on in life. Do mention it to your midwife or GP, if it's a problem. Treatment in the form of physiotherapy, or even surgery, could well be an option.

Meanwhile – and I'm sorry to go on about this, I really am – doing those pesky pelvic floor exercises is the best way you can help yourself to resolve the problem, and/or to prevent it cropping up in the future. Your midwife or a hospital physio *should* have talked you through how to do them soon after birth, and perhaps given you a leaflet or recommended a further source of information, but this can be a bit hit and miss (unlike in France, where getting your nether regions back in order is seen as a post-natal priority, and new mums are offered free pelvic floor physio sessions as a matter of course). If the guidance you've been given is lacking, never fear: there are instructions in the box below, all you have to do is locate the right bits and get squeezing. They may be the last thing you feel like doing – and the unfortunate truth is that lots and lots of women don't bother. But trust me, they could prove to be all-important if you want to avoid leaking wee when coughing, laughing, sneezing, or trying to get through a Zumba class.

> *"Did I do my pelvic floor exercises? Did I fook! I still sometimes wee myself now when I laugh too much or cough."*
>
> ***Celine G***

Doing your pelvic floors can also help to guard against the later possibility of a prolapse, which can happen when a lack of support from the pelvic floor causes a woman's urethra, bladder, uterus, or rectum to drop down into the vagina. Childbirth is one of the main trigger factors for this surprisingly common condition, which – as you can imagine – can have grim consequences in the form of bladder or bowel problems, as well as causing discomfort or pain, and affect your sex life for the worst.

> *"No-one explained to me why you need to do your pelvic floor exercises, and because I didn't, I had a prolapse, two years after having my second child. Not the most serious kind, but enough to cause problems that needed physiotherapy to resolve. Your bottom falling out of your bits is not a consequence of birth you expect, and I think there's a huge conspiracy of silence about it."*
>
> ***Rebecca F***

So, there you go. Pelvic floor exercises: boring, but important. It could be several weeks before any real results kick in, and a couple of months before you've totally regained strength down there, so keep at it. In theory, you should you do them every day – and not just now, but for the rest of your life! The good news is that, once you've worked out where your pelvic floor is and exactly how to move it, these exercises don't require much time or effort and you can do them just about anywhere or any time – while cleaning your teeth, waiting for the kettle to boil, or chatting to your bank manager, for example. As Lauren B advises: 'I did what my midwife recommended, and put a series of little stickers in prominent places round the house. The idea is that every time you see one, it reminds you to do a set. It worked pretty well for me.'

The bad news about pelvic floor exercises is that, yes, they are rather tedious. I recall being a bit of an evader myself, and yes, let's just say that I don't often take to the trampoline like I used to.

A bit of a squeeze: how to do your pelvic floor exercises

- First, identify where your pelvic floor muscles are by squeezing the muscles around the back passage and vagina. The best way to do this is to imagine you're trying to prevent yourself from passing wind, while simultaneously trying to stop yourself from weeing, mid-flow. Alternatively you could insert a clean finger into your vagina, and feel the squeeze that way.
- Don't be tempted to hold your breath, or to tighten your bum or thighs: these aren't the muscles you're looking for so if these bits of you are moving, you're doing it wrong!
- Practise slow contractions first: pull up your pelvic floor muscles gradually and hold the squeeze for up to ten seconds. Release and rest for four seconds, then repeat.
- Then try quick contractions: hold the squeeze for just a second, then relax and repeat up to ten times, in quick succession.
- Aim to do a set of both slow and quick contractions up to four times a day.

Doing a poo

Sluggish bowels after birth are normal because the muscles and nerves down there have been bashed up a bit during delivery, but it's often compounded by the fear of pain or worrying that your stitches will tear apart (although in truth, this is highly unlikely). 'I was badly constipated and it took about ten days for things to get back to normal 'down there' which caused much discomfort,' confesses Molly F. 'I was starving all the time because I was breastfeeding, but the more I ate the worse my stomach ache got because I couldn't get rid of it at the other end. It really added up to making me feel like the least glamorous person alive!'

Chances are, having a poo won't actually be as bad as you think, and holding a clean pad over any stitches or soreness should help bolster your confidence. If constipation is a problem, lots of water and fruit should help, or you could ask your GP, or the pharmacist, to recommend a gentle laxative treatment.

> *“The first poo is the most worrying thing ever. I only managed it by mainlining fruit, sitting gingerly on the pot with my feet on a stool, holding a pad against the perineum, and chanting silent prayers.”*
>
> *Rebecca F*

If your bowels have taken a bashing, or your pelvic floor is letting you down, you might find that excess wind is a problem – a minor one, in the scheme of things. Occasionally, though, leaking poo (more grandly known as postpartum faecal incontinence) can be an issue for the same reasons. If you're suffering, rest assured this should right itself as you regain strength down below, and – yep, you guessed it – faithful attention to your pelvic floor exercises will help. However, do discuss it with your midwife, HV, or GP if it persists as it's not something you have to put up with: as with bladder control issues, there are treatments that can help.

Piles are another common consequence of pressure on the anus at birth (and if you had them during pregnancy, you may find now that they're even worse). This can be particularly miserable if you've got other stuff such as sore stitches going on down there. Eating plenty of fibre and drinking lots of fluids, preferably water, can help. You could also ask your pharmacist about over-the-counter remedies, or if they're really bad, get a prescription for something a bit more heavy duty (usually in the form of a suppository) from your doctor. They will, however, go away on their own, eventually.

Wobbly tummies

Oh dear. At least when you were pregnant, your huge belly was taut and serving a purpose you could be proud of. Now – unless you were able to convince your obstetrician to perform a quick nip/tuck before you checked out of hospital – you undoubtedly have one very wobbly tummy in its place. Your best bet is to learn to love your jelly belly for a little while – or at least to ignore it and perhaps stick with your maternity jeans a bit longer – because right now, it should be the least of your worries. It's definitely not a good idea to think about dieting it off yet. You need all the energy you can muster to get you through the recovery process and if you're breastfeeding, you'll need extra energy for that, too. You can, however, make a gentle start – if you're really worried about it – with short walks and some simple toning exercises (see pages 183–184).

Breastfeeding mums often find it helps them flatten their tummies a bit, and that they quickly shed a certain amount of initial baby weight because it speeds up the shrinking of the uterus and because the extra energy required means it uses up calories. 'I'm sure that breastfeeding helped me lose weight post-birth. I had no idea how many calories it burns but I remember feeling hungry all the time and wondering how I wasn't putting on any weight despite eating for Britain,' recalls Molly F. The flipside is that it can also make you feel ravenous, so you may find yourself 'eating for two' again – fine right now, but something you might need to address when you stop breastfeeding.

> *“I gained aver two-and-a-half stone during pregnancy. It came off quite fast but for a while my stomach had a horrendous flap of skin that I had to tuck into my jeans. I can laugh about it now, but at the time it looked awful. My partner used to tell me not to forget to tuck my belly in! It disappeared after a few months.”*
>
> *Kathryn E*

Getting back into shape

Accepted wisdom is that you shouldn't start exercising for six weeks after birth – and then with caution, once you've got the nod from your GP to do so. You may need a bit longer still if you had a C-section. It makes sense: right now, you're no doubt knackered, very likely unfit, and probably don't have a lot of spare time on your hands. And your body is still vulnerable to the effects of the pregnancy hormones released by your body to loosen joints and ligaments in preparation for birth, so you're more at risk of injury. In fact, it's thought they can hang around for six months or more, so when and if you do start working out, you should be cautious about anything that's high-impact.

Those hormones are also responsible for making the tummy muscles – known as the rectus abdominus – stretch and make way for the growing uterus and, often, after birth, the consequence of this is a significant separation, or gap, between the muscles. It's known as diastasis recti, or divarication of the recti. The gap will usually close and the muscles realign within three to four months after birth, but until that happens, intense sit-ups, curls and crunches are best avoided. Your midwife or GP will carry out a 'rec check' to make sure any gap has closed sufficiently, which it usually does. Occasionally, a large gap can remain, which will make it virtually impossible to get rid of your jelly belly, and if that's the case it may be that physiotherapy or even surgical repair is necessary, so chat to your doc if it seems to be a problem for you.

Meanwhile, the best way to slowly regain some strength and fitness is walking: taking your baby in the sling or pushchair will increase the workout and your baby will inevitably drop off, so you can enjoy the fresh air.

You can also help those stretched abdominal muscles find their way back to where they belong with some gentle tummy-strengthening exercises, as outlined in the box below. It's fine to try these as soon as you feel comfortable enough. Aim to do several sets a day, whenever you can find the time – perhaps in conjunction with your pelvic floors.

TIP Remember, working on your tummy muscles isn't just about getting back into shape: it will help provide support and stability to your back and pelvis, which will really help to ease or protect against back pain – a very common problem for new mums.

Tackling the mum tum: ab-toning exercises you can start straight away

Lower abdominal squeeze:

- Contract the muscles by gently drawing the lower abdomen in towards your spine, and hold them there for a few seconds before releasing.

- Build up gradually until you're holding the squeeze for a maximum of ten seconds.
- Repeat four or five times.

Pelvic tilt:

- You can do this either lying on your back with your hips and knees bent up, or standing against a wall.
- Use your abdominal muscles to tilt your pelvis up – if you slide a hand in the gap between your back and the floor, you'll know you're doing it right when you can feel the small of your back flatten down onto your hand.
- Hold for up to ten seconds before releasing, and repeat.

> *"There's only one Liz Hurley, so there's no point crying when you can't walk out of the maternity ward in your pre-pregnancy size eight jeans. This is the real world: lower your expectations and spend your time enjoying your baby, not worrying about your shape. You'll probably be wearing your PJs a lot of the time anyway."*
>
> *Nicola L*

Stretch marks

Some women get stretch marks as a result of pregnancy, some don't. Whether or not you slathered cocoa butter over your growing belly, you'll either have them or you won't, as the cause is thought to be genetic. They can appear very vivid at first, dark pink, purple, or brown, but – although they'll probably never go altogether – they should fade to fine silvery lines. Breasts and thighs can be affected, as well as tummies. 'I was left with very pronounced stretch marks all over my stomach,' admits Jenny C. 'I remember my mum letting out a screech when she saw them, which I didn't think was very tactful! They did fade in time though and I even braved a bikini again, although I know they'll never disappear completely.'

> *“I have been using Bio Oil on my stretch marks and this is working for me. I cover my belly in it morning and night religiously, and they are definitely fading.”*
>
> *Dani B*

Although there are various lotions and potions which claim to get rid of stretch marks, there isn't really much in the way of evidence that they work, so you may as well keep your cash and just stick with an inexpensive moisturiser containing vitamin E, which is said to help. For the truly desperate, laser or cosmetic surgery now promises to remove stretch marks. Needless to say, neither is available on the NHS, and they're likely to cost some pretty serious money. So for most women, learning to live with their 'baby battlescars' is the only realistic option – and few mums feel they aren't a price worth paying. In the meantime, fake tan's reckoned to be a reasonable way of camouflaging the worst, so maybe you don't have to put your bikini away permanently, after all.

> *“I have horrendous stretch marks, all over my tummy. At first I was really upset by them but after they'd had a chance to fade slightly, I couldn't care less. I'll never be able to wear crop tops or a bikini again but that's a small price to pay. Without them I wouldn't have my son.”*
>
> *Marianne O*

Sagging breasts

It has a medical term – breast ptosis – but they're better known as sagging boobs, and they're a common consequence of having a baby. It occurs when your breasts stretch and swell during pregnancy and milk production, and the ligaments and tissues supporting them are stretched. Some recent research from America found that, contrary to popular belief, breastfeeding in itself won't actually make them drop and any damage will already be done – so don't let fears about how your boobs will be affected put you off if you're keen to breastfeed .

A bit later, when you're ready to exercise, you can firm them up a bit with swimming or weights, but the unfortunate truth is that they'll never really be the same again. If they really bother you – and you're very rich – there's always cosmetic surgery. Please don't consider going under the knife, though. Wear your changed breasts with pride – and a really good uplift bra.

> *"Truth be told they were never that perky, but my breasts are definitely worse now – they point to the floor, and I have to remind myself that they did an amazing job, feeding my baby. I thought about surgery, but ruled it out as I would hate for a bodged operation to leave my children motherless! Press-ups and swimming do actually help, a bit. And a fabulous bra at least means they look great in clothes."*
>
> *Alex G*

Bad backs

Those pregnancy hormones that help make the body more flexible in preparation for birth are all well and good, but the unfortunate upshot of them is that sometimes ligaments in the back and pelvis can be left lax, too, and subject to injury and pain. Your abs play an important role in supporting those areas, and if they're knackered, it won't help. Then of course, there's your new lifestyle: picking up and putting down your baby several dozen times a day, negotiating his seat in and out of the car and bending over to feed, change, or dress him. Your boobs may also be relevant: if they've grown super-heavy with milk, it will just add to the strain. So, all in all, it's not surprising that bad backs are a common affliction after birth (and perhaps for quite some time afterwards).

Usually, there won't be much your GP can do for back pain, but there are some ways you can help yourself significantly, if you're suffering.

- Keep moving, as inactivity makes back pain worse. Try to walk a little way each day, and get to work on your gentle tummy-strengthening exercises, as outlined in the box above. After six weeks, all being well with your recovery, you could try yoga or Pilates as both are said to soothe back pain – but do seek out a qualified instructor, and make sure they know you've recently had a baby.

- Try some gentle, regular neck and back stretches throughout the day to relieve tension and strain. Try pushing your arms up straight over your head, holding for a few seconds, releasing and repeating. Or turn your head slowly to the side and back again. Repeat towards the other side and repeat both movements several times.
- Watch your posture, as best you can: try to keep your back straight whenever you're sitting, standing, holding, pushing, or caring for your baby. When feeding, a footstool to elevate your legs and cushions to support your back and to bring your baby up to the right height will really help. Always bend from the knees. And be sure to brace your abs and pelvic floor before lifting (and avoid lifting anything heavy at all if possible).
- Get yourself a really good bra if big boobs seem to be contributing to the problem. Wear comfortable shoes as well. Heels won't help.
- Treat yourself to a relaxing back massage – or get your other half to do the honours.

Your post-natal check

About six weeks after birth, you should be invited to your GP surgery – or perhaps back to the hospital or birth centre – for a post-natal check. During this routine assessment, the doctor may do the following.

- Take your blood pressure, measure your weight, and check your urine. If you've had low iron levels, he may check those, too.
- Check any remaining stitches and scarring to make sure you're fully healed, or healing well.
- Have a feel of your uterus to make sure it's fully contracted back to its normal state and all's well.
- Ask whether your lochia's stopped, and if you've noticed any strange discharge.
- Ask if your bowels and bladder are in good working order, and recommend you do, or keep up, your pelvic floor exercises.

- Ask if you've had sex and if it was OK; or give you the nod to have sex if you haven't already. He'll probably ask you if you've got some contraception sorted, too.
- Check to see if the abdominal muscles have closed, and give you the go-head to start exercising again, should you want to.
- Offer to make you an appointment for a routine smear test if you're due for one.
- Ask you if you're breastfeeding and, if so, if it's going OK.
- Want to know if you're coping alright, or feeling unduly down.

Do pipe up now if you're worried about these or any other issues. And of course, if you need anything checking out before the six-week check, or indeed after it, don't hesitate to pick up the phone and make an appointment.

Getting used to your new body

Even after the initial recovery period is over, there's likely to be long-term physical differences between your pre-baby body and your new one: perhaps your tummy will never be entirely flat again, your boobs will always head distinctly downwards, your stretch marks never quite fade, or your private bits are irreversibly altered by scar tissue. Some women don't give a toss about changed bodies: they see any flabby, saggy bits as a price worth paying for the privilege of being a mum – and quite rightly so. As Caroline S says, 'It amused me how people thought I would be caring about my weight when I had a baby to show for it.' But for others, the lasting physical legacies of birth are hard to get their heads round – with the knock-on effect of that damage to your self-esteem, or even to your sex life (see page 220). Give yourself loads of time to get used to your new appearance, and remind yourself often what an amazing task your body's undertaken. Practically speaking, some new clothes, shoes, and underwear could give you a boost. They're certainly the very least you deserve.

"It was a shock how much I'd physically changed: that funny saggy tummy, my bits in a total mess. For the first time in my life I didn't feel happy with my body. And there's something very fundamental about these changes. There's no going back. Your body will forever be affected by childbirth. It has real emotional impact."

Rebecca F

Shaping up

If it really matters that you get back in your old jeans – or at least a size somewhere close – then don't just sit there thinking about it, pull your trainers on and start working at it. Some sort of exercise is a great idea for new mums, and not simply to shed weight: it's good for the mind, and, if you can find someone to look after your baby while you're at it, it can be a valuable bit of me-time, too.

It is, however, really important to get the all-clear from your GP before exercising after birth. Going too early could hamper your recovery, and besides, you're sure to be pretty unfit if it's been a while. Added to that, the pregnancy hormone relaxin can hang around in your system for quite a few months after birth, making your joints and ligaments still vulnerable to injury. So stick with low-impact options like swimming, power-walking, buggy-pushing, and Pilates, or better still a specific post-natal exercise class, and steer clear of high-impact, pavement-pounding stuff such as running or heavy-duty aerobic classes, until you know you're strong enough to step things up, should you want to.

Please don't overdo the working out: what you should be aiming for is a very gentle, gradual return to fitness and your former shape. They say it takes nine months to put on and nine months to take off, which seems like a sensible mantra to me. Please steer clear of dieting, especially if you're breastfeeding, because you really do need all the energy you can muster to negotiate your first year of motherhood. Better to eat healthily and make sensible changes (if you need to), cutting out fatty, sugary snacks and watching your portion sizes. If you're really desperate and you're determined to take a structured approach to losing weight, join a slimming club and make sure you do it slowly, sensibly and gradually.

> *“I practically gave myself a coronary trying to fit in walking to the gym, working out, showering and dashing home in time to breastfeed. I was utterly knackered, and wish someone had told me what an idiot I was being. I quickly realised that using the pool and sauna was a much more appropriate use of my time at the gym – and learned not to care too much about getting fit during that mental first year.”*
>
> ***Heidi S***

Meanwhile, don’t be fooled by celebrities who appear to have poured themselves back into skintight leather within a month of birth and want you to think they didn’t try hard to achieve it: they almost certainly nearly *killed* themselves to get there, and furthermore, they would have had a personal trainer providing motivation, and paid help to look after their baby while they did so.

> *“It took nine months to put it on, and at least that much to get it off! I have friends who got back into their skinny jeans (albeit with a bit of muffin top) in three months and couldn’t help but feel envious. Mind you, there are photos of me during pregnancy and it’s reassuring to look back and realise that I’ve come a long way from the beached whale I was then!”*
>
> ***Clare F***

Of course, if you prefer to let any extra weight drop off naturally and your fitness return in its own good time, feel free. You may well get back in shape eventually without much effort and you may even find you’re one of those lucky women who end up slimmer than they were before. This is usually because you’re too busy to eat and you’re running around like a lunatic, either carrying your baby around or – once he’s on the move – just trying to keep him out of mischief. As Molly F testifies, ‘Ironically, I’m now two dress sizes smaller than before I was pregnant. My natural shape just sort of changed on its own. I think it’s because being a mum has made me far more active than I was before. I’m lugging around my daughter, walking lots, and constantly running up and down the stairs at home.’

9

Emotional well-being

Most mums find that life after the birth of their first baby is an emotional rollercoaster, to say the least. The highs can be amazing, but for pretty much all of us, there'll be some lows to contend with, as well. I know some of the stuff covered in this chapter is, frankly, a bit bleak. But for a lot of mums, it's the reality of life after birth. It's not my intention to sound unduly negative, but I do want you to know that if you find yourself pole axed by anxiety, riven by guilt, shellshocked by the demands of your baby, confused by your new identity, angry with your bloke, or simply struggling to find a smile sometimes during this year, it is quite, quite normal. Do find someone to listen and talk openly about how you feel if the going gets tough this year – it's not a good idea to sweep things under the carpet. And please don't ever be ashamed to look around for support, or seek specific help, if you need some. Frankly, it's a rare new mum who doesn't.

> *"I met and spoke to a lot of other mums who felt inadequate, so I know that the 'perfect mum' is just an illusion. The mums you pass in the street all think* you're the *perfect one and* they *are the mess. It's all relative."*
>
> *Charlee C*

A difficult birth

If you've been left badly shaken by your birth experience, you're not alone. It's common to have trouble getting over what happened in the delivery room, whether a particularly difficult labour, interventions you hadn't planned on, a premature or unwell baby, or simply the sense that you lost control, or lacked support. According to the Birth Trauma Association, around 10,000 women in the UK every year develop post-natal post-traumatic stress disorder (PN-PTSD) and as many as 200,000 more will experience at least some of its symptoms: flashbacks and intrusive thoughts, numbed emotions, problems sleeping, irritability, loss of interest in sex, and difficulties in bonding with their baby, for example. If you find yourself affected, you may feel isolated, or perhaps guilty, convinced that what happened was somehow your fault. (In which case, please be assured that it's not. PN-PTSD can happen to anyone.) And it's not an issue that should be ignored, not least because it could leave you with a lasting fear of hospitals or medical treatment, or of the birth process, (a condition known as tokophobia), which could render you too scared to extend your family in the future, should you want to.

> *“I'd planned a home birth because I wanted my baby's entry into the world to be as 'sweet' as possible, but ended up in hospital having all the interventions I'd hoped to avoid. I felt like such a failure. For ten months I was a mess. I felt guilty every time I looked at my son's forehead and saw the scar from the forceps. And it took a long time to bond with him, because I resented what he'd 'done' to my body. Two years on, time has healed, and I finally feel 'at peace' with the birth I had. I've accepted that I can't change how it happened.”*
>
> *Ruth D*

Talking it over

Some say it can really help to go over the finer details of a difficult or traumatic birth with a health professional. You can request your medical notes and ask your GP or community midwife to help you digest them (there's advice on obtaining your notes on the website of the Birth Trauma Association), or contact your hospital or birth centre direct and make an appointment for a chat. Many offer a specific service along these lines, usually known as 'birth debriefing' or 'birth reflections', and while there's debate among the experts about quite how useful this process is, mums who try it often say it was a positive experience.

TIP If you have serious grievances about what happened during birth, you can find out how to make a formal complaint on the website of AIMS, the Association for Improvements in the Maternity Services. Alternatively you could make contact with the hospital's patient advice and liaison service (PALS), which can guide you.

> *"I made use of my hospital's birth reflections service. It was pretty straightforward. The midwife went through my notes and explained what happened, and why certain things were done, and what the terminology meant. I was glad I did it. So many of us have such hideous memories, and it helps to have someone make sense of it, and to know it was all for the greater good."*
>
> ***Alison F***

Hard labour: tips on tackling birth trauma

- Share your feelings, ideally with a health professional such as a GP, HV, midwife or counsellor who can also refer you for help, but otherwise with your partner, a good friend or trusted relative, or with someone else who's been through the same experience.
- Check out the helpful information on the Birth Trauma Association's website. They don't have a telephone helpline, but they do have a team of volunteers who offer support via email.
- Go through your birth records with a health professional.
- Take care of yourself. Keep your expectations low, don't try and do too much, and take life one day at a time. As with PND (see

page 202), eating well, gentle exercise, and finding the time for relaxation can help.
- Write or blog about your birth experiences. You may find it cathartic.
- Ask your GP for a referral to a psychotherapist. PN-PTSD is best treated by 'talking therapies' such as counselling or cognitive behavioural therapy (CBT). Not all health professionals are clued up about PN-PTSD, so if you're getting blank looks from your GP or midwife, download the Birth Trauma Association's advice leaflet and show it to them.

Coping with chaos

Welcome to your new job. Whatever you did career-wise before having a baby, you've undoubtedly never had a role quite as physically and mentally demanding as this one. The hours are erratic but you're more or less permanently on duty, there's no pay rise or positive appraisal to look forward to, your boss is totally dependent on you and frequently unreasonable, and although you're in charge, you've no idea what you're doing and you're not sure you can keep the company afloat. If you feel somewhat panic-stricken by the sheer scale of your new responsibilities, and that you're struggling to cope, it's hardly surprising. But you're definitely not alone. As Emma H confesses, 'I found the 24-hour nature of the job overwhelming, and couldn't believe nobody was going to appear at half past five and say, "ok, you're off duty now, we'll see you in the morning".'

With hindsight, most mums look back on the first couple of months, at least, as 'a bit of a blur' – and tend to recall that 'muddling through' was the only strategy within their grasp. Try to bear that in mind if you're struggling to meet the challenges of your new life: it's absolutely the norm. Dealing with the relentless demands and inevitable chaos can seem impossible – even if you *weren't* someone who particularly relished being in control before giving birth.

> *“The overwhelming sense of responsibility affected me the most. I was the only one who could feed this baby and look after it. And I didn’t really know what I was doing so that sense of responsibility was even more terrifying. Women may excel at multi-tasking, but never is it more necessary than with a new baby: constantly thinking ahead to the next feed, express, bottle, change, or nap, while desperately trying to work out how to slot in a shower. No wonder I was so anxious.”*
>
> *Rebecca F*

Rhythms and routine can certainly make life less head-spinning, and natural patterns of feeding, sleeping and waking will start to emerge once the first few months are under your belt. The confusion and cluelessness of the early weeks will clear as you gain experience, and get things sussed. I'm not saying it then gets easy. (After all, there's teething, weaning, crawling, separation anxiety, tantrums, and much more in the pipeline.) But once you've survived the early months, you're definitely better equipped to survive what comes next. And as your baby gets older, he's going to give a lot back – smiles, gurgles, cuddles, and eventually, words – so, if it hasn't done already, it will all begin to seem worthwhile.

Take it easy

My advice is to take life at the slowest possible pace while at home with your baby, making the most of your maternity leave and – when and if you return to work – any time that you do have to spend with him. Don't aim too high, and cut yourself slack at every opportunity. Above all, keep reminding yourself regularly that life is different now, and make sure you allow for that. A few parents may manage to master the art of carrying on regardless (I remember being utterly gobsmacked one evening at the cinema when I stood up at the end of the movie and realised the woman in the row in front of me had a sleeping baby on her lap), but most don't. We took our firstborn on a mini-break to York, three months after her birth. My plan was to shop, eat in restaurants and enjoy two leisurely nights in a hotel. Needless to say, she cried from the moment we got there and we aborted the mission after a miserable first night trying to settle her in a travel cot. What I'm saying is, don't try too hard to maintain your old lifestyle because you probably won't be able to. Instead, aim to embrace your new one.

> *"You soon realise that the days of grabbing your handbag and walking out of the door are long behind you. Finishing a meal or a conversation becomes something of a rarity. But there's no point lamenting this really. You're at the mercy of your baby, and babies do tend to win out!"*
>
> ***Nicola L***

Order, order: tips for coping with chaos

- Get your priorities right. Work out what matters: usually this will be looking after your baby as best you can; finding a bit of time for yourself and for your partner; keeping on top of basic chores; making friends and getting out and about. For everything else, adjust your expectations to the lowest possible setting, and let it ride. Now is not the time to re-decorate.
- Lean on others and delegate wherever possible. If your mum wants to know what she can do, ask her to run a hoover round; if your partner's hopping about like a spare part while you're feeding, direct him to kitchen duties. Consider establishing an informal rota system: you don't have to write it down if it feels a bit anal, but if everyone takes responsibility for certain roles, it can really help.
- Look to exploit any natural patterns that emerge and make a routine for you and your baby, by aiming to do the same things at the same time each day, where possible.
- Meet up with other mums – and share the chaos! There's more about this on page 207.
- Avoid situations that make you feel stressed. Stick with what's manageable. If you hate taking your baby shopping, for instance, do it online, instead.
- Look for little, practical ways that help you to be organised. Keeping a to-do list on the fridge, for example, or always having your changing bag packed and ready by the door.

- Take life at a snail's pace, for as long as you possibly can. Give yourself loads of time to do anything or get anywhere. What's the hurry?
- Be sanguine. The days of chaos aren't forever – or at least, the days of not being able to cope with them aren't. The first year gets easier as it progresses. Really, it does.

All about anxiety

Some level of anxiety is pretty much par for the course with your first baby. They're so small and vulnerable, it's in our instincts to fear for their health and their safety. And naturally we worry how to meet their needs, whether we're meeting them right, and how to cope with the constant quandaries that have no obvious answer.

I guess there's no point in me advising you not to feel anxious as a first-time mum. I may as well tell you not to breathe. What is worth bearing in mind is that, while it's absolutely normal to worry as a new mum, extreme, all-consuming anxiety can be a symptom of post-natal depression, or even a condition in itself, known as post-natal anxiety, so if you're suffering, keep tabs on it and seek help if you think you need it. There's more about both conditions a bit further on in the chapter.

Stop trying so hard

Natural anxiety is often exacerbated for modern mums by the curse of too-high expectations. Pressure is intense these days to get our 'parenting' right, and for some weird reason – maybe because she features so prominently in our aspiration-obsessed media – many of us are falling over ourselves to be the 'perfect mother' (as well as have the perfect home, the perfect marriage and the perfect career). Then when it turns out, quite inevitably, that it's not possible, we feel guilty. As Alex G puts it: 'Our society is so critical of mothers, whichever decisions we make: if we're not breastfeeding, we're no good, if we breastfeed for too long, we're weird; if we work, we're selfish, if we don't work, we're boring. How are you supposed to win?'

> *“I got quite obsessed with trying to do it all right, trying to follow the dictates of the ‘Baby Whisperer’ book, trying to coerce my baby into being happy and contented. I remember asking my online mum friends if I was supposed to leave the baby to it when he was happily staring into space, or if I should be down on the floor cooing over him and engaging with him at every waking moment.”*
>
> ***Heidi S***

Let me tell you, then, that there's no point trying to be the perfect mother, because you'll fail. Nobody's perfect. And mums in particular are unlikely to achieve those giddy heights, because being a mum is bloody hard. A better aim is to be a ‘good-enough’ mum. Make sure your baby's fed, watered, and thoroughly cuddled, and you should have most of the important bases covered. Don't be put off by all the mums around you, either, who seem to have it so much more sussed than you.

Please don't be tempted to compare your baby to other babies, either, or to ‘compete’ in some way with other parents, or be drawn in by others who insist on being competitive, because that way, madness lies. And do your utmost not to judge other mums, whatever you may think of them. We're all in it together, after all.

> *“My daughter had a cleft palate, making feeding difficult, and a dislocating left hip which meant she had to wear a special harness for the first four months, so the whole ‘perfect’ scenario went out the window. I ended up not wanting to leave the house, and became isolated as I avoided mum and baby groups, to save me explaining about the harness and her special bottles. I envied other mum friends, and their seemingly perfect lives. Actually they probably weren't perfect at all, but that's what it felt like.”*
>
> ***Emily D***

Taking the right advice

The right bit of advice can go a long way to quell any short-term anxieties you might be feeling in your first year of motherhood. And there's certainly no shortage of advice to be had, whether from the horse's mouth of your HV, from the endless thoughts to be found in books, leaflets, and on the internet, or from the anecdotal views – solicited or otherwise – of friends, relatives and, er, complete strangers.

Helpful, useful, sensible advice can be exactly what you need to put a situation into perspective or to solve a problem you were otherwise clueless about. Misguided, old-fashioned, or just plain bad advice you need like a hole in the head – particularly if you didn't ask for it in the first place. As Molly F reveals, 'You literally can't walk down the street without a well-meaning neighbour telling you what method of sleep training you should be following or what type of feeding you should be doing. The advice you get given is constant – and often completely contradictory.'

Try to impose filters on the information you receive. Decide whose views you trust, and ignore everyone else's – but always get a second opinion if you're not sure, even on so-called advice. 'After a few weeks I learned to let it go in one ear and out of the other,' Molly F goes on. 'If I really needed answers I turned to my family, HV or a trusted parenting website.'

Ultimately, you will usually find that the person who knows best, is you – just as Dani B did. 'We must have been given every piece of advice under the sun about babies, but in most cases we chose to go with our instinct,' she admits. 'We did what we *thought* was right – and it always turned out OK.'

> *“One tip about advice from parents, aunties and just plain rude strangers in the street: take it in, and nod in agreement. It's much less painful than arguing and it saves a hell of a lot of time. You know you're going to follow your gut and your own process of trial and error, anyway. Every*

child is different and what worked for Aunt Polly is not necessarily going to work for you. Remember: smile and nod, smile and nod.”

Natasha H

Tired all the time

Lack of sleep is something that can seriously undermine your emotional well-being. Night times may start to bring with them a deep sense of dread that descends like a blanket as you crawl into bed at 8p.m., knowing full well you'll be getting out of its warm depths again before too long. And if you're dead on your feet in the daytime, you're very likely to feel irritable, or low, which can affect your normal functioning and your relationships. Extreme exhaustion can even be a trigger factor for post-natal depression (see page 202).

“For at least the first three months I walked around in a complete haze. I'm a person that really needs my sleep, and I was clumsy, and constantly exhausted – but you just have to learn to live on your baby's timetable. To be honest, the exhaustion is the one thing making us think hard about having a second baby. The thought of going through all that again is horrifying.”

Ruth D

Broken nights come with the territory when you've got a baby, and as a rule, exhaustion is something mums just have to adapt to and live with. However, it's worth trying the following.

- Napping whenever you get the chance. Often easier said than done – not every parent can relax enough to drop off in the daytime, and some babies refuse to nap for long, anyway. And yes, no doubt there's laundry to be done. But if you can, do.
- Going to bed early. Really early. Perhaps even when your baby does. Getting a good chunk of sleep early in the night can help bolster you a bit for a disturbed night ahead.
- Eating well. It will help boost flagging energy reserves and keep you going in the daytime.

- Getting your other half to pull his weight when it comes to night time duties. If you're formula feeding, try a one-night-on/one-night-off rota. If you're breastfeeding, you can still get him on board by mastering the art of expressing, and persuading your baby to drink from a bottle sometimes (see page 85). It is *not* an excuse that he has to be up for work the next day.
- Being philosophical. It's not forever. And if your baby still hasn't started sleeping through the night once he's six months old, you can take positive action – if you want to – with some form of sleep training (see page 127). Meanwhile, developing good sleep habits (see page 119) will help pave the way to more sleep for you all in the long run – and give you something to keep your mind off how tired you are.

> *“I think the key is definitely to nap when you can. Sleep whenever baby sleeps. It may mean you're a bit of a hermit for a few weeks, but it really helps, and I felt it helped me get through the night time feeds if I'd had a nap during the day.”*
>
> ***Rachel G***

Post-natal insomnia

Overtiredness and/or anxiety can result in insomnia for a lot of new mums, so even if their baby goes swiftly back to sleep after waking, they don't; or once their baby has cracked sleeping through the night, they can't. Unfortunately, it can become a cycle that persists for a long time ahead.

> *“My son woke up repeatedly, and I ended up so wired I developed insomnia. I honestly wasn't sure for a while how I could carry on. I was angry all the time, and I was in tears most mornings. I found that long walks with the pram, lots of chocolate, and 7.30p.m. bedtimes helped. Eventually my GP prescribed sleeping pills, which meant I could ask my other half or sister to look after the baby, and take the odd night off. And I finally cracked it by taking a pill three consecutive nights in a row – it seemed to break the pattern. He sleeps fine now. But I look back and shudder.”*
>
> ***Vicky L***

Too tired to sleep: tips for coping with post-natal insomnia

- Get some gentle exercise during the day or early evening. Don't do anything too close to bedtime though, or it might leave you too overstimulated for sleep.
- Play a relaxation CD or download, or try doing some deep breathing, or gentle stretches. Progressive muscle relaxation exercises can help: one by one, tense then release the muscles of your body, starting with your toes and feet before moving up to your legs, arms, shoulders, face and neck.
- Steer clear of caffeine, booze, and shedloads of sugar in the evening: they're all likely to make things worse. Try warm milk or a herbal drink instead.
- Check out alternative remedies which claim to help insomnia such as hypnotherapy, aromatherapy, reiki, acupuncture, and reflexology. As with all alternative treatments there are no guarantees – but you've nothing to lose by trying.
- If you're wide awake, get up, go into another room, and read, listen to your iPod, or watch some (low-key) television until you feel sleepy again.
- Chat to your GP about sleeping tablets. These are generally only prescribed as a last resort and you may be worried about becoming dependent on them, or about possible side effects, but a short-term course might help you break the cycle if you're desperate. They may not be suitable if you're breastfeeding, though.
- Bear in mind that insomnia can be caused by post-natal anxiety or post-natal depression, so if you're experiencing any other likely symptoms, it's important you get professional help.

Post-natal depression

What is it?

Although it's quite normal to feel unhappy, anxious, or inadequate at times in your first year of motherhood, there's a point at which serious, relentless emotional problems such as these can amount to post-natal depression (PND). Typically, PND kicks in within a few months of birth, although it can also strike further down the line, and can hang around for several months – or up to a year. And PND is pretty common. Often it's cited as affecting one in ten, but recent findings suggest it's even more widespread than that, with closer to one in three mums touched by it to some degree. No doubt it's impossible to put a true figure on, because so many women go undiagnosed. The bottom line is that if you're a sufferer, you're far from alone and you don't have to feel ashamed about it. And it's absolutely possible to overcome it.

> *"I firmly believe that everyone has emotional changes after having a baby. Everyone (including me) reports times of blackness, feeling low, feeling useless and that they're a rubbish mother. Not everyone gets a formal diagnosis but I think we all suffer from post-natal depression, to one degree or another."*
>
> ***Zoe M***

What causes it?

No-one knows for sure. PND doesn't have one specific cause, but is probably the result of one of more trigger factors that include a previous history of depression or difficult childhood experiences; a backdrop of other stresses; hormonal upheaval; lack of support; exhaustion, and the sheer shock of birth and motherhood. And while some mums may be more vulnerable than others, anyone can fall prey to it. One thing's certain. If you have PND, it is not your fault.

What are the symptoms?

You may have PND if you're feeling:

- unhappy, tearful; hopeless; irritable
- extremely anxious; fearful that something bad will happen; panic-stricken
- constantly stressed; inadequate; unable to cope
- exhausted; unable to sleep when you need to; lethargic; listless

- numb; unable to relax, enjoy life, laugh, or feel interested in anything
- guilty; ashamed
- physical aches and pains; headaches; tummy aches
- that you don't have an appetite – or want to eat compulsively
- unable to concentrate or make decisions
- indifferent towards your baby; struggling to bond with him; sorry you had him
- thinking about harming yourself or your baby; thinking about death
- indifferent or angry towards your partner; argumentative; uninterested in sex.

TIP If you recognise five or more of these symptoms and they've been affecting you for more than a few weeks, please get some help.

> *"I really went off the rails for a while. I had suicidal thoughts. It was very ugly. I wasn't really prepared for how bad it would get."*
>
> *Charlee C*

What can I do to make it go away?

The most important thing you can do if you suspect you have PND is to find someone you trust who may be able to help, and tell them about it. Your HV would be a good start, but if you don't have a good relationship with her, you could chat to your GP instead, or contact a PND support group or helpline and go from there. Even just chatting to a good friend would be a positive thing, or to your partner, if he's understanding (and some men do find it a problem that's hard to get their heads round).

Your doctor or HV will diagnose PND by asking questions about how you're feeling, and establishing how many of the recognised symptoms you're suffering. It's a condition that strikes at different levels: if you're considered to have a mild case, self-help techniques like those outlined below may be all you need to get through it, but if it's more serious, you should be offered treatment. Counselling or cognitive behaviour therapy (CBT) are generally regarded as the best way forward, but in some cases, medication may be prescribed. Some anti-depressants aren't suitable while breastfeeding, and they need time to work, so you have to be prepared to take them for at least six months. You'll need to talk and think this option through carefully. Meanwhile, there are lots of ways in which you can help yourself.

- Find time and ways to regularly relax. Long baths, deep breathing, yoga, massage, or aromatherapy are all possible options.
- Eat a balanced, healthy diet, and regular meals: lack of nutrients and fluctuating blood sugar levels can have a negative effect on mood. And steer clear of too much coffee and booze. They may offer a short-term buzz but ultimately will make you feel worse.
- Try to get some gentle exercise, as physical activity stimulates endorphins, the 'feel good' hormones. Fresh air's a tonic, too. Taking your baby out and about in the pram or sling is a good start.
- Enlist support from your family and friends. Ask someone you trust to look after your baby so you can get some time to yourself, or with your partner. If anyone doesn't seem to understand what you're going through, explain, downloading information from a relevant charity such as Mind to show them, if necessary.
- Look into alternative treatments. They're not guaranteed, but you never know – you may find a complementary therapy such as acupuncture, homeopathy or cranial osteopathy will help.
- Make friends. Talk to them about what you're going through. But don't hang out with anyone who doesn't sympathise.

> *“Anti-depressants made my PND worse. They gave me terrible skin, and a permanent period. I didn't feel like myself at all. So I just stopped them and decided to fix things my own way. I put my son into nursery two mornings a week, started blogging and took up photography. I went running, too. And, crucially, I went to see an acupuncturist. After a couple of sessions I felt myself again, like I wasn't*

being ruled by my hormones. I know some people dismiss it as hippy bullshit, but for me, it really works. No idea how, but it does. I really believe it saved me."

Ruth D

Don't panic: could it be post-natal anxiety?

Less well known and less common than PND, post-natal anxiety (PNA) is a separate psychological condition that can also hit new mums for six. Sufferers can be consumed with intense, irrational fears and compulsive behaviour that comes to rule their lives and may suffer panic attacks, insomnia, and night terrors. Treatment is available, so do seek help if you're concerned.

Beating boredom and overcoming isolation

Feeling lonely or bored while at home with your baby is a common experience. If you had a busy job, other interests and a good social life before becoming a mum, the loss of those things is bound to hit you hard. And modern mums are particularly vulnerable to feelings of isolation in a way that previous generations of mothers weren't, because it's no longer the norm for extended families and wider communities to pull together after the birth of a baby.

If you're lucky you'll have a handful of reliable relatives around, including your own mum, but as it's not unusual these days for couples to base themselves far away from their families, maybe you won't. (Or, maybe your mum's too busy with her own life, anyway.) You may also be fortunate enough to have a partner who is self-employed, or has a flexible job and can wiggle his hours around, downsize or take extended paternity leave to spend more time at home – but the truth is that even in these enlightened times, the most common set-up is for dad to keep working full-time while mum takes maternity leave and a career break. Furthermore, old friends or colleagues who haven't yet had babies can rapidly become strangers because you don't have the time to catch up, and little in common any more. Hardly surprising, then, if the four walls of your home feel like they're closing in on you, sometimes.

> *"I was happy to be a stay-at-home-mum. I wouldn't have swapped it for the world. But I admit I began to feel incredibly lonely and incredibly bored. My daughter was wonderful, but I felt invisible. I felt unappreciated, and kind of worthless. And I hated the cleaning, the ironing, the cooking. And the seven-day week!"*
>
> ***Alex G***

No need for guilt

You don't have to feel guilty about feeling bored or lonely. It's normal, and it certainly doesn't mean you don't love your baby enough. A return to work when and if the time comes for you may solve the problem (although it may well create others: there's more on the subject in Chapter 11), but in the meantime, your best bet for tackling boredom and loneliness is for you and your baby to get out of the house as much as possible, and/or to spend time with friends.

Why friends matter

Most mums say that spending time with other mums really helped oil the wheels of the first year. Some go so far as to say it was a lifesaver. Friendships that are forged during this time (or old ones, enhanced by the shared experience of parenthood) often go on to be strong and enduring. But even if the bonds don't run deep or for long, any company that you feel positive about can still be a huge boon in the short-term.

> *"It's one massive upside to all the changes post-birth: the deepening of your female relationships through this shared experience."*
>
> ***Rebecca F***

Consider old friendships that might be worth renewing, too. I got back in touch with a previously close school pal, after finding out via a social networking site that she had a baby daughter the same age as mine. We re-bonded over breastfeeding sessions: another two kids later, we're good friends still. (Although thankfully, these days, we no longer have to talk about breastfeeding.)

Not everyone's a parent

Make efforts to hold on to any worthwhile pre-baby friendships, even if you don't have motherhood in common. Apart from the fact that the situation may well change in the future, it's good to have non-parents in your life to keep your horizons open, and it's definitely good to talk about things other than babies, sometimes.

Coffee and more: what good friends who are mums as well can do for you

- Give you a reason to get out of the house, and somewhere else to go.
- Provide company and relieve boredom.
- Digest birth stories with you, offer anecdotal advice, and share helpful information.
- Show empathy if you're struggling, and help you understand you're not alone.
- Provide a potential playmate for your baby.
- Swap babysitting favours sometimes.
- Eventually become part of a core social network; and maybe even a friend for life.

Having fun

Make the most of your mum friends. Coffees and lunches, shopping trips, walks in the wood, days out, shared activity sessions, or just hanging round each other's houses are all great alternatives to feeling isolated alone at home. Don't forget to introduce the friends you value to others – chances are if you get on with both, they'll get on with each other. What you'll probably end up with is a broad social circle which will usually widen and multiply as time goes on, and you encounter many different parents in many different settings. And hopefully you'll secure at least a handful of mum-friends you can pool me-time with eventually and enjoy socialising without your babies.

Stand by, in particular, for some awesome nights out, once you've got the energy and there's nothing else stopping you. It can be a massive thrill rediscovering your social life after birth in the company of like-minded mums who are likewise off the leash. Beware, though: if you're back on the booze after an extended break, it may not take much drinking to get very drunk – and hangovers are a lot harder when you need to be up early. Do also try to remember not to talk about your babies all night!

> *"Four of us from my ante-natal group started a book club. Once a month we leave our babies with their dads and take turns to host, and as time's gone on we've attracted new 'members'. Our nights are pretty legendary now. We sink too much wine, and put the world to rights. There's never been much talking about the book, if I'm honest."*
>
> ***Lauren B***

Friend finder: how to meet other mums

- Check out the list of local groups, classes and events on parenting websites such as Netmums or Mumsnet, or get chatting on their forums.
- Ask your HV if the local clinic or children's centre hosts a regular get-together.
- Contact the NCT in your area to see where your nearest coffee morning takes place.
- Look on noticeboards in individual church halls and community centres to see if mother and baby groups are run there.
- Find out about age-appropriate local classes and activities for parents and babies. The sky's the limit these days, with baby massage, baby gym, baby yoga, baby swimming, soft play sessions, baby music, and baby signing all available options. (Don't do too much though. You and your baby could both end up knackered.)
- Be bold. Strike up conversation whenever you see a mum you like the look of. Even if you're shy, you'll always have a starting point for a chat: your babies.

- Get online. OK, it won't get you out of the house, but social networking while your baby's asleep or otherwise happily engaged is one good way to make contact with other mums, without being restricted to your own town.

> *"Joining the NCT was one of the best things I did, it was such a brilliant support network. We took turns to host coffee and cake mornings every week, and I always looked forward to it. Some are still friends today."*
>
> *Sarah R*

Friends you don't need

However wisely you choose your mum mates, you're sure to also acquire a few who don't float your boat. These you'll probably filter out naturally and gradually over time, with nothing lost. Sometimes of course, far from being helpful, relationships with other mums can become quite fraught – usually where jealousy or competitiveness enter the equation. It's easy to fall into the grip of these tendencies, but they're destructive and pointless. Aim to rise above them. And if you find yourself in friendships that make you unhappy, extricate yourself from them, sharpish. Equally, if you get stuck in a mums' group that seems cliquey and unwelcoming, walk away and find another instead.

Where did the old me go?

You may feel you've become a different person now you're a mum. It's pretty normal to feel this way when your life has changed so profoundly. And lots of new mums really struggle with the loss of, or changes to, their identity. It can feel as though your old self has taken a permanent hike – while the new one is covered in baby sick and too tired to have an intelligent conversation.

> *“It doesn’t matter what I wear, do, or say, or what colour I dye my hair (it’s green at the moment), whenever I see myself in a mirror or shop window, I see ‘Mama Charlee’. I just look like a mum now. I don’t know how it happened.”*
>
> *Charlee C*

You will start to feel yourself again, eventually. Maybe there’ll be a particular turning point, but more likely it will be a gradual process that spreads itself over the first year. And there may be a particular factor, or several, that help you recover your ‘va-va-voom’: a return to work, perhaps; getting physically fit again; rebuilding some sort of social life; or the return of your lost libido (there’s more about that in the next chapter).

Bear in mind though, if it’s the ‘old you’ you’re looking for, she probably won’t come back, entirely, just as your old life is forever gone – after all, you have a whole new role in which your baby is central, and that’s bound to make you a different person. Try to view this change positively. You’re almost certainly stronger, more selfless, more confident, and, well, more grown-up than you used to be. And once the dust has settled after giving birth and you’ve had a chance to adjust, you’ll find there’s also room for work, a social life, friendships, love and sex, other interests or whatever you’ve been missing for a while. You just have to make sure you find the time to slot them in.

> *“For a while I mourned for my old self, seemingly lost forever. Sometimes I’d cry in frustration. I can’t remember the turning point but eventually I gave up fighting for my old identity and embraced the changes brought by motherhood. I didn’t want to waste the precious time I had. Late nights and wine bars went out, and coffee shops and baby massage came in.”*
>
> *Nicola L*

Getting some me-time

It’s a bit of a cliché, but ‘me-time’ does matter. You probably weren’t even aware of the notion, pre-motherhood, because it’s not until you become a mum that you realise how little you have – and how much you'd like more. Think back to life before birth, and you can no doubt recall hours, evening and weekends' worth of the stuff. Now, just being able to take a shower is a bonus. But a bit of me-time can work wonders for your emotional well-being. Even a short burst can help rejuvenate you for a little while to come. And you owe it to your baby to stay rejuvenated, so you can give him your all the rest of the time. So, as soon as it becomes remotely plausible, insist someone else take charge of your baby for a while, and schedule in whatever me-time you can get away with. It doesn't matter what you use it for. The point is, it's for you.

> *"I went back to my old dance classes a few months after the birth, which I absolutely love doing. It's great to do something that's completely and utterly for me."*
>
> *Lucy R*

Mums' panel round-up

How did you get your 'va-va-voom' back?'

Exercise made me feel more positive. I started going for long walks with him in his all-terrain buggy, progressing to a jog after a while. Eventually I felt healthier than before I had him – Kathryn E

I don't think it did come back in a dramatic way, it was more a case of life returning gradually to normal, or at least, a new kind of normal. Making friends, and reigniting our sex life definitely helped – Lorraine B

It took a while: about four months. That's when we started regularly meeting up with two separate ante-natal groups. It made me feel so much better to realise everyone else had the same questions I had – Claire A

I feel a bit guilty saying it, but I felt much more myself when I stopped breastfeeding. I'm glad I did it, but relished the freedom once I stopped. Taking up running proved a big boost. And starting work again helped, too – Jenny C

Returning to work when he was five months old helped me to feel me again. A few months later my husband and I took a holiday together, without him, and that made me feel better too. So much so it resulted in our second child! – **Rachel G**

I remember when my daughter was about three months, leaving her for a whole afternoon and going to the hairdressers on my own and having a major cut and highlights. And going back to work in some new clothes my mum had kindly bought me. So for me it was all about self-image. Shallow? Moi?! – **Rebecca F**

I think it was when I got back in my pre-pregnancy skinny jeans. Going out on a date again really helped, too. Having said that, some days I still don't feel I've got my va-va-voom back completely, and that's 11 months on – **Lucy R**

10

Love and sex

So, you and your man have made a baby – probably your greatest piece of teamwork to date. Becoming parents can strengthen your relationship in wonderful ways and most couples find that ultimately, it brings them closer together. But it can also put a great many pressures on it, and the truth is, there may be a disappointing lack of roses around the door for a while, as you settle into your new roles and get your heads round the business of parenting. In the meantime, you both may find you need plenty of adjustment time, lots of communication, and oodles of understanding – on both sides – to negotiate the rollercoaster ride of being new parents.

> *“It was difficult, at first. I know I pushed my husband out for a while, I was so busy concentrating on our baby. And I must admit, I wasn't that interested in resurrecting our sex life for several months at least. But that changed. I realised what an amazing dad he was and how lucky my daughter and I both were to have him. And my libido came back, thankfully. Things are great between us now.”*
>
> *Lorna B*

Changing relationships

Having a baby is almost certain to change your relationship with his dad (and this chapter assumes that you share your life with your baby's father, as that's probably the most usual set-up at this stage). For most couples, the shift is a wonderful, positive one. But it can take a little while to adjust, and in the meantime, you may find yourself affected by difficult issues you've never had to deal with before. Maybe you're often cross with him, because you feel he's not doing enough to help, he's maddeningly laid back about it all, or you know he's trying his best, but doing it all wrong. Perhaps you're just less interested in him generally, because your baby's number one now. Or maybe you're surprised to find you resent him, because you're stuck at home on maternity leave or you've opted to put work on hold, while his career is unscathed and he still gets to swan out the door every day.

You may also find your relationship comes under pressure for various practical reasons – the stress of trying to find the right work/life balance for you both, for instance, of making sure you've got enough income, or finding acceptable childcare. If you've gone back to work, attempts to thrash out a fair system of childcare and domestic responsibilities may well have caused ructions. And of course, if you're also trying to deal with other forms of emotional upheaval like anxiety, depression or birth trauma, feelings of isolation, loss of identity, difficulties coping, or maybe just a ruinous lack of sleep, then any difficulties with your other half are likely to feel a whole lot worse.

His feelings count, too

But hey, that's just you. It could be that your partner has some difficult feelings to deal with too, now that a third party has muscled in on your double act. Perhaps you're not the only one bewildered by your new role, terrified of the responsibility, and anxious about being the perfect parent. Maybe he feels pushed aside, unsure where he fits in the new set-up, or even jealous of the baby, the extra time you have with him, and the special bond you seem to have. He too could be suffering from exhaustion and perhaps even from depression, or really feeling the pressure if he's the main breadwinner now. And yes, maybe he also feels disgruntled about any new work/life set-up you get into place. If you've decided to stay at home maybe he feels you got the 'easy option'; if you went for the compromise of part-time, perhaps he's jealous that you get the best of both of worlds; and if you've swapped traditional roles altogether, it could be that he's the one left at home, feeling like a desperate housewife.

> *"My husband really struggled at first. He wasn't prepared for fatherhood, and dealt with it by distancing himself, which I found incredibly hard. When my daughter turned six months, his relationship with her turned a corner. Suddenly he could make her laugh and when she cried she didn't just need her mum. It brought us all closer in the end."*
>
> *Molly F*

How to deal with it

Try not to panic if you find your relationship has altered, and problems develop for you and your other half after your baby's born. Remember that it's absolutely normal – and almost certainly temporary. You're facing huge upheaval in your lives, and it's going to take some adjusting to. Meanwhile, try your best to do the following.

- Empathise with him. Bear in mind that he may be struggling, too. Put yourself in his shoes, sometimes.
- Put aside differences in opinion over how you look after your baby. Being mum doesn't necessarily mean you know best – and he has equal say when it comes to rearing your child. If you're disagreeing in a big way, sit down, thrash the issue out, and agree on a compromise before it becomes a serious sticking point.
- Resist the urge to interfere. Let him do as much as possible to care for your baby, and encourage them to spend time alone together, too. Don't be critical or undermine his efforts, even if you do feel they fall short of your own standards.
- Develop a system that means you're both happy with the share of childcare and domestic duties. Work out who does what best, or enjoys it the most, and go from there. And make sure you pipe up if you have a problem with your existing set-up.

- Don't just let it simmer inside you if you're not happy for some reason. Relationship experts say that good communication is all-important. Let him know what's bothering you – politely. And listen carefully if he's got something to say, too.
- Be philosophical. This is a temporary phase in your lives together. Easier times are almost certainly ahead.

> *"My husband and I spent a year working out that it was best for him to get home and cook dinner while I sorted our girls out. It works fine if he does bath and bed and I make tea, but as I can't stand cooking and he makes a mean bolognese, it makes sense. It's silly to have both tired parents doing both jobs together in twice the amount of time."*
>
> *Natasha H*

TIP To get your man clued up about life with a baby, get him a copy of *Babies and Toddlers for Men* by Mark Woods (White Ladder, 2012), which will take him through the first year and up to year three with lots of help from dads who have been there and survived.

Keeping your love alive

There's no doubt about it: you'll have far less time to spend together than you used to now you're parents. And even if you can find a spare moment or two, you might just be too tired or too pre-occupied to devote it to lovin'. Perhaps you've even lost sight of one another in a romantic sense, right now: he's Daddy; you're Mummy. It's cute, but it's not very sexy. All the same, you and he will need to make real efforts to find time for each other and – corny as it sounds – to keep your love alive. Your relationship may be put on the backburner for a while, as you both focus on your baby above all else, but neglect one another for too long, and it could become a serious problem.

Try to use any opportunities you get – once your baby's clean, fed, and content, the laundry's done, and you've caught up on some sleep, that is – to stop, talk, and reconnect with each other. Make physical contact whenever you have the chance. And aim to set aside a regular slot when it really is just about the two of you. As Lara S puts it: 'A bit of time out for us is an absolute must. We've never been away overnight or even out until late, but just a few hours when we're husband and wife rather than Mummy and Daddy are great. It's really important to keep on talking to each other, too. None of us are mind readers.'

Date night

The prospect of getting out on a date with your partner might seem very distant when you first become parents, and nipping to the 24-hour garage for a bag of nappies constitutes a big night out. It's hardly surprising. Maybe your baby's feeding or other needs can only be met by you, or maybe you're just not ready to leave him in someone else's care. Perhaps you're simply too exhausted to even consider staying up beyond 9p.m. However, getting out of the house sometimes with your other half but without your baby is definitely a habit worth developing at some point in the first year. You may find you have to force yourselves to find the time, energy, or inclination, but please do, because a bit of time together will help serve to remind you that in spite of being parents now, you are also still a couple. And it's one of several other good reasons for getting your baby into the swing of an early, regular bedtime (see page 123). It's never too late to start establishing one of these.

Finding a babysitter

One thing you'll have to get sorted before heading off into the sunset together is a reliable babysitter. If you're lucky enough to have a familiar family member around who'll do it for love, then that's wonderful: exploit it while you can. If not, perhaps you could ask a trusted mum-friend if she'll help on a favour-swap basis, with you or your other half doing the same for her on another night. Better still, expand your options by joining, or creating, a babysitting circle.

It does go without saying, though, that when it comes to finding a reliable sitter you should avoid anyone you don't know well – and anyone who's likely to raid your drinks cabinet, snog her boyfriend on your sofa, or panic if your baby wakes up crying.

Staying in

Of course, if actually going out isn't possible, you can still have a date night. You just have to have it at home, instead, as recommended by Caroline S. 'We made Tuesday a date night, and we take turns to organise it,' she explains. 'It's almost always "in", as we prefer to save my parents' babysitting "tokens" for special functions.'

Relight my fire: how to 'date' your baby's dad

- Pick your moment. Choose a time when you're least likely to be knackered or feeling more cold fish than hot lover. And remember that dates don't have to take place in the evening. Maybe you could meet for lunch, instead.
- Don't plan anything too ambitious or tiring at first. Keep your first few dates short and simple.
- If you're staying in, clear away the baby clutter first. Soggy muslins and chewed teething rings won't enhance the ambience.
- Don't let yourself go. Make a little effort for the occasion with your clothes, hair, and make-up and, if you suspect your luck could be in at the close of proceedings, shave your legs and wear nice pants. (At the very least, take off anything that's spattered with baby goo and replace it with something clean. And he should wear nice pants too. Insist on it.)
- Find time to flirt with each other. Hold hands or look into each other's eyes, even if it does seem a bit awkward. Send a cheeky text or email on the day of the date, just to let him know you're looking forward to it.
- Talk as much as possible during your date, even if it's just about the minutiae of your days – and not just about your baby. If that seems a big deal, plan to date round a shared activity instead: watching that DVD, for example, going for a run, signing up for an evening class, or playing Scrabble. As long as you're spending time together, it counts.

> *“We took every opportunity to go out for a lunch or dinner or even just a drink if babysitting allowed. It was the only time we had a proper conversation about how he was feeling, being at work all day, and how I was feeling, being at home with the kids. If we hadn't spent some time reconnecting, we would just have been ships that passed in the night.”*
>
> *Alex G*

Reigniting your sex life

Sex is bound to be pushed to the backburner for a certain period after birth. For many, a lengthy period. But resurrecting it when you're ready is all-important. Having sex again could do great things for your relationship, if it's a little the worse for wear since you became parents. And it will help you reclaim your va-va-voom in general, if it's been missing hitherto. It should also help you solve the mystery of the missing woman, if you've been wondering where exactly the old you went since becoming a mum.

> *“I hated being referred to as 'Mum' by midwives instead of by my name. Re-instating our sex life – which was very much not about being mum – as soon as possible was liberating. Knowing that I was still 'me' in that sense and had an identity beyond being a mum was a real boost.”*
>
> *Rosie C*

Where did my mojo go?

A few lucky mums find they're ready and able to renew their sex lives within weeks of birth. But for most, it's a slower process than that. Even once you feel physically up for it, you might find your mind still isn't willing. Or you may just feel too darn exhausted to prioritise lovemaking over the opportunity for some sleep.

You may also find that sex doesn't feel quite the same, either physically or emotionally, as it did before, and that it can be quite a while before it feels 'normal' again. In fact, some experts warn that you should allow up to a year to *entirely* get your groove back. Meanwhile, you should take whatever time you need to find it again. If your other half's gagging for it and you're not, take time to explain to him how you're feeling and don't feel guilty about it. But do be sure to consider his feelings, too. Be gentle about saying 'no'. And keep on communicating, and making sure he knows you still love him.

> *"After a day looking after my baby and breastfeeding, the last thing I wanted to do was have sex, or even a cuddle. I much preferred a cuppa and bed. Oops. And that lasted longer than it should have done. I know my husband wanted me to make more effort."*
>
> *Jane H*

Physical recovery

There's huge variation in when women feel sufficiently healed and physically ready to make love after having a baby. Convention has it you should wait four to six weeks before having sex after birth (and you'll usually get the nod from your GP at your six-week check to give it a go if you haven't already), but if you're raring to go before then, there's no reason not to – although, it's often advised that you wait for your lochia flow to stop first, because until then your uterus is still healing and there's an increased risk of infection.

If you've been left torn, stitched, or simply bruised and battered by giving birth, you'll very likely want to hold fire on resuming marital relations until you're good and healed, whenever that may be. However, there are no absolute guidelines on this: it comes down to whenever you feel ready for it. And actually that could be months, rather than weeks ahead, for a variety of potential reasons.

No sex, please: why you may not be ready to resume relations yet

- **You're absolutely exhausted.** It goes without saying, really. When you're this tired, going to bed is bound to be more about the wonder of sleep than the joy of sex. And sex requires at least some energy to be expended. After a day spent looking after your baby, you may not have a lot to spare.
- **You're scared it's going to hurt or feel 'weird'.** A deep-rooted dread of making love can, quite understandably, cause you to avoid it. And it's particularly likely to be a problem if you had a difficult birth which left you with a serious tear or episiotomy cut. There's more advice about 'the first time' on page 224.
- **You don't want your baby to know you're doing it.** If you're abiding by safe sleep guidelines, your baby's cot will be close to your own bedside. Unfortunately, it can be a bit of a passion-killer knowing he's there in the room with you – you don't want to let rip for fear of waking him, and even if he'll sleep through anything, you might just feel a bit funny knowing he's there.
- **You're having an identity crisis.** It's not unusual for a woman to lose sight of herself in a sexual sense after giving birth. Your whole life revolves around being a mother now, not a lover. It's a powerful and profound feeling. But if you don't feel sexy, you won't want sex.
- **You're unhappy about your body.** Whether it's extra flab; a C-section scar; those huge, veiny boobs, or changes to your lady bits that bother you, you may find your self-esteem and body image have taken a hefty blow after birth. In particular, lots of women fear their vagina will be somewhat 'slacker' than it was, or that scarring has altered its appearance for the worst.
- **Your partner isn't interested.** Really. Sometimes it's blokes who go off sex after birth. He might just be as tired and overwhelmed as you are, or it could go a bit deeper – maybe he was freaked out by seeing you give birth, or he's scared about hurting you. And maybe he's got a touch of 'Madonna syndrome': you're the mother of his child, now, and he doesn't want to do anything as sordid as shag you. It's also possible he's a bit turned off by your wobbly belly or leaky breasts: harsh, but potentially true.
- **You're keen to keep your boobs to yourself.** If you're breastfeeding, your boobs may be sore or sensitive for quite a while to come, as well as being full of milk and prone to leaking at awkward moments (arousal or orgasm can actually trigger

a rather untimely spurt). And, psychologically speaking, you might just feel your breasts have a higher purpose than just being fun bags, right now.

- **You're worried about pregnancy.** Reluctant to go through the whole pregnancy, birth, and new baby experience again for a while? Not that unreasonable, really. And fear of conception can be a powerful thing.
- **You're just not feeling very sexy at the moment.** No specific reason really, you're just knackered, anxious, preoccupied, and your hormones are all over the shop. You have a new baby. Sex is quite simply the last thing on your mind.
- **Your mental health is stopping you.** If you've got post-natal depression (see page 202), post-natal post-traumatic stress disorder (see page 192), or post-natal anxiety (see page 206), your appetite for sex and intimacy could well be affected for the worst.

Mums' panel round-up

When were you ready for sex again?

It was at least three months before I felt ready. Physically I'd healed long before, but emotionally, I just wasn't up for it. And the longer I left it, the more I dreaded it – **Lauren B**

After about six weeks. It was bizarre and uncomfortable. And to be honest, it didn't actually feel as it once had for a couple of years afterwards – **Jane H**

I had quite a lot of stitches, so I was pretty terrified. I think it was about three months and at first it was painful and quite horrible. It probably took six months for everything to start to feel normal again – **Charlee C**

It was about two weeks. It was a little painful, but it felt good to be intimate again, especially as he hadn't wanted it much when I was very pregnant – **Amanda W**

We gave it six weeks, and it was grand. I had no trouble from my C-section scar – **Melanie F**

We tried after a couple of months but I was still traumatised after a difficult birth, and it didn't go well. A second attempt, a month later, was better – **Sarah N**

The first time

Try not to expect fireworks when you reignite your love life after birth. For most women, the first time after birth is more of an experimental shag than anything else; a chance to work out whether you're still in one piece or not. And yes, it certainly can feel a bit weird and frankly, not that great when you first try, and perhaps for several subsequent tries afterwards. Lots of new mums report feeling 'a bit different down there', or that it was 'odd' or 'not like it used to be'. This will almost certainly be temporary – and it's very common.

> *"The first time was mostly to see if the physical side of things was OK. It was not painful and nothing felt too odd, but it was all quite mechanical. It took me several 'attempts' until I felt totally at ease with it."*
>
> ***Kathryn E***

It might help not to build it up too much: don't plan for a big, candlelit love-fest, just grab the first chance that arises. A glass of wine can be useful if you're tense, but don't have more than that because too much booze can be de-sensitising. And get your timing right – make sure your baby is well fed and fast asleep, or better still, enjoying a couple of hours' quality time with his grandparents. If you're breastfeeding and self-conscious about leakage issues, it would make sense to schedule in sex after feeding when your boobs are as empty as possible.

> *"I found that it was different both emotionally and physically. I felt quite self-conscious despite the fact my hubby kept telling me that I was beautiful. I felt fat and ugly and not at all sexy! Physically it felt tighter, but I'm guessing that was something to do with having lots of stitches."*
>
> ***Jemma P***

Looking good

If you've got body image issues, don't feel ashamed to keep some clothing on: preferably something vaguely sexy, though, not one of his old t-shirts. A bit of fabric can also provide a useful barrier against sore nipples and leaking. (You might even want to make like the *Sex and the City* girls, and keep your bra on. You could also stuff in some breast pads.)

Remind yourself, if you're worried about the way you look, that your body's done an amazing thing: try taking a look at it in the mirror, and appreciating its finer points. Have a look – and a little feel, too – if your new-look vagina's worrying you. Chances are it won't be nearly as much of a mess as you think. And even if it does look different, remember that it's a small adjustment to make, in the scheme of things, for both of you.

Gently does it

Choose a gentle position if you're concerned about pain or discomfort. Anything with very deep penetration is probably best avoided, and if you've had a C-section you probably won't want your man lying on top of you for a while. Go on top yourself, so you can take control, or better still do it 'spoon-style', with you both lying down and him entering from behind. Bear in mind too that lubrication levels can be affected by post-birth hormonal changes and/or breastfeeding, so it may help to have some KY jelly at the ready.

> *“I was terrified about the idea of having sex again because I'd had an episiotomy and stitches. And I have to say that while it was a bit uncomfortable, it wasn't painful and was nowhere near as bad as I had been preparing myself for.”*
>
> ***Lucy R***

Although you absolutely should not try having sex if you don't want to, it's worth bearing in mind that the longer you leave sex after birth, the harder it can become. So, even if you don't really feel much like it, you might want to consider biting the bullet anyway. There's a good chance your worries will turn out to be unfounded. And don't forget that making love doesn't have to involve penetration. If you can't or don't want to take the plunge completely, concentrate on other ways of being intimate, with snogging, cuddles, massage, or mutual masturbation.

TIP Do stop if sex hurts. It may be that tension and anxiety is causing the problem, in which case you may need more time or more foreplay – or you may just need to stop worrying about penetrative sex for a while, and try something gentler, instead. Do, however, get any persistent pain during sex checked out by your GP as there are a number of potential medical causes – including an infection, a problem with the way you were stitched, or a prolapse (see page 179) – for which treatment is required.

If you can't seem to get your love life off the ground at all after birth, try taking it off the menu altogether for a while – putting pressure on yourself to be a sexy mother is only going to make things worse. Aim to find intimacy again in a gradual way, with the focus on hand-holding, cuddling, and talking, and move things along very slowly, making penetration a low priority and your own enjoyment and relaxation a high one. And if things still aren't happening for you, and one or both of you is frustrated or unhappy as a result, do seek some further help. There's lots of good advice to be found on the website of relationship support service The Couple Connection – and counselling is available through Relate, the relationships charity.

> *"My son has been a terrible sleeper and I'm so exhausted, my libido has disappeared completely. Quite frankly, it's all too much effort. My husband isn't happy about it. I do miss the intimacy, but I just can't be bothered."*
>
> *Theresa G*

Family planning

Yes, I expect you *did* let out a hollow laugh when the midwife rounded on you while still in the labour ward and asked if you had your contraception sorted. The bundle of joy in the plastic cot beside you – not to mention the physical wreckage of your body – were probably all the contraception you needed right then. But health professionals ask these silly questions because they know that new parents are going to get their mojo back at some point and, contrary to a lot of people's assumptions, it's quite possible to get pregnant again very soon: within as little as three weeks after birth, regardless of whether your periods have returned. So unless you're dead set on a very small gap between children, it's an issue you should probably address sooner rather than later.

The return of your periods

Your periods will not *usually* start again while you're exclusively breastfeeding, but could return any time after you have begun to breastfeed less often, and if you're formula or mixed feeding from the start, they could come back any time from five to six weeks after the birth. Hormonal upheaval means that you may find your periods are very light, perhaps even nothing more than 'spotting', when they return initially, or conversely that they're heavier than usual. They may also be irregular for a while.

Don't assume you can't conceive until getting your first period after birth: bear in mind that you ovulate about two weeks before your period, so you could well have a short window of fertility without realising.

Which contraceptive?

If you plan to take up with your old contraceptive again, you may need to check it's suitable for you right now, or you may want to use the opportunity to try something new.

The best options if you think you'll want a short gap between kids and you want to try again within a year or so include the combined or progestogen-only pill; contraceptive patch; cap or diaphragm; vaginal ring; condoms; or 'natural family planning'. But bear in mind the following.

- The combined pill, vaginal ring and patch aren't recommended if you're breastfeeding as they contain oestrogen which can affect milk flow.
- Caps or diaphragms should be checked by a doc to make sure they still fit, as the shape of the vagina and cervix can change after birth.

- You should be cautious about relying on natural family planning (also known as the 'rhythm' method) as your cycle may be all over the shop for a while after birth and you won't be able to work out when's 'safe' and when isn't.

If you know you won't want to start trying for another baby for at least a year or more, you might want to consider a long-acting reversible method, which are considered extremely effective and don't run the risk of 'user failure'. These include the contraceptive implant, which works for up to three years; contraceptive injection, which lasts for eight or 12 weeks depending on the type used; intrauterine device (IUD), which can be relied upon for five to ten years depending on the type, or intrauterine system (IUS), effective for five years. If you plump for the injection, bear in mind that it can take up to a year for your fertility to return to normal once you cease use; while it will return quickly after having an implant, IUD, or IUS removed. There's lots more information about all the options above on the website of the Family Planning Association (FPA).

Can I get pregnant while breastfeeding?

Good question. According to the FPA, what's officially known as the lactational amenorrhoea method (LAM) is up to 98% effective in preventing pregnancy but *only* if:

- your baby is less than six months old; **and**
- your periods have not returned; **and**
- you are fully breastfeeding, day and night (or 'nearly fully breastfeeding' – in other words, giving your baby nothing but breastmilk and, just occasionally, other liquids).

TIP Some experts do urge extreme caution when it comes to relying on this method – and some mums have certainly been caught out after assuming they were safe while breastfeeding.

Parental love

Even once you do get your love life up and running again, be prepared for the possibility that your relationship may not ever be quite the same as it once was. Many couples find that lack of opportunity and lack of energy are issues that continue for as long as they have a young family, and that they make love less frequently than they used to. You may also find that some effort is required to keep things interesting – it's normal, especially if you've been together for a while. Meanwhile, as long as you're having reasonably regular sex and you're both enjoying it, that's all that matters. Ignore any other parents who insist they're swinging from the chandeliers on a nightly basis. They're almost certainly lying, anyway.

> *“Our love life did get a bit lacklustre once we were parents, due to tiredness. We found the solution in Ann Summers.”*
>
> *Abi M*

Looking on the bright side, some couples find that a post-natal sex drought leaves them keen to make up for lost time – and others that in the long term, their love life gets even better, ramped up by the increased bond they share.

Red-hot mama: how to keep the love alive now you're parents

- **Make love somewhere different.** Try the sitting room, the dining room, or the stairs, for starters. Avoiding the bedroom is a good idea if your baby's in with you and it's putting you off (and even if he isn't, the variety will spice things up).
- **Be creative about timings.** Don't wait until night time to make love, schedule in a daytime slot which hopefully you'll have more energy for. (Wait until your baby's napping, or better still ask a kindly relative to take him for a walk while you get down to it – obviously you don't have to tell her this is what your plan is.)
- **Try something you've never tried before.** If life is just a bit too tiring to pull on a leather basque at the end of the day, then fair enough, but something low-effort, like a rude movie, can improve things no end.

- **Get away for the odd night, if you can.** Not everyone's lucky enough to have someone willing and able to provide overnight sitting services, but if you do, make the most of it. Your baby will be fine. And a change of environment can really get you in the mood.
- **Master the art of the quickie.** When you don't have that many moments to spare, sometimes you have to make the most of any that do crop up.
- **Be business-like about it.** Get out your diaries and make an appointment for sex. Like exercise, you may have to force yourself to find the energy to make love – but you'll feel so much better when you do.
- **Talk to each other.** Be vocal about what you like and what you want – and don't button up if there's a problem.

“Having a baby in your room puts a bit of a dampener on things. You have to find some creative ways around that. Let's just say our lounge proved popular because we were so terrified of waking him.”

Lucy R

11

Going back to work

You'll likely be returning to work at some point in the first year, or at least considering the alternatives. The decision to go back, stay at home, seek a new balance, or change direction entirely is rarely easy, and you may have some serious thinking to do – not just about the practicalities like finances and childcare, but profound emotional stuff, too, like how you'll cope leaving your baby in someone else's care, or whether you're prepared to forego the professional status you've reached thus far. Even once you've made your mind up and a return to work looms, you still have to pick your way through the minefield of childcare options, and steel yourself for the difficult business of job- and baby-juggling. Whatever your next move is likely to be, take your time working it out – and ease yourself very gently in.

> *“I don't regret or feel like I sacrificed any time with my baby by returning to work after maternity leave. It gave me independence, and something other than nappies to focus on. The money has also given us the opportunity for holidays and days out that we can enjoy together as a family which otherwise we could never have afforded.”*
>
> ***Nicola L***

Weighing up your options

There are many reasons why you might be going back to work or thinking about it. For a lot of mums, it's mainly about the money. For others it's more to do with sanity or self-esteem. Often, there's a bit of both going on. And maybe there are other factors at play, too. There's no standard situation.

You may also be surprised to find the way you feel is not the way you thought you'd feel. Some mums are convinced when they walk out of the office to start their maternity leave that they'll be walking right back in again in six months' time – but after six months with their baby, decide they're less career-driven than they thought. For others it's quite the opposite: an assumption they'd be fulfilled by life as a full-time mum, followed by a discovery that they are not.

> *“I didn't plan to return to work. I wanted to be a stay-at-home-mummy, but it just didn't feel like me in the end. I wanted to earn my share of our spending money, for one thing. Although I knew I was doing half the work – the childcare – it felt like my husband was earning all the money, and I had no right to spend it. I also wanted to keep a part of me alive that wasn't just 'Mama Charlee'. I think that's really important to be a good parent.”*
>
> *Charlee C*

When you're weighing up the big issues, sit down and go through them carefully one by one, perhaps even jotting down your thoughts as you go. You may want to do some soul-searching alone, before talking through your thoughts (and the financials) with your partner. Among the things you might be considering are outlined below.

- **How you feel about leaving your baby.** How much time, ideally, would you (and/or your partner) like to spend with him? Do you (or will you) feel OK about leaving him in someone else's care?
- **How much you value your work.** Is it a career you're keen to keep, and if so, would a break matter much? Are you ready for a change

in any case? Do you need to do something, whatever that may be, other than being a mum?

- **What you can afford.** Do you have no choice but to return to work to pay the bills? Could you manage your money differently so it would allow you to stop working/take longer leave/reduce your hours?
- **What sort of role will make *you* happy.** Is being at home with your baby what will suit you most? Will it affect your self-esteem if you don't work, mix with adults, or contribute financially? Are you determined to have the best of both worlds?
- **What your contract says.** If you've taken advantage of an extended maternity policy, do you have to return, as part of the deal – or pay back part of your maternity pay?
- **Whether flexibility could help.** Could a different working pattern – for you, for your other half, or for both of you – offer a good compromise? If so, is it feasible, either in your current jobs, or in new ones?
- **What the future may hold.** If you know you'd like to have another child before long, would be better to take a long-term career break until your family's complete?

If the issue's throwing up a real dilemma for you, perhaps the decision needn't be set in stone. You could agree to see how things go, and reassess the situation in a couple of months' time, say.

> *“I went back to work, but it wasn't until I did that that I realised how much I wanted more time with him. I always thought I'd be happy to be back at work, but experience is proving different. I don't feel part of the crowd at work anymore, nor am I quite in with the stay-at-home mums I know. Being somewhere in between is quite isolating and lonely. I'm now taking redundancy, intend to study, and change career in due course. I should be ready to go back to work again by the time he's school age.”*
>
> *Clare F*

TIP If, like most new parents, you need to sit down and do some sums before weighing up your back-to-work options, don't forget to find out about any financial help from the government you may be entitled to, including child benefit (currently £20.30 a week for your eldest child and £13.40 a week for each of your other children – you should have got a claim form for this in your Bounty pack while in hospital, or you can download one from the Directgov website); and tax credits. It's also worth seeing if your employer operates a salary sacrifice or childcare voucher scheme. There's lots of good information about financial help for parents on the websites of Working Families, and Paying for Childcare.

NB At the time of writing, qualifying criteria for tax credits and child benefit were due to change, check the HMRC website for more information.

The G word

One emotion is very likely to hold you ransom while you're thinking about a return to work: guilt. As with anxiety, there's probably no point me telling you *not* to feel guilty now you're a mum – it goes with the territory. And few people feel guilt more than the working mum: whether you're heading back to your desk because you've really missed it, or because the coffers are bare, the niggling doubts that you're doing the right thing by your baby can be truly insidious.

Rather than giving in to guilt, remind yourself of all the positives – whatever they may be for you – that returning to work will mean, whether they will be the financial advantage, the company, or an uninterrupted path up the career ladder for you. Doing everything you can to get childcare that's right for your baby and you, and making every second count whilst you *are* at home, should also help. Remember, guilt can become stress, and stress will rub off on your baby. So it's in no-one's interest to indulge it.

Statistically speaking: studies that say it's OK to be a working mum

- In a 2010 study into the effects on babies whose mums made an early return to work, the National Institute of Child Health and Human Development Study of Early Child Care found no evidence that it had an adverse impact on a baby's well-being, and in fact, that it had significant advantages.
- In 2011, a study by the University of North Carolina found that mothers who returned to work in the early years were less likely to suffer health problems and depression than those who didn't.
- Also in 2011, a research team from University College, London, found that there were no detrimental effects for young children growing up in a household with a working mum in it – in fact, where girls are concerned, it can actually be good for them.

“My advice is, get the childcare absolutely right and fight for whatever sort of flexible working that works for you. We found a brilliant (and affordable) nanny, and I fought for a four-day week, with one day working from home. These things made a world of difference to how I feel about being back at work. The balance is absolutely right – or as good as I can get it.”

Rebecca F

Going back to your old job

Unless you left for good before giving birth, a return to your current employers will no doubt be, technically speaking at least, on the cards. All women are legally entitled to take up to a year off work after having a baby – six months of Ordinary Maternity Leave (OML), and a further six months of Additional Maternity Leave (AML) – safe in the knowledge that they can have their job back at the end of it, or sooner, if they want to. (And of course, many *do* head back before the year's up, perhaps because they're keen to get back on the job, or because they can't afford to take 12 months off, since Statutory Maternity Pay (SMP) runs out after 39 weeks, and contractual deals that boost or extend it will rarely cover the entire period.)

Bear in mind that it's your legal *right* to go back to your old job, on your old terms and conditions after taking OML, and indeed after taking any amount of AML, unless it's not 'reasonably practicable', in which case you must be offered a suitable alternative job on your old terms and conditions. So, if for some reason you find your old job, or an acceptable alternative, is not open to you when the time comes to go back, do get some advice: calling the Working Families helpline would be a good start.

TIP Ordinary paternity leave is one or two weeks, but a dad may qualify for up to 26 weeks additional paternity leave if his partner returns to work without using up her full maternity leave entitlement. For dads who don't qualify, there's also the possible option of taking unapid 'parental leave'.

NB A major reform of parental leave laws are afoot, under proposals being made at the time of writing.

Letting them know

Your employer will assume you're going to take the whole 52 weeks maternity leave you're entitled to. You don't even have to formally remind them when you're due back, if you *do* take the whole period, you just have to rock up on the first working day after the 52 weeks are over (although hopefully, they'll be expecting you and will have some kind of plan in place for your return).

If you want or need to go back at any point *before* the year's up, you must give at least eight weeks' notice of your return date. If you're thinking of requesting flexible hours (see below), it's a good idea if you can moot this possibility as early as possible, just in case convincing your boss to go for it turns out to be a lengthy process – allow at least 14 weeks before your return date. It's also a good idea to let your employers know in advance and in writing, if you're planning to carry on breastfeeding, so they can plan for any allowances they need to make (see page 249).

A new arrangement

You may find there's a good compromise to be had in your old job, but with a new pattern. This will often mean going part-time, but there are all sorts of other possibilities for 'flexible working'– and as long as you've been in your job for at least 26 weeks, you have the legal right to request this once you're a mum. The good news is that your employers *must* give your request consideration. The bad news is they can turn you down, if they can show they have good business grounds on which to do so. Among other possibilities, flexible working could mean:

- reducing your hours from full- to part-time
- working from home all or some of the time
- compressing your hours – for instance, working four slightly longer days, and taking the fifth off.
- flexi-time – you choose when you make up your hours (although you'll usually have to agree to work a certain 'core' period)
- job sharing.

Asking for flexible working

Before you ask your boss or your HR department for a change to your old working pattern, sit down and think hard about what sort of arrangement might work best for you. Bear in mind that any new arrangement that's agreed will normally be permanent, so you need to be pretty sure it's going to be a good one. (You might consider asking if you can give it a whirl on a trial basis at first.) Make sure that what you ask for is realistic (not a lot of point, for example, asking if you can work from home two days a week if you're a nurse), and be prepared to be flexible yourself about any alternative suggestions your employer may come back to you with.

> *“I worked full-time hours but managed to get an arrangement to work flexi-time; I started at 7.30a.m. and took a half-hour lunch so that I could leave at 3.30 instead of 5.30.”*
>
> ***Nicola L***

Do your research and have a good think about what the benefits of your proposed arrangement will be to your employer, as well as any likely consequences and how they could be dealt with: put all these thoughts down when you make your application. There are various online tools which you can use to help you put together a case for flexible working – you'll find one on the Working Families website, for starters. Make sure you include all the information that's required when it comes to getting your application down in writing: your employer may have a form you can fill in, but if not, there's a standard template available to download from Directgov. Once you've put in a request, your employer must hold a meeting with you within 28 days, and after that, they must give you a written decision on your request within 14 days.

TIP Don't forget that your partner *may also* be eligible to request flexible working once he becomes a parent. Perhaps you can achieve a happy balance between you.

What if I get turned down?

If your request for flexible working is rejected, your employer needs to outline in writing why (and remember, he can only refuse for good business reasons), and explain the appeal process. If you feel you've a good case for appealing the decision, you have a further 14 days to challenge the reasons given, or provide fresh ammunition for your own case, and a further meeting must follow. If you're still unsuccessful, it may be that you're able to take it further with an appeal on the grounds of sex discrimination, or you may have a case for an industrial tribunal. Get advice if you need it by calling the Working Families helpline.

> *"I wanted to go back to work three days a week. But at the meeting with my manager, I was told that my career progression would freeze unless I came back full time. (I know now they had no right to say that.) So I left, we took a payment holiday from the mortgage, and eventually, I went freelance."*
>
> *Claire A*

If you don't want to go back at all

For some mums, there's just no going back to their old job. Maybe you want more time at home with your baby than a year's maternity leave will provide – or even think you'd rather ditch work altogether, until after you've had another baby, or more, and your family's complete. Or maybe you want fewer hours, or to work from home, and you know that won't be compatible with what you used to do. Perhaps your enthusiasm for your old job had run out in any case. I knew even as I walked out of my office, pregnant with my first baby, that I wouldn't be going back. There may well have been flexible options open to me, but it would still have meant more time away from my baby than I fancied – and the commute was something I'd always found awful. (I also knew I could probably do what I did on a freelance basis, which helped.)

> *"I would find it very hard to work full time and leave my son in childcare every day because he is changing so fast and I enjoy spending so much time with him. We can't get this time back, and I feel so lucky that I've been able to be a stay-at-home mum."*
>
> *Ruth D*

Naturally, you'll need to give your employer notice if you don't want to return to work at all – otherwise, they're just going to assume you'll be walking through the door again a year after you left. You could do this at any time, but you only have to give your normal contractual period of notice, so if you wait until the latest possible point, towards the end of your maternity leave you'll keep any rights that are yours until then – holiday you may have accrued during your leave period, for example. If your employers have been paying you occupational or contractual maternity pay (in other words, anything over and above your statutory pay), they may ask you to pay it (or some of it) back if you don't return, and if you can't afford to do that, you may have no choice but to go back, if only for a while. Some companies, however, are happy to write off contractual maternity pay that's technically owed to them when an employee doesn't come back after having a baby.

“I didn’t go back at all, for a number of reasons: One was the cost of childcare – and the fact that we have no family around to help. Two, I’m still exhausted, and three, I hated all the office politics where I worked anyway. I’d prefer to see if I can get work as a freelance artist, but that may have to be when my children are all at school and I’ve got the time and energy to get a portfolio together.”
Nadine M

Starting all over again

For lots of women, the natural career break of maternity leave offers a good chance to make a fresh start in a whole new company or career, maybe even retraining or studying for qualifications. Some successfully use motherhood as a springboard to (and often, inspiration for) setting up their own business or becoming self-employed. Other mums are happy to take whatever part-time work they can find (even if they’re frankly overqualified for it) on the basis that it gets them out, and earns them a few pennies – as did Amanda G, who formerly worked in an area office for a building society. ‘I didn’t want to return full time, and I knew if I went back part time most of my income would go on childcare,’ she recalls. ‘Fortunately, I was made redundant which suited me fine, and I then got a part-time evening job in a supermarket. It wasn’t very challenging, but it got me out of the house and away from just being a mum.’

Working for yourself

Setting up your own business or going freelance may seem like a fantastic way to get a good work/life balance – and certainly it can work pretty well once you’ve got yourself established. There’s lots of advice available online if you’re looking to find out more about this route. You’d be wise to go about it cautiously, though, and consider the following important points.

- You'll probably still need some kind of childcare. You may be working from home, but you won't get much done with your baby around (unless you can fit it all in during naps and after bedtime).
- It may be quite a while before you actually pull in any money. You'll need to think carefully about how you're going to finance it – and how the bills are going to get paid in the meantime.
- It can be hard work getting a new business off the ground or establishing yourself in self-employment. If you're still up to your neck in nappies, you might find that *now* isn't actually the best time to try.
- If you turn out to be successful, you may end up working harder than ever.

"I always planned to take my full year's maternity leave, but halfway through I realised my pay was barely enough to cover childcare costs, so there seemed little point in returning to my job as a broadcast journalist. I spent the second part of my maternity leave researching and building up a new client base, as a freelance writer and blogger. I know I was lucky to have that option."

Molly F

Mums' panel round-up

When and why did you return to work?

I went back after my first baby when she was eight months old, because I was offered work and I was keen to keep my career going. It was only two days, which suited me – Alex G

I started to work again, on a freelance basis, when my daughter was three months old. I'd decided not to go back to my former job, but felt I needed to do something with my brain – Jenny C

When she was six months old, on a very part-time basis, and from home. I could only do two- to three-hour stints, as she wouldn't take a bottle – Jane H

I took four months off, and was pretty keen to get back. I'd worked bloody hard to get to my managerial position and feared losing my status – **Jess T**

After seven months' maternity leave – and because it was the only way to pay the mortgage, to be honest. I would have liked to have taken longer – **Rebecca F**

I returned to work part time when he was five months old. I cried on the way in that morning. I didn't want to but had no choice, bills needed to be paid – **Rachel G**

Finding the right childcare

Seeking out the right childcare can be a difficult process, and all options will have their benefits, and their drawbacks. – I've outlined the main ones below. But you do need to be confident in the end that you've plumped for the best possible option for your baby – for the sake of his welfare obviously, as well as for your own peace of mind.

When considering your options, try to focus on the positives: remember, if you find the right person to look after your baby for you while you work, you'll be helping him to become confident and independent. It will very likely provide a boost for his developmental and learning skills, too.

Please look after this baby: tips for finding the right childcare provider

- Begin your search well before you're due to go back to work. It may be a long process.
- Check out the results of any inspection reports, but find out about the word on the street too, by asking other parents for their recommendations and views.

- Shop around. Make appointments to visit several possibilities so you can compare, and get a feel for them – you'll be able to tell a lot simply by being there.
- Ask lots of questions. Check out the website of the Daycare Trust for a comprehensive list of the sorts of things you should be asking.
- Consider your baby. What sort of environment is he most likely to thrive in?
- Weigh up all the practicalities: opening times, costs, geography. Write them all down, if it helps.
- Think about back-up options, which you'll need – unless you opt for a nursery – for when your care provider is ill or on holiday.

Easing him in

Once you've found the provision you feel is right, don't forget to allow time to ease your baby in. Individual care providers have different policies about this, but most will offer a handful of short 'settling-in' sessions, usually free of charge, in the run-up to your baby's actual start. Often you'll be invited to stick around for the first of these, and push off for the rest.

Of course, you may not know if your childcare provider of choice is the right one until you've actually tried it for a while. Obviously you don't want to switch unless you really have to, but you'd be wise to keep an open mind while looking at your options – and perhaps have a plan B – just in case it turns out your first choice isn't working.

TIP To access a directory of the childcare providers available in your area, as well as lots of general info and advice, go to the website of your local Family Information Service (in Northern Ireland, this service is known as Family Support NI). You can search for your local branch via the Daycare Trust or Directgov websites.

Your main childcare options

Day nursery

Pros

- No need to consider sick days or holidays, as nurseries are always open.
- They must be registered and inspected by Ofsted (or the equivalent body in Wales, Scotland and Northern Ireland), so must adhere to certain standards.
- Mixing with other children will help boost your baby's social skills and confidence. All day nurseries are expected to conform to a government-set early years 'curriculum' of learning and development – so he may get a positive push in that direction, too.
- With a whole team of staff members in situ, you're not putting your trust in a single person.

Cons

- Less personal attention for your baby (although stringent rules about staff/child ratios mean there should always be one adult on duty, for every three under-twos).
- Lack of flexibility beyond opening hours: you may get charged if you turn up late for collection.
- They won't look after your baby if he's ill, which a childminder or nanny might. (And as nurseries tend to boast lots of germ-ridden charges, he may well be ill more often than you'd like.)

Costs

Rates vary hugely, depending on where you live, but nursery fees are usually somewhere between £25 and £50 per day.

> *“We decided to go for a nursery and tried to be very objective, looking at hours available, cost, care levels, food and so on. When it came down to it though, we chose the one that seemed to match our son's temperament;*

it was very calm. It was tough to start with as it took a while for him to settle in. The staff were really supportive, offering lots of advice and flexibility to help. It was worth persevering; he absolutely loves it now and gets really excited when we arrive."

Clare F

Childminder

Pros

- Generally cheaper than a nursery.
- Offers a home environment.
- Lots of personal attention for your baby (although childminders are allowed to care for up to six children aged under eight at a time, including their own).
- Like nurseries, childminders must be registered and inspected, and conform to the demands of the government's early years' curriculum. They must have undertaken at least introductory training – and many will have secured higher qualifications, too.

Cons

- You're putting your faith in one person. No one's going to blow the whistle if she's not up to scratch.
- You'll need a back-up plan for when she's sick or on holiday.

Costs

Again it's variable but typical childminding rates can be anything from £2.50 to £8 an hour. Don't forget to ask about whether extras like food, nappies and outings are included or whether you'll need to cough up any supplementary cash.

"We chose a childminder. I figured if she couldn't be at home with me then the next best option was for her to be at home with someone else. It's cheaper than a nanny, and as her childminder looks after a couple of other little ones, she gets added stimulation. She's flexible, too. So if I need

to stay an extra half hour at work or finish early then I'm not tied to collecting my daughter at a certain time.”
Molly F

Nanny or nanny share

Pros

- One-to-one care for your baby, in his own home. If you can find someone your baby really likes, it could be the next best thing to being there yourself.
- A nanny will usually be prepared to work long hours, and maybe evenings, too. If you're prepared to have (and can accommodate) a live-in nanny, you potentially have cover whenever you need it.
- You may get extras thrown in, such as housework.
- She'll be (or should be) happy to run things as you dictate.

Cons

- Usually pretty pricey (although if you team up with another set of parents and take on a nanny between you, sharing the fees, it can be cost effective).
- There's no requirement for a nanny to have relevant qualifications or training or to be registered. (However, there is an Ofsted-run voluntary register and the Daycare Trust recommends you always go for a nanny who's signed up to this. As well as assuring certain standards, it means you can claim financial help such as working tax credits – see page 234.)
- The paperwork involved. As your nanny's employer, you'll need to draw up a contract, provide a monthly payslip, and be responsible for paying her tax and national insurance contributions (although there are companies who will provide this service for you).
- If she walks out for some reason, you'll be buggered.
- You may feel resentful that she's 'taken your place'.

Costs

Again, very variable and influenced by many factors, not least geography. Nannies are covered by the national minimum wage, which means, if she's 21 or over, you *must* pay your nanny at least £6.08 per hour – but could end up paying anything up to £15 an hour. Other costs could include providing a car, and agency fees. If she lives in you'll need to factor in the cost of that (although you'll also, no doubt, be paying her less in the way of wages).

> *"For us the nanny route worked. I really wanted one person to provide continuity, security, and a bond. Ours came highly recommended. She's been with us for two years, and is now part of the family. It makes being at work so much easier when I know it's her back at home. And because she comes to our house and brings her own child with her, she charges us an affordable rate."*
>
> *Rebecca F*

Care by a relative

Pros

- You'll probably feel happy leaving your baby with someone he knows and loves, and in an environment (whether your place or theirs) that he's familiar with.
- Cheap – maybe even free.
- Flexible – hopefully.

Cons

- If your relative isn't trained or qualified, or following the early years curriculum, your baby won't get the same level of development and learning as he would (or should) with a registered childcare provider.
- You won't qualify for financial help if you want to pay them (unless the relative in question also happens to be a registered childcare provider, and caring for at least one other child, too).
- It could be awkward if you're not happy about some aspects of the way they care for your baby. (Setting out some basic ground rules before you start may be helpful. You may even want to download and fill in the family childcare agreement template that's available on the website of the Grandparents Association.)

- They may not be prepared or able to offer you consistency and reliability (and if you're not paying them, you certainly wouldn't be able to expect it).

Costs

See above – free, if you're lucky, or perhaps just the price of their expenses, or the odd bottle of wine. (NB. If you *do* pay your relative to look after your baby they probably don't need to be registered, but if you're paying a friend, she does. The rules on this are complex: your best bet is to check out what Ofsted has to say.)

> *"My mum looked after my daughter, luckily for me. I would never have gone back to work if I had to rely on a stranger to look after her. It was mum or nothing."*
>
> *Zoe A*

Gearing up to go back

Give yourself plenty of time to get practically and emotionally ready to work again – it can be a big transition, especially if you've taken the best part of a year off. You'll ease your nerves if you plan your return well in advance: talk to colleagues and undertake any research that might help you catch up on anything missed.

Take some time to thrash out with your partner how your home roles are going to change once you're back at work. If you've been stuck with the lion's share of domestic stuff while you've been at home, clearly you're going to need to reassess the situation. Household chores can be a real sticking point for working couples: agree in advance who's doing what – in writing if necessary – and where you think you can compromise if necessary. Consider any ways you can save yourselves trouble: could you find a few extra quid for a cleaner to come in for a few hours a week, for instance, or to farm your ironing out to a professional service? You'll also need to work out who's in charge of any daycare drop-offs and pick-ups – and who's most likely to carry the can when your baby is ill or your childcare goes up the spout for some reason.

Before the return date itself, write a checklist of whatever you need to get done to get to work on time, and feeling calm. Remember to give yourself loads of time to get you and your baby ready (do as much as you can the night before) and to get to work, factoring in journey times. It's a good idea to have at least one trial run of any new routine ahead of time: if your baby's having one or more trial sessions with his daycare provider, that could be a good time to try.

Breast practice: breastfeeding your baby while you're working

If you're a breastfeeding mum and you don't intend to let a return to employment curtail you, it may mean having to express (see page 81) during breaks from work or, depending on how far away you work, and who's looking after your baby, having him brought to your workplace for feeds. If you're going for the expressing option, it's a good idea to build up a good bank of milk supplies before you start work, and, if you haven't already, you'll need to convince your baby to take milk from a bottle rather than direct from source (see page 85).

Let your employers know before you go back, in writing, if you plan to express or feed your baby while you're at work. By law, they must remove any risks to your or your baby's health or safety (exposure to chemical agents, for example, or adverse working conditions), and they must make sure you have a suitable place to 'rest' if you're breastfeeding. It's not a legal requirement, but if they're following guidelines from the Health and Safety Executive, they should also provide you with a clean, comfortable, private place to express or to feed your baby, and the time you need in which to do that. You'll also need access to a fridge where you can store your expressed milk (and a cool bag, for transporting it back home).

Please don't tie yourself up in knots trying to juggle work and breastfeeding. You may find it a challenge too far to keep up with both – especially if your employers aren't being all that supportive or facilities aren't up to scratch. If it turns out that keeping up with the breastfeeding while trying to hold down your job turns out to be a tall order, but you're keen to carry on, perhaps you can find a good compromise in mixed feeding (see page 86).

> *"I was still breastfeeding my son when I went back to work. In general it was OK, as my boss supported me expressing in the first couple of months. However, I always felt awkward mentioning it at work, as I worried it would make colleagues feel uncomfortable. I must say, I didn't realise until I stopped how much that was tiring me too. I'm glad I stuck it out though."*
>
> *Clare F*

Beating butterflies

You may well have mixed feelings about returning to employment after maternity leave. Nerves are very likely to be among them. Perhaps you're worried that you've forgotten how to do your job, that people will treat you differently, or that things will have changed when you were gone.

If you can, get your boss to agree to an 'easing-in period' – perhaps going back part time for the first week, or simply starting a bit later and finishing a little earlier – and a maternity cover handover period, if someone's been doing your job in your absence and you need to be filled in. It may also be a good idea to schedule in one or more meetings over the first few months with your boss or manager, so you can both review how things are going, and get to grips with any issues that have cropped up.

TIP If you're lacking confidence as you return to work, remind yourself what an amazing job you've been doing in the meantime. You've been caring for your baby – and in doing so, notching up a whole load of useful skills for your CV: personal interaction; time management; multi-tasking; keeping calm under pressure; and decision-making.

Once you're back at work

You may find things feel very different for a while once you're back at work – or maybe it will feel like you've never been away. Chances are you're going to miss your baby, a little bit at least (although you may also feel rather liberated when you look down and realise your little appendage hasn't been sitting on your hip for at least two hours). You're very likely to find you're shattered, too.

All in all, the process of settling back in could be a long one – so give yourself plenty of time, and cut yourself lots of slack. As Zoe A recalls: 'I went back to the same job, part time, when my daughter was ten months old and found it horrible leaving her. I was very sleep deprived so I found it hard to concentrate, avoided development and tried to keep my head down. It's taken time to feel comfortable in the role again.'

> *"I was devastated at first, but also glad of the opportunity to use my brain and engage with other people. There was another plus, too. I hadn't been sleeping very well, waking up in the night even though my baby wasn't. But as soon as I started work I slept properly. My mind obviously needed exercising!"*
>
> ***Alex G***

Back to business: tips for returning to work

- If you haven't done so already, make contact with old colleagues before you go back so you can catch up on any important changes – or even just the hot office gossip.
- Splash out on some new outfits and have your hair styled. Feeling physically confident could make all the difference.
- Show you're keen. Ask to see any documents that might help you catch up on what you've missed, and find out what if anything's changed by asking lots of questions.
- Make life outside work as easy as possible for yourself while you're getting back into the swing of it. Let the housework go

and eat ready meals or takeaways. Go to bed stupidly early, for a while, if you need to. If your baby's still waking you at night, perhaps it's time to think about sleep training (see page 127).

- Look for any positives that could arise from your return to work. For instance, could this be a good chance to come in, refreshed, with a new attitude to your work? Are there different opportunities that the 'new' you could pursue? Can you book a nice holiday now that you wouldn't have been able to afford otherwise?

"Maternity leave worked in my favour. When I went back, my work had been farmed out to other people and I never got it all back. I took that as my opportunity to explore some different positions within the company and started working in the web development team, a radical departure from my previous role in admin."

Nicola L

TIP There's masses of good information about returning to work on the Next Step website, and they also offer an advice service which you can access online, over the phone, or in person. Contact details are in the back of the book.

You made it!

Once you reach the magic milestone of your baby's first birthday, it's truly something to celebrate. Within one short year, he's grown from a tiny, helpless stranger in your arms, to the smiling, mobile child you can't imagine life without. Make sure you take a moment to reflect on the amazing changes of the previous year, to breathe a sigh of relief, and to give yourself a massive pat on the back. Yes, there are many challenges still to come, but once you've got the first 12 months sewn up, you can probably handle anything – even a second baby. (And maybe that's something you're thinking about now – or even a reality already – if you want a short gap between children. Well, at least you know you can do it!)

Be sure to light a candle on your baby's first birthday cake – and crack open a bottle of bubbly to share with his dad, grandparents, or anyone else that matters. And congratulations! You're a first-time mum who's made it through the first year. There are few greater achievements.

Useful contacts

Health and safety

NHS Direct: Advice line 0845 4647; www.nhsdirect.nhs.uk

NHS 24 (for Scotland): Advice line 08454 242 424; www.nhs24.com

NHS Direct Wales: Advice line 0845 4647; www.nhsdirect.wales.nhs.uk

Bliss, the special care baby charity: Family Support Helpline 0500 618 140; www.bliss.org.uk

Cancer Research SunSmart campaign: www.sunsmart.org.uk

Child Accident Prevention Trust: www.capt.org.uk

Living with Reflux: www.livingwithreflux.org

The Meningitis Trust: Helpline 0800 028 18 28; www.meningitis-trust.org

Royal Society for the Prevention of Accidents: www.rospa.com

Which?: www.which.co.uk

Breastfeeding

Association of Breastfeeding Mothers: Helpline 08444 122 949; www.abm.me.uk

Baby Café: www.thebabycafe.org

La Leche League: Helpline 0845 120 2918; www.laleche.org.uk

National Breastfeeding Network: Supporter line 0300 100 0210; www.breastfeedingnetwork.org.uk

National Breastfeeding Helpline: 0300 100 0212; www.nationalbreastfeedinghelpline.org.uk

National Childbirth Trust: Breastfeeding helpline 0300 330 0771; Breast pump hire line 0300 330 0770; www.nct.org.uk

Post-natal support

Cry-sis: Helpline 08451 228 669; www.cry-sis.org.uk

Doula UK: www.doula.org.uk

Family Lives: Helpline 0808 800 2222; www.familylives.org.uk

Independent Midwives UK: 0845 4600 105; www.independentmidwives.org.uk

Midwives Online: www.midwivesonline.com

Weaning

Baby-led weaning: www.babyledweaning.com

British Dietetic Association: www.bda.uk.com

Emotional well-being

Anxiety UK: Helpline 08444 775 774; www.anxietyuk.org.uk

Association for Improvements in the Maternity Services (AIMS): Helpline 0300 365 0663; www.aims.org.uk

The Association for Post-Natal Illness: Helpline 020 7386 0868; www.apni.org

Birth Trauma Association: www.birthtraumaassociation.org.uk

British Association for Behavioural and Cognitive Psychotherapies (BABCP): www.babcp.com

British Association for Counselling and Psychotherapy (BACP): www.bacp.co.uk

Mind: Info line 0300 123 3393; www.mind.org.uk

Patient Advice and Liaison Service (PALS): www.pals.nhs.uk

Perinatal Illness UK: www.pni-uk.com

Alternative and holistic treatments

The Aroma Therapy Council: www.aromatherapycouncil.co.uk

Association of Reflexologists: www.reflexology.org

British Acupuncture Council: www.acupuncture.org.uk

Craniosacral therapy: www.craniosacral.co.uk

Hypnotherapy UK: www.hypnotherapists.org.uk

The Reiki Association: www.reikiassociation.org.uk

The Society of Homeopaths: www.homeopathy-soh.org

The Sutherland Society – the UK organisation for cranial osteopathy: www.cranial.org.uk

Love and sex

The Couple Connection: www.thecoupleconnection.net

Family Planning Association: Helpline 0845 122 8690; www.fpa.org.uk

Relate: www.relate.org.uk; www.relateforparents.org.uk

Going back to work

Direct Gov: Child benefit helpline 0845 3021 444; Tax credit helpline 0345 300 3900; www.directgov.co.uk; www.payingforchildcare.org.uk

Next Step – for careers and retraining advice: 0800 100 900; www.nextstep.direct.gov.uk

Working Families: Parents and carers' helpline 0800 013 0313; www.workingfamilies.org.uk

Other helpful websites

www.mumandworking.co.uk

www.jobs4mothers.com

www.familyfriendlyworking.co.uk

www.workingmums.co.uk

www.netmums.co.uk

Childcare

Daycare Trust: www.daycaretrust.org.uk

Grandparents Association: Helpline 0845 434 9585; www.grandparents-association.org.uk

Nanny Tax: www.nannytax.co.uk

National Childminding Association: 0845 880 0044; www.ncma.org.uk

National Day Nurseries Association: 01484 40 70 70; www.ndna.org.uk

Ofsted: www.ofsted.gov.uk

Voice the Union (for information about nannies): 01332 372337; www.voicetheunion.org.uk

Miscellaneous

Go Real, the real nappy information service: www.goreal.org.uk

Recommended first-time mum bloggers

Charlee C: www.bumpdiaries.com

Molly F: www.mothersalwaysright.wordpress.com

Ruth D: www.dorkymum.wordpress.com

Lucy R: www.dearbeautifulboy.com

Index

GREAT TALES FROM ENGLISH HISTORY

GREAT TALES FROM ENGLISH HISTORY

Chaucer to the Glorious Revolution
1387 - 1688

Robert Lacey

CHIVERS

British Library Cataloguing in Publication Data available

This Large Print edition published by BBC Audiobooks Ltd, Bath, 2005.
Published by arrangement with Time Warner Books Ltd.

U.K. Hardcover ISBN 1 4056 3236 4
U.K. Softcover ISBN 1 4056 3237 2

Copyright © 2004 Robert Lacey

The moral right of the author has been asserted.

All rights reserved.

8396376

942 LAC

LUTON LIBRARIES BOROUGH COUNCIL

Printed and bound in Great Britain by
Antony Rowe Ltd., Chippenham, Wiltshire

FOR SCARLETT

CONTENTS

MAP OF ENGLAND 1387–1688
(SEE MAP ON PAGE XII FOR BATTLES)

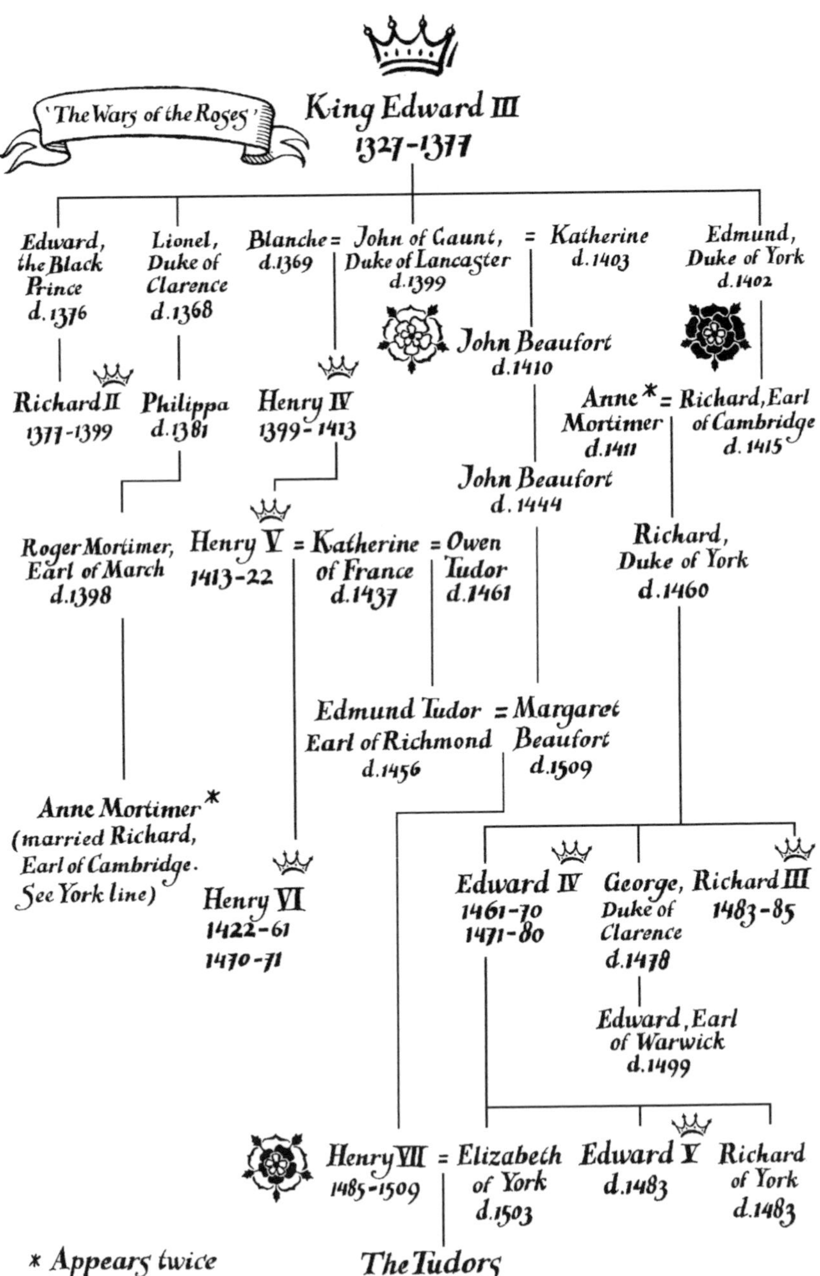

SIMPLIFIED FAMILY TREE, SHOWING THE HOUSES OF YORK, LANCASTER AND TUDOR

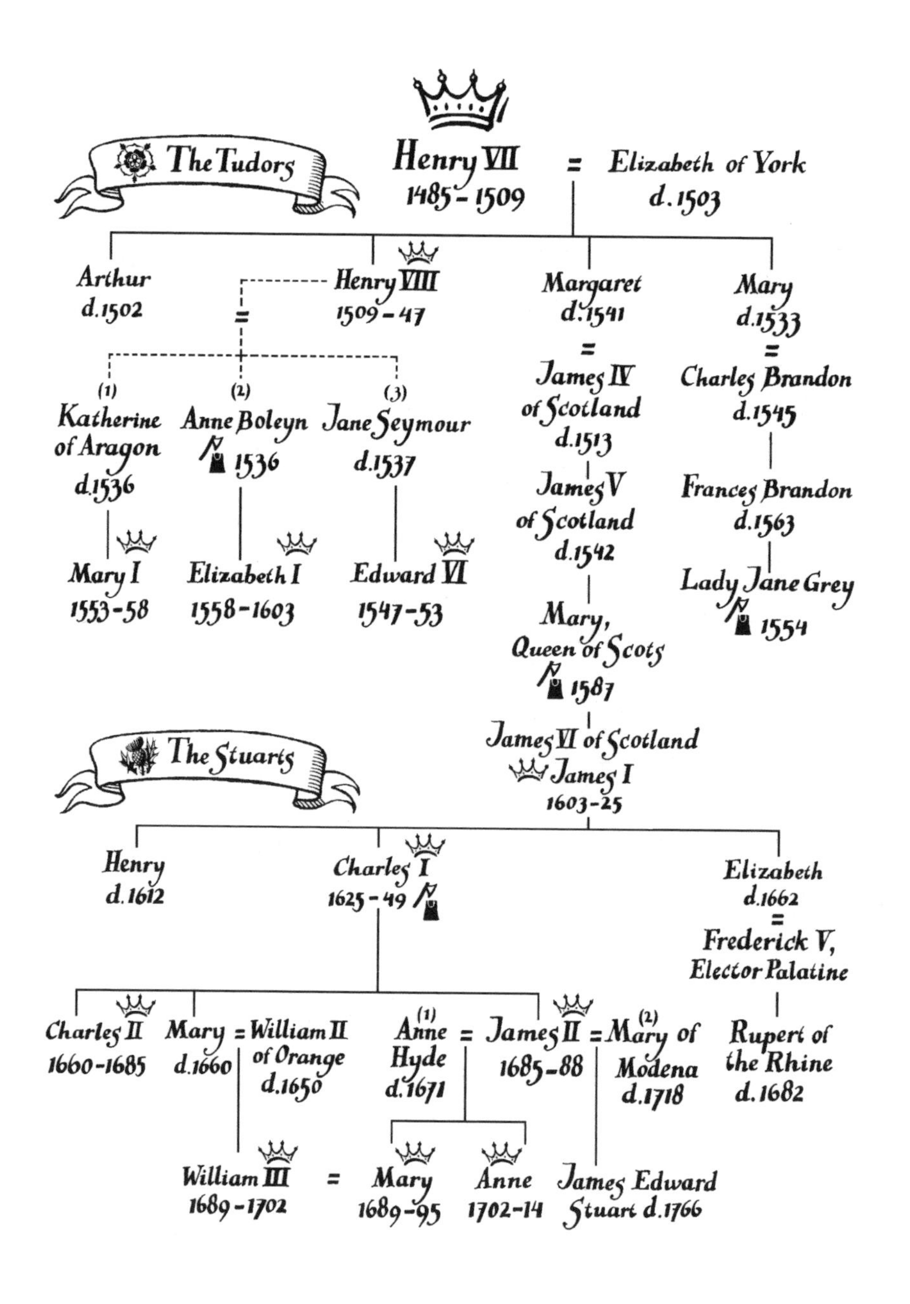

SIMPLIFIED FAMILY TREE OF ENGLAND'S TUDOR AND STUART MONARCHS

MAP OF ENGLAND AND NORTH-WEST EUROPE 1387–1688

HISTORY IN OUR HEADS

For most of us, the history in our heads is a colourful and chaotic kaleidoscope of images—Sir Walter Ralegh laying down his cloak in the puddle, Isaac Newton watching the apple fall, Geoffrey Chaucer setting off for Canterbury with his fellow pilgrims in the dappled medieval sunshine. We are not always sure if the stories embodied by these images are entirely true—or if, in some cases, they are true at all. But they contain a truth, and their narrative power is the secret of their survival over the centuries. You will find these images in the pages that follow—just as colourful as you remember, I hope, but also closer to the available facts, with the connections between them just a little less chaotic.

Our very first historians were storytellers —our best historians still are—and in many languages 'story' and 'history' remain the same word. Our brains are wired to make sense of the world through narrative—what came first and what came next—and once we know the sequence, we can start to work out the how and why. We peer down the kaleidoscope in order to enjoy the sparkling fragments, but as we turn it we also look for the reassuring discipline of pattern. We seek to make sense of the scanty remnants of the lives that preceded ours on the planet.

The lessons we derive from history inevitably resonate with our own code of values. When we go back to the past in search of heroes and heroines, we are looking for personalities to inspire and comfort us, to confirm our view of how things should be. That is why every generation needs to rewrite its history, and if you are a cynic you may conclude that a nation's history is simply its own deluded and self-serving view of its past.

Great Tales from English History is not cynical: it is written by an eternal optimist—albeit one who views the evidence with a sceptical eye. In these books I have endeavoured to do more than just retell the old stories; I have tried to test the accuracy of each tale against the latest research and historical thinking, and to set them in a sequence from which meaning can emerge.

The earlier volume, *Cheddar Man to the Peasants' Revolt,* showed how the beginnings of our history were shaped and reshaped by invasion—Roman, Anglo-Saxon, Danish, Norman. And that was just the armies. The Venerable Bede, our first English historian, described the invasion of the new religion, which, in AD 597, so scared King Ethelbert of Kent that he insisted on meeting the Christian missionaries out of doors, lest he be trapped by their alien magic. We met Richard the Lionheart, England's French-speaking hero-king, who spent only six months living in England and adopted our Turkish-born patron saint, St George, while he was fighting the Crusades. Then, as now, we discovered, some of the things that most define England have come from abroad. Magna Carta was written in Latin, and Parliament, our national 'talking-place', derives its name from the French.

This volume opens in the aftermath of another invasion—by a black rat with an infected flea upon its back. In 1348 and in a succession of subsequent outbreaks, the Black Death wiped out nearly half of England's five million people. Could a society undergo a more ghastly trauma? Yet there were dividends from that disaster: a smaller workforce meant higher wages; fewer purchasers per acre brought property prices down. In 1381 the leaders of the so-called 'Peasants' Revolt' with which we concluded the earlier volume were men of a certain substance. They were taxpayers, the solid, middling folk who have been the backbone of all the profound revolutions of history. Later in this volume we will see their descendants enlisting in an army that would behead a king.

Changing economic circumstances have a way of shaping beliefs, and so it was in the fourteenth century. John Wycliffe told the survivors of plague-stricken England that they should seek a more direct relationship with their God, read His word in their own language, and not rely upon the priest. Wycliffe's persecuted followers, the Lollards, or 'mumblers', as they were called by their detractors, in derision of their privately mouthed prayers, would provide a persistent underground presence in the century and a half that followed. If invasion was the theme of the previous volume, dissent—spiritual, personal and, in due course, political—will take centre stage in the pages that follow.

Sir Walter Ralegh, one of the heroes of this volume—and one of mine—is said to have given up writing his *History of the World* when he looked out of his cell in the Tower of London one day and saw two men arguing in the courtyard. Try as he might, he could not work out what they were quarrelling about: he could not hear them; could only see their angry gestures. So there and then he abandoned his ambitious historical enterprise, concluding that you can never establish the full truth about anything.

In this sobering realisation, Sir Walter was displaying unusual humility—both in himself and as a member of the historical fraternity: the things we do not know about history far outnumber those that we do. But the fragments that survive are precious and bright. They offer us glimpses of drama, humour, frustration, humanity, the banal and the extraordinary—the stuff of life. There are still a good few tales to tell . . .

GEOFFREY CHAUCER AND THE MOTHER TONGUE

1387

Whan that Aprill with his shoures soote
The droghte of March hath perced to the roote . . .

Geoffrey Chaucer's *Canterbury Tales* opens on a green spring morning beside the River Thames, towards the end of the fourteenth century. Birds are singing, the sap is rising, and a group of travellers gathers in the Tabard Inn—one of the rambling wooden hostelries with stables and dormitory-like bedrooms round a courtyard, that clustered around the southern end of London Bridge. At first hearing, Chaucer's 'English' sounds foreign, but in its phrasing we can detect the rhythms and wording of our own speech, especially if we read it aloud, as people usually did six hundred years ago: 'Thanne longen folk to goon on pilgrimages . . .'

The pilgrimage was the package holiday of the Middle Ages, and Chaucer imagines a group of holidaymakers in search of country air, leisurely exercise and spiritual refreshment at England's premier tourist attraction, the tomb of St Thomas Becket at Canterbury: a brawny miller tootling on his bagpipes; a grey-eyed prioress daintily feeding titbits to her lapdogs; a poor knight whose chain mail has left smudgings of rust on his tunic. To read Geoffrey Chaucer is to be transported back in time, to feel the skin and clothes—and sometimes, even, to smell the leek- or onion-laden breath—of people as they went about their daily business in what we call the Middle Ages. For them, of course, it was 'now', one of the oldest words in the English language.

The host of the Tabard, the innkeeper Harry Bailey, suggests a story-telling competition to enliven the journey—free supper to the winner—and so we meet the poor knight, the dainty prioress and the miller, along with a merchant, a sea captain, a cook, and twenty other deeply believable characters plucked from the three or four million or so inhabitants of King Richard II's England. Chaucer includes himself as one of the pilgrims, offering to entertain the company with a rhyming tale of his own. But scarcely has he started when he is cut short by Harry the host:

'By God,' quod he, 'for pleynly, at a word,
Thy drasty ryming is nat worth a toord!'

It is lines like these that have won Chaucer his fondly rude niche in the English folk memory. People's eyes light up at the mention of *The Canterbury Tales*, as they recall embarrassed schoolteachers struggling to explain words like 'turd' and to bypass tales of backsides being stuck out of windows. 'Please, sir, what is this "something" that is "rough and hairy"?'

In one passage Chaucer describes a friar (or religious brother, from the French word frère) who, while visiting hell in the course of a dream, is pleased to detect no trace of other friars, and complacently concludes that all friars must go to heaven.

'Oh *no*, we've got millions of them here!' an angel corrects him, pointing to the Devil's massively broad tail:

'Hold up thy tayl, thou Satanas!' quod he,
'Shewe forth thyn ers, and lat the frere se . . .'

Whereupon twenty thousand friars swarm out

of the Devil's *ers* and fly around hell like angry bees, before creeping back inside their warm and cosy home for eternity.

In gathering for a pilgrimage, Chaucer's travellers were taking part in a Church-inspired ritual. But the poet's message was that the Church—the massive nationalised industry that ran the schools and hospitals of medieval England as well as its worship—was in serious trouble. While his imaginary company of pilgrims included a pious Oxford cleric and a parish priest who was a genuinely good shepherd to his flock, it also included men who were only too happy to make a corrupt living out of God's service on earth: a worldly monk who liked to feast on roast swan; a pimpled 'Summoner' who took bribes from sinners *not* to summon them to the church courts; and a 'Pardoner' who sold bogus relics like the veil of the Virgin Mary (actually an old pillowcase) and a rubble of pig's bones that he labelled as belonging to various saints. Buy one of these, was the message of this medieval insurance salesman, and you would go straight to heaven.

Chaucer humorously but unsparingly describes a country where almost everything is for sale. Four decades earlier England's population had been halved by the onslaught of the 'Black Death'—the bubonic plague that would return several more times before the end of the century—and the consequence of this appalling tragedy had been a sharp-elbowed economic scramble among the survivors. Wages had risen, plague-cleared land was going cheap. For a dozen years before he wrote *The Canterbury Tales* Chaucer had lived over the Aldgate, or 'Old Gate', the most easterly of the six gates in London's fortified wall, and from his windows in the arch he had been able to look down on the changing scene. In 1381 the angry men of Essex had come and gone through the Aldgate, waving their billhooks—the 'mad multitude' known to history as the ill-fated Peasants' Revolt. During the plague years the city's iron-wheeled refuse carts had rumbled beneath the poet's floorboards with their bouncing heaps of corpses, heading for the limepits.

Chaucer paints the keen detail of this reviving community in a newly revived language—the spoken English that the Norman Conquest had threatened to suppress. Written between 1387 and 1400, the year of Chaucer's death, *The Canterbury Tales* is one of the earliest pieces of English that is intelligible to a modern ear. For three hundred years English had endured among the ordinary people, and particularly among the gentry. Even in French-speaking noble households Anglo-Saxon wives and local nursemaids had chattered to children in the native language. English had survived because it was literally the mother tongue, and it was in these post-plague years that it reasserted itself. In 1356 the Mayor of London decreed that English should be the language of council meetings, and in 1363 the Lord Chancellor made a point of opening Parliament in English—not, as had previously been the case, in the language of the enemy across the Channel.

Geoffrey Chaucer's cheery and companionable writing sets out the ideas that are the themes of this volume. In the pages that follow we shall trace the unstoppable spread of the English language—carried from England in the course of the next few centuries to the far side of the world. We shall see men and women reject the commerce of the old religion, while making fortunes from the new. And as they change their views about God, they will also change their views profoundly about the authority of kings and earthly power. They will sharpen their words and start freeing their minds—and in embarking upon that, they will also begin the uncertain process of freeing themselves.

THE DEPOSING OF KING RICHARD II

1399

The last time we met Richard II he was a boy of fourteen, facing down Wat Tyler and his rebels at the climax of the Peasants' Revolt. 'Sirs, will you shoot your king? I will be your captain!' the young man had cried in June 1381 as the 'mad multitude' massed angrily on the grass at Smithfield outside the city walls. His domineering uncle John of Gaunt was away from London, negotiating a truce in Scotland, and Richard's advisers had shown themselves wavering. But the boy king had said his prayers and ridden out to face the brandished billhooks.

An uncomplicated faith brought Richard II a brave and famous triumph, and it was small wonder that he should grow up with an exalted idea of himself and his powers. While waiting for vespers, the evening prayer, the young man who had been treated as a king from the age of ten liked to sit enthroned for hours, doing nothing much more than wearing his crown and 'speaking to no man'. People who entered his presence were expected to bow the knee and lower the eyes. While previous English kings had been content to be addressed as 'My Lord', now the titles of 'Highness' and 'Majesty' were demanded.

Richard came to believe that he was ordained of God. He had himself painted like Christ in Majesty, a golden icon glowing on his throne—the earliest surviving portrait that we have of any English king. When the King of Armenia came to the capital, Richard ordered that Westminster Abbey be opened in the middle of the night and proudly showed his visitor his crown, his sceptre and the other symbols of regality by the flicker of candlelight.

But Richard's public grandeur was a mask for insecurity. The King suffered from a stammer, and by the time he was fully grown, at nearly six feet tall, his fits of anger could be terrifying. Cheeks flushed, and shaking his yellow Plantagenet hair, on one occasion Richard drew his sword on a noble who dared to cross him, and struck another across the cheek. When Parliament was critical of his advisers, he declared that he 'would not even dismiss a scullion' from his kitchens at their request. When Parliament was compliant, he proclaimed proudly that he had no need of Lords or Commons, since the laws of England were 'in his mouth or his breast'.

Richard's dream was to rule without having to answer to anyone, and to that end he made peace with France, calling a truce in the series of draining conflicts that we know as the Hundred Years War. No fighting meant no extra taxes, calculated Richard—and that meant he might never have to call Parliament again.

Some modern historians have frowned on Richard II's ambition to rule without Parliament. They condemn his attempts to interrupt the traditional story of England's march towards democracy—only six Parliaments met during his reign of twenty-two years. But it is by no means certain that Richard's subjects saw this as regrettable. On the contrary. The summoning of Parliament was invariably followed by the appearance of tax assessors in the towns and villages. So there was much to be said for a king who left his people in peace and who managed to 'live of his own'—without levying taxes.

Richard's gilded, image-dazzled style, however, won him few friends. He made no pretence to love the common man, and it was his attempt to 'live of his own' that brought about his downfall. When John of Gaunt died in 1399, aged fifty-eight, Richard could not resist the temptation to seize his uncle's lands. Gaunt's Duchy of Lancaster estates were the largest single landholding in England, and his son Henry Bolingbroke had recently been sent into exile, banished for ten years following a dispute with another nobleman.

Bolingbroke, named after the Lincolnshire castle where he was born in 1366, was the same age as Richard. The two cousins had grown up at court together, sharing the frightening experience of being inside the Tower of London at one stage of the Peasants' Revolt as the angry rebels had flocked outside the walls, yelling and hurling abuse. Some rioters who broke through managed to capture Henry, and he had been lucky to escape the fate of the Archbishop of Canterbury, who was dragged outside to be beaten, then beheaded.

Henry was not one jot less pious than his royal cousin. In 1390, aged twenty-four, he had been on crusade to fight alongside Germany's Teutonic Knights as they took Christianity to Lithuania, and in 1392 he travelled on a pilgrimage to Jerusalem. A tough character, the leading jouster of his generation, he was not the sort to surrender his family inheritance without a fight. Land was sacred to a medieval baron, and many magnates supported

Bolingbroke's quarrel with the King. No one's estates were safe if the great Duchy of Lancaster could be seized at the royal whim.

When Richard decided to go campaigning against Irish rebels in the summer of 1399, his cousin grabbed his chance. Bolingbroke had spent his nine-month exile in France. Now he landed in Yorkshire, to be welcomed by the Earl of Northumberland and his son Henry 'Hotspur', the great warriors of the north. Henry had won control of most of central and eastern England, and was in a position to claim much more than his family's estate. Richard returned from Ireland to find himself facing a coup.

'Now I can see the end of my days coming,' the King mournfully declared as he stood on the ramparts of Flint Castle in north Wales early in August 1399, watching the advance of his cousin's army along the coast.

Captured, escorted to London and imprisoned in the Tower, Richard resisted three attempts to make him renounce in Henry's favour, until he was finally worn down—though he refused to hand the crown directly to his supplanter. Instead, he defiantly placed the gold circlet on God's earth, symbolically resigning his sovereignty to his Maker.

Sent north to the gloomy fortress of Pontefract in Yorkshire, Richard survived only a few months. A Christmas rising by his supporters made him too dangerous to keep alive. According to Shakespeare's play Richard II, the deposed monarch met his end heroically in a scuffle in which he killed two of his would-be assassins before being himself struck down. But the truth was less theatrical. The official story was that Richard went on hunger strike, so that the opening that led to his stomach gradually contracted. His supporters maintained that the gaolers deliberately deprived him of food. Either way, the thirty-three-year-old ex-monarch starved to death. According to one account, in his hunger he gnawed desperately at his own arm.

Of comfort no man speak . . .
Let us sit upon the ground
And tell sad stories of the death
of kings!

Writing two hundred years later, Shakespeare drew a simple moral from the tale of Richard II. Richard may have been a flawed character, but the deposition of an anointed monarch upset the ordained order of things. The playwright knew what would happen next—the generations of conflict between the families of Richard and Henry that have come to be known as the 'Wars of the Roses'.

‘TURN AGAIN, DICK WHITTINGTON!’

1399

As Henry IV took control of his new kingdom at the end of 1399, he pointedly promised that, unlike his wilful predecessor, he would rule with the guidance of ‘wise and discreet’ persons. Richard II had been criticised for shunning the advice of his counsellors. He was nicknamed ‘Richard the Redeless’—the ‘uncounselled’. So Henry made sure that the advisers he summoned to his early council were a sober mixture of bishops and barons.

Then on 8 December that year the new King sent for a different sort of expert—a merchant and businessman, the first ever to sit on the

Royal Council. Sir Richard Whittington was a cloth trader and moneylender from the City of London, who had served as Mayor of the City and who would, in fact, be elected Mayor no less than three times.

'Oh yes he did! Oh no he didn't!' Every Christmas the adventures of Dick Whittington still inspire pantomime audiences in theatres and church halls around the country. We see Whittington, usually played by a pretty girl in tights, striding off from Gloucestershire to seek his fortune in London, only to leave soon afterwards, dispirited to discover that the streets are not paved with gold. But sitting down to rest with his cat, the only friend he has managed to make on his travels, Dick hears the bells of London pealing out behind him.

'Turn again, Dick Whittington,' they seem to be calling, 'thrice Lord Mayor of London!'

Reinvigorated, Dick returns to the city, where he gets a job in the house of Alderman Fitzwarren and falls in love with Fitzwarren's beautiful daughter, Alice. Disaster strikes when Dick is falsely accused of stealing a valuable necklace. So, deciding he had better make himself scarce, he and his cat stow away on one of the alderman's ships trading silks and satins with the Barbary Coast. There Puss wins favour with the local sultan by ridding his palace of rats, and Dick is rewarded with sackfuls of gold and jewels, which he bears home in triumph—more than enough to replace the necklace, which, it turns out, had been stolen by Puss's mortal enemy, King Rat. Alice and Dick are married, and Dick goes on to fulfil the bells' prophecy, becoming thrice Lord Mayor of London.

Much of this is true. Young Richard Whittington, a third son with no chance of an inheritance, did leave the village of Pauntley in Gloucestershire sometime in the 1360s to seek his fortune in London. And there he was indeed apprenticed to one Sir Hugh Fitzwarren, a mercer who dealt in precious cloth, some of it imported from the land of the Berbers, the Barbary Coast of North Africa. Dick became a mercer himself (the word derives from the Latin *merx*, or wares, the same root that gives us 'merchant'). He supplied sumptuous cloth to both Richard II and Henry IV, providing two of Henry's daughters with cloth of gold for their wedding trousseaus. He also became a friendly bank manager to the royal family, extending generous overdrafts whenever they were strapped for cash. In the decades around 1400 Dick Whittington made no less than fifty-three loans to Richard and Henry, and also to Henry's son Henry V. He routinely took royal jewels as security, and on one occasion lost a necklace, whose value he had to repay.

Dick was elected mayor of London in 1397, 1406 and 1419. With the populist flair that a mayor needs to go down in history, he campaigned against watered beer, greedy brewers who overcharged, and the destruction of old walls and monuments. There was a 'green' touch to his removal from the Thames of illegal 'fish weirs', the standing traps of basketwork or netting that threatened fish stocks when their apertures were too small and trapped even the tiniest tiddlers.

Less kind to the river, perhaps, was the money that he left in his will for the building of 'Whittington's Longhouse'. This monster public lavatory contained 128 seats, half for men and half for women, in two very long rows with no partitions and no privacy. It overhung a gully near modern Cannon Street that was flushed by the tide. Dying childless in 1423, Dick spread his vast fortune across a generous range of London almshouses, hospitals and charities.

The trouble is the cat. There is not the slightest evidence that Dick Whittington ever owned any pets, let alone a skilled ratter who might have won the favour of the Sultan of Barbary. Puss does not enter the story for another two hundred years, and was probably introduced into the plot by mummers in early pantomimes.

'To Southwark Fair,' wrote Samuel Pepys in his diary for 21 September 1668. 'Very dirty, and there saw the puppet show of Whittington which was pretty to see.'

Stories of clever cats are found in the earliest

Egyptian and Hindu myths; Portuguese, Spanish and Italian fables tell of men whose fortunes are made by their cats. Puss in Boots, a rival pantomime, also celebrates the exploits of a trickster cat that magically enriches his impoverished master.

Experts call this a 'migratory myth'. Blending the cosy notion of a furry, four-legged partner with the story of the advancement of hard-nosed Richard Whittington, England's biggest moneylender, took the edge off people's envy at the rise of the merchant class in the years after the Black Death—these new magnates who mattered in the reign of King Money. And when it comes to our own day, Dick's tale of luck and ambition provides a timeless stereotype for the pop stars and celebrities who play him in panto: the classless, self-made wannabes who leave their life in the sticks and reinvent themselves in the big city.

HENRY IV AND HIS EXTRA-VIRGIN OIL

1399

When Parliament first welcomed Henry IV as king in September 1399 with cries of 'Yes, Yes, Yes', he told them to shout it again. The first round of yeses had not been loud enough for him. At that moment the deposed Richard II, just a mile or so down-river in the Tower of London, was still alive. The new King quite understood, he told the company who assembled that day in Westminster, that some of them might have reservations.

This may have been a joke on Henry IV's part—he had a self-deprecating sense of humour. But the fact that he had usurped the throne was to be the theme of his reign. For his coronation in October, he introduced a new 'imperial' style of crown consisting of a circlet surmounted by arches that English kings and queens have worn ever since. He commissioned a book to emphasise the significance of England's coronation regalia—and he had himself anointed with an especially potent and prestigious oil that Richard II had located in his increasing obsession with majesty. The Virgin Mary herself, it was said, had given it to St Thomas Becket.

The fancy oil delivered its own verdict on the usurper—an infestation of headlice that afflicted Henry for months. He spent the first half of his reign fighting off challenges, particularly from the fractious Percy family of Northumberland who plotted against him in the north and were behind no less than three dangerous rebellions. In Wales the English King had to contend with the defiance of the charismatic Owain Glyndwr, who kept the red dragon fluttering from castles and misty Celtic mountain-tops.

Henry defeated his enemies in a run of brisk campaigns that confirmed his prowess as a military leader. But he was not able to enjoy his triumphs. In 1406, at the age of forty, the stocky and heavy-jowled monarch was struck down by a mystery illness that made it difficult for him to travel or to communicate verbally.

Modern doctors think that Henry must have suffered a series of strokes. For the rest of his reign he was disabled in both mind and body, though he went to great lengths to conceal his infirmity. Letters went out to the local sheriffs ordering the arrest of those who spread rumours of his sickness, while his bishops received letters requesting prayers to be said for his physical recovery. Depressed and speaking of himself as 'a sinful wretch', Henry came to believe that his salvation rested in a repeat of his youthful pilgrimage to Jerusalem.

One cause of his melancholy was the conflicts that arose with his eldest son, Henry of Monmouth. A brave and forceful warrior who fought alongside his father against the Percys and took charge of the campaign against Owain Glyndwr, 'Prince Hal' was not the dissolute hell-raiser portrayed by Shakespeare. But he was an impatient critic of the ailing King. In 1410 he elbowed aside Henry's advisers to take control of the Royal Council for a spell—it seems possible he was even pushing his father to abdicate.

In 1413 the old King collapsed while at prayer in Westminster Abbey. Carried to the abbot's quarters and placed on a straw mattress beside the fire, he fell into a deep sleep, with his crown placed, as was the medieval custom, on the pillow beside him. Thinking he had breathed his last, his attendants covered his face with a linen cloth, while the Prince of Wales picked up the crown and left the room.

Suddenly the King woke. As he sat up, the cloth fell from his face, and he demanded to know what had happened to the crown. Summoned to his father's bedside, the prince did not beat about the bush.

'Sir,' he said, 'to mine and all men's judgement, you seemed dead in this world. So I, as your next heir apparent, took that as mine own.'

'What right could you have to the crown,' retorted Henry wryly, 'when I have none?'

Richard's usurper never lost his sense of guilt—nor his sense of humour. Looking round the room, the King asked where he was, and was told that he had been brought to the Jerusalem Chamber.

'Praise be to God,' he said, 'for it was foretold me long ago that I would die in Jerusalem.'

WE HAPPY FEW— THE BATTLE OF AZINCOURT

1415

The new King Henry V was a twenty-five-year-old in a hurry. He had been impatient with his disabled father, and he was impatient with just about everyone else. Watching a Lollard blacksmith suffering the recently introduced penalty of being burned at the stake, he had the man dragged out of the flames, then invited him to recant. When the blacksmith refused, the prince thrust him back on to the pyre.

Henry saw himself as God's soldier, and he had a soldier's haircut to match: shaved back and sides with a dark-brown pudding-basin of hair perched on top. This pallid young warrior, with his large, fiercely bright, almond-shaped eyes, brought intense religious conviction to England's long-running quarrel with France.

'My hope is in God,' he declared as he stood with his troops in the pouring rain on the night of Thursday 24 October, 1415. 'If my cause is just I shall prevail, whatever the size of my following.'

He was addressing his small, damp and beleaguered army outside the village of Agincourt in northern France. Here the English had been disconcerted to find their route back to Calais blocked by an immensely larger French army. Modern estimates put the English at 6000, facing as many as 20,000 or even 25,000. Henry's cause looked hopeless. A large number of his men were suffering from dysentery, the bloody diarrhoea that was a major hazard of pre-penicillin warfare. The French were so confident that night that they threw dice, wagering on the rich ransoms they would be extorting for the English nobility they would capture next day.

In contrast to the rowdy chatter and singing around the French campfires, there was silence in the English ranks, where Henry walked among his intimidated little army, doing his best to raise their morale.

'He made fine speeches everywhere,' wrote Jehan de Wavrin, a French knight who fought in the battle and collected eyewitness accounts of how Henry set about encouraging his men:

> *They should remember [the King said] that they were born of the realm of England where they had been brought up, and where their fathers, mothers, wives, and children were living; wherefore it became them to exert themselves that they might return thither with great joy and approval . . . And further he told them and explained how the French were boasting that they would cut off three fingers of the right hand of all the archers that should be taken prisoners, to the end that neither man nor horse should ever again be killed with their arrows.*

Archers made up nearly four thousand of the English force—double the number of men-at-arms—and the English archers were crucial to what happened next day.

The French had chosen the ground on which they wished to fight—an open field, bordered by thick woods. But as their knights advanced in their heavy armour, the effect of the woods was to funnel them into the English bowmen's line of fire. The torrential rain the night before had turned the ground into mud, so the French slithered and stumbled, falling in their dozens beneath the fusillades of arrows. The white-feathered quills littered the battlefield, protruding from the bodies of both horses and men. It looked as if snow had fallen, according to one observer.

At the end of the encounter the English casualties were minimal, no more than two hundred. By contrast, more than seven thousand French lay dead, though many of their nobility died in circumstances their descendants would not forget. Under the pressure of a surprise counterattack, Henry ordered the summary execution of several hundred French noblemen who had surrendered but had not been disarmed. He considered them a threat. But in France to this day, the Battle of Azincourt—as the French call it—is remembered for this shaming betrayal of the traditional rules of chivalry. Modern visitors to the area are told that the battle saw the death not just of thousands of men, but of *'un certain idéal de combat'*—a foretaste of modern mass warfare.

For England, Agincourt has inspired quite a different national myth. London welcomed Henry home with drums, trumpets and tambourines and choirs of children dressed as angels. Flocks of birds were released into the air and gigantic carved effigies spelled out the meaning of the victory—a David defeating Goliath.

'We few, we happy few, we band of brothers', were the words with which Shakespeare would later enshrine Agincourt's model of bravery against the odds—the notion that the English actually do best when they are outnumbered.

This phenomenon came to full flower in 1940 during the Battle of Britain, when Britain faced the might of Germany alone and Churchill spoke so movingly of the 'few'. To further fortify the bulldog spirit, the Ministry of Information financed the actor Laurence Olivier to film a Technicolor version of Agincourt as depicted in Shakespeare's Henry V. 'Dedicated to the Airborne Regiments', read a screen title in medieval script as the opening credits began to roll.

Henry V's own patriotism was deeply infused with religion. Dreaming of England and France unified beneath God, he had crusader ambitions similar to those of Richard the Lionheart, the warrior king he so resembled in charisma and ferocity. Like the Lionheart, Henry could not keep away from battle and, like him, he was struck down, young and unnecessarily, by a hazard of the battlefield when besieging a minor castle in France. Gangrene claimed Richard. Henry was felled by dysentery, contracted at the siege of Meaux. His boiled and flesh-free bones were borne back to England in a coffin topped with his effigy—a death mask of his head, face and upper body that had been moulded in steamed leather.

Just before he died Henry had called for charts of the harbours of Syria and Egypt, and was reading a history of the first Crusade. He was getting ready for his great expedition to

Palestine. His wish to link England and France in this pious joint venture went beyond the simple jingoism of a modern soccer or rugby crowd. But one thing that modern fans might share with holy Henry is the two-fingered, 'Up yours' V-sign, directed derisively at the enemy. Possibly originating from the gesture presumed to have been made by fifteenth-century archers who wished to demonstrate that their bowstring fingers had not been cut off, it is known today as 'the Agincourt salute'.

JOAN OF ARC, THE MAID OF ORLEANS

1429

Joan of Arc was three years old when Henry V won his famous victory in the mud of Azincourt. She was the daughter of a prosperous farmer whose solid stone-built house can still be seen in the village of Domrémy, near the River Meuse in Lorraine, France's eastern border country.

Today the border is with Germany. In 1415, it was with the independent and ambitious Duchy of Burgundy, whose territory stretched down from the prosperous Low Countries towards Switzerland. Joan's village was right in the path of the Burgundians when they came raiding, often in alliance with the English, as the two countries carved out conquests from the incompetently governed territories of France.

Henry V's famous victories, which continued after Agincourt, owed much to the weakness of France's rulers. The French king Charles VI suffered from long periods of madness, when he would run howling like a wolf down the corridors of his palaces. One of his fantasies was to believe himself made of glass and to suspect anyone who came too near of trying to push him over and shatter him. His son Charles, who bore the title of Dauphin, had a phobia about entering houses, believing they would fall down on him (as one once did in the town of La Rochelle).

The title of Dauphin, meaning literally 'dolphin', is the French equivalent of Prince of Wales, a title relating to the heir to the throne. England's heir had three feathers on his crest—the banner of France's sported a playful dolphin. But in the early 1400s the shifty and hesitant Dauphin of France did no credit to the bright and intuitive animal whose name he bore. The Dauphin's court was notorious throughout Europe for harbouring such undesirables as the paedophile Gilles de Rais—the model for the legendary Bluebeard—in whose castle were found the remains of more than fifty children.

France degenerated into civil war. King and

Dauphin were at loggerheads, and England reaped the benefit in 1420 when the unstable Charles VI disinherited his equally unbalanced son. On 20 May, in the Treaty of Troyes, the French king took the humiliating step of appointing England's Henry V as 'regent and heir' to his kingdom, marrying his daughter Catherine to the English warrior monarch. So five years after Agincourt, Henry V had within his grasp the glorious prospect of becoming the first ever King of both France and England—only to die just six weeks before his father-in-law, in August 1422, leaving his title to the long-dreamed-of double monarchy to his nine-month-old son.

It was three years later that the thirteen-year-old Joan first heard God talking to her in her home village of Domrémy.

'And came this voice,' she later remembered, 'about the hour of noon, in the summertime, in my father's garden . . . I heard the voice on the right-hand side, towards the church, and rarely do I hear it without a brightness. This brightness comes from the same side as the voice is heard. It is usually a great light.'

Anyone today who reported hearing voices would probably be sent to a psychiatrist and might well be diagnosed as schizophrenic. But Joan had no doubt who was talking to her. 'After I had thrice heard this voice, I knew that it was the voice of an angel. This voice has always guided me well and I have always understood it clearly.'

The fascination of Joan's story is that a teenage girl should have persuaded ever-widening circles of people to agree with her. 'You are she,' said her angel, 'whom the King of Heaven has chosen to bring reparation to the kingdom.'

It was just what a divided and demoralised France needed to hear. After months of badgering, Joan finally won an audience with the Dauphin, and she galvanised the normally melancholic prince, who was now technically Charles VII but had so far lacked the push to get himself crowned. Dressed in men's clothes, Joan had been led into court as a freak show. But the Dauphin was inspired. After hearing her, recalled one eyewitness, the would-be king 'appeared radiant'. He sent the girl to be cross-examined by a commission of learned clerics, and she confronted them with the same self-confidence.

'Do you believe in God?' asked one theologian.

'Yes,' she retorted, 'better than you.'

The practical proof of Joan's divine mandate came in the spring of 1429 when, aged seventeen, she joined the French army at the town of Orleans, which the English had been besieging for six months. Her timing was perfect—the English, weakened by illness, had been deserted by their Burgundian allies. Within ten days of Joan's arrival they had retreated.

What the English saw as a strategic withdrawal on their part, their opponents interpreted as a glorious victory inspired by '*La Pucelle*'—'the Maid', as the French now called her. Joan symbolised the purity that France had lost and was longing to regain. Her virginity was a curious source of pride to her fellow-soldiers, among whom she dressed and undressed with a remarkable lack of inhibition. Several later testified that they had seen her breasts 'which were beautiful', but found, to their surprise, that their 'carnal desires' were not aroused by the prospect.

Joan's voices had told her to dress as a soldier of God, and her appearance in a specially made suit of armour created a stirring image around which her legend could flourish. As her authority grew, she demanded that France's soldiers should give up swearing, go to church and refrain from looting or harassing the civilians through whose towns and villages they passed.

Volunteers stepped forward in their hundreds, inspired by the idea of joining an army with a saint at its head, while the demoralised English, once so confident that God was on their side, also began to believe the legend. When Joan was captured by Burgundian forces in May 1430, both the Burgundians and the English 'were much more excited than if they had captured five hundred fighting men', wrote the French chronicler de Monstrelet. 'They had never been so afraid of any captain or commander in war.'

The English promptly set up a church tribunal where Joan was condemned as a witch—her habit of wearing men's clothes was taken as particular proof of her damnation. If the Dauphin had exerted himself he might have negotiated her ransom, as was normal with high-profile prisoners-of-war. But he did nothing to help save the girl who had saved *him*. On 30 May 1431 Joan of Arc was led out into the marketplace in Rouen by English soldiers, tied to a stake and burned to death. She was nineteen years old.

'We are all ruined,' said one English witness, 'for a good and holy person was burned.'

Over the centuries England has chosen to remember the Hundred Years War for its great victories like Crécy and Agincourt: but, thanks to Joan of Arc, the bloody 116-year enterprise actually ended, for the English, in miserable defeat. According to one account, a white dove was seen in the sky at the moment of the Maid's death, and the French took this to symbolise God's blessing. They felt inspired to campaign with even more righteous certainty, and by 1453 all that survived of England's once great French empire was the walled port of Calais.

Joan of Arc's scarcely credible adventure remains eternally compelling. The simplicity and purity of her faith have inspired writers and dramatists over the centuries —particularly in times when it has become fashionable not to believe in God.

A 'PROMPTER FOR LITTLE ONES'

1440

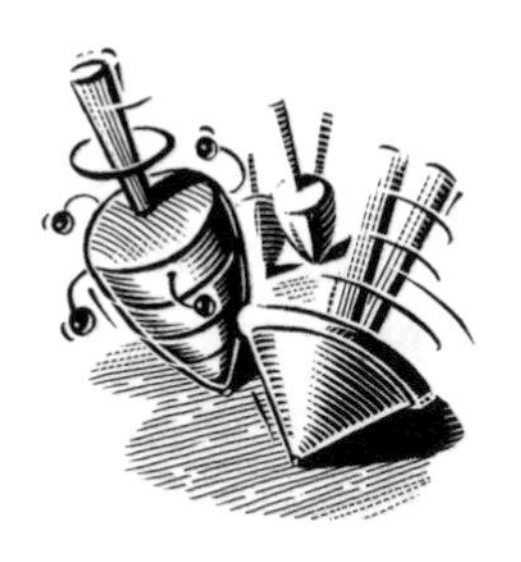

The long lists of Latin words in Geoffrey of Lynn's *Promptorium Parvulorum* would offer tedious reading for modern fans of Harry Potter, but his 'Prompter for Little Ones' has a good claim to being England's first child-friendly book.

Geoffrey was a friar from the Norfolk town known today as King's Lynn, and his 'Prompter' reads like the work of a kindly schoolmaster. It was a dictionary which set out the words that a good medieval pupil might be expected to know—many of them to do with religion. But defying the solemn tone, Geoffrey also listed the names of toys, games and children's playground pastimes. We read of rag dolls, four different types of spinning top, a child's bell; of games of shuttlecock, tennis and leapfrog, three running and chasing games, and games to be played on a swing or seesaw (which Geoffrey calls a 'totter', or 'merry totter').

All this gives us a rare glimpse into childhood in the Middle Ages. Medieval books were for grown-ups—most chronicles tell us of war and arguments over religion. But Geoffrey of Lynn takes us into the world of children, and shows us something of their preoccupations and imaginings.

In recent times this picture has been made real for us thanks to the chirps and bleepings of the modern metal detector. The Thames Mud Larks, named after the Victorian children who used to scavenge flotsam from the banks of the river, are a group of enthusiasts who scour the mudflats of the Thames at low tide. During London's construction boom of the 1980s they were also to be seen raking over the city's building sites, and what they came up with was an extraordinary treasure trove—large numbers of ancient toys.

One Mud Lark, Tony Pilson, retrieved hundreds of tiny pewter playthings dating back as early as AD 1250—miniature jugs, pans, other kitchen and cooking utensils and even bird-cages. He and his fellow-searchers turned up just about everything you would need to equip a doll's house—along with small metal soldiers that included a knight in armour. Mounted on horseback, the little figure had been cast from a mould, so he must originally have been produced in bulk.

When we look at portraits of children in the Middle Ages, they usually stare out at us with formal and stern expressions. But in the pages of Geoffrey's 'Prompter for Little Ones' and in the modern discoveries of the Mud Larks, we find evidence of so much infant fun and laughter. And since all these toys were made by adults, and must, for the most part, have been purchased and given as presents by parents and other fond relations, we can presume that medieval grown-ups recognised and cherished the magic world of childhood.

HOUSE OF LANCASTER: THE TWO REIGNS OF HENRY VI

1422–61, 1470–1

Henry VI was the youngest ever king of England, succeeding his warrior father Henry V at the age of just nine months. When the little boy attended his first opening of Parliament, aged only three, it was hardly surprising that he 'shrieked and cried and sprang', as one report described.

The problem was that in the course of his fifty troubled years, this king never really grew up. Henry VI went from first to second childhood, according to one modern historian, 'without the usual interval'.

This is unfair. Henry was a kindly and

pious man who financed the building of two gems of English architecture—the soaring Perpendicular chapel of Eton College across the Thames from Windsor, and the chapel of King's College, Cambridge. He also ran a court of some magnificence, to which his naïvety brought a charming touch. The 'Royal Book' of court etiquette describes Henry and his French wife Margaret of Anjou waking up early one New Year's morning to receive their presents—then staying in bed to enjoy them.

But Henry showed a disastrous lack of interest in the kingly pursuits of chivalry and war. Faced with the need to command the English army in Normandy at the age of eighteen, three years after he had taken over personal control of government from his father's old councillors, his response was to send a cousin in his place. Henry felt he had quite enough to do supervising the foundation of Eton College. It was not surprising he developed a reputation for namby-pambiness. Riding one day through the Cripplegate in London's city walls, he was shocked to see a decaying section of a human body impaled on a stake above the archway—and was horrified when informed it was the severed quarter of a man who had been 'false to the King's majesty'. 'Take it away!' he cried. 'I will not have any Christian man so cruelly handled for my sake!'

Unfortunately for Henry, respect for human

rights simply did not feature in the job description of a medieval king. Toughness was required. In the absence of a police force or army, a ruler depended on his network of nobles to ensure law and order, and if people lost confidence in the power of the Crown, it was to their local lord that they looked. They wore their lord's livery and badge—and it was these rival badges that would later give the conflicts of this period its famous name.

A memorable scene in Shakespeare's play Henry VI, Part 1 depicts the nobility of England in a garden selecting roses, red or white, to signify their loyalty to the House of York or the House of Lancaster. It did not happen—Shakespeare invented the episode. 'The Wars of the Roses', the romantic title we use today for the succession of battles and dynastic changes that took place in England between 1453 and 1487, was also a later invention, coined by the nineteenth-century romantic novelist Sir Walter Scott. The Yorkists may have sported a rose on occasion, but there is no evidence that the Lancastrians ever did—at the Battle of Barnet in 1471, they started fighting each other because they did not recognise their own liveries. To judge from the profusion of badges and banners that were actually borne into battle during these years, men were fighting the wars of the swans, dogs, boars, bears, lions, stars, suns and daisies.

The struggle for power, money and land,

however, certainly revolved around York and Lancaster, the two rival houses that developed from the numerous descendants of King Edward III (you can see the complications in the family tree on p. xiv). The Lancastrians traced their loyalties back to John of Gaunt, Duke of Lancaster, while the Yorkists rallied round the descendants of Gaunt's younger brother Edmund, Duke of York. Shakespeare dated the trouble from the moment that Gaunt's son Henry Bolingbroke deposed his cousin Richard II. But York and Lancaster would have stuck together under a firm and decisive king—and if Henry V had lived longer he would certainly have passed on a stronger throne. Even the bumbling Henry VI might have avoided trouble if, after years of diminishing mental competence, he had not finally gone mad.

According to one account, in August 1453 the King had 'a sudden fright' that sent him into a sort of coma, a sad echo of his grandfather, Charles VI—the French king who had howled like a wolf and imagined he was made of glass. After sixteen months Henry staged a recovery, but his breakdown had been the trigger for civil disorder, and in the confused sequence of intrigue and conflict that followed he was a helpless cipher. In February 1461 he was reported to have spent the second Battle of St Albans laughing and singing manically to himself, with no apparent awareness of the mayhem in full swing around him. It was hardly a surprise when, later that year, he was deposed, to be replaced by the handsome, strapping young Yorkist candidate, Edward IV (see p. 48).

In this change of regime the key figure was the mightiest of England's over-mighty subjects—Richard Neville, Earl of Warwick, who fought under the badge of the Bear and Ragged Staff. With no claim to the throne, but controlling vast estates with the ability to raise armies, the earl has gone down in history as 'Warwick the Kingmaker'. 'They have two rulers,' remarked a French observer of the English in these years, 'Warwick, and another whose name I have forgotten.'

When Warwick and Edward IV fell out in the late 1460s, the Kingmaker turned against his protégé, chasing him from the country. To replace him, Warwick brought back the deposed Henry VI who had spent the last six years in the Tower: the restored monarch was paraded around London in the spring of 1471. But the confused and shambling king had to be shepherded down Cheapside, his feet tied on to his horse. Never much of a parade-ground figure, he now made a sorry sight, dressed in a decidedly old and drab blue velvet gown that could not fail to prompt scorn—'as though he had no more to change with'. This moth-eaten display, reported the chronicler John Warkworth, was 'more like a play than a showing of a prince to win men's hearts'.

It was the Kingmaker's last throw—and a losing one. Warwick was unable to beat off the challenge of Edward IV, now returned, who soon defeated and killed the earl in battle, regaining the crown for himself.

As for poor Henry, his fate was sealed. Two weeks later he was found dead in the Tower, and history has pointed the finger at his second-time supplanter, Edward. Henry probably *was* murdered—but there is a sad plausibility to the official explanation that the twice-reigning King, who inherited two kingdoms and lost them both, passed away out of 'pure displeasure and melancholy'.

THE HOUSE OF THEODORE

1432–85

If the Wars of the Roses were fought by the men, it was the women who eventually sorted out the mess. By the late 1400s the royal family tree had become a crazy spider's web of possible claimants to the throne, and it took female instinct to tease out the relevant strands from the tangle. The emotions of mothers and wives were to weave new patterns—and eventually they produced a most unlikely solution.

Owain ap Maredudd ap Tydwr was a silver-tongued Welsh gentleman who caught the eye of Henry V's widow, Catherine of France. He was a servant in her household in the

1420s—probably Clerk of her Wardrobe—and being Welsh, he had no surname. The 'ap' in his name meant 'son of', so he was Owen, son of Meredith, son of Theodore.

But once he had captured the heart of the widowed Queen, Owen had needed a surname. According to later gossip, Catherine would spy on her energetic Welsh wardrobe clerk as he bathed naked in the Thames, and she decided she liked what she saw.

The court was outraged. An official inquiry was held. But Catherine stuck by her Owen and in 1432 their marriage was officially recognised. 'Theodore' became 'Tudor', and Owen went through life defiantly proud of the leap in fortune that he owed to love. Thirty years later, in 1461, cornered by his enemies after the Battle of Mortimer's Cross, he would go to the block with insouciance. 'That head shall lie on the stock,' he said jauntily, 'that was wont to lie on Queen Catherine's lap.'

From the outset, the Tudors confronted the world with attitude. Catherine and Owen had two sons, Edmund and Jasper, who were widely viewed as cuckoos in the royal nest. But the dowager Queen resolutely brought up her Welsh boys with her first-born royal son Henry VI, nine or ten years their senior, and the young King became fond of his boisterous half-brothers. In 1452 he raised them both to the peerage, giving Edmund the earldom of Richmond and making Jasper Earl of

Pembroke. The two young Tudors were given precedence over all the earls in England, and Henry, who had produced no children, was rumoured to be considering making Edmund his heir. The new Earl of Richmond was granted a version of the royal arms to wear on his shield.

The Tudors rose still higher in the world a few years later, when Edmund married the twelve-year-old Lady Margaret Beaufort, who had her own claim to the throne. The great-granddaughter of John of Gaunt, she proved to be one of the most remarkable women of her time. Bright-eyed and birdlike, to judge from the portraits still to be seen in the several educational establishments she endowed, she was a woman of learning. She translated into English part of *The Imitation of Christ*, the early-fifteenth-century manual of contemplations in which the German monk Thomas of Kempen (Thomas à Kempis) taught how serenity comes through the judicious acceptance of life's problems. 'Trouble often compels a man to search his own heart: it reminds him he is an exile here, and he can put his trust in nothing in this world.'

Diminutive in stature, Lady Margaret was nonetheless strong in both mind and body. She was married, pregnant and widowed before the age of thirteen, when Edmund died of plague. In the care of his brother Jasper, Margaret gave birth to Edmund's son, Henry, in Jasper's castle at Pembroke in the bleak and windswept south-west corner of Wales. But some complication of the birth, probably to do with her youth or small frame, meant that she had no more children. For the rest of her life she devoted her energies to her son—'my only worldly joy', as she lovingly described him—although circumstances kept them apart.

The young man's links to the succession through his mother—and less directly through his grandmother, the French queen Catherine—made England a dangerous place for Henry Tudor. He spent most of his upbringing in exile, much of it in the company of his uncle Jasper. At the age of four he was separated from his mother, and he scarcely saw her for twenty years.

But Lady Margaret never abandoned the cause. She would later plot a marriage for her son that would make his claim to the throne unassailable, and she had already arranged a marriage for herself that would turn out to be the Tudor trump card. In 1472 she married Thomas, Lord Stanley, a landowner with large estates in Cheshire, Lancashire and other parts of the north-west. The Stanleys were a wily family whose local empire-building typified the rivalries that made up the disorderly jostlings of these years. Allied to Lady Margaret, the Stanleys would prove crucial partners as her son Henry Tudor jostled for the largest prize of all.

HOUSE OF YORK: EDWARD IV, MERCHANT KING

1461–70, 1471–83

The flamboyant Edward IV shares with his luckless rival Henry VI the dubious distinction of being the only king of England to reign twice. In 1461 and 1471, thanks to Warwick the Kingmaker, the two men played box and cox in what turned out to be a humiliating royal timeshare. But after Edward had defeated Warwick and disposed of Henry, he ruled for a dozen prosperous and largely undisturbed years, during which he achieved another distinction. He was the first king for more than a century and a half who did not die in debt—in fact, he actually left his successor a little money in the kitty.

Edward was England's first and last businessman monarch. Clapping folk around the shoulders and cracking dirty jokes, he was also an unashamed wheeler-dealer. He set up his own trading business, making handsome profits on exporting wool and tin to Italy, while importing Mediterranean cargoes like wine, paper, sugar and oranges. He ran the Crown lands with the keen eye of a bailiff, and when it came to PR with the merchant community he was a master of corporate hospitality.

One day in 1482 Edward invited the Lord Mayor of London, the aldermen and 'a certain number of such head commoners as the mayor would assign' to join him in the royal forest at Waltham in Essex. There, in today's golf-course country, they were treated to a morning of sport, then conveyed 'to a strong and pleasant lodge made of green boughs and other pleasant things. Within which lodge were laid certain tables, whereat at once the said mayor and his company were set and served right plenteously with all manner of dainties . . . and especially of venison, both of red deer and of fallow.' After lunch the King took his guests hunting again, and a few days later sent their wives 'two harts and six bucks with a tun of Gascon Wine'.

It could be said that Edward IV invented the seductive flummery of the modern honours list when he made six London aldermen Knights of the Bath. Like the Order of the Garter, the Order of the Bath, which referred to the ritual cleansing that a squire underwent when he became a knight, was primarily a military honour. Now the King extended the bait to rich civilians that he wanted to keep on side: a moneylender would kneel down as Bill Bloggs, the sword would touch his shoulder, and he arose Sir William.

Edward understood that everyone had his price—himself included. In 1475 he had taken an army across the Channel where he met up with the French King at Picquigny near Amiens—and promptly did a deal to take his army home again. For a down payment of 75,000 crowns and a pension of 50,000 a year, he cheerfully sold off his birthright—England's claim to the French territories for which so many of his ancestors had fought so bloodily over the years.

The Treaty of Picquigny brought peace and prosperity to England, but not much honour. Edward's reign was too undramatic for Shakespeare to write a play about—one reason, perhaps, why Edward is sometimes called England's 'forgotten king'. But the beautiful St George's Chapel at Windsor, designed to outshine the chapel that his rival Henry VI had built at Eton College in the valley below, remains his memorial. And the Royal Book reveals a sumptuous court—along with a diverting little insight into how comfortably this fleshly monarch lived. After he had risen every morning, a yeoman was deputed to leap on to his bed and roll up and down so as to level out the lumps in the litter of bracken and straw that made up the royal mattress.

In 1483, Edward IV retired to his mattress unexpectedly, having caught a chill while fishing. He died some days later, aged only forty. Had this cynical yet able man lived just a few years longer, his elder son Edward, only twelve at the time of his death, might have been able to build on his legacy. As it was, young Edward and his younger brother soon found themselves inside the Tower of London, courtesy of their considerate uncle Richard.

WILLIAM CAXTON

1474

Wars and roses . . . We have seen that roses were rare on the battle banners of fifteenth-century England. Let's now take a closer look at the 'wars' themselves. In the thirty-two years that history textbooks conventionally allot to the 'Wars of the Roses', there were long periods of peace. In fact, there were only thirteen weeks of actual fighting—and though the battles themselves were bitter and sometimes very bloody, mayhem and ravaging seldom ensued.

'It is a custom in England,' reported Philippe de Commynes, a shrewd French visitor to

England in the 1470s, 'that the victors in battle kill nobody, especially none of the ordinary soldiers.' In this curiously warless warfare, defeated noblemen could expect prompt and ruthless execution, but 'neither the country nor the people, nor the houses were wasted, destroyed or demolished'. The rank and file returned home as soon as they could, to continue farming their land.

In towns and cities people also got on with their lives. Trade and business positively flourished, generating contracts, ledgers and letters that called for a literate workforce —and it was the 'grammar' schools that taught this emerging class of office workers the practical mechanics of English and Latin. The grammar schools multiplied in the fifteenth century, and the demand for accessible low-price books that they helped generate was met by an invention that was to prove infinitely more important than considerations of who was nudging whom off the throne.

In 1469 William Caxton, an English merchant living in the prosperous Flemish trading town of Bruges, was finishing a book that he had researched. Caxton was a trader in rich cloths—a mercer like Richard Whittington—and books were his passion. He collected rare books, and he wrote for his own pleasure, scratching out the text laboriously with a quill on to parchment. The book he was currently completing was a history of the ancient Greek city of Troy, and the mercer, who was approaching his fiftieth birthday, was feeling weary. 'My pen is worn, mine hand heavy, my eye even dimmed,' he wrote. The prospect of copying out more versions of the manuscript for the friends who had expressed an interest was too much to contemplate. So Caxton decided to see what he could discover about the craft of printing, which had been pioneered by Johann Gutenberg in the 1440s in the Rhine Valley.

Travelling south-east from Bruges, he arrived on the Rhine nearly thirty years after Gutenberg had started work there. And having 'practised and learned' the technique for himself, the mercer turned printer went back to Bruges to set up his own press. In 1474 his History of Troy became the first book to be printed in English, and two years later he brought his press to England, setting up shop near the Chapter House, in the precinct of Westminster Abbey, where Parliament met.

Caxton had an eye for a good location. Along the route between the Palace of Westminster and the Chapter House shuttled lawyers, churchmen, courtiers, MPs—the book-buying elite of England. The former cloth trader also had an eye for a bestseller. The second book he printed was about chess, *The Game and Play of the Chesse*. Then came in fairly quick succession a French–English dictionary, a translation of Aesop's fables, several popular romances, Malory's tale of Camelot in the *Morte D'Arthur*, some school textbooks, a history of England, an encyclopaedia entitled *The Myrrour of the Worlde*, and Chaucer's bawdy evergreen, *The Canterbury Tales.*

More than five hundred years later a copy of Caxton's first edition of Chaucer became the most expensive book ever sold—knocked down at auction for £4.6 million. But in the fifteenth century the obvious appeal of the newly printed books lay in their value for money. Books became so commonplace that snobs sometimes employed scribes to copy Caxton's printed editions back into manuscript—while both Church and government became alarmed at the access to new ideas that the printing press offered to a widening public.

Over the centuries Caxton's innovation would marvellously stimulate diversity in thinking, but in one important respect its impact was to standardise. Caxton loved to write personal prefaces to his publications, explaining the background of the new book he was sharing with his readers, and in one of these he describes the difficulties of being England's first mass publisher. He was in his study, he relates, feeling rather bereft, looking for a new project to get his teeth into, and happened to pick up the recently published French version of Virgil's *Aeneid.* The editor in him couldn't resist trying to translate the great epic poem into English. Taking a pen, he wrote out a page or two. But when he came to read through what he had written, he had to wonder whether his customers in different corners of England would be able to understand it, since 'common English that is spoken in one shire varies from another'.

To make the point he recounted the tale of a group of English merchants who, when their ship was becalmed at the mouth of the Thames, decided to go ashore in search of a good breakfast. One of them asked for some '*eggys*', to be told by the Kentish wife that she did not understand French. Since the merchant himself only spoke and understood English, he started to get angry, until one of his companions said he would like some '*eyren*'– and the woman promptly reached for the egg basket.

'Loo,' exclaimed Caxton, 'what sholde a man in thyse dayes now wryte—egges or eyren?'

Even in this account you may notice that Caxton himself first spelled the word '*eggys*', then '*egges*' a few lines later. As the printer-publisher produced more and more books—and when he died in 1491 he was on the point of printing his hundredth—he made his own decisions about how words should be spelled. His choices tended to reflect the language of the south-east of England, with which he was familiar—he was proud to come from Kent, 'where I doubt not is spoken as broad and rude English as is in any place of England'.

Many of Caxton's spelling decisions and those of the printers who came after him were quite arbitrary. As they matched letters to sounds they followed no particular rules, and we live with the consequences to this day. So if you have ever wondered why a bandage is 'wound' around a 'wound', why 'cough' rhymes with 'off' while 'bough' rhymes with 'cow', and why you might shed a 'tear' after seeing a 'tear' in your best dress or trousers, you have William Caxton to thank for the confusion.

WHODUNIT? THE PRINCES IN THE TOWER

1483

When Edward IV died early in April 1483, his elder son Edward was in Ludlow on the Welsh border, carrying out his duties as Prince of Wales. The twelve-year-old was duly proclaimed King Edward V, and leisurely arrangements were made for him to travel to London for his coronation. But on the 30th of that month, with little more than a day's riding to go, the royal party was intercepted by the King's uncle, Richard, Duke of Gloucester, at Stony Stratford on the outskirts of modern-day Milton Keynes.

The thirty-year-old Richard was the

energetic and ambitious younger brother of Edward IV. He had been ruling the north of England with firm efficiency, and he claimed to have uncovered a conspiracy to seize control of the new King. He took charge of his nephew and escorted him back to London where, after a spell in the bishop's palace, the young Edward V was dispatched for safekeeping into the royal apartments in the Tower. There the boy was joined on 16 June by his nine-year-old brother, Prince Richard of York.

But only ten days later, claiming that the two boys were illegitimate, Uncle Richard proclaimed himself King. It was an outlandish charge, but he was formally crowned King Richard III on 6 July 1483, and the children were never seen at liberty again. With a poignant report in the Great Chronicle of London that they were glimpsed that summer 'shooting and playing in the garden of the Tower', the young Edward V and his brother vanished from history.

Few people at the time doubted that the King had disposed of them. But there was no solid evidence of foul play until, nearly two centuries later, workmen digging at the bottom of a staircase in the Tower of London discovered a wooden chest containing the skeletons of two children. The taller child was lying on his back, with the smaller one face down on top of him. 'They were small bones of lads . . .' wrote one eyewitness, 'and there were pieces of rag and velvet about them.'

The reigning monarch of the time, Charles II, ordered an inquiry. All agreed that the skeletons must be those of the boy king Edward V and his younger brother, murdered in 1483 by their wicked uncle. In 1678 the remains were ceremonially reburied in Westminster Abbey, with full dignity, in an urn beneath a black-and-white marble altar.

But over the years historians and physicians queried the authenticity of the bones. Did they really belong to the so-called 'Princes in the Tower'? And even if they did, what proof was there that they were murdered by anybody, let alone by their uncle? By 1933 the controversy was such that King George V, grandfather of the present Queen, authorised the opening of the tomb.

The two medical experts who examined the contents came to the conclusion that the remains of the young skeletons were almost certainly those of Richard III's nephews. Both indicated a slender build, with very small finger bones. Dental evidence set the age of one at eleven to thirteen years old, the smaller at between nine and eleven. Professor W. Wright, a dental surgeon who was president of the Anatomical Society of Great Britain, declared that the structure of the jaws and other bones in both skeletons established a family link, and he further suggested that a red mark on the facial bones of the elder child was a bloodstain caused by suffocation.

The notion of the victims having been suffocated made a neat connection with the first detailed account of the boys' deaths by Sir Thomas More back in 1514. Writing thirty years after the event, More pieced his story together through first-hand research—plus a certain amount of what he honestly described as 'divining upon conjectures'. Acting on Richard's orders, he alleged, two men had crept into the princes' bedchamber about midnight, 'and suddenly lapped them up among the clothes, so bewrapped them and entangled them, keeping down by force the feather bed and pillows hard into their mouths, that within a while, smothered and stifled, their breath failing, they gave up to God their innocent souls'. More went on to describe how the murderers then buried the bodies 'at the stair foot, meetly deep under the ground, under a great heap of stones'.

We shall meet Thomas More again in a later chapter. His name has become a byword for both learning and courage in standing up for principle, and his unpublished account was written at the behest of no particular patron. While clearly disapproving of Richard III, he nonetheless made several attempts in his story to separate fact from rumour. But his research was seized on by others for commercial and political reasons—most notably by William

Shakespeare, whose *Tragedy of King Richard III*, first performed in 1597, gave birth to one of the most exquisitely chilling villains of English drama: 'Conscience is but a word that cowards use . . .'

In Shakespeare's play we see the King ruthlessly order the murder of his two nephews, along with the deaths of a whole catalogue of other rivals and opponents —actually uttering at one point the immortal words 'Off with his head!' The evil that festers in the usurper's mind is graphically symbolised by his twisted and deformed body, reflecting sixteenth-century superstitions that Richard spent a full two years in his mother's womb, before emerging with teeth fully developed, a mane of black hair and a hideously hunched back.

In reality, King Richard III was lean and athletic. His portraits show quite a handsome-looking man, who may possibly have carried one shoulder a little higher than the other but who was certainly not the crookback of legend. Modern X-rays show that the higher shoulder in one portrait was painted in afterwards. He was a devout Christian—something of a Puritan. He was an efficient administrator. And while he was certainly ruthless in sweeping aside those who stood in his path to the throne—including his helpless nephews—he was not the hissing psychopath of Shakespeare's depiction. The popular image of 'Crookback Dick' is quite certainly a defamation—one of history's most successful hatchet jobs—and it is not surprising that over the centuries people have come to Richard's defence. Founded in 1924, the Fellowship of the White Boar, now known as the Richard III Society, has become the most thriving historical club in the entire English-speaking world, with branches in Britain and North America.

In a testament to the English sense of fair play, the Ricardians, as they call themselves, campaign tirelessly to rescue their hero's reputation, and central to their argument is the absence of solid evidence linking Richard III directly to the disappearance of his nephews. More himself wrote, for example, that, having initially been buried beneath the staircase in the Tower, the princes' bodies were later dug up and reburied some distance away. So, argue the Ricardians, the skeletons discovered in the 1670s could not possibly have been the princes—who might even have escaped from the Tower.

As for the 'experts' of 1933, their techniques do not stand modern forensic scrutiny. To take one instance, there is no possibility that a single stain on an ancient bone could be plausibly linked to suffocation. In 1984 no less than four hours of television were devoted to a court-room inquest and trial in which this evidence and much more was minutely dissected and argued over by prominent lawyers and historians. Did Richard III murder the Princes in the Tower? The jury reached a verdict of 'not guilty'.

The debate will doubtless go on for ever—or, at least, until some conclusive new evidence is discovered. Modern DNA analysis could determine, for example, whether or not the bones that have lain in Westminster Abbey since 1678 are genetically linked to those of the boys' father, Edward IV, lying for over five centuries in his tomb at Windsor—though that would not tell us who disposed of the children.

Richard III's contemporaries had little doubt: 'There was much whispering among the people,' recorded the Great Chronicle, 'that the king had put the children of King Edward to death.'

'I saw men burst into tears when mention was made of [the boy king] after his removal from men's sight,' wrote the Italian traveller, Dominic Mancini, 'and already there was suspicion that he had been done away with.'

Medieval folk were not surprised by skulduggery and death at the top. In the previous two centuries England had seen three kings deposed (Edward II, Richard II, Henry VI), and all were subsequently disposed of in sinister circumstances. But to eliminate children—and your own brother's children—went one big step beyond that. Even if the physical evidence to convict Richard III of murder was missing, he was guilty of appalling neglect, for he had had a duty of care to his nephews. When it came to explaining what had happened to them, he never even tried to offer a cover story.

In any case, history's debate over the 'Princes in the Tower' lets Richard off too lightly. The younger boy was indeed a prince, but the elder one, Edward V, was a properly proclaimed and fully acknowledged king, until his uncle went riding out to meet him at Stony Stratford on that late spring day in 1483. Richard might wriggle off the hook of modern TV justice. But he was found guilty in the court of his own times, and he was soon made to pay the full penalty.

THE CAT AND THE RAT

1484

Europe was scandalised by Richard III's seizure of power. 'See what has happened in England since the death of King Edward,' declared Guillaume de Rochefort, the Chancellor of France, to the Estates-General, France's Parliament, in a speech that positively oozed gloating disapproval. 'His children, already big and courageous, have been slaughtered with impunity, and their murderer, with the support of the people, has received the crown.'

In fact, the support of England's people for their self-appointed monarch was anything but whole-hearted. The opening months of Richard's reign, as he disposed of his critics and enemies, saw five executions, and this made London an uneasy place to be. 'There is much trouble,' reported one newsletter to the provinces, 'and every man doubts the other.'

The new king's favourites ruled the roost, and Richard's roster of unpopular sidekicks prompted a famous piece of doggerel:

> *The Cat, the Rat, and Lovell our Dog*
> *Rule all England under the Hog.*

The Cat was Sir William Catesby, a sharp-witted lawyer who was Speaker of the House of Commons—his job it was to make sure that MPs toed the line with the new regime. The Rat was Sir Richard Ratcliffe, one of Richard's oldest cronies; Francis, Lord Lovell, who had a silver dog on his crest, had grown up with Richard in the household of Warwick the Kingmaker; and the Hog was Richard himself—a derisive reference to the white boar of his crest.

Today it is our sacred right to make fun of our rulers. Satirists and cheeky impersonators make up a major branch of the entertainment business, sometimes becoming so famous in their own right that they outshine the national leaders they deride. But things were very different in 1484, when the authorities tracked down Sir William Collingbourne, the Wiltshire gentleman who had dared pen the scornful verse that had ended up pinned to the door of St Paul's Cathedral. Collingbourne was one of several West-Countrymen accused of plotting rebellion, and while the others were spared, the lampooner received special treatment for his 'rhyme [in] derision of the king and his council'. He was strung up on the gallows, then cut down while still breathing, to be castrated and disembowelled.

To his credit, Collingbourne seems to have retained his sense of humour to the end. 'Oh Lord Jesus, yet more trouble,' he sighed, as the executioner reached inside his body to yank out his intestines.

THE BATTLE OF BOSWORTH FIELD

1485

One day in the summer of 1485, the French chronicler Philippe de Commynes encountered Henry Tudor at the court of the King of France. It was the young Welshman's latest port of call in more than twenty years of exile. Moving from castle to castle across Brittany and France, he knew what it was to live from hand to mouth. From the time he was five years old, Henry told the Frenchman, he 'had always been a fugitive or a prisoner'.

Now all this was about to change. With his faithful uncle Jasper Tudor beside him, Henry was preparing his bid for the English throne.

Since Richard III had seized power two years earlier, an increasing trickle of Englishmen had been making their way across the Channel to throw in their lot with the young man whose descent through his mother Lady Margaret Beaufort—and, to a lesser extent, through his grandfather Owen's romantic marriage to Queen Catherine of France—made Henry the best alternative to Richard.

On 1 August Henry set sail with a force of a thousand or so soldiers, including a group of French pikemen he was paying with borrowed funds. They were heading for the south-west tip of Wales, Jasper's home territory, where Henry himself had been born, and they dropped anchor in Milford Haven on Sunday the 7th. Their plan was to head north in a loop across Wales, gathering support as they marched. Local poets, we are told, had been primed to proclaim the coming of *y mab darogan*, 'the man of destiny'.

In the event, the response was far from overwhelming. Few Welshmen were willing to risk their lives on Henry's threadbare enterprise, and when he reached Shrewsbury and the English Midlands there was further disappointment. Henry had been counting on the support of his stepfather, his mother's third husband Thomas, Lord Stanley. But anticipating such a move, Richard III had seized Stanley's eldest son and was holding him hostage.

The Stanley family certainly had the power to determine the course of the forthcoming conflict—they were the major magnates in the area. But they had not achieved their standing by taking chances. In battle, they had a history of holding back their troops till the very last possible moment—and in the high summer of 1485 this was as far as they were prepared to go for young Henry. When the armies of Henry Tudor and Richard III finally confronted each other on Monday 22 August, Henry's forces were considerably outnumbered by those of the King—though Richard's army also lacked the reinforcements he had been promised, with the Stanleys keeping their troops on the side.

Tradition has set the momentous Battle of Bosworth Field not far from Leicester. But modern research suggests that the armies may have clashed several miles further west near the modern A5 and the village of Mancetter, just north of Coventry, where Boadicea made her last stand fourteen hundred years earlier. The A5 follows the great curve of Watling Street, the Roman road connecting London with north Wales. So as Henry's pikemen made their uncertain way towards Richard's army, they were tracing the route of the Roman legions.

By one account, Richard was plagued by bad dreams and premonitions on the night before the battle. But he put on a brave face. He clad himself ostentatiously in glorious kingly armour, setting the gold circlet of the crown over his helmet. Then, when he caught sight of his rival's standard at the back of the Tudor army, he launched a cavalry charge directly at it.

'This day I will die as a king,' he cried, 'or win.'

There is some speculation as to why Henry was stationed to the rear of his men. The cautious claimant seems to have had an eye to cutting his losses if the battle went against him—he had left his uncle, Jasper, even further to the rear to cover his getaway. But Henry was saved by his French pikemen, who presented Richard's charging horsemen with a tactic never before seen in England. Swiftly, they formed their five-metre-plus steel-headed staves into a bristling defensive wall around their leader, and as Richard's cavalry hit the pike wall, the King was unhorsed. An eyewitness account by one of the mercenaries, written the day after the battle and recently rediscovered in a nineteenth-century transcription, describes Richard crying out in rage and frustration: 'These French traitors are today the cause of our realm's ruin!'

This seems to have been the moment that prompted the Stanleys, at last, to intervene. Cagey as ever, Lord Stanley himself continued to hold back, but his brother Sir William deftly moved his troops across the battlefield, overpowering Richard's soldiers and cornering the King. Richard fought on, bravely refusing his friends' offer of a horse on which to flee.

'A horse! A horse! My kingdom for a horse!' Shakespeare's Tragedy of King Richard III dramatically portrays the hunchback monarch screaming for a fresh mount to carry him to the personal showdown he craved with Henry Tudor. And in this depiction of defiant courage, the playwright finally does right by the King. By most eyewitness and contemporary accounts, Richard fought to the very last, until he was finally overpowered and cut down, his crown rolling off his helmet as he fell. Sir William Stanley picked up the gold circlet and placed it on Henry Tudor's head. 'Sir, here I make you King of England.'

As always after a battle, the victors turned to plunder. Stanley was allowed to take whatever he wished from the dead king's tent—he picked out a set of royal tapestries for the Stanley residence, enduring evidence of the family's decisive, if less than heroic, doings on Bosworth Field. Richard's miniature Book of Hours, his beautifully illustrated personal prayer book, went to Henry's mother Lady Margaret—while Henry himself chose to keep the delicate gold crown.

Richard's corpse, meanwhile, was stripped of all clothing—'naught being left about him so much as would cover his privy member'. The body was then slung over a horse, with arms and legs hanging down on both sides, 'trussed . . . as a hog or other vile beast and so all bespattered with mire and filth'. He was taken to the Greyfriars Church at Leicester, and there he was buried 'without any pomp or solemn funeral'.

Five decades later the tomb was broken open when the friary was destroyed during the Dissolution of the Monasteries. To this day, the bones that are said to have belonged to the little Princes in the Tower rest in honour in Westminster Abbey. But sometime in the 1530s the bones of Richard III were thrown into a river in Leicestershire.

DOUBLE TROUBLE

1486–99

On 18 January 1486 the new King Henry VII, the twenty-eight-year-old victor of Bosworth, married nineteen-year-old Princess Elizabeth of York, the elder sister of the tragic Princes in the Tower. Plotted by Henry's mother, Margaret Beaufort, the marriage was a step towards mending the bitter and bloodstained rift between the House of Lancaster and the House of York.

But the mysterious disappearance of the little princes had left a curious legacy. No one could be quite sure what had happened to them—and, if they *had* been murdered, who was to blame. Despite the suspicion attaching to Richard III, there were no bodies and no closure: the poison had not been drawn. For a dozen years England was haunted by conspiracy theories made flesh. It was the age of the pretenders.

The first was Lambert Simnel, an Oxford tradesman's son who became the tool of Richard Symonds, an ambitious local priest. Symonds took his twelve-year-old protégé to Ireland, claiming that Simnel was Edward, Earl of Warwick, the young nephew of Richard III (see Wars of the Roses family tree, p. xiv). On Whit Sunday 1487 'King Edward VI' was crowned by dissident Irish noblemen in Dublin.

The real Edward was in the Tower of London. Henry had made it a priority to put Warwick away when he came to the throne, and now he lost no time in bringing him out to be paraded through the streets of London. When Simnel and his Irish followers landed at Furness in Lancashire later that June, Henry marched north to defeat them in a rerun of the previous years of disorder.

But the Tudor response in victory was a new departure. Instead of executing 'Edward VI', Henry gave Simnel a job in the royal kitchens, turning the spit that roasted the royal ox. The boy made such a good job of his duties as a scullion that he rapidly earned promotion, rising to take care of Henry's beloved hunting hawks and finishing up as royal falconer.

In his humane, rather humorous treatment of Lambert Simnel, Henry was making a point—this new king did not kill children. He even spared the boy's Svengali, Symonds, who had planned to have himself made Archbishop of Canterbury. But Henry might have done better to be more severe, for within a few years he was confronted with another pretender. This one declared himself to be Richard, Duke of York, the younger of the Princes in the Tower. Apparently, he had made a miraculous escape following his elder brother's murder and had now returned to claim the throne.

'King Richard IV'—by this account, Henry's brother-in-law—would later confess that he was, in fact, one Pierquin Wesbecque (Perkin Warbeck) from Tournai in the Netherlands, the son of a boatman. But it suited all manner of people to believe he was indeed the nephew of Richard III, and he did the rounds of Henry's enemies and neighbours, being treated to banquets and hunting excursions and given money to buy troops. King James IV of Scotland even found him an attractive wife, his own cousin Lady Katherine Gordon.

This pretender's six-year odyssey came to grief in the autumn of 1497, after a failed attempt to raise the West Country against Henry. Captured at Beaulieu in Hampshire, he finally admitted his humble origins. But having heard his confession, Henry again took a conciliatory line, inviting Warbeck and his charming Scottish wife to join his court. It was as if the King was enjoying the fairytale himself. Even when Warbeck tried to escape the following summer, Henry was content merely to put him in the stocks and have him repeat his confession. It was not until Warbeck tried to escape yet again that the King lost patience. On 23 November 1499 the false claimant was hanged, and a few days later the true claimant, the hapless Earl of Warwick, was beheaded on Tower Hill.

Henry gave Warbeck's noble widow a pension and made her lady-in-waiting to the Queen. Lady Katherine Gordon became quite a figure at the Tudor court, marrying no fewer than three more husbands and surviving until 1537. But the King's sharp dose of reality in 1499 had the desired effect—no more pretenders.

FISH 'N' SHIPS

1497

In fourteen hundred ninety-two, Columbus sailed the ocean blue
And found this land, land of the Free, beloved by you, beloved by me.

Fourteen ninety-two is the famous date when Christopher Columbus is credited by history with the 'discovery' of America. But modern archaeologists have shown that the Vikings must have crossed the Atlantic long before him. The remains of Viking homes, cooking pits and metal ornaments on the island of Newfoundland have been dated to around the year 1000. And there is every reason to believe that Columbus was also preceded to the Americas by several shiploads of weather-beaten Englishmen.

The men had set sail from Bristol, heading out from the prosperous port on the River Avon in the west of England, first towards Ireland, then further westwards into the Atlantic. They were fishermen, searching for cod that they could salt and trade for wine, and they brought back tales of remote islands that they called 'The Isle of the Seven Cities' and 'The Isle of Brasil'. Late in the 1490s an English merchant called John Day reported their discoveries to the 'Grand Admiral' of Spain—the *Almirante Major*—who may have been Columbus himself. In a letter that was misfiled for centuries in the National Archives at Simancas, Day pointed out that the New World across the Atlantic had, in fact, already been 'found and discovered in other times by the men of Bristol ... as your Lordship knows'.

The problem with this English claim to transatlantic discovery is that these West Country fishermen had kept their find to themselves, as cagey fishermen tend to do. Harbour records make clear that in the 1480s, if not earlier, ships from Bristol had located the fabulously fecund Grand Banks fishing grounds that lie off New England and Newfoundland. But they did not wish to attract competitors or poachers. Their only interest in terra firma of any sort was as a landmark to guide them to the fishing waters. So Christopher Columbus has retained the glory for 1492—and in any case, 'discovery' now seems the wrong word for landing on a continent that was already occupied by hundreds of thousands, if not millions, of indigenous American Indians.

When a contingent of Bristolians did finally set foot in America in a properly documented fashion, they did so under royal patronage. Around 1494 an Italian navigator, Zuan Caboto, arrived at the court of King Henry VII. Like Columbus, Caboto came from Genoa and he was a skilled propagandist for the exploding world of discovery. Brandishing charts and an impressive globe, he persuaded Henry to grant him a charter to 'seeke out, discover and finde whatsoever isles, countries, regions or provinces of heathens and infidels . . . which before this time have been unknown to all Christians'.

The prudent king was not about to invest any of his own money in the project. On the contrary, royal approval carried a price tag—20 per cent of the profits. But Zuan, now 'John Cabot', was granted permanent tax exemption on whatever he might bring back from the New World for himself. So he went down to Bristol in search of investors. There he was able to fit out a small wooden sailing ship, the *Matthew*, with a crew of eighteen, most of them 'hearty Bristol sailors'.

It might seem surprising that the clannish West-Countrymen should team up with an Italian, an outsider, but there was a fraternity among those who risked their lives on the mysterious western ocean. Cabot was skilled in the latest navigational techniques using the stars, and he needed a crew who would not lose their nerve when out of sight of land for four weeks or more.

In the event, the journey took five. On 24 June 1497, thirty-five days after leaving England, the *Matthew* sighted land and dropped anchor somewhere off the coast of modern Newfoundland, Labrador or Nova Scotia. Cautiously, Cabot and his landing party rowed ashore, where they found the remains of a fire, some snares set for game, a needle for making nets and a trail that headed inland. Obviously, there were humans around; but Cabot was not keen to meet them. 'Since he was with just a few people,' John Day later explained in his letter to the Spanish Grand Admiral, 'he did not dare advance inland beyond the shooting distance of a crossbow.'

The landing party planted four banners: the arms of St George, on behalf of King Henry VII; a papal banner on behalf of the Pope; the flag of Venice, since Cabot had taken Venetian citizenship; and a cross intended for the local 'heathens and infidels'. Then the English mariners set off down the coast in pursuit of their great passion—the waters were 'swarming with fish', Cabot later boasted to the Milanese Ambassador, and there was no need of a net to catch them: they could just lean over the ship's rail and 'let down baskets with a stone'.

Heading for home around the middle of July, captain and crew used the same method that had got them there—the so-called 'dead reckoning'. This involved fixing on one particular angle to the stars and preserving that angle as they sailed, effectively staying on one line of latitude as they moved around the curve of the globe. Contrary to received wisdom, fifteenth-century sailors did not believe the world was flat. Indeed, its roundness was the basis of their adventurous navigation techniques.

By 23 August, Cabot was back in London, reporting on his finds to the King who, never careless with his money, doled out an immediate ten pounds—about four times the average annual wage at the time. Henry also granted the mariner an annual pension of twenty pounds for life, to be paid by the port of Bristol out of its customs receipts. But John Cabot did not live to claim it. The next year he set out on another expedition westwards where, as the Tudor historian Polydore Vergil heartlessly put it, the 'newe founde lande' he discovered was 'nowhere but on the very bottom of the ocean'. Cabot and his ship vanished without trace.

But his death did not discourage other adventurers. In 1501 Henry VII commissioned six more Bristolians to head westwards, and they returned with Arctic hunting falcons —perhaps the King gave them to Lambert Simnel to train—along with a few of the native inhabitants that Cabot had been careful to avoid encountering four years earlier: 'They were clothed in beasts' skins and ate raw flesh,' recorded one awestruck chronicler, 'and spake such speech that no man could understand them ... In their demeanour [they were] like ... brute beasts.'

Falcons, fish and Eskimos—as the Inuit people came to be called at the end of the sixteenth century—were interesting enough, but they bore no comparison to the gold, jewels and, above all, silver that Spain would soon be carrying home in heaving galleon-loads from the southerly lands discovered by Columbus. It would be more than seventy years before England made a determined effort to settle the northern parts of the continent that, after 1507, would be described on the maps as 'America'.

But the Eskimos settled in nicely, thank you. They evidently found themselves a tailor, for just two years after they had first appeared at Henry's court in their animal skins, England's first New World immigrants were spotted by a chronicler strolling around the Palace of Westminster, 'apparelled after the manner of Englishmen'. They were no longer 'brute beasts', he admitted—'I could not discern [them] from Englishmen.'

FORK IN, FORK OUT

1500

For more than half his reign, Henry VII's chief minister was Cardinal John Morton, Archbishop of Canterbury and one of the great church statesmen who shaped England's story during the Middle Ages. Often of lowly birth, these clever individuals rose through the meritocratic system of ecclesiastical education to make their names—in Morton's case, via the challenging task of national fund-raising.

When collecting money for the King, Morton's commissioners are said to have confronted their targets with a truly undodgeable means test. If a likely customer appeared prosperous, he obviously had surplus funds to contribute to the King's coffers. If, on the other hand, he lived modestly, he must have been stashing his wealth away. Either way the victim was compelled to pay—impaled, as it were, upon one or other of the twin prongs of a pitchfork.

Like many of history's chestnuts, the facts behind what came to be known as 'Morton's Fork' are not quite as neat as the story. It was more than 130 years later that the statesman-philosopher Francis Bacon coined the phrase, and the documents of the time make clear that Morton did not wield the pitchfork personally. But the cardinal certainly did work hard to satisfy the appetite of a money-hungry monarch. As well as helping Henry to tighten up parliamentary taxation, he presided over the collection of 'benevolences'—'voluntary' wealth taxes that invited subjects to show their goodwill towards the King. Not surprisingly, these forced loans soon became known as 'malevolences', and Henry himself developed a reputation as a miser. 'In his later days,' wrote the normally loyal Polydore Vergil, 'all [his] virtues were obscured by avarice.'

Henry VII's account ledgers would seem to bear this out. At the foot of page after page are the royal initials, scratched by the careful bookkeeper monarch as he ran his finger down the columns. But Henry could spend lavishly when he wanted to, particularly when it came to making his kingship visibly magnificent. In November 1501 he spent £14,000 (over £8 million today) on jewels alone for the wedding in St Paul's Cathedral of his eldest son Arthur to Katherine of Aragon, daughter of Ferdinand and Isabella of Spain. Ten days of tournaments were staged at Westminster and the feasting went on night after night beneath the hammer-beam roof of the Great Hall, the walls hung with the costliest cloth of Arras.

Two years later Henry splashed out again when he sent his daughter Margaret north to marry King James IV of Scotland, with an escort of two thousand horsemen, a train of magnificently clad noblemen and £16,000 (another £9 million or so) in jewels. Henry VII's marriage-broking proved portentous. It was Margaret's marriage that would one day bring the Stuart dynasty to England, while Katherine of Aragon, following the death of Arthur in 1502, would be passed on as wife to his younger brother Henry, with equally historic consequences.

Henry VII had done well by England when he died, aged fifty-two, in April 1509. You can see his death mask in Westminster Abbey, his face lean and intelligent, his eyes sharp and his mouth shut, concealing the teeth which, according to contemporary description, were 'few, poor and black-stained'. He lies in splendour in the magnificent chapel that he built at the south end of the abbey—another notable item of dynastic extravagance. Beside him lies his wife Elizabeth of York, and not far away, his mother Lady Margaret Beaufort, who had schemed so hard and faithfully to bring her Tudor son to power.

The soaring stone pillars of the chapel are decorated with the Beaufort portcullis and with the double rose that would become the symbol of the Tudors, giving graphic shape to the healing, but oversimplified, myth that the warring flowers had been melded into a flourishing new hybrid. One of the chapel's stained-glass windows shows a crown wreathed in a thorn bush, and later legend relates how Henry actually plucked his crown from such a bush at Bosworth. In fact, contemporary accounts of the battle made no mention of bushes—they describe the crown as simply being picked up off the ground. But it is fair enough to think of Henry as the King who redeemed England from a thorny situation.

KING HENRY VIII'S 'GREAT MATTER'

1509–33

After the penny-pinching ways of Henry VII, the profligate glamour of his red-blooded, redheaded son, the new King Henry VIII, exploded over England like a sunburst. Just seventeen years old, the athletic young monarch was the nation's sporting hero.

'It is the prettiest thing in the world to see him play,' purred an admirer of Henry's exertions at tennis, 'his fair skin glowing through a shirt of the finest texture.' When the young King, tall and energetic, joined the royal bowmen for target practice, his arrow 'cleft the mark in the middle and surpassed them all'.

He was a superlative horseman, a champion in the jousts, an all-round wrestler—and when the music started, he could pluck a mean string on the lute. Recent research has revealed that Henry may even have played football, a game usually considered too rough and common for the well born. In February 2004 a fresh look at the inventory of his Great Wardrobe discovered that alongside forty-five pairs of velvet shoes the King kept a pair of purpose-made football boots.

The other side of bluff King Hal was evident within three days of his accession. With the vicious eye for a scapegoat that was to characterise his ruling style, the King authorised the show trials of Richard Empson and Edmund Dudley, two of his father's most effective and unpopular money-raisers. The pair had done nothing worse than carry out royal orders and line their own pockets. But Henry had both men executed—then promptly embarked on a spending spree with his father's carefully hoarded treasure. He had an insatiable capacity for enjoying himself. Masques, mummeries, jousts, pageants—the festivities went on for days when Henry was crowned in June 1509 alongside his fetching and prestigious new Spanish wife Katherine of Aragon.

Four years older than Henry, Katherine was embarking on her second marriage. Having married Henry's brother Arthur in November

1501, she had found herself widowed before that winter was out. Young Henry had stepped forward to take Arthur's place both as Prince of Wales and as Katherine's betrothed, and when he came to the throne he made their marriage his first order of personal business. The couple exchanged vows and rings in a private ceremony at Greenwich on 11 June 1509, and set about the happy process of procreation. When, after one miscarriage, a son was born on New Year's Day 1511, Henry's joy knew no bounds. As bonfires were lit and salutes cannonaded from the Tower, the proud father staged a vast tournament, mingling with the crowds and delightedly allowing them to tear off as souvenirs the splendid gold letters 'H' and 'K' that adorned his clothes.

But the baby boy, who had been christened Henry, died within two months, and disappointment would prove the pattern of Katherine's childbearing. One daughter, Mary, born in 1516, was the only healthy survivor of a succession of ill-fated pregnancies, births and stillbirths, and after ten years of marriage without a male heir, Henry came to ponder on the reasons for God's displeasure.

He thought he found his answer in the Bible. 'Thou shalt not uncover the nakedness of thy brother's wife,' read chapter 18 of the Old Testament Book of Leviticus—and two chapters later, the consequences were set out clearly: 'If a man shall take his brother's wife, it is an unclean thing ... they shall be childless.' This apparently firm prohibition had been overruled at the time of Henry and Katherine's betrothal in 1504 by special licence from the Pope, who based his action on the contradictory instruction in the Book of Deuteronomy that it was a man's duty to take his brother's widow 'and raise up seed for his brother'. Katherine, for her part, firmly maintained that she was free to marry Henry because her five-month marriage to the fifteen-year-old Arthur had never been consummated.

But as Katherine remained childless through the 1520s, her discontented husband started to lend a ready ear to those who suggested that his wife could easily have been lying. 'Bring me a cup of ale,' brother Arthur was said to have cried out contentedly on the first morning of his married life, 'I have been this night in the midst of Spain!'

To Henry the solution seemed simple. Since a pope had fixed his improper, heirless marriage to Katherine, a pope should now unfix it, freeing the English King to take the fertile young wife his dynastic duty required—and by the spring of 1527 the thirty-six-year-old Henry knew exactly who that wife should be. He had fallen in love with Anne Boleyn, a self-assured beauty ten years or so his junior, notable for a pair of mesmeric dark eyes and a steely sense of purpose.

But as Henry set his mind to making a new marriage, events in Italy made it highly unlikely that the Pope would give him any help. In May that year Rome was captured and sacked by the troops of Charles V, the powerful Habsburg ruler who was also Katherine's nephew. Charles controlled Spain, the Netherlands, much of Germany and Italy—and now the Pope. There was no way he would allow his aunt to be humiliatingly cast aside by the King of England.

Until now Henry had been content to leave the handling of his divorce to Cardinal Thomas Wolsey, the talented church statesman who ran the country for him, as Cardinal Morton had taken care of business for his father. But the normally competent cardinal was left helpless after the shift of power in Rome—and he had made the mistake of offending the now powerful Anne Boleyn. He called her the 'night crow'. After fourteen years of effectively running England, Wolsey was disgraced. Charged with treason, he died from the shock. Henry took over Hampton Court, the magnificent palace the portly cardinal had built for himself down the Thames from Richmond—and started lending an ear to advisers who were considerably more Popo-sceptic.

Chief among these was Anne herself, who had a radical taste in reading. Sometime in

1530 she placed in Henry's hands a copy of the recently published *Obedience of a Christian Man* by the reformer William Tyndale, a controversial little volume that had been denounced as 'a holy boke of disobedyence' by Thomas More, Wolsey's successor as Lord Chancellor. *How Christian Rulers Ought to Govern* was Tyndale's subtitle, and he argued that, since the Bible made no mention of the Pope (nor of bishops, abbots, church courts or of the whole earthly edifice of church power and glory), the Church should be governed like the state, by a 'true Christian prince'—without interference from the so-called 'Bishop of Rome'.

'This book is for me and for all Kings to read,' mused Henry—here was the solution to his troublesome 'Great Matter'. Why should the King not effectively award himself his own divorce, as governor of the English Church, in order to secure the heir that his country needed? 'England cares nothing for popes,' Anne's brother George Boleyn would declare to a papal official visiting England in the summer of 1530. 'The king is absolute emperor and pope in his own kingdom.'

The Boleyns were thrusting members of the rising Tudor gentry—landowners and former merchants whose personal beliefs were traditional but who had no special fondness for the Pope, and still less for the power and privileges of the clergy with their unearned wealth and their special exemptions from the law. Scrounging was the Church's speciality, according to a scurrilous tract of the time, *A Supplication for the Beggars*, which pretended to be a petition from the 'Beggars of England' to the King, complaining that crafty churchmen were putting them out of business by begging so much better than they could. Stealing land, money and even, on occasion, the virtue of good men's wives and daughters, the clerics had filched 'the whole realm', complained the *Supplication*.

This jeering anticlerical sentiment was mobilised in the autumn of 1529, when Parliament gathered for what was to prove an historic series of sessions. Discontented laymen were invited to draw up lists of their grievances against the clergy, and the result, finally codified in May 1532, was a formidable roundup of just about everything that people found irritating about the often complacent and greedy ways of the all-too-earthly Church. It was exactly what the King wanted to hear. 'We thought that the clergy of our realm had been our subjects wholly,' declared Henry menacingly as he studied the list of complaints. 'But now we have well perceived that they be but half our subjects.'

Here was an area where the King and a fair number of the merchants, lawyers, country gentlemen and landed magnates who dominated Parliament clearly felt as one.

England, they argued, should have control over its own Church—and between 1529 and 1536 Parliament passed a series of laws to accomplish that, transferring the many aspects of church life and business to the Crown.

The immediate consequence was that Henry was able to marry Anne and cast off Katherine. But the long-term consequence of these new laws went far beyond Henry and his need for a son. 'This realm of England is an empire . . .' declared the Act in Restraint of Appeals of 1533, 'governed by one supreme head and king . . . furnished with plenary, whole and entire power . . . without restraint or provocation to any foreign princes or potentates of the world'.

Henry's 'Great Matter' turned out to be greater than anyone, including himself, had guessed. English kings now acknowledged no superior under God on earth.

'LET THERE BE LIGHT'— WILLIAM TYNDALE AND THE ENGLISH BIBLE

1525

Henry VIII's historic break with Rome was fundamentally about earthly power, not spiritual belief. Even while Henry was demolishing the Pope's authority over the English Church in the early 1530s, a Sunday service in the average English parish was still shaped by the comforting chants and Catholic rituals hallowed by the centuries.

But in Europe, belief was changing more radically. In October 1517 the rebellious German monk Martin Luther, a miner's son turned theologian and philosophy professor, had nailed his famous ninety-five theses—or 'propositions'—to the church door in Wittenberg in Saxony. Luther was appalled by the materialism of the Roman Church, and his ninety-five propositions were a particular attack on the sale of 'indulgences', Church-approved coupons that people purchased in the belief that they were being let off their sins—printed tickets to heaven. The Pope had no authority to forgive people's sins, argued Luther, let alone offer forgiveness for sale, like bread or beer. It was faith alone that would bring salvation, and men had no need of priests to mediate with God. Believers could commune directly with their Maker through prayer, and by reading God's word in the Bible. Within a few years several dozen of Germany's duchies and principalities had thrown off papal authority and signed up to Luther's protests and to his call for reform—generating the movement that historians would later call the Protestant Reformation.

Henry VIII was outraged. He thought that Luther's views undermined civil obedience, and left people with no reason to be good. When Luther's message reached England, the King was still on warm terms with the Pope, and with the help of Thomas More he fired off an indignant diatribe against the heretical German, earning himself the title *Fidei Defensor*, 'Defender of the Faith'. To this day the abbreviations *Fid. Def.*, or *F.D.*, appear on the face of every English coin, commemorating the title by which in 1521, only a decade before the break with Rome, the grateful Pope declared Henry his favourite and most faithful prince in Europe. On Henry's orders, Cardinal Wolsey organised public burnings of Luther's books, and even hunted down the reformer's translation of the New Testament into German.

The Roman Church's own version of the Bible was in Latin—the fourth-century Latin of St Jerome, whose precise meaning might be accessible to learned priests and scholars but which floated sonorously over the heads of most churchgoers, rather like a magical incantation, heavy on comfort and light on explanation. The Roman priesthood's control over faith relied heavily on its virtual monopoly of Latin, and most churchmen felt deeply threatened by the idea of people reading the Bible in their own language and interpreting it for themselves.

But this was precisely the ambition of the young priest, William Tyndale, who was working in Gloucestershire in the early 1520s. This area, on the border with Wales, had long been a stronghold of the Lollards, the prayer-mumbling disciples of John Wycliffe who, back in the 1380s, had argued that the Bible should be made accessible to ordinary people in their own tongue. 'If God spare my life,' declared

Tyndale in a heated argument with an establishment cleric who had railed against the translating of the Bible, 'ere many years, I wyl cause a boye that dryveth the plough, shall know more the Scripture than thou dost.'

The talented and scholarly Tyndale had command of eight languages, notably Greek and Hebrew, which were virtually unknown in England at this time. He was also blessed with an extraordinary ability to create poetic phrases in his native tongue, and his memorable translations live on to this day—'the salt of the earth', 'signs of the times', 'the powers that be' and even 'bald as a coot' we owe to William Tyndale. All these vibrant expressions flowed from his pen as, through the 1520s, he laboured to render the word of God into ploughboy language. When he could not find the right word, he invented it—'scapegoat' and 'broken-hearted' are two of his coinages. As he translated, he was helping to shape the very rhythm and thought patterns of English: 'eat drink and be merry'—'am I my brother's keeper?'—'fight the good fight'—'blessed are the meek for they shall inherit the earth' . . .

To avoid the wrath of Wolsey, who was having heretics whipped and imprisoned, Tyndale had to compose his fine phrases abroad. In 1524 he travelled to Europe, where he dodged from printing press to printing press in cities like Hamburg and

Brussels—shadowed by the cardinal's agents, who had identified this prolific wordsmith as a home-grown heretic quite as dangerous as Luther. In 1526, Tyndale managed to get three thousand copies of his New Testament printed in the German city of Worms, and within months the books were circulating among freethinkers in England, smuggled in by Hull sailors in casks of wax and grain. It was four years later that a copy of Tyndale's *Obedience of a Christian Man* reached Anne Boleyn, providing encouragement for Henry's break from the Pope.

But then in 1530, Tyndale dared to address the great question of the King's marriage from a biblical point of view, and with the perversity of the dyed-in-the-wool nonconformist he concluded in his book *The Practice of Prelates* that the Bible did *not* authorise Henry to jettison his wife.

It was his death sentence. The growing number of reformers among the English clergy were advocating the use of the Bible in English, and Tyndale's accurate and powerful translation was the obvious version to use. But the King was infuriated by Tyndale's criticism of his divorce and of his proposed marriage to Anne. The English agents kept up their pursuit of the fugitive, and in May 1535 they got their man. Now aged about forty, he was captured in Antwerp, to be condemned as a heretic and sentenced to be burned to death.

On 6 October 1536, William Tyndale was led out to his execution. As a small token of mercy he was granted the kindness of being strangled in the moments before the fire was lit. But the executioner bungled the tightening of the rope, painfully crushing Tyndale's throat while leaving him still alive as the flames licked around him.

'Lord, open the King of England's eyes!' cried the reformer as he died.

The executioner piled on more fuel until the body was totally consumed, since the purpose of burning heretics was to reduce them to ashes that could be thrown to the winds—no trace of their presence should be left on earth. But William Tyndale left more than ashes: 'In the begynnynge was the worde and the worde was with God and the worde was God . . . In it was lyfe and the lyfe was the light of men. And the light shyneth in the darknes, but the darknes comprehended it not.'

THOMAS MORE AND HIS WONDERFUL 'NO-PLACE'
1535

Young Henry VIII loved the company of the learned and witty Thomas More. The King would take him up on to the roof of his palace to gaze skywards and 'consider with him the diversities, courses, motions and operations of the stars'. Travelling in his barge down the Thames one day, he decided to drop in unexpectedly on the Mores' sprawling riverside home in Chelsea. He invited himself for dinner, then walked in the garden with his host 'by the space of an hour, holding his arm about his neck'.

More's son-in-law William Roper was much impressed by this intimacy with the King, but

More himself had no illusions. 'Son Roper, I may tell thee . . .' he confided, 'if my head could win His Majesty a castle in France it should not fail to go.'

Thomas More was literally a Renaissance man, playing his own part in the great 're-birthing' of the fifteenth and sixteenth centuries. South of the Alps, the Renaissance was famously embodied by such artists as Michelangelo and Leonardo. In the north, it was the so-called 'Christian humanists' like More and his Dutch friend Erasmus who struck sparks off each other—to memorable effect. In 1509, Erasmus dedicated his great work *In Praise of Folly* to Thomas (its Latin name, *Encomium Moriae*, was a pun on More's name). More responded with his own flight of intellect, *Utopia*—his inspired combination of the Greek words for 'no' and 'place'.

Utopia is the tale More claimed to have heard when, coming out of church one day, he bumped into an old seaman: 'his face was tanned, he had a long beard, and his cloak was hanging carelessly about him'. This philosopher-sailor had been travelling with the Italian explorer Amerigo Vespucci, after whom the Americas would shortly be named. Having chatted with More for a while about all that was presently wrong with the kingdoms of Europe, he started describing his experiences on the island of 'Utopia' where, he said, there was no shortage of life's essentials. When people went to the market, everything was free, and because of that 'there is no danger of a man's asking for more than he needs ... since they are sure that they shall always be supplied. It is the fear of want that makes any of the whole race of animals either greedy or ravenous.'

Like space travel in our own day, the sixteenth century's voyages of discovery were stirring people's imaginations, and More's *Utopia* was a sort of science fiction, a fantasy about a super-perfect society where thoughtful people had worked out a life of benevolent equality. In this ideal 'No-Place', couples who were 'more fruitful' shared their children with those who were not so blessed, while lawyers were totally banned—they were a profession who disguised the truth, explained More quizzically, whose own wealth came from his prosperous legal practice. Living according to nature, striving for health and dying cheerfully, the Utopians offered a satirical commentary on the 'moth-eaten' laws and the hypocrisy of European society—and More himself tried to put some of Utopia's ideas into practice, encouraging his daughters to debate philosophy in front of him. 'Erudition in women is a new thing,' he wrote, 'and a reproach to the idleness of men.'

But More's visionary thinking was tethered to a deep religious conservatism—he was steadfastly loyal to the Pope and to the old ways of the Church. In the style of Thomas Becket, he wore a hair shirt beneath the glorious liveries of the public offices that he occupied—though unlike Becket, he kept his prickly garment maggot-free: it was regularly laundered by his daughter Margaret Roper. Thomas shared his royal master Henry VIII's indignation at Martin Luther and his reforming ideas, outdoing the King in his furious invective. In one diatribe, More described Luther as *merda*, *stercus*, *lutum*, *coenum*—shit, dung, filth, excrement. And for good measure, he then denounced the German as a drunkard, a liar, an ape and an arsehole who had been vomited on to this earth by the Antichrist.

More joined Henry's Council in 1517, the same year that Luther nailed his theses to the church door in Wittenberg, and set about waging a personal war on the new ideas for reform. He had a little jail and a set of stocks built in his garden so he could cross-question heretics personally, and he nursed a particular hatred for the translations of William Tyndale, whom he described as 'a hell-hound in the kennel of the devil'. When More got back to Chelsea after his work on the King's Council he would spend his evenings penning harangues denouncing Tyndale, while defending the traditional practices of the Church.

But while More and Tyndale might differ

over popes and sacraments, they were agreed on the subject of kings' wives. More actually shared Tyndale's opinion that the Bible did not authorise Henry VIII's annulment of his marriage with Katherine—and their highly inconvenient conviction set both men on a tragic collision course with the King. When, after the disgrace of Wolsey, Henry invited Thomas to become his new Lord Chancellor, More at first refused. He could see the danger ahead. He only accepted after Henry promised not to embroil him in the divorce, leaving the 'Great Matter' to those 'whose consciences could well enough agree therein'.

But detachment became impossible as Henry's quarrel with the Pope grew more bitter. By the early 1530s royal policy was being guided by the gimlet-eyed Thomas Cromwell, a former agent of Wolsey's who, in the spring of 1534, pushed a new statute through Parliament, the Act of Succession. This required men to swear their agreement to the settlement, rejecting the rights of Katherine and her daughter Mary. When More refused to swear, he was promptly escorted to the Tower.

'By the mass, Master More,' warned the Duke of Norfolk, an old friend and one of several visitors who tried to persuade him to change his mind, 'it is perilous striving with princes . . . I would wish you somewhat to incline to the king's pleasure for, by God's body, *indignatio principis mors est*—the wrath of the king is death.'

'Is that all, my lord?' responded Thomas. 'Then in good faith is there no more difference between your Grace and me, but that I shall die today and you tomorrow.'

More was led out to the scaffold early on the morning of 6 July 1535, and he kept up his graceful, ironic humour to the end. 'I pray you, Master Lieutenant, see me safe up,' he said as he mounted the ladder, 'and [for] my coming down, let me shift for myself.'

Worn and thin from his months in prison, loose in his clothes, with a skullcap on his head and a long straggling beard, the former chancellor looked not unlike the old sailor-philosopher he had once imagined telling stories of 'No-Place'—and that name he invented for his imaginary island remains to this day the word people use when they want to describe a wonderful but impossible dream.

DIVORCED, BEHEADED, DIED . . .
1533–7

Anne Boleyn sailed down the Thames to her coronation at the end of May 1533 in a Cleopatra's fleet of vessels. Anne herself rode in Katherine of Aragon's former barge—from which the discarded Queen's coat of arms had been hacked away—and her costume made clear the reason for her triumph. The new Queen had added 'a panel to her skirts' because she was visibly pregnant. In just four months she would be delivered of the heir for which her husband had schemed so hard.

But the child born on 7 September that year turned out to be a girl. She was christened Elizabeth, and the pre-written letters announcing the birth made embarrassingly clear that this had not been the plan—a last-minute stroke of the pen had made the word 'Prince' into 'Princes[s]'. The jousting that had been organised to celebrate the new arrival was cancelled, and it was noted ominously that Henry did not attend the christening. Anne Boleyn might 'spurn our heads off like footballs', prophesied Thomas More, 'but it will not be long ere her head will dance the like dance'.

When Anne's second pregnancy ended in a miscarriage in January 1536 her fate was sealed, since Tudor medical science—or the lack of it—meant that one miscarriage might well be the first of an unbreakable series. This had been the case with Katherine, and once again Henry had not been slow in lining up a possible replacement for his non-productive Queen. He had set his cap at Jane Seymour, a soft-spoken young woman who was as meek and submissive as Anne had proved complicated and assertive.

Having made the Boleyn marriage possible, Thomas Cromwell was now given the job of destroying it. Anne had always been flirtatious, and this proved the route to her undoing. Playful glances and gestures were interpreted as evidence of actual infidelity. Men were tortured and 'confessions' produced. A court musician pleaded guilty to adultery. Her own brother was charged with incest. The facts were outlandish, but the servants of a Tudor government knew that 'proof' had to be found so that the defective Queen could be condemned. As Anne Boleyn prepared to step out on to Tower Green on 19 May 1536, the first Queen of England ever to be executed, she seemed to have reached her own peace. 'I hear the executioner is very good,' she said, 'and I have a little neck.' Then she put her hands around her throat and burst out laughing.

Henry wasted no time. No sooner had he received the news of Anne's beheading than he set off upriver on his barge to see Jane Seymour. Engaged the next day, the couple were married ten days later, and Jane was formally enthroned on Whit Sunday 4 June 1536—in the very chair where Anne had sat only five weeks earlier.

From Henry's point of view, it was third time lucky. A kindly and level-headed woman in her late twenties, Jane worked hard to reconcile Henry with his elder daughter Mary, whose place in the succession he had given to Anne's daughter Elizabeth, and the lottery of fertility finally yielded the King the male heir that he wanted. At Hampton Court on 12 October 1537, Queen Jane was delivered of a healthy baby boy, whom Henry christened Edward, after the Confessor, the patron saint of English royalty. Henry at last had the token of divine blessing he had sought.

But his wife had suffered a disastrous delivery. According to one account, she had undergone the then primitive and almost invariably fatal surgery of a Caesarean section. Other evidence suggests blood poisoning of the placenta—puerperal fever. Either way, Prince Edward's mother died after twelve days of blood loss and infection that the royal doctors were helpless to reverse.

Henry was prostrated with unaccustomed sorrow. Jane Seymour lay in state for three weeks, and then, alone of Henry's wives, she was buried in pomp and glory in St George's Chapel at Windsor. It was later said that her name was on Henry's lips when he died, and certainly his will was to direct that he should be buried beside her. When the King of France sent his congratulations on the birth of a healthy heir, Henry's reply was uncharacteristically subdued. 'Divine Providence,' he wrote, 'hath mingled my joy with the bitterness of the death of her who brought me this happiness.'

Diplomatic dispatches are seldom to be taken at their face value, still less when worded by Henry VIII. But in this case we might, perhaps, give Henry the benefit of the doubt.

THE PILGRIMAGE OF GRACE

1536

Early-sixteenth-century life was interwoven with the joy of religious rite and spectacle—effigies of saints, stained-glass windows; the washing of feet on Maundy Thursday, the 'creeping to the cross' on Good Friday. In London every Whit Sunday, doves were released from the tower of St Paul's Cathedral to symbolise the Holy Spirit winging its way to heaven. This age-old texture of symbol and ritual provided a satisfying structure to most people's lives. The English were devout folk, reported one European traveller: 'they all attend mass every day'.

The miracle of the mass—the Holy

Communion service when bread and wine were offered up at the altar—was graphically described in Thomas Malory's *Morte D'Arthur*, the bestselling epic first printed and published by Caxton in 1485. As the bishop held up a wafer of bread, 'there came a figure in likeness of a child, and the visage was as red and as bright as any fire, and smote himself into the bread, that all they saw it that the bread was formed of a fleshly man'.

This was the moment of 'transubstantiation' when, according to Catholic belief, the bread and wine on the altar were literally transformed into the body and blood of Christ. It provided the awe-inspiring climax of every mass. Bells rang, incense wafted, and heads were bowed as Jesus himself, both child and 'fleshly man', descended from heaven to join that particular human congregation—to be devoured as the people ate his flesh and the priest alone drank his blood (the liquid that had once been wine was too precious to risk being passed around and spilled).

By the 1520s and 30s, the evangelical followers of Luther and Tyndale were openly scoffing at this potent but, to their mind, primitive and sacrilegious Catholic theatre. How could the Lord's sacred body be conjured up on earth by imperfect men in gaudy vestments? The exhilarating idea at the heart of the Reformation, that every man could have his own direct relationship with God, challenged the central role of the priest in religious ceremonies—and from this spiritual doubt followed material consequences. By what right did the clerics control their vast infrastructure of earthly power and possessions, notably the vast landed estates of the monasteries? The Church was by far the largest landowner in England.

In 1535 Henry VIII's chief minister, Thomas Cromwell, seized on this appetising question: if the Church was corrupted by its involvement with worldly goods, why should he not relieve it of the problem? So he sent out his 'visitors', crews of inspectors who descended on the eight hundred or so monasteries and nunneries in England and duly discovered what they were sent to find. Laziness, greed and sexual peccadilloes: it was not difficult to unearth—or indeed, invent—evidence that some of the country's seven thousand monks, nuns and friars had been failing to live up to the high ideals they set themselves. Cromwell's inquisitors gleefully presented to their master plenty of examples of misconduct, along with some improbable relics—the clippings of St Edmund's toenails, St Thomas Becket's penknife. Their hastily gathered dossiers provided the excuse for the biggest land grab in English history, starting in 1536 with the dissolution of the smaller monasteries.

But the destruction of the country's age-old education, employment and social welfare network was not accomplished without protest. The monasteries represented everything that, for centuries, people had been taught to respect, and in October 1536 the north of England rose in revolt. Rallying behind dramatic banners depicting the five wounds of Christ, some forty thousand marchers came to the aid of Mother Church in a rebellion they proudly called the Pilgrimage of Grace.

The 'pilgrims' set about reinstating the monks and nuns in sixteen of the fifty-five houses that had already been suppressed. They demanded the legitimisation of Queen Katherine's daughter, Mary. They also called for the destruction of the disruptive books of Luther and Tyndale, and for the removal of Thomas Cromwell along with his ally Thomas Cranmer, the reforming Archbishop of Canterbury. The rebels had a fundamental faith in the orthodoxy of their monarch—if only King Henry's wicked advisers were removed, they believed, he would return to the good old ways.

This loyalty proved their undoing when Henry, unable to raise sufficient troops against them, bought time by agreeing to concede to the 'pilgrims' some of their demands; he invited their leader, Robert Aske, to come down to London and present his grievances in person, under safe conduct. But once the rebels were safely dispersed back home in their villages, Henry seized on the excuse of new risings in the early months of 1537 to exact revenge. 'Our pleasure,' he instructed his army commander, the Duke of Norfolk, '[is] that you shall cause such dreadful execution to be done upon a good number of every town village and hamlet that have offended as they may be a fearful spectacle to all others hereafter that would practise any like matter.'

Norfolk carried out his orders ruthlessly. Some seventy Cumberland villagers were hanged on trees in their gardens in full sight of their wives and children; the monks of Sawley, one of the monasteries reopened by the pilgrims, were hanged on long timber staves projecting from their steeple. Aske was executed in front of the people who had so enthusiastically cheered him a few months earlier.

The rebels had not been wrong in their hunch that Henry was at heart a traditional Catholic—the King believed in the miracle of transubstantiation to the day he died. Even as the Reformation progressed, he burned the reformers who dared to suggest that the bread and wine of the communion were mere symbols of Christ's body and blood. But he needed to fill his coffers. By 1540 England's last religious house, the rich Augustinian abbey of Waltham, had been closed and the royal treasury was richer by £132,000 (more than £50 million today) from the sale of the monastery lands.

Even richer in the long term were the squires, merchants and magnates who had been conscripted into the new order of things, picking up prime monastic acres all over the country. The Dissolution of the Monasteries was Henry's payoff to the landed classes, and it helped make the Reformation permanent.

But to this day we find corners of the English countryside curiously sanctified by the remains of high gothic arches, haunted towers and long-deserted cloisters. Rievaulx in north Yorkshire, Tintern in the Wye Valley, and Whitby on the windswept North Sea coast where St Hilda preached and the cowherd Caedmon sang: all these ghostly ruins are visible reminders of what was once the heart of English learning, education and history-making—a civilisation that consoled and inspired rich and poor alike for centuries.

. . . DIVORCED, BEHEADED, SURVIVED

1539–47

In the summer of 1539 Henry VIII staged a pageant on the River Thames. Two barges put out on to the water, one manned by a crew representing the King and his Council, the other by sailors in the scarlet costumes of the Pope and his cardinals. As Henry and crowds of Londoners looked on, the two boats met and engaged in mock battle, with much capering and horseplay until the inevitable happened—the scarlet-clad Pope and his cardinals were pitched into the river.

Real life was not so simple. In 1538 the Pope had issued a call to the Catholic powers of

Europe to rally against England's 'most cruel and abominable tyrant' and England now found herself dangerously isolated. Thomas Cromwell's solution was to look for support among the Protestant princes of Germany. He could see how his royal master had been moping since the death of Jane Seymour a year or so earlier: perhaps business and pleasure could be combined by marriage to a comely German princess.

Inquiries established that there were two promising candidates in Cleves, the powerful north German duchy with its capital at Düsseldorf. The duke had a pair of marriageable sisters, Anne and Amelia, and early in 1539 Cromwell asked the English ambassador Christopher Mont to investigate their beauty. Mont reported back positively, and two locally produced portraits were sent off for the King's inspection. But were the likenesses trustworthy?

The answer was to dispatch the King's own painter, Hans Holbein, the talented German artist whose precise and luminous portraits embody for us the personalities and textures of Henry's court. Working quickly as usual, Holbein produced portraits of both sisters in little more than a week. That of Anne showed a serene and pleasant-looking woman, and legend has it that Henry fell in love with the portrait. In fact, the King had already decided that now, at forty-eight, he should go for the elder of the two sisters—the twenty-four-year-old Anne. The gentle, modest face that he saw in Holbein's canvas simply confirmed all the written reports he had received.

When Henry met his bride-to-be, however, he found her downright plain. 'I see nothing in this woman as men report of her,' he said, speaking 'very sadly and pensively' soon after he had greeted Anne on New Year's Day 1540. 'I marvel that wise men would make such report as they have done.'

Four days later Henry VIII went to his fourth marriage ceremony with a heavy heart. 'If it were not to satisfy the world and my realm,' he told Cromwell reproachfully on their way to the service, 'I would not do that I must do this day for none earthly thing.'

Next morning, Henry was in a thoroughly bad mood: there were still more grounds for reproach.

'Surely, as ye know,' he said to Cromwell, 'I liked her before not well, but now I like her much worse, for I have felt her belly and her breasts, and thereby, as I can judge, she should be no maid.' He added the indelicate detail that Anne suffered from bad body odour, and went on to describe the deflating effect this had on his ardour. 'I had neither will nor courage to proceed any further in other matters . . .' he confessed. 'I have left her as good a maid as I found her.'

The royal doctors were called in. It was a

serious matter when a king could not consummate his marriage, but all they could offer was the age-old advice in such circumstances—not to worry too much. They advised Henry to take a night off.

But when the King returned to the fray, he found that nothing had changed—as Anne confirmed with charming innocence. 'When he comes to bed,' she told one of her ladies-in-waiting, 'he kisses me and taketh me by the hand and biddeth me "Goodnight, sweetheart". And in the morning [he] kisses me and biddeth me "Farewell, darling". Is this not enough?'

We know these extraordinary details because, not for the first time, Thomas Cromwell was allotted the task of undoing what he had done. A widely unpopular figure, he had pushed the reforming agenda too far for the tastes of many, and landing his master with a wife that Henry disparagingly called 'the Flanders Mare' proved the last straw. In June 1540 Cromwell became the latest of Henry's scapegoats, condemned for treason by act of Parliament and facing the dreadful penalties of hanging, drawing and quartering. If he wished to avoid this particular fate, the minister's final duty was to set down on paper the circumstantial evidence that would make possible the annulment of Henry's non-marriage to Anne.

Thomas Cromwell was executed—with an

axe—on 28 July 1540; the paperwork he produced at the eleventh hour helped Henry secure annulment of the Cleves marriage. Just ten days later the King was married again, to Katherine Howard, the twenty-year-old niece of his fierce general in the north, the Duke of Norfolk. For nearly a year the traditionalist duke, a Catholic and a bitter enemy of Cromwell's, had been pushing the enticing Katherine into Henry's path while plotting his rival's downfall.

Unfortunately, the new Queen's lively allure was accompanied by a lively sexual appetite, and little more than a year after her marriage, rumours circulated about Katherine's promiscuity. As an unmarried girl in the unsupervised surroundings of the Norfolk household, she was said to have romped with Henry Manox her music teacher and also with her cousin Thomas Dereham—whom she then had the nerve to employ as her private secretary when she became Queen. In the autumn of 1541, during a royal progress to the north, inquiries revealed that she had waited till Henry was asleep before cavorting with another young lover, Thomas Culpeper.

Henry wept openly before his Council when finally confronted with proof of his wife's betrayal. Katherine was beheaded in February the next year, along with Culpeper, Manox the music teacher, her cousin Dereham and Lady Rochford, the lady-in-waiting who had facilitated the backstairs liaisons after the King had gone to sleep.

Henry was by now a gross and lumbering man-mountain, ‘moved by engines and art rather than by nature’, as the Duke of Norfolk put it. Arthritic and ulcerous, the ageing King had to be manhandled up staircases—a little cart was built to transport him around Hampton Court. His apothecary’s accounts list dam-busting quantities of liquorice, rhubarb and other laxatives, along with grease for the royal haemorrhoids.

What Henry needed was a reliable and experienced wife, and he finally found one in Catherine Parr, thirty-one years old and twice widowed—which gave her the distinction of being England’s most married Queen. In July 1543 she embarked sagely on the awesome challenge of life with England’s most married king, bringing together his children Mary, Elizabeth and Edward to create, for the first time, something like a functional royal family household. Catherine was sympathetic to the new faith, and her most significant achievement, apart from surviving, was probably to ensure that the two younger children, Edward and Elizabeth, were educated by tutors who favoured reform.

When Henry died on 28 January 1547, the news was kept secret for three days. It was difficult to imagine England without the lustful, self-indulgent tyrant who had once been the beautiful young sportsman-king. In moral terms the tale of his reign was one of remorseless decline, of power corrupting absolutely. By no measure of virtue could Henry VIII be called a good man.

But he was a great one—and arguably England's greatest ever king. Take virtue out of the equation, and his accomplishments were formidable. He destroyed the centuries-old medieval Church. He revolutionised the ownership of English land. He increased the power of central government to unprecedented heights, and though he ruled England as a despot, he did so without the support of an army. The new Church of England was Henry VIII's most obvious legacy. And in the turbulent years that followed his death the country's destiny would also be decisively shaped by the institution that he had enlisted—and thus, in the process, strengthened—to help him break from Rome: the Houses of Parliament and, in particular, the House of Commons.

BOY KING—EDWARD VI, 'THE GODLY IMP'

1547–53

After all the trouble that Henry VIII and England had gone through to get a male heir, Henry made sure that his son Edward received the best education that could be devised for a future king. The boy's tutors, Richard Cox and John Cheke, were the leading humanist scholars of the day, and they redoubled their efforts with the nine-year-old when he succeeded his father in January 1547. In his geography lessons Edward learned by heart the names of all the ports in England, Scotland and France, together with the prevailing winds and tides; in history he studied the long and disastrous reign of Henry VI, an object lesson in how *not* to rule. By the age of twelve, the 'godly imp' was reading twelve chapters of the Bible every day and taking notes as he listened to the Sunday sermon. In a display of cunning reminiscent of his grandfather Henry VII, the boy king devised his own secret code of Greek letters so no one could read his personal jottings.

Except for rejecting the authority of the Pope, Henry VIII had gone to his grave a pretty traditional Catholic. But he seems to have accepted that change must come: the two tutors he engaged for his son were prominent evangelicals, and he was well aware of the radical sympathies of his Archbishop of Canterbury Thomas Cranmer, who had been secretly preparing a programme of Protestant reform. For nearly twenty years Cranmer had hidden from his master the fact that he was married—Henry did not approve of married priests—but with Henry's death the archbishop's wife became public, and so did his programme of reform.

Out went the candles, the stained-glass windows, the statues of the Virgin and the colourful tableaux that had embellished the walls of the churches, which were now slapped over with a virtuous coat of whitewash. No more ashes on Ash Wednesday, no palms on Palm Sunday, and no creeping to the cross on Good Friday. Bells were pulled down from belfries, altar hangings and vestments were cut up to be used as saddle-cloths—and doves no longer flew from the tower of St Paul's on Whit Sunday. In just six years the changes were remarkable.

Today we delight in the beautiful and sonorous phrases of the Book of Common Prayer, first framed by Thomas Cranmer in 1548–9, then revised in 1552. But this was a strange, discordant new language to the people of the time. While reformers obviously welcomed the change, they were in the minority. Most people felt themselves deprived of something they had known and loved all their lives.

Times were already unsettling enough. Inflation was rampant. By 1550, a silver penny contained a fifth of the silver content of 1500, having been so debased by the addition of red copper that, as Bishop Latimer put it, the coin literally 'blushed in shame'. Farming, the mainstay of the economy, was being transformed by rich landowners fencing in the common land. Large flocks of sheep, tended by a single shepherd boy, now grazed on pasture that had once supported half a dozen families ploughing their own strips.

These new fields, or 'enclosures', were helping enrich the Tudor squirearchy, but less affluent country-dwellers—the vast majority of the population—felt dispossessed. In the summer of 1549, villagers in East Anglia started uprooting hedges and seizing sheep by the thousand. They gathered on Mousehold Heath, outside Norwich, around a massive oak tree they called the Reformation Oak. Since Christ had died to make men free, they reasoned, they were demanding an end to bondage. In the West Country, the Cornish-speaking men of Cornwall had already risen in revolt, calling for the restoration of the mass in Latin, since they spoke little English. They had marched eastwards, besieging Exeter for thirty-five days.

Edward's tough councillors dealt with these and other risings in the traditional way—promising to listen to grievances, then meting out mortal punishment as soon as they had mustered their military strength. But inside his own family, Edward found a nut that could not be cracked. His elder sister Mary, thirty-two years old in January 1549, was an unashamed champion of the old faith, and she refused to prohibit the reading of the mass in her household as her brother requested. 'Death shall be more welcome to me,' she declared, 'than life with a troubled conscience.'

Edward's councillors tried for a compromise, but the boy king refused to give in on the matter. 'He would spend his life,' he said, 'and all he had, rather than agree and grant to what he knew certainly to be against the truth.'

His sister tried a mixture of flattery and

condescension. 'Although your Majesty hath far more knowledge and greater gifts than others of your years, yet it is not possible that your Highness can at these years be a judge in matters of religion.'

Edward confirmed what a child he still was by breaking down in a fit of sobbing, 'his tender heart bursting out'. All the same, he refused to budge, as did Mary, who responded to his tears by repeating her willingness to be a martyr. 'Take away my life,' she said, 'rather than the old religion.'

This bitter clash between brother and sister showed that the obstinacy of Henry VIII lived on in both of them—as it did, for that matter, in their strong-willed half-sister Elizabeth, in 1553 approaching her twentieth birthday. It also suggested that the religious differences in their respective parentings might, in the future, cause turbulence and division. When Edward came down with a feverish cold in the spring of that year and could not shake it off, the whole programme of evangelical reform was suddenly in jeopardy. Edward's Protestant advisers had no doubt that if the boy were to die and Mary succeed him, she would immediately set about dismantling all the changes they had put in place. England would once again be subject to the Bishop of Rome. So what was to be done?

LADY JANE GREY — THE NINE-DAY QUEEN

1553

As the fifteen-year-old Edward VI lay sick at Greenwich in April and May 1553, his doctors were baffled by his 'weakness and faintness of spirit'. They noted a 'tough, strong, straining cough'—a possible sign of tuberculosis. Edward was coughing up blood; his body was covered with ulcers. In addition, there had been rumours that he was a victim of poison, so to protect themselves the doctors formally notified the Council that they feared the King had less than nine months to live.

On the death of Henry VIII, Edward's uncle Edward Seymour, Duke of Somerset, had taken charge of the boy king as 'Protector of the Realm'. Seymour was the elder brother of Henry's beloved third wife Jane, and it was under his auspices that the new Prayer Book of 1549 was introduced. But the risings of that year had marked the end of the Protector's power and provided an opening for John Dudley, son of Edmund Dudley, the overzealous fund-raiser that Henry VIII had executed at the beginning of his reign.

His father's fate had not deterred John Dudley from the perilous path of Tudor royal service. In the autumn of 1549 his contribution to the crushing defeat of the Norfolk rebels at the Battle of Dussindale opened the way to him becoming Lord President of Edward's Council, and two years later he awarded himself the dukedom of Northumberland. With a boy king on the throne, the new duke was the effective ruler of England.

Yet Northumberland's power rested entirely on the fragile health of the real King, and as Edward sickened, the duke resorted to desperate measures. He persuaded the fevered young monarch to keep the throne from his Catholic sister by altering the succession in favour of Lady Jane Grey, Edward's cousin and great-granddaughter of Henry VII (see Tudor family tree, p. xv). Jane was intelligent and well educated, versed in Greek, Latin and Hebrew—and reliably Protestant. Born in October 1537, the same month as Edward, she had been brought up with him in the reform-minded household of Henry VIII's last Queen, Catherine Parr—Jane and Edward often attended the same lessons.

But the young woman's greatest attraction, from the Lord President's point of view, was that she offered a way of entrenching the Northumberlands in the royal succession. On 26 May 1553 the sixteen-year-old Lady Jane was married, against her will, to Northumberland's fourth son Guildford Dudley—her protests overruled by her father Henry Grey, Duke of Suffolk, who owed his elevated title to his old crony Northumberland.

Most of Northumberland's fellow-councillors were aghast at his naked grab for power. Archbishop Cranmer said he could not agree to the change until he had spoken personally with the King—but Edward, though drifting in and out of consciousness, was still set on denying England to Rome. He ordered Cranmer to endorse his Protestant cousin, and the archbishop reluctantly obeyed. The rest of the Council went along with him.

As letters patent were hastily drawn up declaring that Edward's two elder sisters Mary and Elizabeth were illegitimate, writs went out to summon a Parliament that would confirm the new succession. But the royal health was fast failing. By now Edward's digestion had ceased to function, and his hair and nails were dropping out. When he coughed he brought up foul-smelling black sputum. Death came, on 6 July, as a merciful release.

Two days earlier, Northumberland had summoned Princesses Mary and Elizabeth to their brother's deathbed. But Elizabeth declined the trap and Mary would move only cautiously. The moment the news of Edward's death reached her, she retired to Framlingham Castle in East Anglia and defiantly proclaimed her right to the throne. Down in London, meanwhile, Northumberland was proclaiming the new Queen Jane. But as two heralds and a trumpeter made their way through the city, they met with a cold and indifferent response.

'No one present showed any sign of rejoicing,' reported one diplomat. When one herald cried, 'Long live the Queen', the only response came from the few archers who joined the sad trio.

In East Anglia it was equally clear where people's sympathies lay. Local gentlemen flocked to Framlingham with horsemen and retainers to pledge their loyalty to Mary. People who were unable to fight sent money or carts full of beer, bread and freshly slaughtered meat for the volunteer army, which by 19 July numbered nearly twenty thousand. When Mary rode out to thank them, she was greeted with 'shouts and acclamations' as men threw their helmets in the air. The noise frightened her horse so much she had to dismount and continue on foot through the mile-long encampment, greeting the soldiers personally and thanking them for their goodwill. Across the country there were enthusiastic demonstrations of support for Henry VIII's firstborn child, and local forces were quickly mustered.

It did not take long for the Council in London to get the message. Northumberland had headed north to arrest Mary, but his venture was clearly doomed. To save their own skins the colleagues he left in London, in a deft about-turn, offered a reward for his capture and proclaimed Mary's accession. In an explosion of popular joy people ran wild, crying out the news and dancing in the streets. As darkness fell, bonfires were lit. 'I am unable to describe to you,' wrote one visiting Italian, 'nor would you believe the exultation of all men. From a distance the earth must have looked like Mount Etna.'

When Mary entered London on 3 August 1553, the celebrations knew no bounds. By then Northumberland had surrendered and had been sent to the Tower, where he was executed before the month was out. Lady Jane Grey was also imprisoned, but spared by Mary—she had clearly been only a pawn in the game.

Unfortunately for Jane, however, one of Mary's first decisions as Queen was to arrange a marriage for herself to the Catholic Philip of

Spain. Early in 1554 the unpopularity of this 'Spanish match' prompted an uprising by Kentish rebels who reached the walls of London, and it became clear that the nine-day Queen, who embodied the hope for a Protestant succession, was too dangerous to be kept alive.

On 12 February 1554, Lady Jane Grey was led out to the block. It was some sort of poetic justice that along with her went Guildford Dudley, the husband she had not wished to marry, and Henry Grey, the father who had forced her into it.

BLOODY MARY AND THE FIRES OF SMITHFIELD

1553–8

The spontaneous revolt that put Mary Tudor on the throne of England was the only popular uprising to succeed in the 118 years of her dynasty's rule. '*Vox Populi, Vox Dei*', read the banners that welcomed the daughter of Henry VIII and Katherine of Aragon to London in the summer of 1553—'The voice of the people is the voice of God.'

England had always felt sympathy, and perhaps a little guilt, over the way that both Mary and her mother had been treated during the break from Rome. Both women had stayed true to their faith, and now the old religion was back. The altars and vestments came out of hiding, and once again on feast days people could process and chant in church.

Mary believed in putting her intense personal piety into practice. She took the ceremonies of Maundy Thursday particularly seriously, covering her finery with a long linen apron to kneel in front of poor women, humbly washing, drying and kissing their feet. She would turn up at the door of needy households and of poor widows, in particular, dressed not as a queen but as a gentlewoman with offers of help. She liked to mingle with ordinary villagers, asking if they had enough to live on and, if they lived on royal estates, whether they were being fairly treated by the officers of the Crown. To judge by the folk tales told of Mary Tudor's charitable exploits, the Catholic Queen was a sixteenth-century combination of Mother Teresa and Diana, Princess of Wales.

But that is not, of course, how 'Bloody Mary' has been remembered by history, for there was a fanatical and unforgiving core to her faith. On 30 November 1554, the long and complicated legal process of reuniting the English Church with Rome was finally completed, with Parliament reinstating the medieval heresy statutes. If condemned by the church courts, heretics would now be handed over to the civil authorities to endure the grim penalty of burning to death at the stake. Less than three months later, the executions began.

Before the Reformation the public burning of heretics, which horrifies us today, was generally accepted—even popular. Since 1401, when the activities of the Lollards put burning on the Statute Book, the orthodox Catholic majority had felt strengthened in their own prospects for salvation by the sight of dissidents being reduced to ashes. Even as Henry VIII was breaking with Rome in the 1530s, his burning of especially vocal Protestants could be taken as demonstrating a sensible middle way. But by the 1550s the Protestants were no longer a crazy fringe. They made up a solid and respected minority of believers, and it was on them that Mary's zeal now focused.

From an early date, Mary's fervour worried those around her. In July 1554 she had provoked Protestant sensibilities by her marriage to the Catholic Philip of Spain—the Kent uprising that cost Lady Jane Grey her life only made Mary more determined—and even Philip's Spanish advisers counselled her against inflaming feelings further. But Mary felt she had compromised enough. Under pressure from her English councillors, many of them inherited from her brother Edward, she had reluctantly agreed to leave the monastery lands with those who had purchased them. But when it came to dogma, she had God's work to do. The burnings started in February 1555 with a selection of heretics both humble and mighty, among them the puritanical former Bishop of Gloucester, John Hooper.

Hooper was a victim of the local authorities' inexperience at the practicalities of this rare and specialised form of execution. They had supplied only two saddle-loads of reeds and faggots—and because the wood was green it burned slowly. Hooper desperately clasped bundles of reeds to his chest in a vain attempt to hasten the process, but only the bottom half of his body was burning. 'For God's love, good people,' he cried out, 'let me have more fire!'

In these early days the burnings were well attended. For the citizens of Gloucester there was a novelty value, and perhaps even a ghoulish attraction, in watching their once high-and-mighty bishop agonise in front of their eyes. But the very suffering began to alter opinion—the smell of burning human flesh turns even the strongest stomach—and the executions of Bishops Hugh Latimer and Nicholas Ridley at Oxford on 16 October that same year came to symbolise the tragedy of good men being tortured for their sincere beliefs.

Ridley had been Bishop of London and had played a major role in drafting the Book of Common Prayer of 1549. Latimer was a populist preacher well known for his sympathy for the poor. Famous for blending theology with everyday social concerns in open-air sermons that he delivered to large crowds, he had proudly refused the escape route that many radicals took to the German states and Swiss cities where Protestants were safe. As he and Ridley were being trussed to the same stake, he uttered the words that would forever evoke Mary's martyrs: 'Be of good comfort, Master Ridley, and play the man; we shall this day, by God's grace, light such a candle in England as I trust shall never be put out.'

Though Latimer died quite quickly, suffocated by the smoke and losing consciousness, the fire burned more slowly on Ridley's side. As was becoming the custom, his family had bribed the executioner to tie a bag of gunpowder around his neck, but the flames were not reaching high enough to trigger this ghastly if merciful release. 'I cannot burn,' Ridley cried, screaming in pain until a guard pulled away some of the damp faggots. Immediately the flames leapt upwards, and as Ridley swung his head down towards them the gunpowder exploded.

Watching this excruciating agony was the former Archbishop of Canterbury, Thomas Cranmer. The Catholic authorities were trying to terrify him into recanting his faith—and they succeeded. Under the pressures of prison life, constant hectoring and sheer fear, Cranmer signed no less than six recantations, each more abject than the one before. The great architect of England's Protestant

Reformation was even driven to accept the Catholic doctrine of transubstantiation and the authority of the Pope.

But Cranmer still was not spared. Mary's determination to punish the archbishop who had annulled her mother's marriage and proclaimed her a bastard was unassailable. His burning was set for 21 March 1556, on the same spot in Oxford where Ridley and Latimer had died, and he was led into the university church to pronounce his final, public recantation.

But having embarked on the preamble that the authorities were expecting, Cranmer suddenly changed course. He wished to address, he said, 'the great thing which so much troubleth my conscience', and he began to explain that the recantations he had signed were 'contrary to the truth which I thought in my heart'. As uproar broke out in the church, he raised his voice to a shout: 'As for the Pope, I refuse him, as Christ's enemy and Antichrist!'

The white-bearded ex-archbishop was dragged out and hurried to the stake, where fire was put to the wood without delay. As the flames licked around him, he extended towards them the 'unworthy right hand' with which he had signed his recantations.

Cranmer's death was a propaganda disaster for Mary's government. Even loyal Catholics could see the unfairness in someone who had repeatedly recanted being punished just the same. In the forty-five killing months between 4 February 1555 and 10 November 1558, 283 martyrs—227 men and 56 women—were burned alive for their faith. By June of that final year Londoners were reacting with anger and distaste: the burnings, hitherto held in front of St Bartholomew's Hospital in Smithfield, had to be shifted to secret places of execution. And elsewhere, things were looking no better for Henry VIII's eldest child. Earlier in 1558 her armies had been driven out of the fortified port of Calais, the last vestige of England's empire across the Channel; and she herself was mortally ill, dying of a stomach tumour that she had imagined to be a baby that would keep the Catholic cause alive.

The very opposite proved the case—for the reign which began with such popular promise ended by inspiring a hostility to 'popery' in England that is embedded to this day. It is still impossible for a British king or queen to be Roman Catholic or to marry a Roman Catholic, and the roots of the bitter hatreds that divide Northern Ireland can be similarly traced back to the fires of Smithfield. Stubborn, pious, Catholic Mary had helped make England a Protestant nation.

ROBERT RECORDE AND HIS INTELLIGENCE SHARPENER

1557

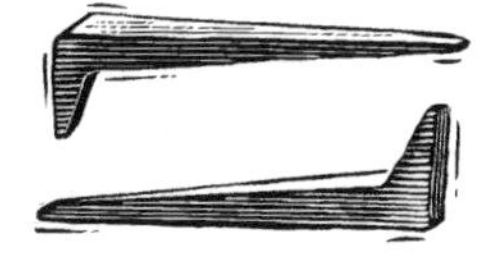

Robert Recorde was a Welshman who studied at both Oxford and Cambridge in the reign of Henry VIII, before moving down to London to work as a doctor—he was consulted, on occasion, by both Edward VI and Mary. But it is for his maths that he is remembered. In 1543 he published *The Ground of Arts*, the first ever maths book in English, which ran through over fifty editions and introduced English schoolchildren to the tortured delights of such problems as: 'If a horse has four shoes, each with six nails, and you pay half a penny for the first nail, one penny for the second, two for the third, four for the fourth, and so on, doubling every time, how much will the shoeing of the horse cost?'

The modern historian Adam Hart-Davis has pointed out that there are, in fact, two answers to this problem: 126 pence, if the shoes are counted separately—that is, 4 lots of 6 nails—or 8,388,607.5 pence (£34,952) if you continue the doubling process as you move through all the shoes and nails.

In 1556, in *The Castle of Knowledge*, Recorde set out some of the revolutionary ideas of the Polish astronomer Nicolaus Copernicus who had died in 1543. After a lifetime of studying the stars, Copernicus had come to the conclusion that the earth is *not* the centre of the universe, but moves around the sun, while also spinning on its own axis. Copernicus had been careful to keep his heretical observations to himself in his lifetime—it was an article of Catholic faith that the heavens moved around God's earth—and Recorde, writing in the reign of Bloody Mary, exercised similar prudence: 'I will let it pass till some other time,' he wrote.

But the innovation for which the Welshman is remembered today appeared the following year in his algebra book, *The Whetstone of Wit* ('The Intelligence Sharpener'). Until 1557, mathematicians had finished off a calculation by laboriously writing out the words '. . . is equal to . . .', which was sometimes abbreviated to *ae* (or *oe*), from the Latin word for equal—*aequalis.* But Recorde had a better idea: why not use a symbol? 'To avoide the tedious repetition of these woords', he proposed the use of a pair of parallel lines: =.

Using the simple device that we now call 'the equals sign' released an enormous log jam in the efficient handling of numbers, and the implications extended far beyond pure maths. It immensely speeded up the calculations of astronomers and navigators—even shopkeepers—and what could be more satisfying for everyone than to round off a calculation with two elegant little parallel lines? As Recorde himself put it—'noe two things can be moare equalle'.

ELIZABETH—QUEEN OF HEARTS

1559

Elizabeth I was crowned in Westminster Abbey on 15 January 1559—a date selected by her astrologer, Dr John Dee. Cheering crowds had lined the route as she set off from the City of London the previous day, and the red-haired Queen had time for everyone, holding hands, cracking jokes and watching with rapt attention the loyal pageants staged in her honour. When the figure of Truth approached her, carrying a Bible, the twenty-five-year-old monarch kissed the holy book fervently and clasped it to her breast.

Flamboyant and theatrical, Elizabeth was very much her father's daughter—with the dash and temper (as well as the piercing dark eyes) of her mother Anne Boleyn. Tudor to the core, she was spiky, vain and bloody-minded, with the distrustfulness of her grandfather Henry VII whose penny-pinching she also matched. At the receiving end of arbitrary power during her youth, she had lived with rejection and danger and survived to boast about it. 'I thank God,' she told her Members of Parliament a few years after she came to power, 'that I am endued with such qualities that if I were turned out of the Realm in my petticoat, I were able to live in any place in Christendom.'

On the first day of her reign, the new Queen selected as her principal adviser William Cecil, her efficient estate manager whom she liked to call her 'spirit'. In fact, this hardworking servant of the Crown was anything but airy-fairy—Cecil provided ballast to the royal flightiness. At nine o'clock on the dot, three mornings a week, the dry little secretary summoned the Council to plough through the detail of administration. One early reform was to call in the much-debased 'pink' silver pennies for re-minting: within two years the coinage was so well re-established that the government actually made a profit. Her reign also saw the creation of England's first stock exchange. And to build up the nation's shipping capacity—as well as its seafarers—it became compulsory in Elizabeth's England to eat fish on Wednesdays and Saturdays.

But it was religion that was the priority after the trauma of Mary's excesses. Traditionally minded, like her father, Elizabeth favoured beautiful vestments, crucifixes and candlesticks, insisting there should be ceremony at the heart of Sunday worship. Also like her father, she disliked the new-fangled Protestant notion of allowing the clergy to marry, and made clear her disapproval of their wives. England's Catholics were also reassured when she declined to reclaim her father's title as Supreme Head of the Church. It was a subtle distinction, but she settled for Supreme Governor.

For their part, Protestants were pleased to see the powerful rhythms of Cranmer's Book of Common Prayer restored, and hear again William Tyndale's robust English ringing out when the gospel was read. Elizabeth offered both sides a compromise, and she promised no trouble to those who would live and let live—she did not wish to make, in Francis Bacon's words, 'windows into men's souls'. Elizabeth's attempt at a tolerant middle way came to define a certain strand of Englishness.

One subject on which she disagreed, however, with virtually every man in England —including William Cecil—was on her need to take a husband. It was inconceivable in the sixteenth century that a woman could lead a proper life, let alone run a country, without a better half: in 1566, in a telling display of insubordination, Parliament threatened to refuse to levy taxes unless the Queen took a husband. But Elizabeth was only too aware that if she married a foreign prince England would get embroiled in European wars, while an English husband could not help but provoke domestic jealousies. 'I am already bound to a husband,' she liked to say, 'which is the kingdom of England.'

Thus came into being the powerful myth of Gloriana the Virgin Queen—bedecked in jewels and an endless succession of spectacular dresses that took on the status of semi-sacred vestments. Homage to this stylised, white-faced icon became compulsory—a draft proclamation of 1563 sought to insist that all portraits of Elizabeth had to be copied from one approved template. When John Stubbs, an evangelical pamphleteer, dared to criticise the Queen's marriage policy in 1579, he was sentenced to have his writing hand chopped off with a cleaver. 'God save the Queen!' he cried out after his right hand was severed, raising his hat with his left.

This tyrannical, capricious monarch was the inspiration for the most glittering and creative court England has ever seen. Every year Elizabeth would embark on her 'progresses' —glorified summer holidays—in which the Queen, accompanied by her court and by a veritable army of horses and carts, set off to cadge free hospitality from the great of the land in their magnificent new windowed country houses.

Well before the end of the century, Elizabeth's accession day, 17 November, had come to be celebrated as a national holiday. Bells would be rung, toasts drunk, and poems composed in praise of the Faerie Queen who had made herself the embodiment of a dynamic and thrusting nation. And if by the end of the century the physical reality of Elizabeth in her sixties, lined and black-toothed, scarcely matched the idealised prints and portraits of the young monarch she once had been, people willingly suspended disbelief.

In 1601 she received a deputation from the House of Commons, furious at the many abuses and shortcomings of her government in these her declining years. But when, bewigged, bejewelled and beruffed, she responded to them directly yet again, they fell willingly under her spell. 'Though God has raised me high,' she declaimed, in what became known as her 'Golden Speech', 'yet this I count the glory of my crown, that I have reigned with your loves . . . Though you have had and may have many mightier and wiser princes sitting on this seat, yet you never had nor shall have any that will love you better.' The frail and fractious old lady was sixty-seven years old. But to her listeners she remained Gloriana, and one by one they shuffled forward to kiss her hand.

THAT'S ENTERTAINMENT

1571

As you approached Queen Elizabeth's London from the south you were confronted by a ghastly sight. Down from the stone gateway above London Bridge grimaced a row of rotting and weathered skulls—the severed heads of traitors, some of them generations old. Every sixteenth-century town had its hanging place, a purpose-built gallows or a tree where malefactors were executed and left to putrefy, dangling there as a warning to others. There were several gallows in London. Twenty to thirty offenders were hanged every day the law courts sat, reported one Swiss-German traveller in 1599, who was clearly rather impressed.

In a field to the west of London stood Tyburn Tree, the capital's busiest hanging place—and hence a major venue for popular entertainment, where rowdy crowds gathered and children, straining to get a glimpse, would be hoisted on to their parents' shoulders to cheer and jeer. Food and drink stalls did a brisk trade in pies, fruit and sweetmeats at the spot that is marked today by an iron plaque in the middle of the traffic island, near Speakers' Corner, just across from the fast food and takeaway shops of Marble Arch.

By 1571 the gallows traffic was such that a large wooden contraption had to be built on which as many as twenty-four bodies could be strung at once. The executioner was a local butcher who would tie a rope round the criminal's neck while he sat in a cart. When the cart moved on, the victim was left dangling, and his friends ran forward to hang on his legs and try to hasten his painful strangulation. In 1577 the topographer-chronologist William Harrison's *Description of England* listed the hanging crimes as buggery, murder, manslaughter, treason, rape, felony, hawk-stealing, witchcraft, desertion in the field of battle, highway robbery and the malicious letting-out of ponds.

Many Elizabethan amusements were brutal by our tastes. In 1562 an Italian visitor,

Alessandro Magno, described a Sunday-afternoon session at one of London's animal-baiting pits, where admission cost the modern equivalent of £2 for standing room and £4 for a seat:

First they take into the ring a cheap horse . . . and a monkey in the saddle. Then they attack the horse with 5 or 6 of the youngest dogs. Then they change the dogs for more experienced ones . . . It is wonderful to see the horse galloping along . . . with the monkey holding on tightly to the saddle and crying out frequently when he is bitten by the dogs. After they have entertained the audience for a while with this sport, which often results in the death of the horse, they lead him out and bring in bears—sometimes one at a time, sometimes all together. But this sport is not very pleasant to watch. At the end, they bring on a fierce bull and tie it with a rope about two paces long to a stake fixed in the middle of the ring. This sport is the best one to see, and more dangerous for the dogs than the others: many of them are wounded and die. This goes on until evening.

It is a relief to turn to descriptions of the innovative wooden structures that were being built among the bear-pits of Southwark—the playhouses. In the early Tudor decades, pageants and rudimentary plays had been performed in tavern courtyards and in noble households by touring companies of players. But 1587 saw the construction of England's first modern theatre, the Rose, an open-air stage and arena surrounded by wooden galleries—an enlarged and exalted version, in effect, of the tavern courtyard. 'They play on a raised platform,' wrote the Swiss traveller Thomas Platter, 'so that everyone has a good view. There are different galleries and places, however, where the seating is better and more comfortable and therefore more expensive . . . During the performance food and drink are carried round the audience . . . The actors are most expensively and elaborately costumed.'

Today one can get a taste of Elizabethan theatregoing by visiting the Globe, a modern reconstruction of the original theatre that opened in Southwark in January 1599. By that date there was a little clutch of playhouses on the south bank of the Thames, safely outside the jurisdiction of London's City Fathers, who disapproved of the low and licentious shows that tempted people away from work in the afternoons. The best-designed playhouses faced south-west so they could catch the afternoon sun as it set; the outstanding productions were honoured by an invitation to go and perform at court in the presence of Elizabeth.

William Shakespeare is the most famous of an entire school of English playwrights who were the equivalent of the TV programme makers of today, churning out soap operas, thrillers, comedies and even multi-part series: we watch docudramas on the world wars and on twentieth-century history—the Elizabethans sat through Henry VI Parts 1, 2 and 3. To appeal to the groundlings in the pit, the playwrights wrote slapstick comedies at which the Queen herself was known to slap a thigh—Shakespeare's most farcical play, *The Merry Wives of Windsor*, was written at her request. But they also invented a new dramatic form—the introspective soliloquy that showed how a harsh age was also becoming reflective and questioning: 'To be, or not to be—that is the question . . .'

SIR WALTER RALEGH AND THE LOST COLONY

1585

Walter Ralegh was a swaggering West Country lad who started his career as a soldier of fortune. He was only sixteen when he crossed the Channel to fight on the side of the Huguenots, the French Protestants, in the religious wars that divided France for much of the sixteenth century. Later he fought against the Catholics in Ireland.

Ralegh was six feet tall by the time he came to court in the late 1570s, handsome and well built, with a jutting chin and dark curling hair shown off to perfection with a double pearl drop-earring. He has gone down in history for his rich and flashy clothes, and for many twentieth-century British schoolchildren the name Ralegh (or Raleigh—the 'i' was added in later years) stood for sturdy bicycles and for cloaks in the mud:

This Captain Ralegh, [runs the earliest version of the famous story] coming out of Ireland to the English court in good habit—his clothes being then a considerable part of his estate—found the Queen walking, till, meeting with a plashy place, she seemed to scruple going thereon. Presently Ralegh cast and spread his new plush cloak on the ground; whereon the Queen trod gently over, rewarding him afterwards with many suits for his so free and seasonable tender of so fair a foot cloth.

This gallant tale was not recorded for another eighty years, but something like it almost certainly happened: one version of Ralegh's coat of arms featured a visual pun on the story—a plush and swirling cloak. Sir Walter epitomised the peacockery that danced attendance on the Virgin Queen, and Elizabeth was entranced by the style with which he played her game. She made him her Captain of the Guard. She liked 'proper men' and Ralegh was certainly one of those —though, not quite properly, 'he spake broad Devonshire till his dying day'.

As a West Countryman, Ralegh made himself the champion at court for the growing number of Elizabethans who were drawn towards the New World. Among these were relatives like his half-brother Humphrey Gilbert, who vanished in 1583 while searching for a route that would lead him to the riches of China through the ice floes and mist-laden inlets that lay beyond Newfoundland—the 'North West Passage'. Adventurers such as Francis Drake and Richard Grenville saw good Protestant duty, as well as piracy and plunder, in capturing Spanish galleons and challenging the Catholic King of Spain (who after 1581 also took over Portugal and its colonies). The guru of the New World enthusiasts was Dr John Dee, the Merlin-like figure who had cast the Queen's coronation horoscope. Dee put forward the ambitious idea of a 'British Impire' across the Atlantic—a land first discovered, he said, not by John Cabot in 1497 but by Madoc, a Welsh prince in the King Arthur mould, who was said to have crossed the Atlantic centuries previously.

In the early 1580s Dee provided Ralegh with a map of the American coastline north of Florida. Ralegh dispatched scouts to search for a suitable settlement, and in 1585 he presented the results of their prospecting to Elizabeth—two native Indians, some potatoes, and the curious leaf smoked by the natives: tobacco.

The Elizabethans considered the potato an exotic and aphrodisiac vegetable. When Sir John Falstaff was attempting to have his wicked way with the merry wives of Windsor, he called on the sky to 'rain potatoes'. As for tobacco, the 'herb' was considered a health-giving medicine, which 'purgeth superfluous phlegm and other gross humours and openeth all the pores and passages of the body'.

Sir John Hawkins had introduced tobacco to England twenty years earlier, but it was typical of Ralegh to hijack the brand identity with a stunt to match the cloak and puddle. Talking to the Queen one day he boasted he could weigh tobacco smoke. Not surprisingly, Elizabeth challenged him, and he called for scales. Having weighed some tobacco, he smoked it in his long-stemmed pipe, then weighed the ashes and calculated the difference. As a final flourish, he proposed that the land where this remarkable plant grew should be named in her honour—Virginia.

Ralegh's prospective colonists set sail for the New World in May 1587—ninety men, seventeen women and nine children—with all the supplies they needed to establish a self-sustaining and civilised community, including books, maps, pictures and a ceremonial suit of armour for John White, who was to be the governor. They landed on the island of Roanoke off modern North Carolina, and established what seemed to be relatively friendly relations with the local Croatoan Indians. But only a month after landing it became clear that more supplies would be needed, so Governor White set sail to organise a relief expedition for the following spring.

But White arrived home to find England transfixed by the threat of Spanish invasion. Though chief promoter of the Virginia colony, Ralegh had not sailed himself with his adventurers, and now he was tied up organising ships to combat the threat of King Philip's Armada. There was not a vessel to be spared, so it was August 1590 before Governor White could finally drop anchor off Roanoke again—nearly three years after he had departed. To his delight he saw smoke rising from the island, but when he landed he discovered it was only a forest fire. There was no trace of the colonists.

'We let fall our grapnel near the shore,' White related poignantly, 'and sounded with a trumpet and call, and afterwards many familiar English tunes of songs, and called to them friendly. But we had no answer.'

Locating the ruins of the palisade and cabins that he had helped to build, White discovered only grass, weeds and pumpkin creepers. But there were fresh native footprints in the sand—and one sign of Western habitation: a post on which were carved the letters, 'CROATOAN'. White had agreed with the colonists that if they moved to a new settlement, they would leave its name carved somewhere on Roanoke. But when he investigated the nearby Croatoan Island, he found no sign of human habitation.

In later years archaeologists and historians would search for evidence of what might have happened to Walter Ralegh's 'lost colony'. Recent diggings have uncovered the English fort and what appears from the assembled samples of flora and fauna to be a primitive science and research centre, North America's first. But the only clue to what happened to the colonists—and that is tenuous—has been found in modern Robertson County in North Carolina. Survivors of an Indian tribe there, called the Croatoans, speak a dialect containing words that sound a little like Elizabethan English—and some of these modern Croatoans have fair skin and blue eyes.

MARY QUEEN OF SCOTS

1560–87

When it came to dealing with the other kingdom that occupied their island, English monarchs sometimes sent armies north of the border, and sometimes brides. Henry VII's daughter Margaret Tudor had been the last bridal export—she had married James Stuart, King of the Scots, in 1503 (see p. 78), and her glamorous but troubled granddaughter Mary was to provide Elizabeth I with the longest-running drama of her reign.

Mary's life was dramatic from the start. Her father James V of Scotland died when she was only six days old—and for the rest of her life she bore her famous title Queen of Scots. She was Queen of France too for a time, thanks to her brief first marriage to the French King François II. But François died in 1560, and his eighteen-year-old widow returned to the turmoil of the Scottish Reformation.

The young Queen was not well received by John Knox, the fiery leader of Scotland's evangelicals, who had just published his virulent denunciation of female rulers, *The First Blast of the Trumpet against the Monstrous Regiment of Women*. Mary's Catholicism was another black mark against her in Knox's eyes, and as Protestantism became the official religion of Scotland in the early 1560s she had to pick her way carefully, prudently confining her beliefs to her own household.

But after several years of delicate and quite skilful balancing, Mary succumbed to the first of the headstrong impulses that would turn her promising young life to tragedy. In July 1565, she plunged into a passionate marriage with her cousin Henry Stuart, Lord Darnley, whose good looks masked a vain, drunken, jealous and violent nature—as he proved within months, when he arranged for a gang of cronies to set upon Mary's Italian private secretary, David Rizzio. Darnley's possessiveness could not tolerate the trust that his wife placed in her chief of staff, and as the hapless Italian clung screaming to the Queen's skirts—she was now six months pregnant—he was murdered in front of her eyes.

Compared to the canniness with which her English cousin Elizabeth steered clear of marital entanglement, Mary was worse than impulsive: she was self-destructive. Within a year of Rizzio's murder she was romantically involved with another homicidal aristocrat, James, Earl of Bothwell, who devised nothing less than the blowing-up of the bedridden Darnley who, after a youth of debauchery, had been laid low by the ravages of syphilis. Mary herself may even have been complicit in the murder. She had spent the evening of 10 February 1567 visiting her ailing husband in his house at Kirk o' Field, Edinburgh, before leaving for Holyrood Palace between ten and eleven o'clock. Two hours after midnight all Edinburgh was rocked as the house exploded. Darnley's lifeless body was found in the garden.

Mary's marriage to Bothwell only three months later confirmed Scottish suspicions of her involvement, and ended her last chance of being a credible ruler. In July that year she was compelled to abdicate in favour of her thirteen-month-old son James (Darnley's child), and in May 1568 at the age of twenty-five she fled from Scotland in disgrace to throw herself on the mercy of her cousin Elizabeth.

Elizabeth had been viewing Mary's melodramatic adventures across the border with fascination—and not a little rivalry. Nine years younger than Elizabeth, Mary was generally reckoned a beauty, and this piqued the jealousy of the English Queen. In 1564 she had cornered the Scottish ambassador Sir James Melville, putting his diplomacy to the test as she cross-questioned him on the looks of his Scottish mistress. Elizabeth got crosser and crosser as Melville dodged her traps—until he let slip that Mary was taller. 'Then she is too high,' exclaimed Gloriana in triumph. 'I myself am neither too high, nor too low!'

Mary's arrival as an uninvited asylum seeker placed Elizabeth in a dilemma. England could hardly provide money, still less an army, to restore the deposed Queen—this would impose an unpopular Catholic monarch on Scotland's staunch Protestants. But since blood made Mary next in line to Elizabeth's own throne, she could not, either, be allowed to leave England lest she fall into the clutches of France or Spain. The Queen of Scots would have to be kept in some kind of limbo.

To start with, the fiction was maintained that Mary, as a cousin and anointed monarch, was being received in England as Elizabeth's honoured guest. Yet Elizabeth did not visit Mary—the two women never met—and as the Queen of Scots was shifted across the north of England from one residence to another, it became clear that she was under house arrest.

With a bodyguard that was curiously large for a cousin who was supposed to be trusty and beloved, Mary was shuttled from Carlisle to Bolton, then on to Tutbury in Staffordshire.

The transfer that made her captivity plain occurred late in 1569, when the Catholics of the north rose in revolt. As the rebels burned the English prayer books and Bibles, restoring church altars so as to celebrate the Roman mass in all its splendour, the earls who headed the rising dispatched a kidnap squad to Tutbury. Only in the nick of time did William Cecil have Mary whisked southwards to the fortified walls of the city of Coventry, and though the revolt collapsed, the Queen of Scots was now clearly identified as the focus of Catholic hopes. In February 1570, Pope Pius V formally excommunicated Elizabeth and called on all Catholics to rise up, depose and, if necessary, murder the 'heretic Queen'.

The papal decree was to become Mary's death sentence, but Elizabeth could not bring herself to go along with the simple but ruthless solution proposed by her anxious councillors, and particularly by her spymaster Sir Francis Walsingham—England would not be safe, in their opinion, until the Queen of Scots was dead. In the meantime, the bodyguards kept moving Mary onwards—from Coventry to Chatsworth, then on to Sheffield, Buxton, Chartley, and finally to Fotheringhay Castle in Rutland, now Northamptonshire. As she travelled, Walsingham's network of secret agents kept working to entrap her and, after a decade and a half, in October 1586 they had finally secured the evidence they required.

Imprudently, Mary had been plotting with fellow-Catholics through coded letters smuggled in waterproof pouches hidden in beer casks. But the whole scheme was of Walsingham's invention—a sting devised to incriminate Mary—and when she was put on trial at Fotheringhay it was revealed that his cipher clerks had been decoding her messages within hours of her sending them off.

Mary Queen of Scots was found guilty of treason and sentenced to death on 4 December that year. But again Elizabeth hesitated, and for weeks she could not bring herself to sign the death warrant—and then only in a contradictory fashion, first ordering her secretary William Davison to seal it, then instructing that it should not be sealed until further ordered. It was her councillors who took matters into their own hands by sealing the warrant and sending it north without informing the Queen.

On 8 February 1587, in the great hall at Fotheringhay, Mary went to the block with dignity, dressed dramatically in a blood-red shift, her eyes blindfolded with a white silk cloth. She was praying as the axe descended, and as the second blow severed her head, some witnesses maintained they could see her lips still moving in silent prayer.

'God save the Queen!' cried the executioner —but as he reached down to grasp Mary's head, her auburn hair came off in his hands: her wigless, grey-stubbled head fell to the ground and rolled unceremoniously across it.

Down in London, Elizabeth threw a fit of sorrow, surprise and anger at the death of her royal cousin. She raged at the councillors who had sent off the warrant without her final authority. She dispatched Secretary Davison to the Tower for eighteen months, and he was never restored to royal favour. When it came to necessary brutalities, Gloriana was as skilled at finding scapegoats as her father Henry VIII.

SIR FRANCIS DRAKE AND THE SPANISH ARMADA

1588

In England his name described a male waterfowl that might be seen bobbing placidly on the village pond—but in Spanish the drake became a dragon. El Draque was a name with which to frighten naughty children, a fire-breathing monster whose steely, glittering scales 'remained impregnable', wrote the sixteenth-century dramatist Lope de Vega, 'to all the spears and all the darts of Spain'.

By the 1580s, Francis Drake's reputation provoked panic in the seaports of Spain and in its New World colonies. In a series of daring raids, the rotund Devon-born pirate had pillaged Spanish harbours, looted Catholic churches and hijacked King Philip's silver bullion as it travelled from the mines of the Andes to the Spanish treasury in Seville. In his most famous exploit, during 1577–80, Drake had sailed round the world claiming California for Queen Elizabeth and arriving home laden with treasure. No wonder she knighted him—and that his ship the Golden Hind, moored at Deptford near London, became the tourist attraction of the day.

Now, on 20 July 1588, Sir Francis was taking his ease at Plymouth with the other commanders of the English navy, preparing to confront the great war fleet—*armada* in Spanish—that Philip II had marshalled to punish the English for their piracy and Protestantism. According to the chronicler John Stow, writing a dozen years after the event, the English officers were dancing and revelling on the shore as the Spanish Armada hove into sight.

It was not until 1736, 148 years later, that the famous tale was published of how Drake insisted on finishing his game of bowls before he went to join his ship. But the story could well be true. The tide conditions were such on that day in 1588 that it was not possible to sail out of Plymouth Sound until the evening, and the Spanish ships were scarcely moving fast. Indeed, their speed has been calculated at a stately walking pace—just two miles an hour—as they moved eastwards in a vast crescent, heading for the Straits of Dover, then for the Low Countries, where they were planning to link up with the Duke of Parma and his army of invasion.

According to folklore, the Spanish galleons were massive and lumbering castles of the sea that towered over the vessels of the English fleet. In fact, the records show the chief fighting ships on both sides to have been of roughly similar size—about a thousand tons. The difference lay in the ships' designs, for while the English galleons were sleek and nippy, custom-made for piracy and for manoeuvring in coastal waters, the Spanish ships were full-bellied, built for steadiness as they transported their cargo on the long transatlantic run.

More significantly, the English ships carried twice the cannon power of their enemies', thanks, in no small part, to the zeal of Henry VIII. Elizabeth's polymath father had taken an interest in artillery, encouraging a new gun-building technology developed from bell-founding techniques: in 1588 some of the older English cannon that blasted out at the Spanish galleons had been recast from the copper and tin alloy melted down from the bells of the dissolved monasteries.

Popular history has assigned Francis Drake the credit for defeating the Spanish Armada. In fact, Drake almost scuppered the enterprise on the very first night: he broke formation to go off and seize a disabled Spanish vessel for himself. The overall commander of the fleet was Lord Howard of Effingham, and it was his steady strategy to keep pushing the Spanish up the Channel, harrying them as they went. 'Their force is wonderful great and strong,' wrote Howard to Elizabeth on the evening of 29 July, 'and yet we pluck their feathers by little and little.'

Ashore in England, meanwhile, the beacons had been lit. A chain of hilltop bonfires had spread the news of the Armada's sighting, and the militia rallied for the defence of the shires. Lit today to celebrate coronations and royal jubilees, this network of 'fires over England' dated back to medieval times. Seventeen thousand men rapidly mustered in the south-east, and early in August Queen Elizabeth travelled to inspect them at Tilbury as they drilled in preparation for confronting Parma's invasion force. According to one account, the fifty-four-year-old Queen strapped on a breastplate herself to deliver the most famous of the well-worded speeches that have gilded her reputation:

> *I am come amongst you, as you see . . . in the midst and heat of the battle, to live and die amongst you all . . . I know I have the body of a weak and feeble woman, but I have the heart and the stomach of a king, and a king*

of England too, and think it foul scorn that Parma, or Spain, or any prince of Europe should dare to invade the borders of my realm . . . We shall shortly have a famous victory over those enemies of my God, my kingdom and my people.

By the time Elizabeth delivered this speech, on 9 August 1588, the famous victory had already been won. Several nights previously, Howard had dispatched fire ships into the Spanish fleet as it lay at anchor off the Flanders coast, and in the resulting confusion the Spanish had headed north, abandoning their rendezvous with Parma. Fleeing in front of their English pursuers, they took the long way home, heading round the top of Scotland and Ireland. Almost half the Armada, including many of the best warships, managed to make it back to Spain. But over eleven thousand Spaniards perished, and the great crusade to which the Pope and several Catholic nations had contributed ended in humiliation.

Drake himself died eight years later on a raiding expedition in the Caribbean that went disastrously wrong. He was buried at sea, and great was the celebration when the news of his death reached Spain. In England, however, he became an instant hero, inspiring implausible tales of wizardry. According to one, he increased the size of his fleet by cutting a piece of wood into chips, each of which became—hey-presto!—a man-o'-war.

His legend has been revived particularly at times of national danger. In the early 1800s, when Napoleon's troops were poised to cross the Channel, an ancient drum was discovered which was said to have travelled everywhere with Drake, and the Victorian poet Sir Henry Newbolt imagined the old sea dog dying in the tropics on his final voyage, promising to heed the summons whenever England had need of him:

Take my drum to England, hang et by the
shore,
Strike et when your powder's runnin' low;
If the Dons sight Devon, I'll quit the port o'
Heaven,
An' drum them up the Channel as we
drummed them long ago.

SIR JOHN'S JAKES

1592

Today we associate sewage disposal with water—the push of a button, the pull of a chain and whoosh . . . But conveniences were rarely so convenient in Tudor times. A few castles had 'houses of easement' situated over the waters of the moat, and Dick Whittington's famous 'Longhouse' (see p.16) had been built over the River Thames. One of the advantages of occupying the hundred or so homes built on the sixteenth-century London Bridge was the straight drop from privy to river—though this was also a hazard for passing boatmen.

For most people, a hole in the earth did the

job—inside a fenced enclosure or little hut at the back of the house. Moss or leaves served for toilet paper and a shovelful of earth for a flush. When the hole was full, you simply upped sticks and found, or made, a new hole.

At the other end of the social scale, Henry VIII had a private throne to suit his style and status. Decorated with ribbons, fringes and two thousand gold nails, his 'close stool' was a black velvet box concealing a pewter chamber pot whose regular clearing and cleaning was the job of the 'groom of the stool'.

His daughter Queen Elizabeth probably had a similar device, but in 1592 she was offered a novel alternative. While staying with her godson Sir John Harington at Kelston near Bath, she was invited to test his invention—the first modern water closet, complete with a seat and a lever by means of which you could flush water down from a cistern above. The Queen liked it so much she had one installed in her palace at Richmond.

Harington publicised his invention in a joke-filled book, *The Metamorphosis of Ajax*. The title itself was a pun—'jakes' was the Elizabethan slang for lavatory—and the author supplied a helpful diagram for do-it-yourselfers showing how, for 30s 8d (around £250 today), you could build your own WC. It would make 'your worst privy as sweet as your best chamber', he promised—and his drawing showed that you could even keep your pet goldfish in the cistern.

Harington's WC was not the first. The Romans had flushing cisterns. But his design does seem to have been the original product of a lively mind. Elizabeth's multi-gifted godson amused her court with his translations of risqué foreign verses and, not surprisingly, bold wit that he was, he was never afraid to mention the unmentionable:

If leeks you leake, but do their smell disleeke, eat onions and you shall not smell the leek.
If you of onions would the scent expel,
Eat garlic—that shall drown the onion smell.
But against garlic's savour, if you smart,
I know but one receipt. What's that? A fart.

BY TIME SURPRISED

1603

By March 1603 it was clear that Elizabeth was dying. The faithful Doctor Dee had looked at the stars and advised her to move from Whitehall to her palace at airy Richmond. There she sat on the floor for days, propped up with embroidered cushions. With her finger in her mouth and her features, as ever, plastered with white, lead-based make-up, the sixty-nine-year-old monarch refused to eat, sleep or change her clothes.

'Madam, you must to bed,' urged Robert Cecil, who had become her chief minister following the death of his father William, Lord Burghley, in 1598.

'Little man! Little man!' retorted the Queen. 'Your father would have known that "must" is not a word we use to princes.'

The closing years of her reign had not been happy ones. The great triumph of the Armada had been followed by still more warfare—with Spain, in Ireland, in France and in the Netherlands. War cost money, and three times more taxes had been levied in the fifteen years since 1588 than in the first thirty years of her reign. Harvests had been poor, prices high, trade depressed. Parliament complained bitterly at the growth of 'monopolies', the exclusive trading licences the Queen granted to favourites like Ralegh, who controlled the sales of tin and playing cards, and also the licensing of taverns. Steel, starch, salt, imported drinking glasses . . . the list of these privately controlled and taxed commodities was read out one day in Parliament. 'Is not bread there?' called out a sarcastic voice.

In 1601 discontented citizens had marched through the streets of London in support of the Earl of Essex, the arrogant young aristocrat who had dared to criticise and defy Elizabeth. She sent him to the block—a last flourish of the standard Tudor remedy for troublemakers—but that did not stop people laughing at her behind her back. Even her godson John Harington, the Jakes inventor, sniggered uncharitably at the out-of-touch monarch 'shut up in a chamber from her subjects and most of her servants . . . seldom seen but on holy days'. Sir Walter Ralegh put it more gallantly. The Queen, he said, was 'a lady whom time had surprised'.

Elizabeth had always refused to nominate an heir. She had no wish, she said, to contemplate her 'own winding sheet'. But by 1603 it was clear there could be only one successor—King James VI of Scotland, the son of Mary Queen of Scots. Now thirty-six, James had proved himself a canny ruler north of the border, and his bloodline was impeccable. He was the great-great-grandson of the first Tudor, Henry VII.

Robert Cecil had been corresponding secretly with James for months, and all through February and March the horses stood ready, staged at ten-mile intervals so that news of the Queen's death would reach Scotland without delay. On the evening of 23 March she fell unconscious and, waking only briefly, she died in the small hours of the 24th. As the messenger headed north, trumpeters, heralds, judges and barons were already processing through the streets of London to proclaim the new King James I.

Elizabeth I, Queen of Shakespeare, Ralegh, Drake and the Armada, had presided over one of the most glorious flowerings of English history and culture, and her success owed not a little to the adroitness with which she had avoided marriage. But this also meant that she was the last of her line. Her successor James Stuart and every subsequent English and British monarch has taken their descent not from Gloriana, but from Elizabeth's hated rival, Mary Queen of Scots.

5/11: ENGLAND'S FIRST TERRORIST

1605

With his flowing moustache and luxurious beard, Guy Fawkes cut an elegant figure—he looked like anything but a household servant as he lurked in one of the cellars-to-rent below the Houses of Parliament on the afternoon of 4 November 1605. He was wearing a dark hat and cloak, and had strapped his spurs on to his riding boots, ready for a quick escape. But when the Lord Chamberlain's guards came upon Guy in the candlelit cellar, they believed his story. He was a domestic servant, he told them—'John Johnson' was the cover name he had prepared—and he had been checking on the piles of firewood stacked against the wall. The search party went on their way, not thinking to rummage behind the dry kindling, where, if they had looked, they would have discovered thirty-six large barrels of gunpowder . . .

The notorious Gunpowder Plot was born of the injustice and disappointment that many English Catholics came to feel at the beginning of the reign of King James I. Their hopes had been high that the son of Mary Queen of Scots, their Catholic champion and martyr, would ease the legal persecution from which they suffered—and James duly had his mother's body dug up and reburied in Westminster Abbey. Mary lies there to this day, in a splendid tomb alongside Elizabeth —the two cousins, Catholic and Protestant, honoured equally in death.

But James knew he must live with the reality of a nation that defined itself as Protestant, and soon after his arrival in England he summoned a conference at Hampton Court to submit the Church of England to review by the growing number of evangelicals who wanted to weed out the 'impure' practices left over from Catholicism. As far as doctrine was concerned, the new King gave these 'Puritans' less than they wanted, but he did bow to their demands to enforce the anti-Catholic laws that Elizabeth had applied with a relatively light touch.

These laws were fierce. Anyone caught hearing the mass could be fined and sent to jail. Priests—many of whom survived in 'priest holes' hidden behind the panelling in the homes of rich Catholics—were liable to be punished by imprisonment or even death. Catholic children could not be baptised. The dying were denied the ceremony of extreme unction, their crucial step to heaven. Catholics could not study at university. If they failed to attend their local Anglican church they were classed as 'recusants' (we might say 'refuseniks'), and became liable to fines of £20 a month. The enforcement of recusancy fines was patchy, but £20 was a quite impossible penalty at a time when a yeoman, or 'middling', farmer was legally defined as someone whose land brought him forty shillings, or £2, per year.

'Catholics now saw their own country,' wrote Father William Weston, 'the country of their birth, turned into a ruthless and unloving land.'

State-sponsored oppression, frustration, hopelessness—from these bitter ingredients stemmed the extravagant scheme of Guy Fawkes and a dozen aggrieved young Catholics to blow up the King, his family, the Royal Council and all the members of the Protestant-dominated Houses of Parliament in one spectacular blast. Modern explosives experts have calculated that Guy's thirty-six barrels

(5,500 pounds) of gunpowder would have caused 'severe structural damage' to an area within a radius of five hundred metres. Not only the Houses of Parliament, but Westminster Abbey and much of Whitehall would have been demolished in a terrorist gesture whose imaginative and destructive power stands comparison, for its time, with the planes that al-Qaeda's pilots crashed into New York's World Trade Center on 11 September 2001.

But as the Gunpowder Plotters' plan for scarcely imaginable slaughter became known in Catholic circles, someone felt they had to blow the whistle:

> *My Lord, out of the love I bear to some of your friends, I have a care of your preservation . . . [read an anonymous letter sent to a Catholic peer, Lord Monteagle, on* 26 *October* 1605*] I would advise you, as you tender your life, to devise some excuse to shift of your attendance at this Parliament . . . [and] retire yourself into your country where you may expect the event in safety.*

Delivered at dusk by a tall stranger to a servant of Monteagle's outside his house in Hoxton on the north-east outskirts of London, this 'dark and doubtful letter' can be seen today in the National Archives, and has inspired fevered debate among scholars: who betrayed the plot? The letter's authorship has been attributed to almost every one of Guy Fawkes's confederates—and even to Robert Cecil, Lord Salisbury, James's chief minister, who organised the investigation after Monteagle handed over the letter.

'John Johnson' fooled the first search party on the afternoon of 4 November, but not the second, who, lanterns in hand, prodded their way through the cellars in the early hours of the 5th, the very day Parliament was due to assemble. Once arrested, he made no secret of his intention to blow up King and lords. His only regret, he said, was that his plan had not succeeded. It was 'the devil and not God' who had betrayed the plot.

Torture soon extracted from Guy Fawkes that he was a thirty-four-year-old Catholic from York who had fought in the Netherlands on the Spanish side against the Dutch Protestants. Like the letter that betrayed him, his successive confessions can be read today: his signature starts off firm and black, then degenerates to a tremulous and scarcely legible scratching as the rack does its dreadful work. Once Parliament had been destroyed, it turned out, the conspirators were planning to seize the King's nine-year-old daughter Princess Elizabeth, and install her as their puppet ruler.

Guy and his fellow-plotters suffered the

ghastly penalties prescribed for traitors: they were hung, drawn and quartered. When Parliament reassembled, the first order of business was to institute 'a public thanksgiving to Almighty God every year on the fifth day of November'—the origin of our modern 'Bonfire Night'. But furious Protestants were not content with executions and prayers.

'This bloody stain and mark will never be washed out of Popish religion,' declared Sir Thomas Smith, one of the many who called for vengeance. Half a century after the fires of Smithfield, the Gunpowder Plot marked a further stage in the demonising of English Catholics, who, in the years that followed, were banned from practising law, serving in the army or navy as officers, or voting in elections. In 1614 one MP suggested Catholics be compelled to wear a yellow hat and shoes so they could be easily identified and 'hooted at' by true Englishmen.

This last proposal was, happily, judged to be unEnglish and went no further. But the Gunpowder Plot raises important moral issues to this day. Is violence permissible to a persecuted minority? And if you do strike back against a government that subjects you to state-sponsored terror—why are you the one called a terrorist?

KING JAMES'S 'AUTHENTICAL' BIBLE

1611

'No mor England bot Grate Britaine,' noted a patriotic Scot in his diary, as James VI of Scotland and I of England rode out from Edinburgh to claim his southern kingdom in the spring of 1603. When the new King opened his first Parliament in London, he urged his English subjects to join more closely with Scotland—he called for a 'Union of Love'—and on 16 November he signed a decree creating a new Anglo-Scottish currency featuring a twenty-shilling piece called 'the Unite'. Sadly for James, his McPound proved impractical, but in 1604 he did initiate a project that would, over the years, make for unity in another sense, and in a context far wider than England and Scotland.

As the clerics debated at the Hampton Court conference in 1604 one of them suggested that there should be 'one only translation of the Bible to be authentical', and the King seized on the idea. 'One uniform translation' should be produced, he agreed, 'by the learned of both universities', to be reviewed by the 'chief learned of the church', then ratified by himself. 'Were I not a King,' he informed his bishops proudly, 'I would be a University man.'

Seven years, fifty-four translators and six committees later, the result of the King's initiative was the 'Authorised Version' that bears his name—the so-called King James Bible, 'Newly Translated out of the Originall tongues & with the former Translations diligently compared and revised by his Maiesties Speciall Comandement—Appointed to be read in Churches'.

For two hundred and fifty years the King James Bible would set the standard for phraseology, rhythm and syntax wherever in the world English speakers gathered—an English grammar and literature lesson in its own right. Sunday after Sunday its sonorous cadences filtered into the English consciousness, shaping thought patterns as well as language—and this was just as King James's scholarly committees intended: the surviving records of their deliberations make clear that they searched constantly for the words that would not only read better but sound better, for this was a lectern Bible, designed above all to be read out and listened to.

The dream of William Tyndale—and before that of John Wycliffe—had finally come true. Here was a Bible that could be understood by every ploughboy, built on a spare and simple vocabulary of only eight thousand different words—and time after time the reviewing committees decided that William Tyndale's translations were the best. They made only small changes to his original phrases, so that, in the end, eighty per cent of this royally 'authorised' version came from the man who had been tracked down by Henry VIII's agents seventy-five years earlier and had been burned at the stake.

'Our Father, which art in heaven, hallowed be thy name . . .' Even today, in our relatively non-religious age, these memorable Tyndale-King James lines may well be the most frequently repeated set of sentences in the English language.

'SPOILT CHILD' AND THE PILGRIM FATHERS

1616

In the spring of 1616 the toast of London was an exotic young arrival from the New World—'Pocahontas', the beautiful twenty-one-year-old daughter of Powhatan, chief of the Algonquins of coastal Virginia. Her tribal name had been Matoaka, but her family had nicknamed her the 'naughty one', or 'spoilt child'—and it was under her nickname that she had been brought to London to celebrate the nine-year survival of Jamestown, Virginia. This was England's first permanent colony in North America, established in Chesapeake Bay, a hundred miles or so north of Ralegh's 'lost colony' of Roanoke.

Wined and dined and taken to London's flourishing theatres, Pocahontas was presented to King James I, after whom the new settlement had been named. Her visit spearheaded a publicity drive by the investors of the Virginia Company who were looking for new colonists and partners. Much was made of the young woman's conversion to Christianity and her marriage to a wealthy tobacco planter, John Rolfe, by whom she had a son. Even before Pocahontas died of pneumonia (or possibly tuberculosis) in March 1617, to be buried at Gravesend in Kent, the Indian 'princess' had come to symbolise the prospect of good relations between the new colonists and the native population.

That hope, we now know, was a cruel illusion. The modern United States of America has been built upon the systematic destruction and dispossession of its native population—and the few reliable facts we possess about the life of Pocahontas place a question mark over her myth. In 1612 she had been captured and held to ransom in the course of a savage series of attacks and reprisals between colonists and locals, and according to the Powhatan nation of American Indians who champion her cause today, the marriage of Pocahontas to the older, wealthy widower John Rolfe was anything but a love match: it was the price of her release.

The Never-Never Land aspects of transatlantic exploration were made clear the following year when Sir Walter Ralegh, now sixty-seven and a creaking relic of the glory days of Elizabeth, sailed into Plymouth after a failed attempt to locate El Dorado, the fabled city of gold that was said to lie in the rainforests of South America. Having flirted with ill-judged notions of conspiracy in the early months of James's reign, Ralegh had spent a dozen years imprisoned in the Tower before winning temporary release on his far-fetched promise to bring back the treasures of El Dorado. But he failed to locate the city. Furthermore, his frustrated followers attacked a Spanish settlement, and it suited James to sacrifice the old Elizabethan to the Spanish protests that followed. ' 'Tis a sharp remedy,' Ralegh remarked as he felt the edge of the axe in New Palace Yard on 29 October 1618, 'but a sure one for all ills.'

The flamboyant champion of England's empire overseas went to his death not long before his dream—or something like it—became reality. In September 1620 the Pilgrim Fathers set sail from Plymouth in their merchant ship, the Mayflower. They came mainly from the village of Scrooby in Nottinghamshire, where they had pursued a category of Puritanism known as 'Separatism'. Abandoning the hope that they could 'purify' the Church of England of its papist taints, the

Scrooby Separatists looked abroad, and in 1608 had exiled themselves to Protestant Holland. Among their leaders were the local postmaster William Brewster, and a fervent Yorkshireman, William Bradford, who would later write the story of their great adventure.

But Bradford, Brewster and their companions did not find the welcome they expected in Holland. While they were allowed to practise their religion, Dutch guild regulations prevented them from practising their trades. So they were after economic as well as religious freedom when they boarded the Mayflower in the summer of 1620, landing on Cape Cod, in modern Massachusetts, on 9 November. To govern themselves they drew up the 'Mayflower Compact', the first written constitution in the Americas—indeed, the first written constitution in the English language, in which the authority of government was explicitly based on the consent of the governed. And having sailed from Plymouth, they named their colony Plymouth.

In the next two decades Plymouth Colony inspired more than twenty thousand settlers to create new lives for themselves in the stockaded villages of 'New England'—and it also inspired the great American festival of Thanksgiving. Tradition dates this back to November 1621 when, after half Plymouth's pilgrims had died of disease and famine, the local Indians came to their rescue with a feast of turkey, corn on the cob, sweet potatoes and cranberries.

The rescue of 1621 is well documented, but more than two centuries were to elapse before we find Thanksgiving being celebrated routinely on an annual basis. Not until 1863 was Abraham Lincoln encouraged by the rediscovery of William Bradford's history *Of Plymouth Plantation* to reinvent the tradition and declare Thanksgiving a national holiday.

We should also, perhaps, revise our image of the Pilgrim Fathers all wearing sober black costumes with white collars and big buckles on their shoes. Shoe buckles did not come into fashion until the late 1660s, and, as for the colonists' costumes, as inventoried on their deaths by the Plymouth plantation court, they sound more like those of pixies than pilgrims: *Mayflower* passenger John Howland died with two red waistcoats in his travelling chest; William Bradford also owned a red waistcoat, along with a green gown and a suit with silver buttons, while the wardrobe of William Brewster, the former postmaster of Scrooby, featured green breeches, a red cap and a fine 'violet' coat.

THE ARK OF THE JOHN TRADESCANTS

1622

Ananas comosus

The John Tradescants, father and son, were England's first master gardeners. John Sr made his name in the final years of Elizabeth's reign, and was then hired in 1609 by Robert Cecil, 1st Lord Salisbury, to beautify the gardens of his grand new home, Hatfield House in Hertfordshire. John travelled to Holland to purchase the newly fashionable flower, the tulip, and spent no less than eighty shillings of Cecil's money (the equivalent of £440 today) on sacks of bulbs. In search of more exotic plants, he joined a trading expedition to Russia in 1618, and two years later accompanied a squadron of English warships sent to North Africa to quell the Barbary pirates. Among the specimens he brought home was the hardy perennial beloved of modern gardeners, tradescantia.

But John was interested in more than plants. He started collecting local artefacts and curiosities on his travels, and this passion of his received a powerful boost in 1622 when he became gardener to George Villiers, Duke of Buckingham, the controversial favourite of King James I. Buckingham was Lord Admiral, and it was not long before the navy was instructing all English merchants engaged in trade with the New World to be on the lookout for a lengthy list of rarities—in fact 'any thing that is strange'—drawn up by John Tradescant.

By the 1630s, the Tradescant collection filled several rooms of the family house at Lambeth, just across the Thames from Westminster, and John decided to open his 'rarities' to the public. Taking biblical inspiration, he called England's first ever museum 'The Ark'. The public flocked to gaze at such novelties as the hat and lantern taken from Guy Fawkes when he was arrested under the Houses of Parliament, alongside over a thousand named varieties of plants, flowers and trees—an apparently odd but enduring combination of English enthusiasms that lives on in the popularity of such TV programmes as

Gardeners' World and Antiques Roadshow.

After John's death in 1638, his son took over the collection, proving an even more adventurous traveller than his father. He crossed the Atlantic three times to bring back the pineapple, the yucca and the scarlet runner bean, along with the Virginia creeper whose green leaves go flame-red in autumn. In his later years John Jr joined forces with Elias Ashmole, an ambitious lawyer who had helped catalogue the collection, but after John's death Ashmole became embroiled in a series of disputes with Tradescant's widow Hester.

One morning, in April 1678, Hester Tradescant was found dead, apparently drowned in the garden pool at her Lambeth home. Foul play was ruled out, but Ashmole took control of Tradescant's Ark. The collection came to form the nucleus of the Ashmolean Museum at Oxford—where you can still see Guy Fawkes's hat and lantern.

GOD'S LIEUTENANT IN EARTH

1629

When James I's second-born son Prince Charles arrived in London at the beginning of his father's reign, courtiers hesitated to join his retinue. The child was sickly and backward—he could easily die and his household vanish, leaving them high and dry. By his fourth birthday in November 1604 the young prince was still not walking properly, and his father was so worried by his slow speech and stutter that he 'was desirous that the string under his tongue should be cut'.

But Charles was not a quitter. The plodding prince worked hard at overcoming his disabilities, particularly after 1612 when his more obviously gifted elder brother Henry died of typhoid. By the time Charles I succeeded his father in March 1625, he was a young man of some grit, principle and piety, already displaying the taste that would make him, arguably, England's greatest royal patron of the arts. But the admirable determination he had shown in his childhood now verged on obstinacy, which was fed by the big idea that would eventually bring disaster on his family—the Divine Right of Kings.

The notion had been planted by his writerly father, James, who quoted lengthy passages from the Bible in his pamphlet *The Trew Law of Free Monarchies* in support of his argument that an anointed monarch was 'God's Lieutenant in earth'. This view was taken for granted by the absolute monarchs of early modern Europe, but the self-righteous James had turned it into a lecture directed at his 'honest and obedient subjects'. A people could no more depose their King, he told them, than sons could replace their father. 'I have at length prooved,' he concluded, 'that the King is above the law.'

When it came to practical politics, James himself had never pushed his ideas to the limit, particularly when, south of the border, he found himself dealing with the touchy squires and merchants who dominated England's House of Commons. But Charles lacked his father's subtlety. He felt personally affronted when on his accession Parliament declined to vote him the usual supply of customs revenues for life, granting the money for one year only. Puritan MPs were suspicious of Charles's French Catholic wife and of his personal preference for church ceremonial—and no one liked his reliance on the Duke of Buckingham, the unpopular favourite he had taken over from his father. 'In the government,' complained one member, 'there wanteth good advice.'

But rather than negotiate in the style of his father—or cajole, as the imperious Queen Elizabeth would have done—Charles lost his temper. He dissolved Parliament in August 1625 and the following year started raising funds with 'forced loans', the ancient, discredited tactic of Empson and Dudley (see p. 91) which Charles now extended from a handful of rich targets to most of the tax-paying community. When his Chief Justice, Sir Randolph Crew, questioned the legality of this non-parliamentary levy, Charles dismissed him; more than seventy non-payers were sent to prison.

These were serious issues to the MPs whose predecessors had made the laws that had helped Henry VIII break with Rome. James had written about kings being above the law—Charles was trying to put theory into practice. When a shortage of funds compelled him to summon Parliament again in 1628, an angry House of Commons wasted no time in preparing a statement of fundamental principles, the Petition of Right, which prohibited non-parliamentary taxation and arbitrary imprisonment. After some prevarication, Charles signed the petition, but he did so with ill grace—and then, that August, his friend and confidant Buckingham was assassinated in Portsmouth.

The murder was the work of a deranged Puritan, John Felton, who had been incited by parliamentary denunciations of Buckingham as 'the grievance of all grievances', and Charles blamed his critics in Parliament for the killing. He felt bitterly wounded by the explosion of popular joy that greeted the news of Buckingham's death, and it turned his deepening dislike of Parliament into a grudge match that came to a head in the spring of 1629.

The issue was religion. Sir John Eliot, the eloquent Puritan MP who had led the assaults on both Buckingham and forced loans, had produced a resolution against what were known as 'Arminian' church practices, so-called after the Dutch theologian Jacob Arminius whose English admirers had called for a return to church ceremonial. This cause was championed by Charles's recently appointed Bishop of London, William Laud, who was busy restoring neglected rituals to the

Church of England. In what we would describe as a battle between High and Low Church, Charles sided enthusiastically with ritual, and rightly interpreted the Puritan attack on Arminianism as a snub to his royal authority. He sent orders to Westminster to halt all discussion immediately.

The Commons responded with a defiance that would become historic. Heedless of the King's words, the debate continued. One MP, Sir Miles Hobart, locked the door against the indignant hammerings of the King's messenger, while the burly MP for Dorchester, Denzil Holles, forcibly held down the Speaker, Sir John Finch, in his chair. The Speaker was the Commons' servant, not the King's, Finch was told, and Sir John Eliot took the floor to denounce 'innovations in religion' and royal interference with Parliament's right to speak. 'None had gone about to break parliaments,' he declared, 'but in the end parliaments had broken them.'

Cries of 'Aye, Aye, Aye' rang out around the chamber, and Eliot's resolution against 'Popery or Arminianism' was duly acclaimed, along with a further condemnation of taxation without parliamentary assent. Anyone who disagreed or disobeyed—and this presumably included the King—'shall be reputed a capital enemy to this kingdom and commonwealth . . . He shall likewise be reputed a betrayer of the liberties of England.'

But two days later, Hobart, Holles, Eliot and six other leaders of the protest were on their way to the Tower. Charles had the dissidents arrested, then dissolved Parliament on 10 March. God's Lieutenant had decided he could rule England more smoothly without it.

'ALL MY BIRDS HAVE FLOWN'

1642

Charles I attempted to rule England without Parliament for eleven years, from 1629 to 1640, and he started off well enough. He made peace with Spain and France and, alongside his French wife Henrietta Maria, presided over a well-ordered court where art, music and drama flourished. Under his auspices, the Church of England was stringently administered by William Laud who, as Archbishop of Canterbury after 1633, organised diocesan inspections that tested the conformity of every priest and parish. Laud's efficient policy style came to be known as

'Thorough', and it was matched by Sir Thomas Wentworth, a former Member of Parliament who administered first the north and then Ireland for Charles, before rising to become his principal minister, ennobled as the Earl of Strafford.

Back in 1628, as MP for Yorkshire, Wentworth had spoken out in favour of the Petition of Right, yet he came to feel that many of his fellow-parliamentarians went too far in their attacks on King and Crown—a view that was shared by many. The austere and driven Puritans whose voices rang out loudest in the Commons were even calling for the removal of bishops from the Church of England. Such extremism fortified moderate support for the King, and it was Charles's tragedy that he would waste England's deep-rooted conservatism and loyalty to the Crown. As his own man Laud later put it, Charles I was 'a gracious prince who neither knew how to be, nor to be made, great'.

One of the virtues of raising money through Parliament was that it minimised direct conflict between taxpayer and King. But as Charles exploited ancient and obscure sources of revenue like the duty of seaport towns to supply the King with ships, solid citizens came into head-to-head conflict with the Crown. To widespread support, the opposition to 'ship money' was led by a prosperous Buckinghamshire landowner, John Hampden, who fought the tax in court, effectively contending that it was the King who was the law-breaker here.

As so often, religion provoked even deeper issues of due process and fair play. When in 1634 the Puritan lawyer William Prynne denounced as immoral the court masques in which the King and his wife liked to dance, Charles's arbitrary Court of Star Chamber (evolved from the Royal Council of earlier times) ordered that his ears be cut off. Three years later the incorrigible Prynne turned his holy criticism on the bishops—only to have what survived of his ears sliced away.

Hampden and Prynne became national heroes thanks to the printed newsletters —early versions of newspapers—that were beginning to circulate between London and the provinces. These publicised the political and religious issues at stake, usually favouring the underdog, while primitive woodcuts provided dramatic images that got the message to the two-thirds of the population who could not read. One cartoon showed a smiling Archbishop Laud dining off a dish of Prynne's severed ears.

Feelings were running high in 1640 when Charles reluctantly resumed dealing with Parliament. His attempt to take 'Thorough' to Scotland and to impose the English Prayer Book (against Laud's better judgement) on Scotland's Presbyterians had led to the so-called Bishops' Wars that drained the royal treasury dry. The early months of 1640 had seen an army of rebellious Scots occupying the north of England, and the King was urgently in need of money. But his parliamentary critics were bitterly determined that he should pay a price for it.

Strafford and Laud were their first targets, both indicted for treason as Charles's accomplices in what would later be known as the 'Eleven Years Tyranny'. Strafford was sent to trial in March 1641, charged with being the 'principal author and promoter of all those counsels which had exposed the kingdom to so much ruin'. When he defended himself so ably in court that an acquittal seemed possible, the Commons contrived another way to get him. They quickly passed a bill of attainder, a blunt instrument that baldly declared Strafford's guilt without need of legal process, and as Charles hesitated to sign the attainder, mobs of shaven-headed apprentices roamed the London streets baying for the blood of 'Black Tom the Tyrant'.

The campaign against Thomas Strafford was directed by John Pym, the veteran MP for Calne in Wiltshire who, a dozen years earlier, had been Sir John Eliot's principal lieutenant in the battle for the Petition of Right. Now Pym masterminded the entire parliamentary assault on royal powers, plotting with the Scottish rebels to maintain pressure on the

King while also stirring up the London mobs. On 10 May 1641, fearing for the safety of his wife and children, Charles signed Strafford's attainder, and two days later his faithful servant went to the block in front of a jubilant crowd over one hundred thousand strong.

Having secured one victim, Parliament's radicals turned to the practical business of ensuring that personal rule could never be revived. In February that year the Triennial Act had held that Parliament, if not summoned by the King, must automatically reassemble after three years. Now followed an act against dissolving Parliament without its consent, another to abolish ship money, and acts to shut down the Court of Star Chamber, which had sliced off Prynne's ears, along with the Court of High Commission through which Laud had exercised his control over the Church.

On 1 December came the climax—a 'Grand Remonstrance on the State of the Kingdom', which set out no less than 204 complaints against Charles and his eleven years of personal rule. As the Commons went through their list of grievances, the debates escalated into a raucous public event to match the dragging-down of Strafford, with delegations riding in from Essex, Kent and Sussex to shout their protests outside Parliament. Many moderates became alarmed. They rallied to the royal cause and Pym's Remonstrance only just scraped through the Commons, by 159 votes to 148.

One hundred and forty-eight worried MPs was a workable base on which Charles I might have moved towards compromise—and there was every possibility that the Lords would reject the Remonstrance. But God's Lieutenant did not do compromise, and his hurt pride would not let him delay. Bitterly remorseful and blaming himself for Strafford's fate, on Monday 3 January 1642 Charles instructed his Attorney General to commence treason proceedings against his five bitterest critics in the Commons: John Pym, John Hampden, Denzil Holles, Arthur Hazelrig and William Strode, along with Viscount Mandeville, a leading reformer in the House of Lords.

Next day Charles marched to the Parliament House in Westminster with a party of guards, intending to lay hands on the culprits himself—an extraordinarily risky and melodramatic gesture into which he was tempted by Pym and his four companions, who had set themselves up as bait. Having advertised their presence in the Commons that morning, the five Members then monitored the King's progress down Whitehall.

When Charles entered the Commons chamber, he requested the Speaker, William Lenthall, to yield him his seat and to point out Pym and the others. Falling to his knees,

Lenthall replied that it was not for him to either see or speak but as the House desired. There was no precedent for this situation. No King of England had ever interrupted a session of the House of Commons. ' 'Tis no matter,' declared Charles, 'I think my eyes are as good as another's', and he cast his eyes along the benches as the MPs stood bareheaded and in silence. Through the open door they could see the royal guards, some of whom were cocking their pistols, playfully pretending to mark down their men—until melodrama turned to anticlimax.

'All my birds have flown,' admitted Charles, disconsolately conceding defeat. Having set their trap, the five had made good their escape, slipping down to the river, where a boat took them into hiding in the City. As the crestfallen King turned on his heel to leave the chamber, the suddenly emboldened Members reminded him of their rights and let out catcalls of 'Privilege! Privilege!' at his retreating and humiliated back.

The debacle marked a breaking point. Compromise was no longer possible between an obstinate monarch and a defiant Parliament, and six days later, on 10 January 1642, Charles slipped out of Whitehall with his family. He stopped briefly at Hampton Court. Then Henrietta Maria headed for Holland with the crown jewels, hoping to raise money, while Charles rode towards York, intent on raising the army he would need to fight the Civil War.

ROUNDHEADS V. CAVALIERS

1642–8

Lady Mary Bankes was a formidable woman, the mother of fourteen children. When the Civil War broke out in August 1642 it fell to her to defend the family home at Corfe Castle in Dorset. Her husband was a senior judge and a privy councillor, so when the King had gone north to raise his standard that summer Sir John Bankes followed. He soon found himself, like all the King's councillors, denounced by Parliament as a traitor.

Down in Dorset, the local parliamentary commander anticipated little trouble when he arrived at Corfe to take the surrender of the

Bankes's home. But he had not reckoned on the valiant Lady Mary, who shut the gates against him. When his men attempted to scale the walls they found themselves showered with rocks and burning embers thrown by the family's loyal retainers—cooks and chambermaids included. Even a prize of £20 (£2,240 today) offered to the first man to reach the battlements attracted no takers. Hearing of royalist troops in the nearby town of Dorchester, the parliamentarians slunk away.

It took an act of treachery to capture Corfe three years later. One February night in 1646, an accomplice in the garrison opened the gates to fifty parliamentary troops disguised as royalists, and Lady Bankes, a widow since her husband's death at Oxford two years previously, was arrested. Parliament confiscated their lands and decided to 'slight' Corfe Castle: they stacked the main towers with gunpowder barrels, then exploded them.

The bravery of Lady Mary and the spectacular ruins of her castle that loom over Corfe to this day illustrate the drama of England's Civil War and the damage it wreaked. Modern estimates suggest that one in every four or five adult males was caught up in the fighting: 150 towns suffered serious destruction; 11,000 houses were burned or demolished and 55,000 people made homeless—these were the years when the German word *plündern*, to plunder, came into the language, brought over by Charles's loot-happy cavalry commander, his nephew Prince Rupert of the Rhine. Nearly 4 per cent of England's population died in the fighting or from war-related disease—a higher proportion, even, than died in World War I. 'Whose blood stains the walls of our towns and defiles our land?' lamented Bulstrode Whitelock to the House of Commons in 1643. 'Is it not all English?'

The Civil War was not like the Wars of the Roses, when everyday life had largely carried on as normal. The clash between King and Parliament involved the most fundamental question—how should the country be ruled? And to this was added the profound differences in religion that bitterly divided families and split friend from friend. Sir William Waller and Sir Ralph Hopton had been comrades-in-arms in the early 1620s, fighting Catholics on the continent. But now they found themselves on opposing sides, Sir William supporting Parliament because of his Puritan beliefs, Sir Ralph feeling that he must stay loyal to his monarch. 'That great God which is the searcher of my heart knows with what a sad sense I go upon this service,' wrote Waller in distress to his old friend in 1643, 'and with what a perfect hatred I detest this war without an enemy . . . [But] we are both upon the stage and must act those parts that are assigned us in this tragedy.'

Both 'Roundhead' and 'Cavalier' were originally terms of abuse. Before the war began, royalists derided the 'round heads' of the crop-haired London apprentices who had rioted outside Parliament in late December 1641 calling for the exclusion of bishops and Catholic peers from the House of Lords. In retaliation the parliamentarians dubbed their opponents caballeros, after the Spanish troopers notorious for their brutality against the Dutch Protestants. When Charles I heard this rendered into English as 'cavalier' he decided that he liked the associations of nobility and horsemanship, and encouraged his followers to adopt the word.

In October 1642 came the first great battle of the Civil War, at Edgehill, north of the royal headquarters at Oxford. Outcome: indecisive. In the year that followed, the balance swung the King's way. But in July 1644 the two sides met en masse at Marston Moor, outside York, and Parliament was triumphant.

'God made them as stubble to our swords,' boasted the plain-spoken commander of the parliamentary cavalry, Oliver Cromwell. In a famous letter to his fellow-officers from East Anglia, this stocky gentleman farmer who was fast becoming the inspiration of the parliamentary cause described what he looked for in his soldiers: 'I had rather have a plain russet-coated captain what knows what he fights for, and loves what he knows,' he wrote, 'than that which you call a gentleman and is nothing else.' When it came to recruiting, explained the Puritan preacher Richard Baxter, 'none would be such engaged fighting men as the religious'.

Religion was the inspiration of the New Model Army, the 22,000-strong professional fighting force that Cromwell and the parliamentary commander Sir Thomas Fairfax were now organising to replace the system of regional militias. Its regiments sang hymns, refrained from drinking, and made a point of listening to sermons. Royalists nicknamed this new army the 'Noddle' in mockery of its constant godly head-bobbing in prayer, but sober discipline and holy certainty brought results. On 14 June 1645 at Naseby, just south of Leicester, the red-tunicked Noddle won the decisive victory of the Civil War, taking some five thousand prisoners, securing £100,000 in jewels and booty, and—worst of all from Charles's point of view—capturing the King's private correspondence. Soon published in pamphlet form, *The King's Cabinet Opened* revealed that Charles had been plotting to hire foreign mercenaries and to repeal the laws against Roman Catholics.

For Oliver Cromwell and the Puritan members of the New Model Army, this was the ultimate betrayal. It was proof that the King could never be trusted. Righteous voices were raised demanding the ultimate accounting with 'Charles Stuart, that man of blood'.

The Battle of Naseby left Charles I at the mercy of an army as convinced of their divine right as he was.

BEHOLD THE HEAD OF A TRAITOR!

1649

Early in June 1647 cornet George Joyce led five hundred horsemen of the New Model Army to Holmby House in Northamptonshire. In civilian life, Joyce was a tailor. Now he was a cornet of horse, an officer who carried the flag—and his orders were to capture the King.

The Battle of Naseby had finished the Cavaliers as a fighting force, and having vainly tried to play off his English and Scottish enemies against each other, Charles had ended up in parliamentary custody at Holmby. But Parliament and the army had fallen out over what should be done with their tricky royal prisoner, and now the army took the initiative. They would seize Charles for themselves. At dawn on 3 June, the King walked through the gates of Holmby to find Cornet Joyce waiting for him, with his fully armed fighting men lined up at attention.

'I pray you, Mr Joyce . . .' asked the King, 'tell me what commission you have?'

'Here is my commission,' replied the cornet of horse.

'Where?' asked the King.

'Behind,' replied Joyce, pointing to his ranks of red-coated troopers.

The dramatic break between army and Parliament had occurred four months earlier, in February 1647, when MPs had voted to disband the New Model Army and to send its members home. England was exhausted by war, and reflecting the national mood, Parliament's leaders set about negotiating a settlement with the King.

But the men who had risked their lives and seen their companions fall in battle were incensed. Parliament was not only dismissing them with pay owing, it was negotiating with the Antichrist, planning to restore Charles—along with his popish wife and advisers—to the throne. 'We were not a mere mercenary army,' complained 'The Declaration of the Army' of June that year, 'hired to serve any arbitrary power of the state, but [were] called forth . . . to the defence of the people's just right and liberties.'

Radical ideas had flourished in the war years. Once the army had taken custody of the King it had the power to shape the way England would be governed, and in October 1647 the Council of the Army met at St Mary's Church in the village of Putney, south-west of London, to discuss future action. The agenda was set by the utopian ideas of the 'Levellers', who were demanding that Parliament be elected by all men, not just on the existing franchise of property-holders and tradesmen. The Levellers wanted no less than to get rid of the lords and the monarchy. 'The poorest he that is in England has a life to live as the greatest he,' declared Colonel Thomas Rainsborough, as he kicked off discussion in what became known as 'the Putney Debates'.

The case for the 'grandees'—the established property-holders and others who held a 'fixed interest in the kingdom'—was put by Cromwell's son-in-law Henry Ireton. But the army's groundbreaking discussions were cut short. Ensconced upriver at Hampton Court, Charles took fright at the reports reaching him from Putney, and on 11 November he escaped under cover of darkness, riding south towards the Channel.

There is no telling what might have happened if, having reached the coast, Charles had then taken ship for France. But, not for the first time, the King turned in the wrong direction, heading for the Isle of Wight, where he had been informed—incorrectly—that the governor had royalist sympathies. In no time Charles found himself behind bars, in Carisbrook Castle, his abortive escape bid the prelude to what became known as the Second Civil War. Royalists now rose in revolt in Kent, Essex, Yorkshire and Wales, to be followed by an invasion by a Scottish army, lured south on a secret promise from Charles that he would introduce Presbyterianism to England and suppress the wilder Puritan sects.

It was the last straw. Parliament and the New Model Army were reunited in their fury at Charles's enduring intransigence, and these risings of the Second Civil War were put down with unforgiving savagery. When the King's chaplain, Michael Hudson, was cornered on the roof at Woodcroft Hall in Lincolnshire, parliamentary troopers refused his appeal for mercy, flinging him and his companions into the moat below. As Hudson clung on to a drainage spout, his fingers were slashed off, and he was retrieved from the moat only to have his tongue cut out before being executed.

The King was treated no less ruthlessly. Cromwell and the generals were now resolved to bring him to trial, and realising that a majority of MPs still favoured some sort of compromise, they organised a *coup d'état*. Early on the morning of 6 December 1648, a detachment of horsemen and foot-soldiers under Colonel Thomas Pride surrounded both Houses of Parliament and arrested or turned away all suspected compromisers and royalist sympathisers—more than 140 members.

'Pride's purge' made possible the final act of the drama. On New Year's Day 1649, the hard-core of MPs remaining voted 'to erect a high Court of Justice to try King Charles for treason', and on 20 January the trial began. The only judge who would risk the terrible responsibility of presiding over the court was an obscure provincial justice, John Bradshaw. But even he, despite being a committed republican, was so fearful that he wore armour beneath his robes and had had his beaver hat lined with steel. The King, for his part, contemptuously declined to remove his own hat as he took his seat beneath the hammer-beam roof of Westminster Hall. This contrived court, he maintained doggedly during one hearing after another, had no right to try him: he, more than his judges, stood for the liberties of the people. 'If power without law may make laws . . .' he declared, 'I do not know what subject he is in England that can be sure of his life.'

It was to no avail. Witnesses were summoned to testify they had seen the King rallying his troops at Edgehill, Naseby and on other battlefields, thus proving him guilty of waging war on Parliament and people. He was thus found guilty as a 'Tyrant, Traitor, Murderer, and Public Enemy to the good people of this Nation'. Death 'by severing the head from his body' was to be his fate.

Ten days later, on 30 January, Charles walked out on to the raised scaffold outside his splendid Banqueting House that stands to this day, just across Whitehall from Downing Street. It was a piercingly cold afternoon. The Thames had frozen, and the King had put on an extra shirt so he should not be seen to shiver.

'A subject and a sovereign are clean different things,' he declared defiantly in a long oration in which he denounced the arbitrary power of the sword that had made him 'the Martyr of the People'. Then, more prosaically, he asked the executioner, 'Does my hair trouble you?'—tucking his straggling grey locks into a nightcap to leave his neck bare.

The axe fell, severing the King's head with a single blow, and the executioner leaned down to pick it up with the standard cry—'Behold the head of a traitor!' But the crowd, estimated at several thousand, scarcely cheered. Instead, recalled one seventeen-year-old boy later, the cry was greeted with 'such a groan as I have never heard before and desire I may never hear again'.

'TAKE AWAY THIS BAUBLE!'

1653

The execution of Charles I was the single most remarkable event in the course of English history—and the person who brought it to pass has a claim to being England's most remarkable man. Until almost the last moment, Oliver Cromwell had shared the fears many felt at the enormity of cutting off the King's head. But when the death warrant was finally presented for signature to the apprehensive judges, it was Cromwell who bullied the requisite number into signing. He shouted down the waverers, flicked ink at them, and, in one case, actually held down a doubter's hand to the page until he signed.

In a portrait by the painter Samuel Cooper we can study the features of the fifty-year-old Cromwell at the moment he became the most powerful living Englishman. His nose is bulbous, his eyes large and strikingly blue; a dusting of salt-and-pepper whiskers conceals a mole beneath his lower lip and there is another, the size of a pea, dark and shiny, above his right brow. 'The mirror does not flatter me,' he told the painter. 'Nor should you, Mr Cooper. I'll have it warts and all.'

Cromwell was a curious mixture of arrogance and humility, ruthlessly sweeping aside obstacles, while also prey to depression in the opinion of some modern historians—he was once treated for 'melancholy' by the exiled Huguenot physician Turquet de Mayerne. In addition, he suffered from bronchitis, though his wheeziness didn't inhibit the 'eloquence full of fervour' with which he came to the attention of the House of Commons; the MP for Huntingdon was sometimes seen with a piece of red flannel wrapped comfortingly around his throat.

His certainty of the rightness of his cause came from a deep and austere Puritan faith that set him on an inescapable collision course with the High Church policies of Charles I. At one stage Cromwell contemplated joining the thousands of Separatists who were seeking their religious freedom in the Americas.

Instead he stayed, rising meteorically through the ranks of the parliamentary armies to find himself charged with the task of creating a New World at home.

Following Charles I's execution, a series of votes in the purged House of Commons abolished the House of Lords and the monarchy, and on 16 May 1649 England was declared a 'Commonwealth', ruled through Parliament by a Council of State of which Cromwell was a member. He was appointed Lieutenant General of the Commonwealth's armies, and in 1649–50 commanded ruthless campaigns against revolts in Ireland—where he massacred Catholics with a brutality that stirs resentful memories to this day—and also in Scotland, which had briefly dared to crown Charles's twenty-year-old son as Charles II. These successes capped a military career that gave Cromwell a victory tally of won 30, lost 0. As he returned triumphantly from each campaign, he was fêted like Caesar.

Like Caesar, too, he was drawn irresistibly towards political power. 'Take away this bauble!' he angrily declared in April 1653, as he strode into the House of Commons with a company of musketeers and pointed at the symbol of parliamentary authority, the ceremonial golden staff, or mace, which was set on the table in front of the Speaker.

Since 1648, when Colonel Thomas Pride had excluded those MPs likely to oppose putting

Charles I on trial, the House of Commons had been a wildly unrepresentative body. Derided as the 'Rump', or remnant, its little clique of surviving members—just 140 or so—had only paid lip service to the problem, solemnly debating the surrender of their power for more than four years, while greedily hanging on to its perks and profits. 'You are no parliament, I say you are no parliament,' declaimed the exasperated Cromwell. 'I will put an end to your sitting.'

His alternative fared no better. The Nominated, or 'Barebones', Parliament (so nicknamed after the MP for London, the leather-seller turned preacher, Praise-God Barbon) was an assembly of Puritan worthies selected by local churches on such criteria as how many times the candidates prayed each day. First meeting in July 1653, this 'Parliament of Saints' dissolved itself after only five months, pushing Cromwell ever closer towards the option by which he had been tempted, but had been resisting, for so long.

King Oliver I? Cromwell's critics had long accused him of desiring nothing less; and his supporters urged him to take the crown. A royal House of Cromwell was not an impossible concept in a society that found it difficult to imagine life without a king. But Cromwell's conscience would not let him. It would have betrayed everything he stood for—and the idea was, in any case, totally unacceptable to the army. In December 1653 he was proclaimed Lord Protector of England, and when he accepted this new dignity he was careful to dress in a plain black outfit with grey worsted stockings to emphasise that this was not a coronation.

The new Lord Protector believed that government should be 'for the people's good, not what pleases them', and for nearly five years he force-fed England a diet of godliness. Since the start of the Civil War, Parliament's Puritans had been legislating for virtue, and now Cromwell put this into practice —particularly after July 1655 when he set up a network of military governors, the 'major generals'. Sunday sports were quite literally spoiled: horseracing, cockfighting, bear-baiting, bowling, shooting, dancing, wrestling —all were banned on the Sabbath. It was an offence on any day to dance around a maypole or to be caught swearing: children under twelve who uttered profanities could be whipped. Fornicators were sent to prison, and for the only time in English history (apart from the reign of King Canute), adultery was punishable by death.

Human nature won through, of course. In many localities these Puritan regulations were scarcely enforced. But they have rather unfairly defined Cromwell's place in history. He never became King Oliver, but he *was* crowned King Kill-Joy—and when he died of malaria in September 1658 there was dancing in the streets. It was 'the joyfullest funeral that ever I saw', wrote John Evelyn, 'for there was none that cried but dogs'.

Today the statue of Cromwell—sword in one hand, Bible in the other—rightly enjoys pride of place outside the Houses of Parliament. But the father of the great English Revolution actually proved how little revolution England could take, inoculating us permanently against deposing monarchs, rule by armies or morality by decree. It is the measure of his achievement that there are more roads and streets in England named after Oliver Cromwell than anyone except Queen Victoria—and none in Ireland.

RABBI MANASSEH AND THE RETURN OF THE JEWS

1655

Manasseh Ben Israel made it his mission to secure freedom of worship for his fellow Jews. He was a rabbi living in Amsterdam during the years of the English Commonwealth, and, like many in Europe, he was fascinated by England's great experiment in the aftermath of killing its king. He particularly pondered the burgeoning of cults and religions that followed the Civil War, for Parliament's victorious Puritans had wasted no time in abolishing the Church of England and its monopoly over worship. Bishops, prayer books and compulsory churchgoing—all the mechanisms of an established state religion—were swept away: people were free to work out their own route to salvation.

'After the Bible was translated into English,' wrote the political theorist Thomas Hobbes, 'Everyman, nay, every boy and wench that could read English, thought they spoke with God Almighty and understood what he said.' An outspoken royalist, Hobbes had spent the Civil War in exile in Paris. There he gave maths lessons to Charles, the teenage Prince of Wales, while writing his great work of philosophy, *Leviathan*. Human life, said Hobbes, was 'solitary, poor, nasty, brutish and short'. In his opinion, humans needed a strong ruler—a Leviathan or giant—to impose order upon their unruly natures. A king was the obvious candidate, but England's King had been destroyed, and two years after Charles's execution the inquiring philosopher went bravely back to England to investigate life in the absence of the royal Leviathan.

Hobbes found the Commonwealth teeming with the new faiths, many with names that reflected their aims. The Levellers (see p. 223) were fighting for social equality; the Diggers prayed and campaigned for land reform; the Baptists favoured adult baptism; the Quakers trembled at the name of the Lord; the Ranters, for their part, believed that nothing human was wrong, permitting them to 'rant'—meaning to swear blasphemously

—while also smoking and drinking and practising free love. The Muggletonians took their name from their spokesman Ludovicke Muggleton, who claimed to be one of the godly witnesses mentioned in the Book of Revelation; while the Fifth Monarchists derived their theories from Daniel's Old Testament dream: they interpreted the four beasts he saw as the four great empires of the ancient world, which were now being succeeded by a fifth, the reign of Christ —whose saints they were.

Hobbes threw up his hands at this bewildering array of creeds. These manifestly contradictory views of God confirmed his amoral and very post-modern view of life's essential chaos. But the Commonwealth's closest thing to Leviathan, Oliver Cromwell, rather welcomed the diversity. 'I had rather that Mahometanism were permitted amongst us,' he said, 'than that one of God's children should be persecuted.'

When the Diggers and Levellers had threatened property and public order immediately after the death of the King and again during the Protectorate, Cromwell had gone along with the army's suppression of their disorder. He expected his major generals to be stern in their enforcement of the new regime. But when it came to the faith inside a man's heart and head, he held firmly that freedom of worship was the right of 'the most mistaken Christian [who] should desire to live peaceably and quietly under you, [and] soberly and humbly desire to live a life of godliness and honesty'. Liberty of conscience was 'a natural right, and he that would have it ought to give it'.

This was the cue for Rabbi Manasseh Ben Israel. In 1654 he sent his son to see the Lord Protector, and the following year he left Amsterdam for London and was granted a personal audience. The Jews had been expelled from England three hundred and fifty years earlier by Edward I (see Great Tales, vol. 1, p. 174), and prejudice still lingered. Indeed, rumours of the letters the rabbi had been sending to Cromwell had prompted speculation that the Lord Protector might be planning to sell St Paul's to the Jews, to be turned into a synagogue: Christian merchants, it was feared, would be elbowed aside by ringleted Shylocks.

Cromwell was too clever to exacerbate such feeling with a formal decree or invitation of readmission to Jews. But he used his personal authority to make sure that they could now benefit from the toleration being enjoyed by other religious groups. In 1656 Jews started worshipping openly in their own synagogue in Creechurch Lane, near London's Aldgate, and within a few years there were thirty to forty Jewish families, mostly of Portuguese origin, operating in the capital as bankers and as dealers in gold and gemstones. The centuries of exclusion were over.

CHARLES II AND THE ROYAL OAK

1660

In September 1651, King Charles II climbed up a makeshift wooden ladder to hide in the branches of a leafy oak tree near Boscobel House in Shropshire. His face was blackened with soot scraped from inside a chimney and his hair had been hastily cropped. Wearing the rough breeches and shirt of a simple woodman, he carried enough bread, cheese and beer to sustain him till nightfall. The twenty-one-year-old, who had been claiming the English throne since the execution of his father eighteen months earlier, was on the run. The royalist army he had led down from

Scotland had been routed at Worcester two days earlier, and now the Roundhead search parties were scouring the countryside. 'While we were in this tree,' he later recalled, 'we see soldiers going up and down in the thicket of the wood, searching for persons escaped, we seeing them, now and then, peeping out of the wood.'

In later life, Charles loved telling the story of his refuge in the Royal Oak—how sore his feet had felt in his badly fitting shoes and how he had actually spent most of his time in the tree asleep. Thirty years later he related the full story: on one occasion he had hidden in a barn behind mounds of corn and hay, on another the sound of galloping hooves had made him dive behind a hedge for cover.

Charles was a fugitive for no less than six weeks, first heading north from Worcester, then doubling back south, finally making his escape to France from the little port of Shoreham in Sussex. Along the way he was sheltered by dozens of ordinary folk—millers, shepherds, farmers—as well as by prosperous landowners, many of them Catholics, who would hide him behind the panelling in their priest holes. There was a price of £1,000 on Charles's head, and the death penalty for anyone who helped him. But the King, as this young man already was in the eyes of most, would not be betrayed.

The Crown exercised an enduring hold on

England's affections. The many faults of Charles I were forgotten in the shock of what came to be seen as his martyrdom, and the succession of republican experiments from Commonwealth to Protectorate made a restoration of the monarchy seem the best guarantee of stability. But the death of Cromwell in September 1658 did not immediately lead to the return of Charles II. Power rested with the thirty thousand officers and men of the Puritan army who were, for the most part, fiercely opposed to the return of the monarch, not to mention the 'popish' Church of England. The title of Protector had been taken over by Oliver's son Richard, and so long as the victors of the Civil War hung together it seemed likely that Charles would remain in exile. As his shrewd adviser Edward Hyde put it, for the monarchy to be restored, its enemies—Puritans, parliamentarians and soldiers—would have to become 'each other's executioners'.

It happened more quickly than anyone had imagined. Richard Cromwell was no leader—he lacked his father's sense of purpose and the very particular prestige that old 'Ironsides' had always enjoyed with his fellow-generals and other ranks too. After only seven months the army removed Richard, and May 1659 saw the return of the forty or so remaining members of the 'Rump' Parliament. This little band of veterans who had survived

Pride's purge and dismissal by Oliver Cromwell could claim a distant, if slightly tortuous, legitimacy that went back, through all the travails of the Commonwealth and Civil Wars, to England's last full-scale elections in 1640. But they handled their comeback no more competently than their previous spell in power. By the end of 1659 they were again presiding over chaos, with taxes unpaid and rioters calling for proper elections.

Watching this slide into disorder was George Monck, commander of the English army occupying Scotland. Of solid Devon stock, the fifty-one-year-old Monck was a tough professional soldier, but he hated what he called the 'slavery of sword government' as fiercely as any civilian. In the closing days of the year he mobilised his forces at Coldstream, where they were stationed on the Scottish border, and started the march south. When he reached London in February 1660, he insisted that Parliament's deliberations could not continue without the participation of the MPs who had been excluded by Pride's purge and he finally put an end to the infamous Rump. London celebrated with revelling and barbecues. That night, 11 February, the streets smelt of roasting meat as rumps were turned on open-air spits in every corner of the city—thirty-one bonfires were counted on London Bridge alone.

Monck was now England's undisputed ruler,

but he refused to make himself Lord Protector. Instead he opened negotiations with Charles II, whose little government-in-exile was gathered at Breda in Holland, and on 4 April 1660, Charles issued the Declaration of Breda, effectively his contract for restoration. Shrewdly heeding the advice of Edward Hyde, he kept his promises vague, placing his destiny in the hands of 'a free parliament'. Charles undertook to grant liberty to 'tender consciences' and a free pardon to all who had fought for Parliament—with the exception of the 'regicides' who had signed his father's death warrant. The army was promised settlement of all pay arrears in full.

The following month, the diarist and naval administrator Samuel Pepys joined Charles and his brother James, at Scheveningen near The Hague, on the ship that would bring them back to a triumphant reception in London. It was the Commonwealth's flagship the *Naseby*, named after the parliamentary victory in the Civil War, and after dinner its name was repainted—as the *Royal Charles*. England was royal again.

As sailors shinned up the rigging, setting the sails for England, Pepys fell into conversation with the tall, dark thirty-year-old who would shortly be crowned Charles II. Walking up and down the quarterdeck with him, the diarist was impressed. He found Charles 'very active and stirring . . . quite contrary to what I thought him to have been'—and scarcely able to believe quite how dramatically his fortunes had been transformed in a mere nine years. 'He fell into discourse of his escape from Worcester . . . where it made me ready to weep to hear the stories that he told of his difficulties that he had passed through.'

THE VILLAGE THAT CHOSE TO DIE

1665

Plague came to England with the Black Death in 1348, and it stayed. According to London's 'bills of mortality', people died quite regularly from the infection, which had ballooned to epidemic proportions in 1563, 1593, 1603, 1625 and 1636. The rich studied the bills of mortality as a guide to their holiday plans. When the weekly plague rate started rising, it was time for a trip to the country.

The Latin *plaga* means a blow or knock, and in those days people often interpreted the erratic pattern of plague infections as punishing blows from an angry God. A more earthly explanation was that poisonous vapours lurked beneath the earth's crust, symptom of a cosmic constipation that could only be cured 'by expiring those Arsenical Fumes that have been retained so long in her bowels'.

Modern science remains baffled by the comings and goings of this deadly contagion. We know that bubonic plague is spread by infected fleas living on rats and humans. It is *not* spread from human to human by physical contact or even by human breath, except in the comparatively rare cases of pneumonic plague where the infection, having penetrated the lungs, is then breathed out by the sufferer in his or her brief remaining hours of painful life. The multiplication of rats and their fleas can be related to climactic factors—the rat flea *Xenopsylla cheopis* hibernates in frosty weather and flourishes at 20–25 degrees Celsius. But no one has convincingly connected particular conditions of heat or cold to the epidemic years—not least to September 1665, when plague hit England again with a vengeance. The bills of mortality mounted alarmingly—to seven thousand deaths a week by the end of the month—and the city streets sounded to the tolling of bells and the rumbling of plague carts as their drivers hooked up bodies left in doorways to convey them to the burial pits outside the city walls. Crosses were daubed on homes where infection had struck and their doors were boarded up, condemning those inside to almost certain death or—in just a few unexplained cases—to miraculous recovery.

Outside London, the plague spread wherever *X. cheopis* travelled, and it is thought to have reached the village of Eyam in Derbyshire that September in a box of tailor's samples and old clothing sent to Edward Cooper, a village trader. The clothes were damp on arrival, so Cooper's servant, George Vickers, placed them before the fire to dry. Within three days, a bluish-black plague-spot appeared on Vickers's chest, and he died the next day. Cooper followed him to the graveyard two weeks later, and by the end of October Eyam had suffered another twenty-six deaths. The mortality rate slowed during the hard Peak District winter to between four and nine a month, but with spring it rose again, and by midsummer 1666 over seventy of the village's 360 inhabitants had succumbed.

The old rector of Eyam, Thomas Stanley, had recently been ousted. A dissenter, he was one of the thousand or so Puritans who had refused to conform to the Church of England when, along with the monarchy, it had been restored six years earlier. So Stanley was deprived of his living, but he stayed on in Eyam, and seems to have collaborated with his young successor, the Revd William Mompesson, in face of the terrifying threat to their flock.

It was Mompesson, a married man with two children, who took the step that made Eyam famous—he urged his congregation to follow Jesus's words in the Gospel of St John: 'Greater love hath no man than this, that a man lay down his life for his friends.' Rather than fleeing the village and spreading the infection around the Peak District, argued the young rector, the community should stick together and help their fellow-men. This, clearly, was to risk their own lives in an act of extraordinary self-sacrifice. The congregation agreed, and for more than a year Eyam became effectively a huge plague house, shut off from the world. Their neighbours, meanwhile, who included the Earl of Devonshire at nearby Chatsworth, responded to their gesture by leaving food and other provisions at the outskirts of the village. Derbyshire was spared further plague, and Eyam paid the price, losing more than 260 inhabitants, some three-quarters of the population. Among the last to die was Mompesson's wife Catherine, who had gone from house to house during the outbreak, ministering to the sick.

The final burial took place on 11 October 1666, and Mompesson started assessing the damage. 'Our town has become a Golgotha, the place of a skull . . .' he wrote in November. 'I intend, God willing, to spend this week in seeing all woollen clothes fumed and purified . . .' Modern quarantine procedure suggests that this is the very first thing Eyam should have done. Had the fleas that were lurking in Edward Cooper's box of clothing been destroyed on day one, the villagers would have posed no threat to their neighbours. And even if the fleas had not been destroyed, those who left the village flealess could not have infected anyone they met.

In scientific terms, we can now say that the sacrifice of Eyam's villagers was probably unnecessary, and quite certainly counterproductive. By staying together they actually brought more humans, fleas and rats into close proximity, hugely increasing the mortality from a single source of infection. But if their lack of knowledge now seems a tragedy, does that invalidate the brave and selfless decision they took?

LONDON BURNING

1666

At two o'clock on the morning of Sunday 2 September 1666, Thomas Farynor awoke to the smell of burning. Farynor bore the title of King's Baker—meaning that he baked ships' biscuits for the navy rather than bread for the King—and he lived above his bakery in Pudding Lane, not far from London Bridge. Dashing downstairs, he met with a blaze of such intensity that he snatched up his family and fled. Modern excavations have unearthed the carbonised remains of twenty tar barrels in the cellar below Pudding Lane, and it was probably their explosion that catapulted burning debris into the stables of the inn next door, setting fire to the hay piled up in the yard.

It had been a long hot summer. London's wood and wattle houses, roofed with straw, were tinderbox-dry, and a warm wind was blowing from the east. By three a.m. the city's fire-fighters were on hand, accompanied by the Lord Mayor Sir Thomas Bloodworth, tetchy at having had his sleep disturbed. He gave the conflagration a cursory glance, then returned to his bed. 'Pish!' he sniffed, 'a woman might piss it out!'

But while the Lord Mayor slept, the flames licked their way to the riverside, enveloping the wooden wharves and warehouses that were stacked to the rafters with merchandise waiting to burn. Tallow, oil, timber, coal—in no time an inferno was raging up the shoreline and had consumed a third of the houses on London Bridge. 'Rattle, rattle, rattle . . .' wrote one eyewitness, 'as if there had been a thousand iron chariots, beating together on the stones.' The fire was roaring along so fast that it caught any pigeons too slow to get out of its path, setting their feathers alight.

By Sunday lunchtime, Mayor Bloodworth's coarse complacency had turned to panic. Samuel Pepys found him sweating helplessly at the front line, a handkerchief tied round his neck. 'Lord, what can I do?' he cried. 'People will not obey me!'

Bloodworth's only recourse was the one reliable defence that the seventeenth century could offer against fire—to pull down blocks of houses to create firebreaks. But he found himself up against the fiercely protective instincts of some of the city's most powerful property owners, and it took royal intervention to get the firebreak policy under way. In fact, King Charles and his brother James were the fire-fighting heroes of that day, and of the three further days it took to bring the blaze under control. The King sent his Life Guards along to help, and the two brothers were soon out on the streets themselves, setting to with shovels and buckets of water. Working from five in the morning until nearly midnight, James came in for particular praise. 'If the Lord Mayor had done as much,' said one citizen, 'his example might have gone far towards saving the city.'

Thirteen thousand two hundred houses, 87 churches, and 44 merchant guild halls, along with the City's own Guildhall, Exchange, Custom House and the Bridewell Prison, were destroyed in the fire that started at Pudding Lane. For several nights the flames burned so brightly that they lit the horizon at Oxford, fifty miles away. One hundred thousand were made homeless—tent cities sprang up in the fields around the capital. And with no compensation available for rebuilding—at this date insurance existed only for ships—many were left destitute.

It was hardly surprising that a catastrophe of such magnitude should prompt a witch-hunt. When MPs gathered at the end of September they agreed to a man that papist saboteurs were to blame, and they set up a commission to prove it, solemnly gathering gossip about sinister French firework-makers and Catholic housewives from Ilford overheard predicting hot weather.

In fact, there is not the slightest evidence that the fire which started in Thomas Farynor's biscuit bakery in Pudding Lane in September 1666 was anything but an accident. And there was a certain half-heartedness in the Protestant attempts to pin the blame on the papists. Coupled with the 'blow' of the plague the previous year, people felt a depressing anxiety that the punishment might be the work of God himself—His judgement on a king and a monarchy that, in just a few years, had fallen sadly short of all that its restoration had promised.

TITUS OATES AND THE POPISH PLOT

1678/9

King Charles II was proud to have fathered no less than fourteen illegitimate children. His pursuit of pleasure summed up the spirit with which Restoration England threw off the drab constraints of the Puritan years. Strolling in the park with his knock-kneed, floppy-eared spaniels, the 'Merry Monarch' privately believed in his divine right to rule as totally as his father had, but unlike his father, Charles II masked his mission with the common touch. Orange-seller turned actress Nell Gwynne was the most popular of his many mistresses, famously turning jeers to cheers when anti-

Catholic demonstrators jostled her carriage. Red-haired Nelly leaned out of the window. 'I am the *Protestant* whore!' she cried.

'King Charles II,' wrote John Evelyn, 'would doubtless have been an excellent prince had he been less addicted to women.' The King, explained Evelyn, was 'always in want to supply their immeasurable profusion'.

Women and wars drained the royal coffers. Under Charles, England's taxes rose to even higher levels than under the Commonwealth and Protectorate, but without the military triumphs that had made Cromwell's wars palatable. In June 1667 a marauding Dutch fleet entered the Thames estuary and sailed up the River Medway, where its fire ships destroyed half the English fleet. The Dutch cannon were clearly heard many miles away in fire-devastated London, while the newly renamed *Royal Charles* was captured and towed ignominiously back to Holland.

The humiliation in the Medway ended the Restoration honeymoon. Charles had been careful to avoid dissolving the 'Cavalier' Parliament that had been elected in the first joyously royalist flush of his return—at the end of every session he used the mechanism of prorogation (the temporary suspension of the Lords and Commons) to keep the Cavaliers returning. But these loyal merchants and country gentlemen distrusted the Roman Catholicism that permeated the royal court, and they disliked wasted taxes as much as the next man.

In 1670 Charles embarked on a disastrous course. Seeking extra funds that would diminish his reliance on Parliament, he made a secret pact with his cousin, the French King Louis XIV. In return for a French pension that, in the event, would be paid intermittently for the rest of his reign, he agreed not only to restore the rights of English Catholics but also, when the moment was right, personally to acknowledge the Catholic faith in which he had been brought up by his devout French mother, Henrietta Maria.

The secret clauses were negotiated at Dover as part of a deal creating an Anglo-French alliance against the Dutch, and to camouflage his betrayal Charles appointed two of his ministers to negotiate a 'cover' Treaty of Dover—without the sell-out over Catholicism. But it was not long before suspicions of under-the-table dealings emerged, and when Charles went before Parliament in 1674 to swear there had been no secret clauses, it was observed that his hand shook.

The King's problems were intensified by the fact that, despite his profusion of bastard children, he had produced no legitimate heirs. His marriage to the Portuguese Catherine of Braganza remained obstinately childless, and though faithless to his spouse in so many ways, Charles refused to discard her. This handed the succession squarely to his brother James, Duke of York, who, unlike Charles, was not prepared to disguise his faith. In 1673 James had resigned his post as Lord High Admiral rather than denounce the doctrine of transubstantiation (see p. 115) as required by the Test Act, Parliament's attempt to exclude non-Anglicans from public office. Thus the heir to England's ultimate public office openly declared himself a Roman Catholic.

With the present King living a lie and his successor conjuring up the prospect of a re-enactment of the fires of Smithfield, it was small wonder that Protestant England felt under threat—and on 17 October 1678 came the event that seemed to justify their wildest fears. The body of Sir Edmund Berry Godfrey, a prominent London magistrate, was found face down in a ditch on Primrose Hill, run through with a sword. Godfrey had been a rare London hero of the plague year. He had stayed in the capital overseeing mass burials and prosecuting grave robbers, and shortly before his death, it now turned out, he had embarked on a still more heroic mission: he was investigating allegations of a sinister 'Popish Plot' to murder the King and place James on the throne.

The allegations had been laid before the magistrate by one Titus Oates, an oily and pompous con man of the cloth, who had been expelled from his school, two Cambridge colleges, his Church of England ministry, the navy, and two Catholic colleges in Europe for offences that ranged from drunkenness to sodomy—with an ongoing strand of perjury. Oates's tabloid tales of dagger-wielding Jesuit assassins might normally have commanded little credence, but the murder of Sir Edmund Berry Godfrey—which was never solved—gave his 'Popish Plot' a horrid plausibility. The magistrate's body was put on public display, and enterprising tradesfolk hawked 'Edmund Berry Godfrey' daggers to citizens newly concerned with self-defence. In the panic that followed, further informers came crawling out of the woodwork, leading to the prosecution of more than twelve hundred Catholics in London alone and the execution of twenty-four innocent men and women on charges of treason.

Parliamentarians and Puritans now saw a pressing need to exclude the King's popish brother from the succession, and the bitter battle to impose this 'exclusion' on Charles produced rudimentary political parties. Campaigning for exclusion was a 'country' alliance of Puritans, populists and old parliamentary diehards—derided by their opponents as 'Whiggamores', a term of abuse for Scottish Presbyterian outlaws. In response, the 'Whigs' denounced the 'court' party of High Anglicans and loyal monarchists as 'Tories' (from the Gaelic word *toraighe*—an

Irish label for Catholic bandits).

Outlaws versus bandits, Whigs versus Tories: thus, in mutual insult, was born the British two-party political system. By the early 1680s the rival groupings were proudly proclaiming their names, printing manifestos, financing newspapers and choosing candidates. They even issued coloured rosettes—red for Tories and true blue for Whigs—and in this, the first of their many great confrontations, the Whigs managed to build up the larger majorities in the House of Commons.

But though the Whigs had the votes, they found themselves helpless in face of the King's prerogative powers, which were still essentially those enjoyed by Charles I—it was as if Commonwealth, Protectorate and Restoration had never been. Whenever the Whigs got close to passing a bill that would exclude James, his brother dissolved Parliament, and after three bitterly debated sessions and three dissolutions, the exclusion crisis ran out of steam. The fabrications of Titus Oates were exposed, and for the last five years of his reign Charles II was able to rule without Parliament.

The King's guiding principle had always been that he 'did not wish to go again on his travels', and through charm, deceit and a general unwillingness on the part of his subjects to fight another Civil War, he succeeded. Charles II never had to climb another oak tree or blacken his face with soot again. On his deathbed, he called for a priest and formally converted to the faith of his childhood. But as the Merry Monarch headed for his Catholic heaven, his farewell words paid due homage to his licentious past—'Let not poor Nelly starve'.

MONMOUTH'S REBELLION AND THE BLOODY ASSIZES

1685

James, Duke of Monmouth, was Charles II's eldest and favourite son, the product of his first serious love affair—in 1649, with Lucy Walter, an attractive, dark-eyed Englishwoman living in Paris. This was the year of Charles I's execution, and it was later recounted that the nineteen-year-old prince, suddenly and tragically King-in-exile, fell so deeply in love with Lucy that he secretly married her.

Charles always denied that Lucy was his legitimate wife, but he showed great favour to his handsome firstborn, awarding him the dukedom—the highest rank of aristocracy

—when the boy was only fourteen, and arranging his marriage to a rich heiress. Sixteen years later, in 1679, Charles entrusted him with the command of an English army sent to subdue Scottish rebels, and the thirty-year-old returned home a conquering hero.

As the exclusion crisis intensified, the Whigs embraced Monmouth as their candidate for the throne—here was a dashing 'Protestant Duke' to replace the popish James—and Monmouth threw himself into the part. He embarked on royal progresses, currying popular favour by taking part in village running races, and even touching scrofula sufferers for the King's Evil (see *Great Tales*, vol. 1, p. 81). But Charles was livid at this attempt by his charming but bastard son to subvert the line of lawful succession. He twice issued proclamations reasserting Monmouth's illegitimacy.

The transition of rule from Charles to James II in February 1685 was marked by a widespread acceptance—even a warmth—that had seemed impossible in the hysterical days of the Popish Plot. Without forswearing his Catholic loyalties, James pledged that he would 'undertake nothing against the religion [the Church of England] which is established by law', and most people gave him the benefit of the doubt. At the relatively advanced age of fifty-two, the new King cut a competent figure, reassuringly more serious and hardworking than his elder brother.

But Monmouth, in exile with his Whig clique in the Netherlands, totally misjudged the national mood. On 11 June that year he landed at the port of Lyme Regis in Dorset with just eighty-two supporters and equipment for a thousand more. Though his promises of toleration for dissenters drew the support of several thousand West Country artisans and labourers, the local gentry raised the militia against him, and the duke was soon taking refuge in the swamps of Sedgemoor where King Alfred had hidden from the Vikings eight hundred years earlier. Lacking Alfred's command of the terrain, however, Monmouth got lost in the mists during an attempted night attack, and as dawn broke on 6 July his men were cut to pieces.

Nine days later the 'Protestant Duke' was dead, executed in London despite grovelling to his victorious uncle and offering to turn Catholic in exchange for his life. It was a sorry betrayal of the Somerset dissenters who had signed up for what would prove the last popular rebellion in English history—and there was worse to come. Not content with the slaughter of Sedgemoor and the summary executions of those caught fleeing from the field, James insisted that a judicial commission headed by the Lord Chief Justice, George Jeffreys, should go down to the West Country to root out the last traces of revolt.

Travelling with four other judges and a public executioner, Jeffreys started his cull in Winchester, where Alice Lisle, the seventy-year-old widow of the regicide Sir John Lisle, was found guilty of harbouring a rebel and condemned to be burned at the stake. When Jeffreys suggested that she might plead to the King for mercy, Widow Lisle took his advice—and was spared burning to be beheaded in the marketplace. Moving on to Dorchester on 5 September, Jeffreys was annoyed to be confronted by a first batch of thirty suspects all pleading 'not guilty': he sentenced all but one of them to death. Then, in the interests of speed, he offered more lenient treatment to those pleading 'guilty'. Out of 233, only eighty were hanged.

By the time the work of the Bloody Assizes was finished, 480 men and women had been sentenced to death, 260 whipped or fined, and 850 transported to the colonies, where the profits from their sale were enjoyed by a syndicate that included James's wife, Mary of Modena. The tarred bodies and heads pickled in vinegar that Judge Jeffreys distributed around the gibbets of the West Country were less shocking to his contemporaries than they would be to subsequent generations. But his Bloody Assizes did raise questions about the new Catholic King, and how moderately he could be trusted to use his powers.

THE GLORIOUS INVASION

1688–9

Those who disliked England having an openly Catholic monarch took comfort from the thought that James II could not live for ever. The King was comparatively old by seventeenth-century standards—in October 1687 he turned fifty-four, the age at which his brother had died—and his immediate heirs, his daughters Mary (twenty-five) and Anne (twenty-three), were both staunch Protestants. Mary, indeed, was married to the Dutch Protestant hero William of Orange, who had his own place in the English succession (see family tree p. xv), and who was leading Holland's battle against the empire-building ambitions of Catholic France. (The 'Orange' in William's title referred to the French town near Avignon that had once belonged to his family.)

Mary and Anne were the surviving offspring of James's first marriage, to Anne Hyde, the daughter of Charles II's adviser in exile, Edward Hyde. Following her death in 1671 James had married an Italian Catholic, Mary, daughter of the Duke of Modena, and the couple had worked hard to produce a Catholic heir—Mary of Modena went through ten pregnancies in the decade 1674–84. But these had produced five stillbirths and five who died in infancy, so by the time James II came to the throne, Protestants could safely feel that his wife's reproductive capacity posed them no threat.

They had not reckoned on the visits that Queen Mary started making to the ancient city of Bath with its curative spa waters, and just before Christmas 1687 came alarming news—the Bath fertility treatment had worked. Mary of Modena was pregnant for an eleventh time, and early in June 1688, she gave birth to a healthy baby boy. Named James and styled Prince of Wales, this new arrival displaced his Protestant sisters from the succession and suddenly offered England the prospect of a Catholic Stuart monarchy in perpetuity.

English Protestants refused to believe

James's luck—the birth had to be a fake. Pamphlets were rushed out asserting that the strapping baby was a miller's son, smuggled into the royal bed in a long-handled warming-pan. Vivid graphic images circulated, showing how the deception must have been carried out, and it was in vain that the King marshalled a chamberful of respected Protestant witnesses to swear to the genuineness of the birth. The story of the 'baby in the warming-pan' proved one of history's most persuasive conspiracy theories.

After three years on the throne, James was arousing widespread suspicion. He had promised not to undermine the established Church, but evidence was mounting that his true purpose was to steer England back towards Rome. By March 1688 a succession of moves favouring Catholics and dissenters had ousted more than twelve hundred members of the Church of England from public office, and though James claimed to be unbiased, even his own family dismissed as a popish ploy his recently cultivated tolerance towards nonconformists. 'Things are come to that pass now,' wrote his daughter Anne from London to her elder sister in Holland, 'that if they go on much longer, I believe no Protestant will be able to live.'

James was knocking the stilts from under his own conservative powerbase. The Anglican Tory squires who had welcomed his accession were incensed to see their own kind being replaced on the magistrates' benches by papists and Puritans—and seriously alarmed when Catholics were given positions of command in the King's rapidly growing standing army. On 30 June, less than three weeks after the birth of the Prince of Wales, seven senior peers, their signatures in code, sent a secret invitation to Mary's husband William of Orange to come over to England.

William needed no prompting. He spent that summer preparing an army and an invasion fleet—463 vessels and forty thousand troops—along with sixty thousand pamphlets to explain his purpose. He did not intend to seize the crown, he said. His expedition was 'intended for no other design, but to have a free and lawful parliament assembled as soon as possible'—and to inquire, among other matters, 'into the birth of the pretended Prince of Wales'.

William's Dutch and German invasion force was larger than Philip of Spain had assembled for the Armada of 1588, but when the Dutch prince landed in Torbay in November a hundred years later, his success was by no means guaranteed. His foreign mercenaries might well have it in them to defeat the twenty-thousand-strong English army that was blocking their way to London. But shedding English blood would have ruined William's claim to be acting in English interests, and would also have exposed his basic reason for invading England—he wanted England's military might on Holland's side in its ongoing battle against Louis XIV.

William was fortunate that, at the moment of confrontation, James lost his nerve. Though debilitated by nosebleeds and insomnia, the King made haste to join his army on Salisbury Plain—only to return abruptly to London, where he discovered that his daughter Anne had deserted and joined the cause of her sister and brother-in-law. Lear-like, James raged against the perfidy of his daughters. Having sent the Queen and the Prince of Wales ahead of him, he fled Whitehall on 11 December by a secret passage, throwing the Great Seal of England petulantly into the Thames as he left.

At this point a band of overzealous Kent fishermen spoiled the plot. They arrested James at Faversham and dispatched him back to London—to William's embarrassed fury. The Dutch prince promptly returned his father-in-law to Kent, with an escort briefed to look the other way when they got the King to Rochester. At the second attempt, James made good his escape.

Six weeks later, on 13 February 1689, William and Mary accepted the English crown as joint sovereigns in return for their agreement to the passing by Parliament of a 'Bill of Rights'—a mutually convenient deal that has gone down in history as 'the Glorious

Revolution'. This is generally taken to mean that 1688/9 marked the inauguration of England's constitutional monarchy—the moment when Parliament finally codified the control over the Crown that it had won in the Civil War, but had failed to secure in the reigns of Charles II and James II.

In fact, the Bill of Rights of 1689 said very little about the rights of individuals, and it would be more than a century before England's monarchy could truly be called 'constitutional'. In the horse-trading with Parliament that followed James II's effective abdication, the hard-headed William coolly defended his royal prerogatives, retaining his right to select his own ministers and to control the length of parliamentary sessions. Revolution? The year 1688/9 witnessed nothing so grass-roots or drastic in England—though from William's point of view his invasion had certainly enjoyed a glorious outcome.

ISAAC NEWTON AND THE PRINCIPLES OF THE UNIVERSE

1687

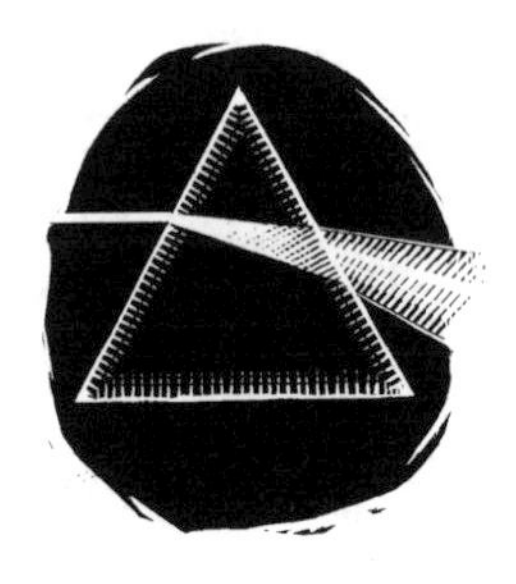

Isaac Newton was born in the Lincolnshire village of Woolsthorpe in 1642, the year that England's Civil War began. A small and sickly baby, he had an unhappy childhood, discarded by his widowed mother at the age of three when she remarried a rich clergyman who had no time for Isaac. But a kindly uncle helped him to school in the nearby market town of Grantham, and in 1661 the nineteen-year-old won admission to Trinity College, Cambridge.

Newton was not an outstanding student. But in 1665 the plague came to Cambridge, the students were sent home, and it was back in

Woolsthorpe that he experienced the revelation he loved to recount in later life. Sitting in the shade of an apple tree one day, he watched an apple drop to the ground. 'Why should this apple always invariably fall to the earth in a perpendicular line?' he remembered thinking. 'Why should it not fall upwards, sideways, or obliquely?'

Newton did not publish his ideas about the law of gravity for another twenty years, and some have suggested that his subsequent description of his famous Eureka moment was nothing more than an exercise in myth-making. But Isaac had come up with another big idea during his plague-enforced gap year at Woolsthorpe, and it is not surprising that falling apples should take a back seat while he explored this equally intriguing—and literally dazzling—phenomenon: the structure of light. 'In the beginning of the year 1666 . . .' he later wrote, 'I procured me a triangular glass prism, to try therewith the celebrated phenomena of colours . . . Having darkened my chamber, and made a small hole in my window shuts [shutters] to let in a convenient quantity of the sun's light, I placed my prism at his entrance that it might be thereby refracted to the opposite wall.'

The prevailing theory at this time was that a prism produced colours by staining, or dyeing, the light that passed through it. But in his study at Woolsthorpe, where we can see today exactly where the twenty-five-year-old boffin played with the colours of the rainbow, Newton set up a second prism. If each prism coloured the light, the hues should have deepened as they passed through the second refraction. In fact, they returned to being bright and clear—Newton had put white light's component colours back together again.

This was the discovery that made his name. In 1672 he was invited to publish his findings by the Royal Society of London for Improving Knowledge. This fellowship of inquiring minds had started life in Oxford and London during the Civil War when, lacking a fixed base, they called themselves the 'Invisible College'. Science was one of Charles II's more constructive interests, and in 1662 he had chartered the 'Invisible College' as the Royal Society, bestowing his patronage on the meeting and mingling of some extraordinary minds: Robert Boyle was working on the definition of chemical elements, together with the density, pressure and behaviour of gases; Robert Hooke was publicising the hidden world revealed by the microscope; Edmund Halley was investigating the movement of heavenly bodies like comets; and Christopher Wren, surveying the almost limitless architectural opportunities offered by fire-devastated London, was formulating a fresh vision of the structures required by city living.

Immediately elected a Fellow of the Royal

Society for his work on 'opticks', Isaac Newton did not, in fact, get on very well with this illustrious fraternity. His troubled childhood had left him a solitary character, untrusting and morose. But it was a gathering of three more sociable Fellows that prompted the publication of his greatest work. Sitting in one of London's newly fashionable coffee houses one day in 1684, Halley, Wren and Hooke fell to discussing how to describe the movements of the planets, and shortly afterwards Halley visited Newton to put the question to him. Newton replied without hesitation: the planets moved in an ellipse. He had worked it out years earlier, he said, and when Halley asked to see his calculations, Newton promised to write them out for him.

The result was his *Principia Mathematica*, often described as the most important book in the history of science. In it Newton set out his three laws of motion, the second of these explaining the power of gravity and how it determined the motion of the planets and their moons, the movement of the tides and the apparently eccentric behaviour of comets. Halley used Newton's calculations to predict the course of the comet that would make him famous—Halley's Comet, which passed over England in 1682 and which he linked to reports of previous comet sightings in 1456, 1531 and 1607.

Having prompted Newton to write the

Principia, it was Halley who extracted the manuscript from him, paid with his own money for its printing, and acted as its chief publicist, preparing reader-friendly summaries of Newton's often severely complicated ideas. Newton himself expressed his thoughts so dourly that students often avoided his lectures at Cambridge, and he spent his time 'lecturing to the walls'.

Today we see Isaac Newton as a pioneering scientist and the father of physics. In fact, the terms 'scientist' and 'physics' did not exist in his lifetime. Newton devoted long years of research to the ancient mysteries of alchemy and how base metals could be turned into gold. The modern scientists and historians involved in the 'Newton Project', a venture that will put all his ten million or so words on to the World Wide Web, report that more than a million of those words are devoted to alchemy, and another four million to lurid biblical prophecy—and particularly to the book of Revelation: the Whore of Babylon, the nature of the two-horned and ten-horned beasts and the Four Horsemen of the Apocalypse.

Yet between the lines of this ancient-sounding discourse lurks a radical and forward-thinking vision. Newton eagerly awaits the moment when 'the Word of God makes war with ye Beasts & Kings of ye earth' to create a 'new heaven, new earth & new

Jerusalem'. This man, born with the Civil War and producing his master work in the years when the absolutist Stuart monarchy finally collapsed, is rightly identified with modernity. He prepared the brief by which Cambridge University would defend its independence against King James II, and in 1689 he was elected to the Parliament that put William and Mary on the throne.

More important, his explanation of how the universe operated by logical mechanical laws was to cause a profound alteration in human thought. The work of Newton, Halley, Hooke and their contemporaries upended the very basis of philosophy and human inquiry, making once divine areas the province of their own earthly research. All things were possible. Reason, logic and deduction would replace blind faith. Old ideas were questioned. New ideas were explored. No longer did God reside in the heavens; he existed in your mind if you could find him there—a transformation in thinking that truly was a glorious revolution.

BIBLIOGRAPHY AND SOURCE NOTES

The excellent general histories of Britain by Norman Davies, Simon Schama, Roy Strong, Michael Wood and others were set out in the bibliography to the previous volume of *Great Tales*. For the fifteenth, sixteenth and seventeenth centuries they are joined by:

Brigden, Susan, *New Worlds, Lost Worlds: The Rule of the Tudors, 1485–1603* (London, Penguin Books), 2000.

Guy, John, *Tudor England* (Oxford, Oxford University Press), 1988.

Haigh, Christopher, *English Reformations: Religion, Politics and Society under the Tudors* (Oxford, Oxford University Press), 1993.

Kishlansky, Mark, *A Monarchy Transformed: Britain 1603–1714*
(London, Penguin Books), 1996.

Saul, Nigel (ed.), *The Oxford Illustrated History of Medieval England* (Oxford, Oxford University Press), 1997.

For a wide range of original documents, some in facsimile and all usually in translation, visit the following:

www.bl.com

www.fordham.edu/halsall
www.history.ac.uk/iht/resources/index.html
www.library.rdg.ac.uk/home.html
eebo.chadwyck.com/home

This last excellent website, Early English Books Online, is set up for institutions—your local library can apply for a free trial—but not individuals. You can find a backdoors way in, however, if you go to the interface supplied by the University of Michigan on www.hti.umich.edu/e/eebodemo/

FURTHER READING AND PLACES TO VISIT

1387: Geoffrey Chaucer and the Mother Tongue
You can visit Chaucer's grave in Westminster Abbey, the memorial that inspired Poets' Corner. To read the very earliest editions of *The Canterbury Tales* as printed by William Caxton in the 1470s and 1480s, visit the British Library website, www.bl.uk/treasures/caxton/homepage.html—and for a wonderfully bawdy modern English version, read the classic translation by Nevill Coghill.

Coghill, Nevill, *The Canterbury Tales* (Harmondsworth, Penguin Books), 1951.

1399: The Deposing of King Richard II

Nigel Saul has written the definitive biography. Christopher Given Wilson has pulled together the contemporary sources.

Given Wilson, Christopher (ed.), *Chronicles of the Revolution, 1397–1400: The Reign of Richard II* (Manchester, Manchester University Press), 1993.

Saul, Nigel, *Richard II* (London, Yale University Press), 1997.

1399: *'Turn Again, Dick Whittington!'*

For an evocative flavour of Whittington's London, visit the medieval gallery at the Museum of London, or its website: www.museumof london.org.uk.

1399: *Henry IV and His Extra-virgin Oil*

A recent academic conference has assembled the latest research and thinking on this enigmatic king.

Dodd, Gwilym, and Biggs, Douglas, *Henry IV: The Establishment of the Regime, 1399–1406* (York, Medieval Press), 2003.

1415: *We Happy Few—the Battle of Azincourt*

The two English films of *Henry V* by the Shakespearian giants of their respective generations are regularly rerun on television. Laurence Olivier's sun-filled idyll was shot in neutral Ireland during World War II, with the Irish army playing the bowmen of England.

Kenneth Branagh's 1989 version presents, surely in deliberate contrast, a dark, brooding and rain-drenched interpretation.

1429: Joan of Arc, the Maid of Orleans
Marina Warner has written the definitive interpretation; George Bernard Shaw, the classic play. For transcriptions of Joan's trial, visit: archive.joan-of-arc.org.

Warner, Marina, *Joan of Arc, the Image of Female Heroism* (London, Weidenfeld & Nicolson), 1981.

1440: A 'Prompter for Little Ones'
Nicholas Orme's playful and original book is the inspiration for this chapter. The metal toys uncovered by Tony Pilson and the Mud Larks are exhibited in the medieval galleries at the Museum of London: www.museumof london.org.uk.

Orme, Nicholas, *Medieval Children* (London, Yale University Press), 2001.

1422–61, 1470–1: House of Lancaster: the Two Reigns of Henry VI
David Starkey's rereading of the 'Royal Book' of court etiquette has cast a new light on the supposed shabbiness of Henry VI. The Paston Letters, England's earliest set of family correspondence, provides a human picture of how the wars disturbed—and did not disturb—

ordinary life. To get the flavour of one conflict, visit www.bloreheath.org, which walks you round the site of the 1459 battle. Eagle Media's DVD (emdv354) has preserved the History Channel's excellent series 'The Wars of the Roses'.

The original manuscripts of the Paston Letters are in the British Library (Catalogue nos. 27443–58, 34888–9, 43488–91, 39848–9, 36988, 33597, 45099), but you can read them online in several versions from the Old English to the modern abridged edition on various electronic libraries most easily accessed from www.google.com (because individual addresses tend to be long and change frequently). The University of Virginia's online library at www.lib.virginia.edu has all 421 letters or 1380 kilobytes' worth!

Starkey, David, 'Henry VI's Old Blue Gown', *The Court Historian,* vol. 4.1 (April 1999).

1432–85: *The House of Theodore*

Knowing that Pembrokeshire is Tudor country gives an extra dimension to visiting this south-west corner of Wales. Henry VII was born inside the dramatic thirteenth-century curtain walls of Pembroke Castle, www.pembrokecastle.co.uk, ten miles from Milford Haven where he landed in 1485 to claim the throne.

1461–70, 1471–83: *House of York: Edward IV, Merchant King*
Warwick Castle, the home of Warwick the Kingmaker, who made and was then unmade by Edward IV, was recently voted Britain's most popular castle, ahead of the Tower of London. With its gardens landscaped by 'Capability' Brown in a later century, it is today impressively maintained by Madame Tussaud's: www.warwick-castle.co.uk.

Seward, Desmond, *The Wars of the Roses* (London, Robinson), 1995.

1474: William Caxton
Caxton is buried within yards of the site of his printing press, in St Margaret's, the little church that is so often overlooked in the shadow of Westminster Abbey. Along with his edition of *The Canterbury Tales*, the British Library has digitised a number of his works on www.bl.uk. To read his charming, often eccentric, publisher's prefaces, visit www.bartleby.com.

Painter, George, *William Caxton: A Quincentenary Biography of England's First Printer* (London, Chatto & Windus), 1976.

1483: Whodunit? The Princes in the Tower
The little princes were lodged by their uncle in the relatively luxurious royal apartments of the Tower. Visit the dungeons and watch the

water come creeping under Traitors' Gate to enjoy the sinister chill of this fortress, prison, and high-class beheading place: www.hrp.org.uk. Dockray presents the contemporary evidence on the mystery, so you can make up your own mind.

Dockray, Keith, *Richard II: A Source Book* (Stroud, Sutton), 1997.

1484: The Cat and the Rat
'Now is the winter of our discontent . . .' Laurence Olivier's 1955 film portrayal of Richard III is the ultimate version of Shakespeare's crookback baddie. It might seem strange that the fullest and fairest account of this film is to be found on www.r3.org, the website of the Richard III Society, founded to clear and glorify the King's name. But that is the nature of this deservedly thriving association of historical enthusiasts.

1485: The Battle of Bosworth Field
This account of the Battle of Bosworth is based on the recent book by Michael K. Jones. Virginia Henderson examines the legend of the Tudor Rose in her article on Henry VII's chapel in Westminster Abbey, while Illuminata's definitive compendium on heraldic badges contains all you could possibly need to know about symbolic roses, Tudor and otherwise.

Henderson, Virginia, 'Retrieving the "Crown in the Hawthorn Bush": the origins of the badges of Henry VII', in *Traditions and Transformations in Late Medieval England*, ed. Douglas Biggs, Sharon D. Michalove and A. Compton Reeves (Leiden, Brill), 2002.
Jones, Michael K., *Bosworth 1485* (Stroud, Tempus), 2002.
Siddons, Michael Powell, *Heraldic Badges of England and Wales*, (London, Illuminata Publishers for the Society of Antiquaries of London), 2005.

1486–99: Double Trouble
Again, www.r3.org, the website dedicated to his bitterest enemy, contains the most comprehensive and the latest material on Henry VII, and it is difficult not to recommend another visit to Westminster Abbey to view Henry's eerily lifelike death mask in the museum in the corner of the Cloisters.

1497: Fish 'n' Ships
www.matthew.co.uk relates the recent recreation of Cabot's historic voyage of exploration and the building of the modern replica *Matthew*, which can be visited in Bristol and, on Tuesday and Thursday evenings, cruised upon in the still waters of Bristol Harbour.

Pope, Peter E., *The Many Landfalls of John Cabot* (Toronto, University of Toronto Press), 1976.

1500: Fork in, Fork Out

Stanley Chrimes wrote the classic biography. Thompson's collection of essays re-evaluates the idea that Henry was a 'new' and non-medieval monarch.

Chrimes, Stanley B., *Henry VII* (Yale, Yale University Press), 1999

Thompson, B. (ed.), *The Reign of Henry VII* (Stanford, Stanford University Press), 1995.

1509–33: King Henry VIII's 'Great Matter'

Built by Thomas Wolsey, Hampton Court breathes the grandiose spirit of its founder and, even more, that of the man who confiscated it from the cardinal, Henry VIII. The King enjoyed three honeymoons here, could entertain five hundred diners at one sitting, and worked up a sweat in the 'real' tennis court. In the garden is the famous maze. www.hrp.org.uk.

Thurley, Simon, *Hampton Court: A Social and Architectural History* (London, Yale University Press), 2003.

1525: 'Let There Be Light'—William Tyndale and the English Bible

This account is largely based upon Brian

Moynahan's revealing and passionate book.

Moynahan, Brian, *William Tyndale: If God Spare My Life* (London, Little, Brown), 2002.

1535: Thomas More and His Wonderful 'No-Place'

To read the complete text of *Utopia* visit the electronic library of Fordham University that contains so many wonderful original sources: www. fordham.edu/halsall/mod/thomasmore-utopia.html. Thomas More himself is buried in two places: his body in the Tower of London, and his head, retrieved by his devoted daughter Margaret Roper, in the Roper Vault at St Dunstan's Church, Canterbury.

1533–7: Divorced, Beheaded, Died . . .

Scarisbrick and Starkey share the honours in the large and distinguished field of those who have written about Henry VIII, his wives and his world.

Scarisbrick, J. J., *Henry VIII* (London, Eyre & Spottiswoode), 1968.

Starkey, David, *Six Wives: The Queens of Henry VIII* (London, Chatto & Windus), 2003.

1536: The Pilgrimage of Grace

In recent years the work of Eamon Duffy, Christopher Haigh and Diarmaid MacCulloch has done honour to the strength of traditional Catholic faith and practice in sixteenth-century

England. They have shown how the Reformation did not so much reform as re-form—and in a variety of complex ways.

Duffy, Eamon, *The Stripping of the Altars: Traditional Religion in England* c.1400–c.1580 (London, Yale University Press), 1992.
Haigh, Christopher (ed.), *The English Reformation Revised* (Cambridge, Cambridge University Press), 1987.
MacCulloch, Diarmaid, *Reformation: Europe's House Divided 1490–1700* (London, Penguin Books), 2004.

1539–47: . . . Divorced, Beheaded, Survived

Henry VIII is buried in the centre of the nave in St George's Chapel, Windsor, in the company of the wife for whom he overturned his country and who bore him the healthy male heir he desired so much. www.royal.gov.uk.

1547–53: Boy King—Edward VI, 'The Godly Imp'

Some grammar schools apart, there are few Tudor remnants dating from the boy king's short reign—and, sadly, an almost endless catalogue of Christian art was destroyed by the whitewash brush and the plundering fingers of those who 'purified' the Church in his name. Jordan's two-volume work is the best survey of the reign.

Jordan, W. K., vol. 1, *Edward VI: The Young*

King; vol. 2, *Edward VI: The Threshold of Power* (London, George Allen & Unwin), 1968, 1970.

1553: Lady Jane Grey—the Nine-day Queen

Jane Grey spent her youth in Sudeley Castle at Winchcombe near Cheltenham in Gloucestershire, where Henry VIII's last wife, Catherine Parr, lies buried. In the Civil War it was for a time the headquarters of the dashing Prince Rupert. www.sudeleycastle. co.uk.

1553–8: Bloody Mary and the Fires of Smithfield

If one man created the legend of Bloody Mary, it was John Foxe, who painstakingly compiled the stories of her victims and brought them together in his *Book of Martyrs*—probably the bestselling book of the sixteenth-century and, arguably, the most influential. For the complete text visit www.ccel.org/f/foxe. Jasper Ridley's lucid modern account is largely based on Foxe.

Ridley, Jasper, *Bloody Mary's Martyrs* (London, Constable), 2001.

1557: Robert Recorde and His Intelligence Sharpener

The School of Mathematics and Statistics at Scotland's University of St Andrews has produced an excellent account of Recorde's life and work on: www-gap.dcs.st-and.ac. You can find the details of his horseshoe brainteaser in Adam Hart-Davis's book:

Hart-Davis, Adam, *What the Tudors and Stuarts Did for Us* (London, Boxtree), 2002.

1559: Elizabeth—Queen of Hearts

David Starkey concentrates on the early years of Elizabeth. Christopher Haigh's 'profile in power' is the best condensed analysis of her life.

Haigh, Christopher, *Elizabeth I* (London, Longman), 1988.

Starkey, David, *Elizabeth* (London, Chatto & Windus), 2000.

1571: That's Entertainment

The contemporary descriptions in this chapter come from Liza Picard's brilliant evocation. If you can't visit the Globe in Southwark, you can enjoy Tom Stoppard's whimsical but scenically accurate *Shakespeare in Love*, now on DVD.

Picard, Liza, *Elizabeth's London: Everyday Life in Elizabethan London* (Weidenfeld & Nicolson), 2003.

1585: Sir Walter Ralegh and the Lost Colony

Ralegh once owned Sherborne Castle in Dorset, though there is not much left of it today after Oliver Cromwell's Civil War siege: www.sherbornecastle.com. And, in the spirit of Sir Walter himself, let me not forget to mention my own biography of the great adventurer, happily still in print.

Lacey, Robert, *Sir Walter Ralegh* (London, Phoenix Press), 2000.

1560–87: Mary Queen of Scots

Inns and castles where Mary Queen of Scots is said to have stayed are almost as numerous as those that boast 'Queen Elizabeth Slept Here'. Tutbury overlooks the Dove Valley in Staffordshire: tel.: 01283 812129. Nothing much remains of Fotheringhay on the River Nene near Oundle in Northamptonshire where she was executed, but nearby is the beautiful fifteenth-century church of St Mary and All Saints. Antonia Fraser's biography is definitive.

Fraser, Antonia, *Mary Queen of Scots* (London, Weidenfeld & Nicolson), 1969.

1588: Sir Francis Drake and the Spanish Armada

Drake lived at Buckland Abbey, eleven miles north of Plymouth. This beautiful thirteenth-century Cistercian monastery had been spared destruction in the Dissolution when Henry VIII granted it to Sir Richard Grenville, whose grandson Richard, himself a naval hero, sold it to Sir Francis. Tel.: 01822 853607.

Cummings, John, *Francis Drake: The Lives of a Hero* (London, Weidenfeld & Nicolson), 1995.

1592: Sir John's Jakes

Named in honour of the modern populariser of the water closet, www.thomas-crapper.com graphically sets out the tale of sewage through the ages in more detail than most would consider strictly necessary. Again, Adam Hart-Davis provides a lively and intelligent summary.

Hart-Davis, Adam, *What the Tudors and Stuarts Did for U*s (London, Boxtree), 2002.

1603: By Time Surprised

Outliving three husbands, that other Elizabeth, Bess of Hardwick, Countess of Shrewsbury, built up a fortune that she devoted to building the redoubtable Hardwick Hall, near Chesterfield in Derbyshire. Tel.: 01246 850430. Mercifully spared the 'improvements' of later generations, it is a remarkably vivid and accurate example of a great Elizabethan country house.

1605: 5 / 11: England's First Terrorist

The cellar where Guy Fawkes stacked his gunpowder was destroyed in the fire of 1834 that devastated the medieval Houses of Parliament, but thanks to the Tradescants you can still see the lantern Guy Fawkes carried in 1605 in the Ashmolean Museum, Oxford.

Fraser, Antonia, *The Gunpowder Plot: Terror*

and Faith in 1605 (London, Weidenfeld & Nicolson), 1996.

1611: King James's 'Authentical' Bible

James VI and I's own prolific writings have been skilfully edited by Rhodes, Richards and Marshall. McGrath tells the story of the Bible he inspired.

McGrath, Alister, *In the Beginning: The Story of the King James Bible* (London, Hodder & Stoughton), 2001.

Rhodes, Neil, Richards, Jennifer, and Marshall, Joseph, *King James VI and I: Selected Writings* (Aldershot, Ashgate), 2003.

1616: 'Spoilt Child' and the Pilgrim Fathers

The sentimental Disney cartoon film *Pocahontas* enraged her descendants, who set out their objections on their website: www.powhatan.org. The best source on the Pilgrim Fathers remains William Bradford's first-hand account which is extracted, along with many other original documents, on the excellent www.mayflowerhistory.com.

Bradford, William (ed. S. E. Morison), *Of Plymouth Plantation 1620–47* (New York, Alfred A. Knopf), 1954.

1622: The Ark of the John Tradescants

The Tradescants, father and son, are buried in the beautiful St Mary-at-Lambeth, just across the Thames from the House of Commons. The church was saved from destruction in 1977 by the Tradescant Trust, who turned it into the world's first Museum of Garden History, complete with its own replica seventeenth-century knot garden of miniature box trees. www.museumgardenhistory. org.

Leith-Ross, Prudence, *The John Tradescants* (London, Peter Owen), 1984.

1629: God's Lieutenant in Earth

Charles I's cradle can be seen at Hatfield House in Hertfordshire where Elizabeth I, a virtual prisoner, was brought the news that her sister Mary had died and she had become Queen. The Tudor building was largely torn down and we see Hatfield today as it was rebuilt in the reign of James I by Robert Cecil. Tel.: 01707 287010.

1642: 'All My Birds Have Flown'

It is difficult to better C. V. Wedgwood's classic account of this episode. Tristram Hunt movingly brings together the voices of the time.

Hunt, Tristram, *The English Civil War at First Hand* (London, Phoenix), 2003.
Wedgwood, C. V., *The King's War* (London, HarperCollins), 1955.

1642–8: Roundheads v. Cavaliers

No study of the Civil War can omit the inspired and seminal work of Christopher Hill. Royle shows the impact of the wars on Scotland and Ireland. Blair Worden brilliantly shows how the Civil Wars have been fought through the subsequent centuries.

Hill, Christopher, *Puritanism and Revolution: Studies in Interpretation of the English Revolution of the Seventeenth Century* (London, Secker & Warburg), 1958.

Royle, Trevor, *The Wars of the Three Kingdoms 1638–1660* (London, Little, Brown), 2004.

Worden, Blair, *Roundhead Reputations Ltd: The English Civil Wars and the Passions of Posterity* (London, Penguin Books) 2001.

1649: *Behold the Head of a Traitor!*

The magnificent Banqueting House from which Charles I walked to his execution still stands opposite Horse Guards Parade in Whitehall. Designed by Inigo Jones as a setting for the plays and pageants of Ben Jonson, it is decorated with ceiling panels that illustrate Charles's disastrous theories on the nature of kingship: one tableau shows James I rising to heaven after his death like a latter-day Christ, to take his place among the immortals. www.hrp.org.

1653: *'Take Away This Bauble!'*

The remains of Oliver Cromwell, like those of

the other regicides, were dug up and dismembered after the Restoration. His rotting head was set on a pole outside Westminster Hall for a quarter of a century. But you can see his death mask, warts and all, in the Museum of London, www.museumoflondon.org.uk, and you can visit the house where he lived from 1636 to 1647 in St Mary's Street, Ely. Tel.: 01353 662062.

Hill, Christopher, *God's Englishman: Oliver Cromwell and the English Revolution* (London, Weidenfeld & Nicolson), 1970.
Morrill, John (ed.), *Oliver Cromwell and the English Revolution* (London, Longman), 1990.

1655: Rabbi Manasseh and the Return of the Jews

The dark oak benches from the Creechurch Lane synagogue, which opened in 1656, were moved in 1701 to the Spanish and Portuguese Synagogue in Bevis Marks Street, now Britain's oldest synagogue. Built by a Quaker, the exterior resembles a nonconformist chapel, while the interior reflects the influence of Sir Christopher Wren. Tel.: 020 7626 1274.

1660: Charles II and the Royal Oak

Richard Ollard colourfully recreates Charles II's adventures after the Battle of Worcester—

and we are now entering the age of the great diarists, whom Liza Picard quotes along with a host of other contemporary sources in her charming and intimate-feeling social history.

Bowle, John (ed.), *The Diary of John Evelyn* (Oxford, Oxford University Press), 1983.
Latham, R. (ed.), *The Shorter Pepys* (London, Bell & Hyman), 1985.
Ollard, Richard, *The Escape of Charles II* (London, Constable), 1986.
Picard, Liza, *Restoration London* (London, Weidenfeld & Nicolson), 2001.

1665: The Village That Chose to Die
Every year on Plague Sunday (the last Sunday in August) the modern inhabitants of Eyam hold an outdoor service to commemorate the heroic sacrifice of their predecessors. In 2000, Eyam's enterprising little museum was awarded the Museum of the Year Shoestring Award. www.eyammuseum.demon.co.uk. The Folio Society has recently republished Walter George Bell's classic account of the plague year.

Bell, Walter George, *The Great Plague in London* (London, Folio Society), 2001.

1666: London Burning
The tragedy of the Great Fire produced the finest building of the seventeenth century, and arguably England's finest building ever.

'Lector, Si Monumentum Requeris, Circumspice' ('Reader, if you seek a monument, then look around you') runs Sir Christopher Wren's inscription beneath the dome of St Paul's. Since Saxon times all five churches on this spot had been destroyed by fire. Wren designed the sixth as a sparkling symbol of London's rebirth, and he was there to witness its completion thirty-five years later. In the cathedral library you can see the huge and fabulously expensive oak model that the architect constructed to persuade Charles II to back his revolutionary concept. www.stpauls.co.uk.

Bell, George Walter, *The Great Fire of London in 1666* (London, Folio Society), 2003.

1678/9: Titus Oates and the Popish Plot

John Dryden's poem *Absalom and Achitophel* feverishly evokes the hysteria of the Popish Plot and the exclusion crisis. J. P. Kenyon recounts the story masterfully.

Kenyon, J. P., *The Popish Plot* (New York, Sterling), 2001.

1685: Monmouth's Rebellion and the Bloody Assizes

Christopher Lee starred as Judge Jeffreys in *The Bloody Judge* (1970), a film that has now acquired cult status. It is available on the DVD *The Christopher Lee Collection* by Blue

Underground.

1688–9: The Glorious Invasion

Lord Macaulay virtually invented modern history, and his great five-volume work remains the classic study of the 1688/9 turning-point. Eveline Cruickshanks coldly dissects his Whig interpretation, but without destroying it.

Cruickshanks, Eveline, *The Glorious Revolution* (London, Macmillan), 2000.

Macaulay, T. B., *The History of England from the Accession of James II 1849–61*. The five volumes of Macaulay's classic are currently in print at three publishers (R.A. Kessinger Publishing, the University Press of the Pacific, and Indypublish.com) and also accessible online at various locations, including www.strecorsoc.org/macaulay/title.html#contents and www.gutenburg.net/etext/1468.

1687: Isaac Newton and the Principles of the Universe

There are modern apple trees in the orchard of Woolsthorpe Manor near Grantham in Lincolnshire, Isaac Newton's birthplace. Tel.: 01476 860338. The best account of the ferment of science and superstition surrounding the birth of the Royal Society is Lisa Jardine's sparkling study of Newton's great rival. The project to put all Newton's words on the web can be accessed on www.newtonproject.ic.ac.uk.

Jardine, Lisa, *The Curious Life of Robert Hooke* (London, HarperCollins), 2004.

ACKNOWLEDGEMENTS

The preceding source notes set out the books, articles and historical research on which I have relied in writing this book, but I owe a special debt to the historians who have given me personal help and advice—Dr Jacqueline Eales, Richard Eales, Dr Christopher Haigh, J. Patrick Hornbeck II, John McSween, Christopher Skidmore, Yvonne Ward and Patrick Wormald. I have also derived particular stimulation from my fellow committee members of the Society of Court Studies—Dr Andrew Barclay, Dr Anna Keay, our esteemed president Dr David Starkey, Dr Simon Thurley and Dr Mary Hollingsworth, who organises our seminars and the convivial evenings that follow. Thanks to Nabil Al-Khowaiter for his data on the Newton Project.

Nigel Rees once again helped me track down several fugitive quotations, and the National Archives joined the quest—but we are still looking for the first reliably recorded utterance of the words 'Glorious Revolution'. Nautical gratitude is due to the crew of *The Matthew* for their guidance in Bristol harbour, and to my mother for her hospitality while I was in Bristol and for her support at all times. Thanks, when it came to reference resources, to the librarians of the British Library, the London Library, and the Westminster public library, as well as to the partners of the John Sandoe bookshop.

As with several previous projects, writing this book with the assistance of Moyra Ashford has made the process a pleasure. My wife Sandi—ever my best friend and critic—has been a particular support in helping to devise the illustrations so beautifully drawn by Fred van Deelen. In recent months I have been especially strengthened by the clarity offered by Prentis Hancock, Gregorio Kohon and Belinda Shand.

My thanks at Time Warner to Peter Cotton, David Young, Ursula Mackenzie, Sue Phillpott, David Atkinson, Jane Birkett and, in particular, to Roger Cazalet and the endlessly patient Viv Redman. Jonathan Pegg, my new agent at Curtis Brown, has worked hard on my behalf with Camilla Goslett and, more recently, with Shaheeda Sabir.

This volume, the second of three, is dedicated to my second child and only daughter Scarlett. She adds wonderful freshness to the ideas that I bounce off her in our transatlantic telephone calls, and I am deeply grateful for her unfailing emotional wisdom and support. She helped me think through the imagery of history as a kaleidoscope, and it is also thanks to her that I find myself revising the manuscript and writing these final words in the serene and stimulating atmosphere of the Esalen Institute at Big Sur, California.

Robert Lacey, August 2004

LC 8/06
LE 01113